AP

Advanced Placement

Psychology

Kimberley O'Steen

XAMonline

Copyright © 2017

To obtain permission(s) to use the material from this work for any purpose including workshops or seminars, please submit a written request to:

XAMonline, Inc.
21 Orient Avenue
Melrose, MA 02176
Toll Free: 1-800-301-4647
Email: info@xamonline.com
Web: www.xamonline.com
Fax: 1-617-583-5552

Library of Congress Cataloging-in-Publication Data

O'Steen, Kimberley

AP Psychology/ Kimberley O'Steen

ISBN: 978-1-60787-634-2

1. AP   2. Study Guides   3. Psychology

Disclaimer:

The opinions expressed in this publication are the sole works of XAMonline and were created independently from the College Board, or other testing affiliates. Between the time of publication and printing, specific test standards as well as testing formats and website information may change that are not included in part or in whole within this product. XAMonline develops sample test questions, and they reflect similar content as on real tests; however, they are not former tests. XAMonline assembles content that aligns with test standards but makes no claims nor guarantees candidates a passing score.

Cover photos provided by © Can Stock Photo Inc./lucidwaters/9437211, © Can Stock Photo Inc./scanrail/3495380, © Can Stock Photo Inc./kentoh/6613671, © Can Stock Photo Inc./GeorgiosArt/10056954, © Can Stock Photo Inc./ingri-dat/24290240

Printed in the United States of America

AP Psychology
ISBN: 978-1-60787-634-2

Table of Contents

Chapter 12: Abnormal Psychology 207

Chapter 13: Treatment of Psychological Disorders 219

Chapter 14: Social Psychology 229

Section III: Practice Tests

MEET THE AUTHOR

Kimberley O' Steen graduated from the University of Southern Mississippi with a Bachelor of Science degree in Psychology in 1994. Kimberley has a Master's degree in Counseling Psychology from the University of Southern Mississippi in Hattiesburg, Mississippi. She also has a Master of Arts in Teaching from Kaplan University. In her spare time, Kimberley enjoys reading, writing, listening to music, spending time with her family, watching crime/drama television, and gardening.

SECTION I:
About the Advanced Placement Psychology Program

Overview

The Advanced Placement® program is designed to offer students college credit while still in high school. More than 30 AP courses culminate in an intensive final exam given every year in May.

AP Psychology is a college-level psychology course students take in high school. Many students take this course to earn college credit. However, they can also be used to demonstrate to college admissions offices that they can do well in rigorous college-level course.

Successful completion of the course and a passing score on the exam not only provides students with a deep sense of accomplishment, but also gives them a jump-start on their college careers. AP credit is almost universally accepted by post-secondary schools, however each school has different guidelines as to what scores they will accept.

There are no prerequisites for AP Psychology. Students should be able to read a college-level textbook and write grammatically correct, complete sentences.

The AP Psychology course introduces students to the systematic and scientific study of human behavior and mental processes of human beings and other animals. Students are exposed to the psychological facts, principles, and phenomena associated with each of the major subfields within psychology. They also learn about the ethics and methods psychologists use in their practice.

Throughout an AP Psychology course, students are given opportunities to employ psychological research methods, analyze bias, evaluate claims and evidence, and effectively communicate ideas.

About the Exam

The AP Psychology Exam measures a students knowledge of the 14 key topics and fields of study in psychology and tests their ability to define, compare, and apply concepts and research findings. Multiple choice and free response questions are based on key terminology, scientific methodology, and theories associated with each sub-field.

Free-response questions may require students to interrelate different content areas and to analyze and evaluate psychological constructs and, more generally, theoretical perspectives.

The exam includes a 70-minute multiple-choice section (100 questions) that accounts for two-thirds of the exam grade and a 50-minute free-response section made up of two questions, accounting for one-third of the exam grade.

Multiple choice scores are based on the number of questions answered correctly. Points are not deducted for incorrect answers, and no points are awarded for unanswered questions. Because points are not deducted for incorrect answers, students are encouraged to answer all multiple choice questions. On questions they do not know the correct answer to, students should eliminate as many choices as they can, and then select the best answer among the remaining choices.

Free-response questions are an appropriate tool for evaluating a student's mastery of scientific research principles and ability to make connections among constructs from different psychological domains (e.g., development, personality, learning). Students may be asked to analyze a general problem in psychology (e.g., depression, adaptation) using concepts from different theoretical frameworks or subdomains in the field, or to design, analyze, or critique a research study.

Beginning with the 2015 AP Psychology Exam, all terminology, criteria and classifications referred to among multiple-choice and free-response questions will adhere to the new fifth edition of the *Diagnostic and Statistical Manual* (DSM-5).

The fifth edition of the *Diagnostic and Statistical Manual of Mental Disorders* (DSM-5) was published in May 2013 with revisions to the criteria for the diagnosis and classifications of mental disorders.

The Make Up of the Exam

The AP Psychology exam is administered annually in May. Students are given 2 hours to complete the test, which consists of 100 multiple choice questions and 2 free-response (short essay) questions. Students are given 70 minutes for the multiple choice questions and 50 minutes for the free-response section.

Part I: Multiple Choice

Question Format	Number of Questions	Time	% of Exam Score
Multiple Choice	100	70 minutes	2/3

Multiple choice questions will focus on psychologists and studies that have shaped the field, psychological theories, key concepts, and phenomena associated with the following topics:

- History and Approaches
- Research Methods
- Biological Bases of Behavior

- Sensation and Perception
- States of Consciousness
- Learning
- Cognition
- Motivation and Emotion
- Developmental Psychology
- Personality
- Testing and Individual Differences
- Abnormal Behavior
- Treatment of Abnormal Behavior
- Social Psychology

Multiple choice questions will range in difficulty. Some questions will rely heavily on definitions and recognition of terms that have been heavily reviewed in their AP Psychology course, referred to as lower order. More difficult questions, known as higher order, will require thoughtful analysis and interpretation. For example, a lower order question might ask for a word that best matches a definition, while higher order will ask for an interpretation of a chart or graph. The practice tests included in this book will cover a range of difficulty, which will prepare you for the variety of questions that you will be given on the AP Psychology exam.

Part II: Free-Response

Question Format	Number of Questions	Time	% of Exam Score
Free-response	2	50 minutes	1/3

The free-response portion of the exam prompts students to write short essays that require students to analyze and interpret psychological concepts and/or theoretical perspectives. To obtain a high score, students must demonstrate analytical and organizational skills in their writing.

Free-response questions will ask students to go above and beyond defining a theory and may include words such as: analyze, interpret, relate, discuss, and explain within the prompt. There are several free-response examples included in this book. Review the samples of quality writing and practice responding to two prompts within 50 minutes to give yourself the best opportunity for a high score.

How the Exam is Scored

The exam scoring process, like the course and exam development process, relies on the expertise of both AP teachers and college faculty. While multiple-choice questions are scored by machine, the free-response questions are scored by thousands of college faculty and expert AP teachers at the annual AP Reading. AP Exam Readers are thoroughly trained, and their work is monitored throughout the Reading for fairness and consistency.

Scores on the free-response questions are weighted and combined with the results of the computer-scored multiple-choice questions, and this raw score is converted into a composite AP Exam score of 5, 4, 3, 2, or 1.

In general, the AP composite score points are set so that the lowest raw score needed to earn an AP Exam score of 5 is equivalent to the average score among college students earning grades of A in the college course.

The College Board proposes the following qualifications for each of the potential score:

Exam Grade	Recommendation
5	Extremely Well Qualified
4	Well Qualified
3	Qualified
2	Possibly Qualified
1	No recommendation

The minimum score required for college credit to be granted is a 3. As mentioned above, many schools require scores of 4 or 5 in order to grant credit.

For comparison, the College Board makes the equivalents of the AP Exam scores at follows:

AP Exam Grade	Letter Grade Equivalent
5	A
4	A-, B+, B
3	B-, C+, C
2	None
1	None

For reference, the 2015 administration of the AP Psychology exam had this distribution:

Exam Score	Percentage of Students
5	20.2
4	26.2
3	19.8
2	13.1
1	20.7

Hints for Taking the Test

Part I – Multiple Choice Questions (70 minutes)

Multiple choice questions can be tricky. Many times it is possible to eliminate one or two of the answers right away, but then get stuck with the others. On the AP Psychology exam, there is no penalty for incorrect answers, so be sure to record an answer for every question, even if it is a complete guess.

It is also very important to know what the question is asking of you. The College Board is notorious for saying things like, "All of the following are examples, EXCEPT…" or, "Which of these is NOT…" These words can change the entire meaning of the sentence. Be on alert for qualifiers like this.

You will be using a number 2 pencil to bubble in your answers on an answer sheet. At this stage your academic career you have taken enough tests of this type that hopefully you know how to properly fill in the circles. If you need to erase an answer, be sure to do it completely.

Remember your timing. Sure, 100 questions in 70 minutes sounds easy enough. But remember, some of these questions are going to take longer to answer. Keep record of your time throughout the exam to ensure you stay on track. Questions that take longer than 3 minutes should be skipped and returned to when you have finished answering all other questions. If you find yourself running out of time, guess on the last few answers. Again, you are not penalized for incorrect answers, so your score will not be negatively impacted by guessing.

Part II – Free-Response (50 minutes)

The free-response questions are usually the items that give students the most difficulty. This is not because they do not they know the answers. The problem usually results from not organizing one's thoughts sufficiently and then getting them down on paper fast enough. There are two free-response questions total, so you should expect to devote approximately 25 minutes to each. You may split this 50 minutes up to allow for 10 minutes of planning and organizing your thoughts on scrap paper and then 40 minutes of writing. Be sure to write down any key terms that will be important to incorporate during this planning time.

The free-response questions are graded on a point scale, with different key topics being worth different amounts. The maximum a question can be worth is 10 points (for example, of the question has two parts, each part is worth five. If the question has three parts, then each part would be worth three and the extra point would be given if all three parts are answered completely). In order to get full credit for each question, you must answer in sufficient enough detail that the reader believes you have a complete understanding of the topic.

Like the multiple choice, you do not lose credit for presenting incorrect information. However, you do lose time. Other things the readers do not care about include: spelling, grammar, and penmanship. Obviously, if a reader in unable to determine what is was you wrote, they cannot grade it, but they do their best to interpret a student's "chicken scratch." Be certain your writing is in essay form (tell a story). Do NOT just list important concepts in an outline.

Also like the multiple choice questions, the free response questions have key terms about which you should pay particular attention. These terms include, "Compare,' "Contrast," Describe,' and their favorite, "Explain." Pay particular attention to these terms and be sure to do what they ask.

Be aware of what you are writing. You do not want to say one thing in the first paragraph and then say the complete opposite in the second paragraph. If you do this, you will not get any credit, even if one of them is correct. This is because the reader does not know if you knew which was correct or just took a guess and got lucky.

It is acceptable to include diagrams or graphs in your answers. If you do, be sure to properly number the visual so the reader knows to which question and part of the question it belongs. Additionally, make certain to label everything!! The last thing you want is not receive points because your beautifully constructed graph or data table was missing a title.

Finally, the biggest piece of advice for answering the free response questions is to answer the question and then move on. Certainly reread it to make sure it makes sense, but do not spend time going back over and editing it to turn it into a major piece of literature. You do not have time for this. Write what the question asks you to write and then move on. This will be the fastest 50 minutes you have ever experiences and you have a lot, a TON of information to get through, so writing brief, but detailed, essays are essential.

What To Expect In This Book

As you move forward through these next pages, you will see a variety of information. The first section is a review of major psychology concepts that you should know, or at least with which you should be familiar. You will see they are broken down by main topic (Biological Bases of Behavior, Sensation and Perception, etc.). Additionally, you will also find sample multiple choice questions for each topic. While these are not necessarily in the same format you will see on the AP Psychology exam, they will help you to assess your knowledge of the different concepts.

You will also find some sample tests at the end of this book. These are designed to give you hands-on experience that simulates the actual exam you will be taking. Each question on these tests has a detailed answer as to why it is correct and why the incorrect answers are wrong. Use this information to help guide your learning.

Tips:

1. **Don't read anything into the question.** Don't make an assumption that the test writer is looking for something other than what is asked. Stick to the question as written and don't read extra things into it.
2. **Carefully read the question and ALL answer options before answering the question.** You may miss something by not carefully reading both the question and the answers.

3. **When in doubt, move on.** If you really don't have a clue as to the right answer, leave it blank on the first time through. Go on to the other questions, as they may provide a clue as to how to answer the skipped questions. If time remains, you can go back to questions you've missed and provide your best guess.

4. **Turn the question into a statement.** Look at the way the questions are worded. The syntax of the question usually provides a clue. Does it seem more familiar as a statement rather than as a question? Does it sound strange?

   By turning a question into a statement, you may be able to spot if an answer sounds right, and it may also trigger memories of material you have read.

5. **Look for hidden clues.** It's actually very difficult to compose multiple-foil (choice) questions without giving away part of the answer in the options presented.

   In most multiple-choice questions you can often readily eliminate one or two of the potential answers. This leaves you with only two real possibilities and automatically your odds go to fifty-fifty for very little work.

6. **Trust your instincts.** For every fact that you have read, you subconsciously retain something of that knowledge. On questions that you aren't really certain about, go with your basic instincts. **Your first impression on how to answer a question is usually correct.**

7. **Mark your answers directly on the test booklet.** Don't bother trying to fill in the optical scan sheet on the first pass through the test.

   Also, be *very careful* not to mis-mark your answers when you eventually transcribe them to the scan sheet.

8. **Watch the clock!** You have a set amount of time to answer the questions. Don't get bogged down trying to answer a single question at the expense of 10 questions you can more readily answer.

Study and Test Tips:

What to study in order to prepare for the subject assessments is the focus of this study guide but equally important is *how* you study.

You can increase your chances of truly mastering the information by taking some simple, but effective steps.

Study Tips:

1. **Some foods aid the learning process.** Foods such as milk, nuts, seeds, rice, and oats help your study efforts by releasing natural memory enhancers called CCKs (*cholecystokinin*) composed of *tryptophan*, *choline*, and *phenylalanine*. All of these chemicals enhance the neurotransmitters associated with memory. Before studying, try a light, protein-rich meal of eggs, turkey, and fish. All of these foods release the memory enhancing chemicals. The better the connections, the more you comprehend.

   Likewise, before you take a test, stick to a light snack of energy boosting and relaxing foods. A glass of milk, a piece of fruit, or some peanuts all release various memory-boosting chemicals and help you to relax and focus on the subject at hand.

2. **Learn to take great notes.** A by-product of our modern culture is that we have grown accustomed to getting our information in short doses (i.e., TV news sound bites or USA Today style newspaper articles).

Consequently, we've subconsciously trained ourselves to assimilate information better in neat little packages. If your notes are scrawled all over the paper, it fragments the flow of the information. Strive for clarity. Newspapers use a standard format to achieve clarity. Your notes can be much clearer through use of proper formatting. A very effective format is called the *"Cornell Method."*

> Take a sheet of loose-leaf lined notebook paper and draw a line all the way down the paper about 1-2" from the left-hand edge.

> Draw another line across the width of the paper about 1-2" up from the bottom. Repeat this process on the reverse side of the page.

> Look at the highly effective result. You have ample room for notes, a left hand margin for special emphasis items or inserting supplementary data from the textbook, a large area at the bottom for a brief summary, and a little rectangular space for just about anything you want.

3. **Get the concept then the details.** Too often we focus on the details and don't gather an understanding of the concept. However, if you simply memorize only dates, places, or names, you may well miss the whole point of the subject.

A key way to understand things is to put them in your own words. If you are working from a textbook, automatically summarize each paragraph in your mind. If you are outlining text, don't simply copy the author's words.

Rephrase them in your own words. You remember your own thoughts and words much better than someone else's, and subconsciously tend to associate the important details to the core concepts.

4. **Ask Why?** Pull apart written material paragraph by paragraph and don't forget the captions under the illustrations.

Example: If the heading is "Stream Erosion," flip it around to read "Why do streams erode?" Then answer the questions.

If you train your mind to think in a series of questions and answers, not only will you learn more, but it also helps to lessen the test anxiety because you are used to answering questions.

5. **Read for reinforcement and future needs.** Even if you only have 10 minutes, put your notes or a book in your hand. Your mind is similar to a computer; you have to input data in order to have it processed. *By reading, you are creating the neural connections for future retrieval.* The more times you read something, the more you reinforce the learning of ideas.

Even if you don't fully understand something on the first pass, your mind stores much of the material for later recall.

6. **Relax.** Our bodies respond to an inner clock called biorhythms. Burning the midnight oil works well for some people, but not everyone.

   If possible, set aside a particular place to study that is free of distractions. Shut off the television, cell phone, and pager and exile your friends and family during your study period. If you really are bothered by silence, try background music. Light classical music at a low volume has been shown to aid in concentration over other types. Music that evokes pleasant emotions without lyrics is highly suggested. Try just about anything by Mozart. It relaxes you.

7. **Use arrows not highlighters.** At best, it's difficult to read a page full of yellow, pink, blue, and green streaks. Try staring at a neon sign for a while and you'll soon see that the horde of colors obscures the message.

   A quick note, a brief dash of color, an underline, and an arrow pointing to a particular passage is much clearer than a horde of highlighted words.

8. **Budget your study time.** Although you shouldn't ignore any of the material, allocate your available study time in the same ratio that topics may appear on the test.

SECTION II:
Review of Content

Chapter 1: History and Approaches

Key Terms, Concepts, and People

Psychology	Behavior	Mind
Eclectic approach	Dualism	Empiricism
Materialism	Structuralism	Introspection
Structuralism	Functionalism	Gestalt psychology
Biological psychology	Behaviorism	Classical conditioning
Stimuli	Responses	Operant conditioning
Reinforcement	Behavior modification	Cognitive psychology
Humanistic psychology	Self-actualization	Unconditional positive regard
Psychodynamic approach	Unconscious mind	Conscious mind
Repressed	Dream analysis	Free association
Sociocultural approach	Evolutionary psychology	Natural selection
Biopsychosocial approach	Clinical psychology	Counseling psychology
Developmental psychology	Educational psychology	Experimental psychology
Human factors psychology	Industrial-organizational psychology	
Personality psychology	Psychometric psychology	Social psychology

Key People: Mary Whiton Calkins, Charles Darwin, Dorothea Dix, Sigmund Freud, G. Stanley Hall, William James, Ivan Pavlov, Jean Piaget, Carl Rogers, B.F. Skinner, Margaret Floy Washburn, John B. Watson, Wilhelm Wundt

Overview

Psychology is the scientific study of the human mind and behavior. *Behavior* refers to the way in which a person acts and can be observed. The *mind* refers to that part of an individual that consists of their cognitions, memories, sensations, emotions, motives, and perceptions. The mind is what enables individuals to think and reason. It consists of conscious and unconscious mental processes. Psychology attempts to explain and describe behavior and the cognitive processes behind behavior.

Psychology is a science based on experimentation and systematic observation, enabling psychologists to form assumptions about behavior, the mind, and human functioning. These assumptions lead to the development of theories that attempt to explain aspects of human behavior or mental processes. As with all sciences, knowledge about general laws and patterns are obtained through experimentation and observation. The field of psychology consists of several different theoretical perspectives, and most psychologists closely adhere to the theoretical approach that most closely fits their perspective. However, many psychologists see value in different theories, and an *eclectic approach* to the study of psychology. These psychologists believe that no single theory perfectly explains human thoughts and behavior, but rather attempt to explain behavior and cognitive processes by drawing upon different theoretical perspectives.

History of Psychology

Early Greek Philosophers

Throughout history, humankind has been interested in the nature of the mind and the factors affecting behavior. Many ancient Greek philosophers, such as Plato, Socrates, and Aristotle presented differing perspectives on human thought and behavior. Aristotle's beliefs about logic, reasoning, and careful observation of the world formed the underpinnings of the scientific method. These philosophers believed the world, and by extension, human nature, could be divided into two parts: the body and the spirit. This concept is known as *dualism*. The debate over which aspect of a person is more powerful in determining behavior and cognitions is still relevant today as the field of psychology continues to expand.

The Scientific Revolution

During the scientific revolution, a great philosophical shift occurred. Whereas religion had asserted that the spirit of a person could not be studied using scientific means, a new generation of philosophers and scientists challenged these religious beliefs. Advances in astronomy, biology, and other areas demonstrated that human behavior could be scientifically studied.

Rene Descartes (1596-1650) believed that the physical world behaved according to patterns and natural laws. However, Descartes did not believe the human mind and its processes could be observed or predicted, because the mind does not follow natural laws. He envisioned an interaction between the mind and body, with the mind controlling the body and the body constantly supplying sensory information to the mind. Descartes believed that some parts of the body, such as reflexes, are not under the control of the mind but are simply reactions to external stimuli.

Descartes's ideas were expanded upon by John Locke (1632-1704). Locke believed that even the mind is subject to natural laws. Locke's perspective that truth and knowledge can be acquired through experiences and observations is referred to as *empiricism*. Locke is perhaps best known for his concept of "tabula rasa," a term that refers to the belief that humans are born knowing nothing, or are essentially "blank slates." According to this perspective, no knowledge is innate; everything a person knows must be learned from experience.

Thomas Hobbes (1588-1679) rejected the idea of a soul and spirit. He believed that matter and energy are the only things that exist, a philosophy referred to as *materialism*. Everything experienced in a person's conscious awareness is a result of processes of the brain. The field of behaviorism was greatly impacted by Hobbes's philosophy.

Theory of Natural Selection

Discoveries in medicine and biology strongly influenced the field of psychology during the nineteenth century. Charles Darwin (1809-1882) proposed the idea of *natural selection*. This evolutionary theory asserted that all living things evolved over a period of millions of years. Natural selection assumes that variations among humans naturally exist, and the individuals most likely to survive and reproduce are those that are the strongest and fittest, or those that have adapted to their environment. Through the process of natural selection, the characteristics that ensure a species' survival are the ones selected. Evolutionary theory is one way that differences between species can be understood and explained.

The Science of Psychology Begins

Wilhelm Wundt (1832-1920) is considered to be the founder of the science of psychology in the year 1879. Wundt hoped to use the process of *introspection*, in which individuals observe and record their mental states, including thoughts and feelings, in response to various stimuli, in order to understand more about basic cognitive processes. From this experiment, Wundt and his mentee, Edward Titchener (1867-1927), developed the theory of *structuralism*, in which the mind can be broken down into its simplest components and then those components can be combined in order to make up the sum total of the individual's experiences. Titchener is credited for bringing the science of psychology to the United States.

William James (1842-1910), an American psychologist, disagreed with the idea of structuralism and offered the view that the function and uses of cognitive processes, or the mind, is more important than the structures of the mind, an approach known as *functionalism*. James is also the author of the first psychology textbook. One of James's students, Mary Whiton Calkins (1863-1930), became the first female president of the American Psychological Association. Calkins is also credited with starting the first women's psychology lab. She is noted for her studies of memory, which led to the development of the *paired association technique*. She was a highly influential professor of psychology and philosophy. Another female pioneer in the field of psychology is Margaret Floy Washburn

(1871-1939). Washburn was the first woman to receive a Ph.D. in psychology. She is noted for her work in animal behavior development and for motor theory. G. Stanley Hall (1844-1924), who also studied under William James, is considered to be the founder of child psychology and educational psychology; he was also interested in evolutionary psychology. Hall was the first president of the American Psychological Association.

Max Wertheimer (1880-1943) was one of the three founders of *Gestalt psychology*. He believed that thinking moves from the whole to the parts, and focused on the total experiences of an individual. Gestalt psychology takes a holistic approach to understanding the individual, and this approach rejects the idea that human thought and behavior can be separated.

Dorothea Dix (1802-1887) was a social activist and reformer who advocated for mentally insane, indigent people. After visiting hospitals and noting the terrible ways the mentally ill were treated and abused, she successfully lobbied for the establishment and expansion of state hospitals for the mentally ill.

Theoretical Approaches

The theoretical perspectives above show an evolution of thinking in science that gradually moves away from using reason and logic alone, to become more and more scientific in nature.

There are ten main schools of thought in contemporary psychology. It is absolutely essential that you understand each one, and know what distinguishes each approach.

School of Psychology (starting year)	Description	Important contributors
Evolutionary 1850s	Process of natural selection determines behaviors and thoughts that promote survival. The behaviors, traits and thought processes that are most beneficial to survival will be passed to the next generation.	Charles Darwin
Structuralism 1880s	Used introspection to identify basic elements or "structures" of psychological experience. To understand "reading", for example, research participants would describe their experience while reading. First laboratory dedicated to psychological research, University of Leipzig, Germany 1879.	Wilhelm Wundt, Edward B. Titchener
Functionalism 1890s	Related to Darwinism, consciousness must have evolved because it was *useful* for something; it had a function. To understand the origins and purpose of psychological phenomenon we should ask what it is used for.	William James, Father of American Psy.

School of Psychology (starting year)	Description	Important contributors
Psychodynamic 1890s	The unconscious mind determines thoughts and behaviors. The *unconscious mind* cannot easily be accessed, but influences our behavior. The *conscious mind* includes cognitive processes that we can access and for which we are aware. Early childhood experiences shape personality and determine behavior	Sigmund Freud Carl Jung Alfred Adler Erik Erickson
Behaviorism early 1900s	Not possible to objectively study the mind, therefore study should focus on observable behavior. *Classical conditioning* was the basis for *learning by association*. *Operant conditioning* refers to the effect of *reinforcers* (positive or negative) that strengthen or weaken the likelihood the behavior happens again.	Ivan Pavlov John B. Watson, B. F. Skinner
Cognitive late 1800s, 1960s, 1990s	The study of mental processes, including perception, thinking, memory, and judgments. Computer analogies guided research and have now evolved to include neuroimaging of the brain.	Hermann Ebbinghaus, Albert Ellis Jean Piaget
Sociocultural 1950s	Social situations and culture influence thinking and behavior. Explains variations in behavior and thoughts as influenced by different social environments, roles, norms and values among people of different cultural groups.	Fritz Heider Leon Festinger Stanley Milgram
Humanistic 1950s	Study of the person, the self-concept, self-esteem and an appreciation for the human condition. Takes a holistic approach to understanding human behavior and improving the growth of the individual person. Maslow's hierarchy of needs and Roger's concept of unconditional positive regard are central concepts.	Abraham Maslow, Carl Rogers
Biological 1990s	Attempts to understand how biology, physiology, and genes affect behavior. Cognitive processes, emotions, and behaviors are seen as direct results of biological factors.	No single researcher recognized
Biopsychosocial	Human behavior is the result of an interaction between biological, psychological, and social factors. Each factor is equally important in determining thoughts and behavior.	George Engel

Modern Subfields in Psychology

The AP Psychology exam requires you to be familiar with the subfields of psychology. Different schools of psychological thought have led to different subfields and professions in the 21st century. The following is a list of the subfields and their definitions. Many universities offer masters or doctoral degrees in these subfields.

Modern Subfields of Psychology

Biological psychology	Examines the mind-body connection. Understand how biology, physiology, and genes affect behavior.
Clinical psychology	Diagnose, assess, treat, and prevent emotional, behavioral, and psychological disorders
Counseling psychology	Help individuals achieve and maintain healthy functioning. Includes social, vocational, educational, developmental, and healthy habits
Developmental psychology	Studies how and why children/adults change over the lifespan. Can include various theoretical approaches.
Cognitive psychology	Examines mental processes involved in social settings, information processing and decision-making.
Educational psychology	Studies learning, motivation, instruction, and assessment in educational settings. Examines and improves the interaction between teaching and learning.
Experimental psychology	Studies humans and animals to understand sensation, perception, memory, learning and motivation.
Human factors psychology	Design products, equipment and technology for human interaction. Often focused on performance and safety.
I/O psychology	How people act in organizations and the workplace. Goal is to increase performance, motivation, and job satisfaction.

Personality psychology	Studies individual differences in emotions, cognitions, and behavior. How cultural factors influence personality development and expression.
Psychometric psychology	Examines the design, administration and interpretation of tests. Measures variables such as aptitude, personality, abilities, and interests.
Experimental Social psychology	Examines the way people relate to others using experimental methods. How attitudes are formed, changed, and affect the behavior of others.

Practice Questions

1. **Which approach deals with issues of self-concept and free choice?**
   (Lower order)

   (A) sociocultural approach
   (B) biological approach
   (C) humanistic approach
   (D) functionalism
   (E) Gestalt psychology

The correct answer is C: humanistic approach
Humanistic psychology focuses on the study of free will, self-concept, awareness of the human condition and aspects of consciousness. The sociocultural approach studies how social and cultural factors influence thoughts and behavior. The biological approach views behavior as being a result of biological and genetic factors. Functionalism is a theory that states that the functions of the mind are more important than the actual components of the mind. Gestalt psychology seeks to understand the individual in view of the person's total experiences. Although very similar to humanistic psychology, gestalt psychology does not focus on self-concept.

2. **Which early theoretical perspective had the greatest influence on the field of behavioral psychology?**
   (Higher order)

   (A) empiricism
   (B) dualism
   (C) natural selection
   (D) materialism
   (E) tabula rasa

The correct answer is D: Materialism

Materialism is the belief that matter and energy are the only things that exist. It rejects the idea of a soul and spirit and proposes that all things in a person's conscious awareness are results of processes of the brain. Since behavioral psychology focuses only on what can be observed, no attention is given to cognitive processes, emotions, or any other part of the human experience, such as the soul and spirit. Empiricism refers to the belief that truth and knowledge can be acquired through experiences and observations. Dualism refers to the idea that the world and human nature can be divided into two parts, the body and the spirit. Natural selection is a theory proposed by Charles Darwin that states that only behaviors and thoughts that promote survival and adaptation are selected and passed down to other generations. Tabula rasa is the theory that all humans are born knowing nothing; they are essentially blank states. Knowledge is gained through experiences.

Challenge Question:

3. **Linda is seeing a therapist because she is having problems in her relationships. Linda reports being moody and grouchy due to a problem with her thyroid. She also states that she feels like she has no one to talk to because her family has never been one that talks about feelings. Linda expresses some negative and self-defeating thoughts. Which of the following statements best reflects the approach Linda's therapist should take?**

   (A) The therapist needs to treat Linda from a cognitive psychology approach because Linda's thoughts are the cause of her problems.
   (B) The therapist should use a sociocultural approach to help Linda understand how her family's views have caused her interpersonal difficulties.
   (C) The therapist should help Linda improve her self-concept and take responsibility for her choices.
   (D) The therapist should focus more on making sure Linda is treated for her thyroid problem since that is affecting her moods, which affect her relationships.
   (E) The therapist should take an approach that addresses Linda's medical issues, familial influences, and thought processes because they are all contributing to Linda's problems.

The correct answer is. D:

The therapist should take an approach that addresses Linda's medical issues, familial influences, and thought processes because they are all contributing to Linda's problems. The problem with Linda's thyroid affects her moods, which has a negative impact on her relationships. However, Linda's culture does not seem to value discussing feelings, but Linda needs to be able to talk about her feelings and how things are affecting her. Linda's thoughts are also negatively affecting her feelings and her relationships. Therefore, the therapist should not ignore any one of these areas because all of these areas are contributing to Linda's difficulties. Neither Linda's thoughts nor her family environment are solely responsible for contributing to her interpersonal problems. While there is nothing wrong with addressing self-concept issues with a client or working with a client to help the client accept responsibility for her problems, there is no indication that either of these scenarios is what is causing Linda's problems. Linda does need to be receiving treatment for her thyroid problem because it is affecting her moods, but focusing more on that issue will not address the cognitive or sociocultural factors that are also contributing to Linda's difficulties.

Chapter 2: Research Methods

Key Terms, Concepts, and People

Descriptive	Correlational	Experimental
Naturalistic	Observational	Archival
Case study	Longitudinal	Cross-sectional
Controlled	Matched pairs	Self-selection
Confounding variables	Internal validity	Generalizability
Sampling bias	Sample characteristics	Sample size
Heterogeneous	Homogeneous	Response rate
Correlation coefficient	Predictor variable	Criterion variable
Scatterplot	Statistical analysis	Missing records
Selective attrition	Historical differences	Experimental research
Independent variable	Dependent variable	Control group
Treatment group	Operational definition	Random Selection
Random assignment	Confound	Participant
Repeated measures		
Independent samples	Demand characteristics	Experimenter bias
External validity	P-value	Sampling error
Null hypothesis	Statistical significance	Frequency distribution
Normal curve	Standard deviation	Skewness
Positive skew	Negative skew	IQ distribution curve
Z score	Nuremberg trials	Tuskegee study
Informedconsent	Confidentiality	Deception
Ethical	guidelines	Debriefing

Methodologies

There are 3 categories of research methods: *Descriptive, Correlational,* and *Experimental.* Within each category are different types of methods that each have strengths and weaknesses.

Descriptive	Correlational	Experimental
• Observational • Case Study • Survey	• Longitudinal • Cross-sectional • Archival	• Independent Samples • Repeated Measures • Matched Pairs

Descriptive Research

The first step when scientifically studying something (anything) is to describe it in as much detail as possible. Just like the first time a botanist ran across a new species of tree, she/he makes a drawing, takes measurements, describes its lifespan, conducts a chemical analysis of inner structures, and so on.

Likewise, when Jane Goodall went into the jungle to observe the great apes, she did so simply by sitting and watching, and taking very detailed notes. The goal of descriptive research therefore is to describe the object of study in as much detail as possible.

Three Main Types of Descriptive Research	
1. Observational:	The number one goal is to describe what is observed; "paint a picture" of the behavior under study; 3 main types of observational research.
Naturalistic	Behavior is observed in its natural environment; no attempt to influence behavior. To hide and not be seen is best.
Controlled	Behavior is observed in a laboratory; researcher controls many factors such as time, setting, participants; behavior is recorded using systematic criteria.

Participant	Researcher interacts with and may become a member of the studied group.
2. Case Study	Involves an in-depth examination and study of a single participant, group, or event; can take weeks or years to complete; can lead to valuable first insights.
3. Survey	People respond to various statements on paper or interview; questions can be *open-ended* or on *rating scales*; responses analyzed with *descriptive statistics*.

Problems with Observational Research:

All research methodologies have flaws. This is one reason why it takes scientists so long to all agree to call something a "fact". The number one flaw with observational research is that it lacks "causality". Since researchers cannot manipulate variables and then see what happens, we cannot answer the question of "why". There will always be a possible alternative explanation for the results based on variables that cannot be controlled.

For example, if we think violent movies will make aggressive actions more likely, we could perform a naturalistic observation of people exiting the cinema. If we observe people coming from violent movies are more aggressive than people that just watched a comedy, we will have many problems drawing a conclusion that violent movies makes people more aggressive.

Self-Selection:

Because the researcher does not control who watches the violent movie and who watches the comedy, it means that the people in our sample chose the movie type themselves. We call this *self-selection*. Of course we can reason that maybe people with aggressive personalities are going to choose violent movies, and the easygoing type will choose a comedy. So we don't know if our results are due to the movie *or* the personality of the moviegoers.

Confounding Variables:

A confounder is a variable that makes the interpretation of our results questionable. For example, if we do our movie study in the summer, when it is really hot, and our results show that there is no difference in aggression between people who watched a violent or comedic movie, we have a confounder. Since it was so hot, everybody was in a bad mood and was a bit aggressive, regardless of which movie they watched. In this example, we say that "temperature" is a cofounding variable.

When researchers cannot control confounding variables it makes the results of the study less *internally valid*. The more problems with the design and procedures of the study, the lower the internal validity.

Problems with Case Studies:

Generalizability:

The biggest problem with case studies is that the researcher cannot generalize to the larger population. The in-depth analysis of a single individual or case can lead to early and valuable insights into human behavior, but the results are scientifically limited and need to be supplemented with other research methodologies. By studying one individual we can learn a lot about that one person, but we cannot say what we learned is true of other people.

Problems with Survey Research: Sampling Bias

The *sample* is the group of people in our survey. *Sampling Bias* is when there is a problem with the sample, and there can be many.

For example, if we are working in an HR Department of a large corporation with thousands of employees, we may be asked to conduct an employee satisfaction survey. Right away we have to make decisions about how many employees will be in our survey, what age groups, which departments, how to ensure all ethnicities are included, as well as if we should include overseas employees or not. Some specific examples of sampling bias include:

Sample Characteristics:

The sample will be *heterogeneous* or *homogeneous*. A heterogeneous sample is diverse and the people in it vary from each other on many characteristics, such as: age, gender, ethnicity, profession, SES status. A homogeneous sample involves the people being similar to each other on one or more characteristics (everyone in the sample is from the same SES group, for example).

If the sample includes everyone from everywhere and does not leave out any single identifiable group, then the researcher can say that the *sample is heterogeneous and representative* of the employees. If however, through bad planning or accident, most of the people in our survey come from the East Coast and only from middle-management, then we must conclude that *the sample is homogeneous and biased*, and therefore *not representative*.

Sample Size:

The size of the sample is very important and one of the biggest shortcomings of psychological research. Unfortunately research is costly and very time-consuming and so researchers often use smaller sample sizes than ideal. In survey research it is common to have only a few hundred respondents. Low sample size makes the results less valid and limits our ability to generalize to the population.

Low Response Rate:

If only 20% of the people asked to be in the survey respond, then the sample size will be too low to be representative. It would be very difficult to say anything about the opinions of the other 80% of employees. There can be many reasons for a low response rate, but they each have the same effect of making the results less valid and less generalizable to the population.

Generalizability:

All of the above problems make our results and conclusions questionable, therefore creating a problem with *generalizing the results* to a larger population. Since we want to know something about all the people, but it is impossible to study them all, we are especially concerned about sampling issues.

Correlational Research

The goal of correlational research is to add further insight to our understanding of behavior by examining how specific variables are related. Researchers measure two or more variables, then conduct a *statistical analysis* to determine if there is a relationship or not. The statistical analysis is called the *correlation coefficient*, and it is a single number between -1 and +1.

For example, if we have a theory about temperature and aggression, then we can compare the temperature of each day of summer with police arrest records. The hypothesis is: the higher the temperature the higher the number of arrests. We use the terms *predictor variable* and *criterion variable* (sometimes called *outcome variable*) when discussing correlational research.

If the correlation coefficient is close to +1, then it means there is a *strong positive relationship* between temperature and arrest. As the temperature increases, arrests increase.

If the correlation coefficient is 0, then it means there is no relationship between those two variables.

If the correlation coefficient is close to -1, then it means there is a *strong negative relationship* between temperature and arrest. As the temperature increases, arrests decrease.

Of course, in reality, there are many variables that are related to police arrest records; we could probably list 10 or 12 easily. Unfortunately it can be nearly impossible to study all variables in one study, so we choose one or two, understand how those variables affect our criterion variable as much as possible, and then study other variables.

The four graphs below show different hypothetical situations between the 2 variables. One variable is represented on the x-axis (temperature) and the other on the y-axis (arrests). The predictor variable goes on the x-axis and the criterion variable goes on the y-axis. Values on the axes are arranged from smallest to largest, starting from left to right (x-axis) and bottom to top (y-axis).

By plotting the data on the axes we create a *scatterplot* that presents the data visually.

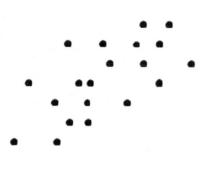

Strong Positive Correlation

As temperature increases in value on the horizontal x-axis, number of arrests also increases on the y-axis.

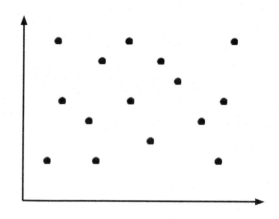

Zero Correlation

As temperature increases in value on the horizontal x-axis, there is no systematic change in number of arrests on the y-axis.

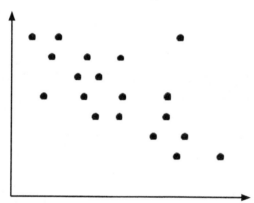

Strong Negative Correlation

As temperature increases in value on the horizontal x-axis, number of arrests actually decreases on the y-axis.

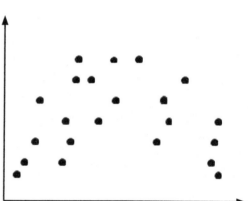

Curvilinear Correlation

As temperature increases in value on the horizontal x-axis, number of arrests also increases on the y-axis, up to a point. Then, as temperature increases, arrests decline.

Three Types of Correlational Research	
Strong Negative Correlation	Curvilinear Correlation
Correlational:	Examines relationship between two or more variables using a statistical technique called the correlation coefficient; can identify variables that are related to each other but not determine "cause".
1. Longitudinal	Involves studying a sample of people over a long period of time, usually years or decades. After a sample is selected all variables are measured at the beginning of the study, and then at the end of the study. Allows the researchers to examine how variables affect behavior over a long period of time.
2. Cross-Sectional	Involves collecting data at one point in time, but including many different groups. The groups are similar on many characteristics but different on the key variable of interest such as age, income level or geographic location.
3. Archival	Involves examining historical records, and identifying relationships among variables under study.

Problems with Correlational Research:

Correlation does not mean causation. This is the biggest problem with all correlational research. Even if we can identify very strong relationships between two variables, the researcher cannot state that one causes the other. There is always the possibility of a *third variable* that can be the cause.

For example, if research reveals a strong positive correlation between eating chocolate and acne, it might be easy to conclude that chocolate makes your face break-out. However, there is the possibility of a third variable which is really the culprit. Perhaps people eat chocolate when they feel stressed, and also, independently, stress causes acne. So the third variable is stress and it is actually the cause of the other two variables. Therefore, correlation does not mean causation due to the possibility of a potential third variable.

Problems with Longitudinal Research:

Selective Attrition:

The biggest problem with longitudinal research is that over time the sample becomes smaller and smaller. This is especially bad if the people dropping out of the study are all similar to one another on a key variable. For example, if we want to know if bad parenting leads to criminal behavior 30 years later, we can follow the sample from preschool to adulthood. But, people will drop out of the study over time. This can be a problem if they drop out for reasons related to the variable of interest.

Problems with Cross-sectional Research:

Historical Differences:

Although studying different age groups simultaneously, instead of tracking one age group for decades, yields a lot of data, the groups often differ from one another on several characteristics in addition to age. For example, a group of 50-60 year olds differ in many ways compared to a group of 20-30 year olds. Major events in history tend to shape attitudes and values of people, so an older age group will have many different historical experiences compared to a younger age group.

Problems with Archival Research:

Missing Records:

The main problem with archival research is that often records are incomplete or missing. Sometimes the information recorded at the time was selected in a biased manner and so may not represent the situation under study accurately. Although archival research can yield a lot of data, the quality and accuracy of the data can make the results less valid.

So, once researchers have described and defined a specific behavior, using descriptive and correlational research, we then take the next step to understanding behavior and try to answer the question "why". The only research method that allows the determination of causality is called the *experiment.*

Experimental Research

Psychologists ultimately want to know exactly *why* people do what they do. But human behavior can be complicated and influenced by a multitude of factors. It is impossible to study all factors at once, so researchers try to focus on 1 or 2 factors at a time. By eliminating the influence of all factors except 1 or 2, the research can determine the *cause* of a behavior.

There are 7 main terms to know:

Independent Variable IV	The causal variable being studied; the researcher manipulates the level of the IV and looks for changes in behavior on the DV.
Dependent Variable DV	The behavior observed; if the IV causes the DV, then it should change based on the level of the IV.

Confounding Variable	A variable that may have a causal relation with the DV; makes interpretation of results difficult; can be controlled by 3 methods.
Control group	The people in the study that will not be exposed to the IV
Treatment group	The people in the study that will receive the IV
Random selection	When every person in the population has an equal chance of being selected for the study.
Random Assignment	When each person in the study has an equal chance of being assigned to the control or treatment group.

Before we describe the 3 main types of the experiment, let's walk through one example first. On the AP exam you will be asked to design a study.

A developmental psychologist wants to know if playing violent video games (IV) will make young children more aggressive (DV). They could use the experiment to isolate one factor (IV: video game violence), and determine if it has an affect on behavior (DV: aggression).

In this hypothetical study, we could have 2 levels of the IV: zero violence and medium violence. But how exactly do we mean by "violence"? There can be many different definitions and examples, so we must make a very detailed definition called an *operational definition*. In our study we will operationally define violence as the actions portrayed in the fighting game Mortal Kombat, and zero violence will be the action portrayed in the puzzle game Tetris.

So, some children in the study will play a game with no violence (Tetris), and some will play a game with a medium level of violence (Mortal Kombat). The zero violence group is called the *control group*, and the medium violence group is called the *treatment group*.

The DV in this study is aggression, but how exactly will we define and measure it? The meaning of "aggression" can be very encompassing, and some may agree or disagree with what we consider aggressive. So, we must be as specific as possible by what we mean by "aggression". In this hypothetical example, the *operational definition of aggression* is: the number of times the child plays with a large inflatable toy in an aggressive manner by pushing, punching, kicking, or throwing the object.

Operational definitions are extremely important. Because scientists and researchers can disagree on the definition of concepts like aggression, we must be very specific with exactly how the concept will be realized in the study. In addition, good operational definitions allow other researchers to *replicate* each other's research. We cannot simply accept the results of one study to understand a specific behavior and declare that we know what causes aggression. It takes many studies, using many different methodologies, over a long period of time.

So our hypothesis is that the IV will cause changes in the DV. Children that play violent video games will be more aggressive than children that play games with zero violence.

Of course, there are many factors that will influence whether a child is aggressive or not, such as parenting practices, personality characteristics, school environment, perhaps time of day, just to name a few. What do we do about those? Each of those factors is related to aggression and are called *confounding variables*. A *confounding variable* is a factor that is related to our DV, but which we do not want to study.

In this example, let's suppose that all the children that played the violent games also came from hostile home environments, while the children that played the zero violence games came from well-adjusted households. In this case family background is a confound. Now there are 2 possible explanations for the results. One explanation is consistent with our hypothesis, but the alternative explanation says our results are due to the family household, not the games.

Confounding variables are a big problem in research. Fortunately there are 3 main ways to control their influence when using the experimental method.

Random Selection	Random Assignment	Statistical Analysis
• choose people who will be in the study randomly so that each person has an equal chance of being in the study • For example, we obtain a list of all 200 students' names in grade 3. We put all the names in a hat and draw 40 names, one by one • Therefore the sample (n=40) was randomly selected from the grade 3 population	• each person in the sample has an equal chance of being in either the control or treatment group • For example, when the first research participant comes to our lab, we flip a coin; heads = control group, tails = treatment group • Therefore, both groups will be the same on all confounds	• measure the confounding variables • statistical techniques can allow the researcher to determine if the confound is affecting the DV, or not • Often used in medical researach that allow doctors to determine that smoking and diet have independent effects on health

In our hypothetical experiment, two groups of participants were randomly assigned to either the control group or the treatment group. This *experimental design* is called an *independent samples* design, because we used two unrelated groups of participants.

The 3 main versions of the experiment.

Three Main Types of Experiments	
Independent Samples	Two groups of participants involved. One group gets the control and the other group gets the treatment.
Repeated Measures	One group of participants gets both the control and treatment.
Matched Pairs	Two groups of participants are purposely matched on one characteristic. One group receives the control and the other group receives the treatment.

In a *repeated measures* design, the participants will be in both the control group and the treatment group. So, first the participants will play the game with zero violence and then we observe their behavior on the DV. Then, the same participants will play the game with medium violence after which we observe their behavior on the DV.

With the *matched pairs* design, there are two groups of participants. One group receives the control and the other the treatment. But, each participant in the control group has been matched to be similar to one participant in the treatment group. So, if we think that IQ level is a confounding variable, we can make sure that the groups are equal to each other in IQ by forming pairs of participants that match each other on IQ, and then randomly assign one person from each pair to either the control or treatment groups.

Problems with Experimental Research:_____

Demand Characteristics:

Demand characteristics are when the research participants change their behavior because they know too much about the study. They may know which group (control or treatment) they are in, they may try to guess the hypotheses and act accordingly (or not), or they may try to make a good impression and alter their behavior in some manner (the *Hawthorne effect*). All of these *demand characteristics* make the results invalid.

Most research attempts to resolve demand characteristics by using a *single-blind* design. A single-blind study is when the participants do not know which group they are in, but the experimenter collecting the data does.

Experimenter Bias:

If the person collecting the data (the experimenter) knows the hypothesis of the study then they may inadvertently influence the participants' behavior. This will make the results invalid.

Most research eliminates *experimenter bias* by using a *double-blind* design. A double-blind design means that neither the research participants nor the experimenter collecting the data knows who gets the control or treatment. Double-blind design eliminates experimenter bias.

External Validity:

External validity refers to how well the results of the study relate to the real world environment. Although the experiment allows the researcher to control and eliminate the effects of confounding variables, it comes with a price. Real behavior does not happen in the absence of confounding variables and the amount of control the researcher has means the results apply less to the real world.

In the lab, the participants play a video game and then we observe their behavior. In the real world, children play video games in a home environment, sometimes with friends, at different times of the day, in different moods, hungry or not hungry, with parental commentary and supervision, or not. The number of differences between the researcher's lab and the real environment make the results of the experiment lower in *external validity*.

Practice Research Design

On the AP Psychology Exam, one of the most likely free response questions asks you to design a research study to evaluate a certain hypothesis. Your task will be to design a study that minimizes all potential confounding variables and shows the strongest results that indicate whether or not the hypothesis is likely true or not true. Look at the following research question and then try to design an experiment to test your hypothesis.

Research Question: Does taking vitamin B12 improve your memory?

This is a good example of how cognitive psychology has evolved over the years to now include examination of brain functioning. How would you design an *experiment* to test the hypothesis that taking B12 improves memory?

Be sure to include the basic concepts and terms in the box below.

hypothesis	random selection
independent variable	random assignment
dependent variable	control group
confounding variable	treatment group

When writing your answer to this question first state the hypothesis in as specific terms as possible.

For example, below are 3 possible hypotheses. Which one is the most specific?

a) Vitamins will help memory
b) Taking vitamin B12 everyday will help memory
c) The intake of 50 mgs. of vitamin B12 daily for 3 months will improve the performance on a memory task of 100 words

Then, define the IV and DV as specifically as possible. That should take no more than 2 sentences. Next, define the control group and treatment group and briefly describe what the research participants will experience (one sentence for each group). The final step is to describe how you will use random selection and random assignment to decide which participants go to which group.

Here is an example:

The researchers theorize that vitamins can help memory. The hypothesis is that taking small doses of vitamin B12 every day for 6 weeks will improve participant's performance on a memory task of 100 words. To test the hypothesis, the researchers will use an independent samples experiment. Participants will be randomly selected high-school seniors from 3 schools and then randomly assigned to either the control or treatment groups. The design will be double-blind, such that neither the participants nor the experimenters collecting the data will know which participants will be in which groups. The control group will not receive any vitamins and will only perform the memory task at the end of the 6-week study. The treatment group will receive 50 mgs. of vitamin B12 for 6 weeks and then take the memory task at the end of the study.

This design has all the key terms and concepts included. You can also include how you will analyze the data to determine if the hypothesis was supported or rejected.

Statistics

The use of statistics in any research is crucial. Statistics allow us to make decisions about our results as meaningful or not. Researchers may disagree about the results of a study, but using statistics takes the bias out of the debate. If the statistics say the results are meaningful then it is very difficult to argue otherwise.

Remember our example using correlation? We performed an archival study that involved looking at the relation between 2 variables: temperature and arrests. Our hypothesis was that temperature and aggression would be related, such that the higher the temperature the higher the number of arrest. However, we always state an alternative hypothesis that says the results are due to random chance. This alternative hypothesis is called the *null hypothesis*. The researcher's hypothesis states that there is a relation between the two variables, and the null hypothesis states that the results are just due to chance.

So, how do we know if a correlation of .39 is real or due to chance? One person might think that it is, but another person may argue that it is not. The solution is called the *p-value*.

P Values and the Null Hypothesis

Just looking at a scatterplot or correlation coefficient will not tell us if the results are real or due to some chance event. Fortunately, statistics will give us the answer by calculating the *p-value*. A statistical program calculates the *p-value* automatically, and it tells us the likelihood that the results are due to chance, or are real.

Let's use another hypothetical study to illustrate the concept of the *p-value* and the *null hypothesis*. Suppose we do a medical experiment using a drug that we already know is completely ineffective. The null hypothesis in reality is true. There should be no difference on the DV between the control and the treatment groups.

Even though we know the drug does not work, it is entirely possible that the two groups in our study might differ on the DV before they even took part in the research, just as a matter of chance. Even if we use random selection and random assignment, it is still a possibility. When this happens it is called *sampling error*. So, the null hypothesis is true and there should be no difference between the groups, but our data might show a difference due to sampling error and chance alone.

When the stats program is finished analyzing the data, it will reveal the p-value. If the p-value is equal to or less than .05, then it means that there is a 5% chance that the results are due to *sampling error*, or chance. That is a very low percentage and therefore researchers will conclude that the results are real and not due chance. The exact term used is *statistically significant*.

However, if the p-value is greater than .05, then researchers will conclude that the results are *not statistically significant*, and probably due to chance. This is a very stringent cut-off point for when results are considered real or not.

Frequency Distribution

A frequency distribution is a graph that shows how many times something occurred. For example, if we measure the height of every person in the world, and then plot the data on a frequency distribution, the results would look like this:

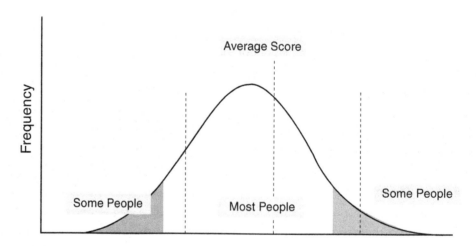

At the extremes, there is a small percentage of people that are very tall, and very short. Most people are somewhere in between. Every human characteristic we can think of shows a similar shaped distribution: height, weight, musical talent, math ability, IQ, etc. This kind of frequency distribution is sometimes called the *Bell Curve* or the *Normal Curve*.

The normal curve has many interesting statistical properties. We use basic descriptive statistics to describe the distribution: range, mean, median, mode, standard deviation, and skewness.

The *range* is the lowest and highest numbers in the distribution. The *mean* of a set of numerical values is the *average* of the numerical values after adding all the numerical values and dividing that sum by the total number of numerical values. The *median* is the numerical value in which half of the other numerical values fall below, and half fall above. The *mode* of the distribution is the value that occurs most frequently and is in the very middle of the distribution curve.

The *standard deviation* is a bit more complex to calculate and beyond the scope of this study guide. However, conceptually it is an extremely important concept to understand in psychology. The standard deviation is a measure of how much the values in the frequency distribution are spread out (or deviate) from the mean.

Below is a hypothetical example showing 3 standard deviations. The larger the standard deviation the more the values in the distribution deviate from the mean.

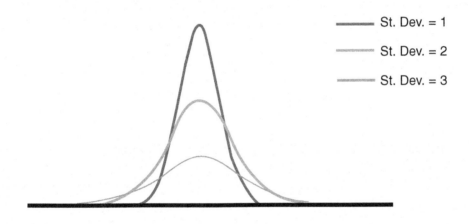

Although human characteristics form a normal distribution, sometimes the data from research is different. Samples are smaller than the population so there can be *sampling error*. Another way to describe a distribution is in terms of *skewness*. When the distribution has a disproportionate number of high values, we say the distribution is *negatively skewed*. When the distribution has a disproportionate number of low values, we say the distribution is *positively skewed*. The figure below shows the two types of *skewness* in relation to the normal curve.

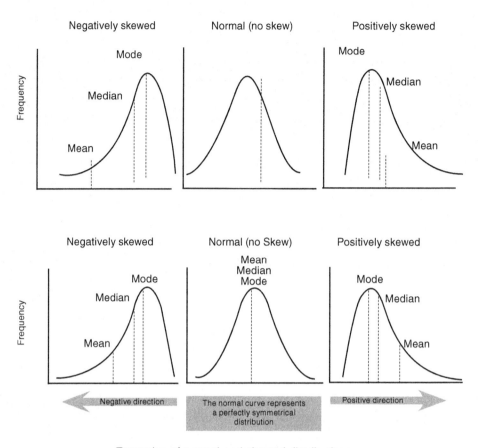

Examples of normal and skewed distributions

Approximating Percentiles Using Standard Deviations

An *IQ distribution curve*, for large samples, is an almost perfect Gaussian distribution where each standard deviation up or down is 15 points away from the median *score of 100*. Those who score one standard deviation above the mean, i.e. 115, have higher scores than about 85% of all test takers. Those who score two standard deviations above the mean, 130, have higher scores than about 98% of all test takers. Scores that are three standard deviations above the mean, 145, represent scores that are higher than 99.9% of all test takers. These percentile values (not the actual value of the standard deviation, which can be any value) are roughly the same for all standard deviations and you should be able to recognize this if you are given standard deviation questions on the AP Psychology Exam.

One other notable descriptive statistic in terms of the AP Psychology Exam is the *Z score*. Z scores are converted values derived from standard deviation values. Z scores can be compared between different distributions. Z scores below the mean have negative values and Z scores above the mean have positive values.

Ethics in Research

Historical Antecedents

There was a time when scientists could conduct research on humans and animals without any oversight. However, after WWII many horrific accounts of human experimentation emerged and eventually resulted in many people being convicted of crimes in the *Nuremberg Trials*.

In addition, the *Tuskegee study* is a famous example from the United States where doctors purposefully administered a disease to unknowing citizens in the name of research. Several other examples can be described, but now scientists must follow very strict government regulations regarding their research. Some of the considerations are listed below.

APA Ethical Guidelines

For Animals

- Research should be undertaken with a clear scientific purpose.
- The scientific purpose of the research should be of sufficient potential significance to justify the use of nonhuman animals.
- Research on nonhuman animals may not be conducted until the protocol has been reviewed by an appropriate animal care committee.
- The facilities housing laboratory animals should meet or exceed current regulations and guidelines and are required to be inspected twice a year.
- All procedures carried out on nonhuman animals are to be reviewed by an institutional animal care and use committee to ensure that the procedures are appropriate and humane.
- Laboratory animals not bred in the psychologist's facility are to be acquired lawfully.
- Nonhuman animals taken from the wild should be trapped in a humane manner.
- Whenever possible behavioral procedures should be used that minimize discomfort to the nonhuman animal.

For Humans

Informed Consent

- Researchers are required in some, but not all, circumstances obtain the *informed consent* of the individual.
- When obtaining informed consent researchers should inform participants about the purpose of the research, and give the right to decline to participate or withdraw from the research once participation has begun (no coercion).
- Researchers must also inform potential participants of reasonably foreseeable factors such as potential risks, discomfort, or adverse effects.
- Researchers may dispense with informed consent only where research would not be reasonably assumed to create distress or harm.

Researchers should:

- Advise subjects on questions about the research and research participants' rights.
- Provide an opportunity for the prospective participants to ask questions and receive answers.
- Have a primary obligation and take reasonable precautions to protect confidential information.
- Not disclose *confidential* information without the consent of the individual except when it is mandated by law, or where it is permitted by law for a valid purpose.
- Take reasonable steps to protect the identity of the research subjects.

Deception in Research

- Researchers do not conduct a study involving *deception* unless they have determined that the use of deceptive techniques is justified by the study's significant prospective value, and effective nondeceptive alternative procedures are not feasible.
- Researchers do not deceive prospective participants about research that is reasonably expected to cause physical pain or severe emotional distress.
- Researchers explain any deception that is an integral feature of the design and conduct of an experiment to participants as early as feasible, preferably at the conclusion of their participation, but no later than at the conclusion of the data collection.

Debriefing

Psychologist researchers provide a prompt opportunity for participants to obtain appropriate information about the nature, results, and conclusions of the research.

Chapter 3: Biological Bases of Behavior

Neuroanatomy

Neuroanatomy is the study of the physical architecture of the nervous system.

At the cellular level, the nervous system is composed primarily of neurons, highly specialized cells that conduct electrical signals, and other cells that provide metabolic and structural roles within the nervous system. These other cell include glial cells and hormone-secreting cells that are located in various glands and other regions throughout the body.

Neurons are by far the most important cells within the nervous system. They are the major component of all the nerves in the body. Within the brain, neurons are first organized in small clusters of cells called *ganglia* and then in increasingly more complex structures that finally result in a vast and immensely complicated interconnected information processing network. Some individual neurons within the brain can have direct neurochemical communication with over 10,000 other neurons.

Nerves, Axons and Action Potentials

A *nerve* is primarily composed of nerve fibers. A *nerve fiber* is a thread-like extension of a single neuron. These extensions are called *axons*. Axons always transmit electrical signals away from the parent neuron and towards the end of the nerve fiber. These electrical signals are called *action potentials*.

Efferent Nerves

Electrical signals that travel from the brain or spinal cord to peripheral targets are called *efferent signals*. The nerves that transmit these signals are called *efferent nerves*. Efferent nerves almost always send signals to muscles or glands These nerves are also called *motor nerves*, and the neurons that form these nerves are called *motor neurons*.

Afferent nerves

Nerve signals that travel from the periphery to the brain or spinal cord, or from the spinal cord to the brain, are called *afferent signals*. The nerves that transmit these electrical signals are called *afferent nerves*. Afferent nerves are almost always sending sensory information to the brain and/or spinal cord. These nerves are also called *sensory nerves*, and the neurons that form these nerves are called *sensory neurons*.

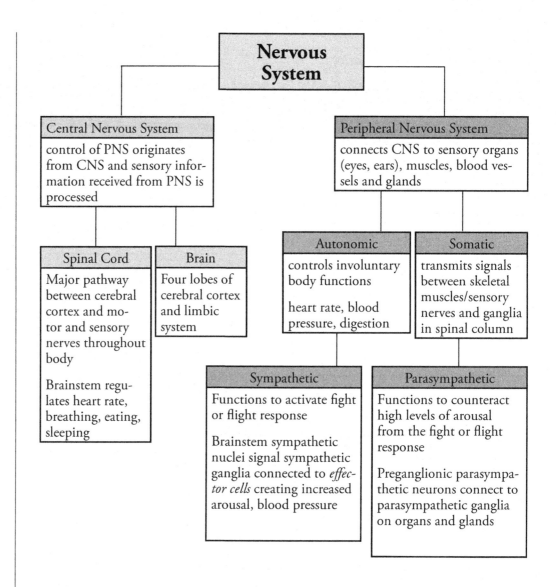

The Peripheral Nervous System_____

Outside of the central nervous system, neurons exist in numerous ganglia and form nerves that are the primary components of the peripheral nervous system. One excellent definition of the peripheral nervous system is that it is the portion of the nervous system that is not encased in bone (the skull and the vertebrae of the spinal column). The peripheral nervous system has two major divisions, the *somatic* nervous system, and the *autonomic* nervous system.

The Somatic Nervous system_____

The somatic nervous system is also referred to as the *voluntary nervous system*. The nerves of the somatic nervous system transmit signals between skeletal muscle fibers sensory organs,\ and ganglia located in the vertebrae of the spinal column.

Motor Division of the Somatic Nervous System

When you make a voluntary decision to move a part of your body, *upper motor neurons* located in the *motor cortex* of the brain send signals to *lower motor neurons* in ganglia located either in the head and neck or in the *ventral* (toward the front of the body) portions of individual *vertebrae* of the spinal column. The lower motor neurons then relay these signals to the voluntary muscles via somatic motor nerves. Somatic motor nerves connected to vertebral ganglia are called *spinal motor nerves*. Somatic motor nerves connected to ganglia located in the head and neck are from the motor divisions of the *cranial nerves*.

Sensory Division of the Somatic Nervous System

Sensory information originating from locations below the neck travel in *spinal sensory nerves* to ganglia located in the *dorsal* (toward the back of the body) portions of individual vertebrae of the spinal column. Sensory information from the head and neck, including visual (sight), olfactory (smell), auditory (hearing) and gustatory (taste) information also travel in the cranial nerves. Nerves that carry both sensory and motor signals are called *mixed nerves*.

Sensory information transmitted through the somatic nervous system travels many locations in the brain, including the visual cortex located in the occipital lobes, the somatosensory cortex located in the parietal lobes, the auditory cortex located in the temporal lobes.

The Autonomic Nervous System

The other major division of the peripheral nervous system is the *autonomic nervous system*. The autonomic nervous system controls and regulates involuntary body functions. Some examples of these functions are regulation of heart rate, blood pressure and digestion. In most cases, you have very limited, if any, conscious control over your autonomic nervous system. The autonomic nervous system sends and receives information through nerves that travel between the central nervous system and autonomic ganglia that are located in widespread locations throughout the body. Most of the motor activity of the autonomic nervous system is under the control of specialized regions of neurons called *nuclei* located in the brainstem.

The autonomic nervous system consists of two subdivisions, the *sympathetic* nervous system and the *parasympathetic* nervous system. Traditionally the sympathetic system is referred to as the "fight or flight" nervous system, and the parasympathetic system is referred to as the "rest and digest" nervous system. In general, the sympathetic system tends to act rapidly to raise the body's level of arousal in the form of increased alertness, heart rate, blood pressure and energy production. Parasympathetic actions act more gradually and tend to lower the body's overall state of arousal and to increase the process of digestion.

In reality, the two systems are constantly interacting and fine-tuning the body's involuntary sensory and motor functions. This interaction between the two systems is critical to maintaining the optimum homeostatic levels within the body.

The Sympathetic Nervous System

The sympathetic motor pathways begin in sympathetic ganglia mostly located in the head and neck or along either side of the vertebrae of the spine (the paraspinal or chain ganglia). Brainstem sympathetic nuclei transmit signals to the sympathetic ganglia, sympathetic nerves connect the ganglia to many target cell, called *effector cells*, located throughout the body. Sensory information is transmitted to the central nervous system through sensory sympathetic nerves.

The Parasympathetic Nervous System

All of the motor neural pathways of the parasympathetic nervous system begin with parasympathetic neurons located either in the brainstem region of the brain or in the spinal cord. These neurons are called preganglionic parasympathetic neurons. All preganglionic parasympathetic neurons send their axons via parasympathetic nerves to various parasympathetic ganglia located close to organs, glands and other structures throughout the body. Sensory information is transmitted to the central nervous system through sensory parasympathetic nerves sympathetic nerves.

Reflex Arcs

Reflex arcs are a special case of automatic motor function. Reflex arcs are basically involuntary (although you can sometimes override them if you know they are coming). The classic example of a reflex arc is the patellar tendon reflex. When the patellar tendon of a bent (flexed) knee is tapped by a blunt instrument - like a reflex hammer, the tendon is suddenly stretched. This stimulates specialized sensory receptor cells, called *stretch receptors*, to fire action potentials to motor neurons located in the spinal cord.

In response, these neurons fire action potentials to neuromuscular junctions located at muscles that extend the knee. This stimulates the muscles to contract, causing the lower leg to straighten (extend), thereby reducing the stretching force on the patellar tendon. Notice that this neural circuit requires only two neurons and one synapse. This is the simplest type of reflex. It is called a monosynapicareflex.

Be careful of the terminology here, the two neurons are the motor neuron and the stretch receptor cell, which is considered to be a highly specialized type of neuron. In fact, nearly all sensory receptor cells are considered to be highly specialized types of neurons. Also, as we have previously advised, the neuromuscular junction is not formally considered to be a synapse, even though it is nearly identical to a synapse.

The next more complex type of reflex arc consists of a three-neuron sequence. It is nearly identical to the monosynaptic reflex except that another neuron, called an *interneuron*, relays the electrical signals from the sensory receptor cell to the motor neuron.

NOTE: Autonomic sensory and motor neural innervation can be quite diffuse and you are not expected to know the precise neural pathways of the autonomic nervous system, but in general autonomic nerves can be purely sensory, motor or mixed. In the head and neck, these nerves often travel alongside somatic cranial nerves.

The Central Nervous System_____

The central nervous system is where nearly all control of the peripheral nervous system originates and it is where nearly all of the sensory information from the peripheral nervous system is processed. One of the best way to describe the anatomical structures of the central nervous system is to begin with the oldest structures. The central nervous system has evolved over time beginning with the earliest organisms that first developed the most rudimentary types of nervous systems.

The Spinal Cord and the Brainstem

The evolution of central nervous system began with the notochord. The notochord is a tube of neural tissue that was the first neural structure that began to process sensory information and coordinate motor activities in simple multicellular organisms. As animals evolved, the complexity and capabilities of the notochord increased. In higher animals including humans the notochord evolved into the spinal cord.

One end of the spinal cord evolved into an enlarged, more highly differentiated structure that in humans is the brainstem. The most basic functions of the central nervous system are under the direct control of the brainstem including control of the majority of the autonomic nervous system. Regions of the brainstem regulate heart rate, breathing, eating and sleeping

The Myelencephalon

The region of the brainstem closest to the spinal cord is the *medulla oblongata*. The medulla oblongata is also called the *myelencephalon*. It is composed primarily of nerve tracts that transmit information between the peripheral nervous system and higher brain centers.

The Metencephalon

Adjacent to the medulla are the *pons* and the *cerebellum*, together they comprise the *metencephalon*. The pons, like the medulla, is primarily a relay center between lower and higher levels of the nervous system. The cerebellum represents a significantly more complex brain structure. It coordinates basic types of motor activities. Well-coordinated movement sequences are impossible without a functional cerebellum. The myelencephalon and the metencephalon together are referred to as the *hindbrain.*

The third region of the brainstem is the *midbrain* or *mesencephalon*. Regions of the mesencephalon are involved in visual and auditory processing, motor control, regulation of body temperature, sleep/wake cycles and maintaining alertness.

As we move forward to more recently evolved brain structures we begin to see the emergence of central nervous system functions that have great significance to psychologists. The anatomical elements of these structures are not nearly important as their functional roles in sensation, perception, cognition, motivation, emotion, personality and social behavior. The functional aspects of the following brain structures will be discussed in greater detail later in the chapter.

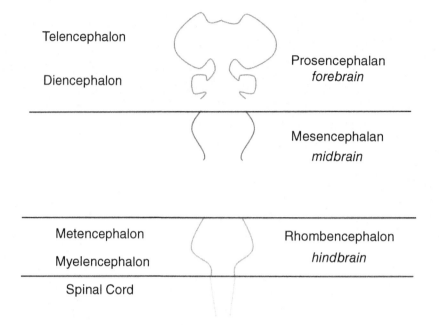

| Telencephalon | | Prosencephalan |
| Diencephalon | | *forebrain* |

| | Mesencephalan |
| | *midbrain* |

Metencephalon	Rhombencephalon
Myelencephalon	*hindbrain*
Spinal Cord	

The Diencephalon

The diencephalon is a division of the *forebrain*. The forebrain is the most complex and recently evolved anatomical division of the brain. The diencephalon is contiguous with the midbrain and the adjacent division of the forebrain, the *telencephalon*. Important structures of the *diencephalon* are the *thalamus* and the *hypothalamus*.

The Limbic System

The Hypothalamus

The hypothalamus is remarkable for its role as a *neurosecretory organ*. It synthesizes and secretes hormones that control other hormone secreting glands. It also is involved in generating the sensations of thirst and hunger. Significantly to psychology, the hypothalamus appears to play an important role in behaviors related to parenting and interpersonal attachment. Adjacent to the hypothalamus are the *amygdala* and the *hippocampus*.

The Amygdala

The *amygdala* is part of the limbic system of the brain, which plays a central role in the integration of basic emotions into more complex emotional and motivational behaviors.

The Hippocampus

The hippocampus is also part of the *limbic system*. The hippocampus is critically important for the consolidation of short-term memory into long-term memories. It is one of the first structures to degenerate in patients with Alzheimer's disease.

The Cerebral Cortex

The cerebral cortex is the other major division of the forebrain. It is the final level of central nervous system evolution and it reaches its peak complexity and functionality in humans. At the most basic anatomical level the cerebral cortex is notable for its differentiation into two hemispheres, the right hemisphere and the left hemisphere, and its highly convoluted structure, which vastly increases its total surface area. The two hemispheres are connected by several very large nerve tracts, the largest being the corpus callosum. There is heavy information flow between the two hemispheres and most of this occurs through the corpus callosum.

The cerebral hemispheres are subdivided into four major regions called lobes. These are the *frontal* lobes, the *temporal* lobes, the *parietal* lobes and the *occipital* lobes. There is a high degree of specialization of function among the lobes. Many functions are lateralized, meaning that they are localized to either the left hemisphere or the right hemisphere. The functional aspects of the regions of the cerebral cortex will be discussed in detail later in the chapter.

Anatomy of a Neuron

Neurons can be classified based on various characteristics. One of these methods of classifying defines neurons as bipolar, unipolar or multipolar. The classic description of a neuron is the bipolar neuron.

The two poles of a bipolar neuron refer to the location of the neuron's primary signal receiving structures, the dendrites, which are tree-like branched extrusions extending from one end of the neuron, and the signal transmitting structure, and the axon, a thread-like extrusion extending from the opposite end of the neuron.

The axon is the nerve fiber of the neuron. As we have discussed, nerves are composed of nerve fibers. The sciatic nerve is a peripheral somatic motor nerve that can be over two feet long. The nerve fibers within the sciatic nerve are all individual axons extending from motor neurons located in the spinal column. We usually think of cells as microscopic structures, but a single sciatic nerve motor neuron can be over two feet long!

The remainder, or main body of the neuron, is located between the two poles of the neuron, the axon and dendrites. This main body of the neuron is called the *soma* and it contains the cellular nucleus and a major percentage of the cell's other organelles.

Electrically Excitable Cells

The key feature of neurons is that they are electrically excitable cells. *Electrically excitable cells* can transmit electrical signals along their cell membranes. Muscle cells and sensory receptor cells are the other major types of electrically excitable cells (sensory receptor cell are actually considered highly specialized types of neurons). Electrically excitable cells, like nearly all cells in the human body, have a transmembrane electrical potential. The interior of these cells are negatively charged relative to the exterior of the cells.

This has been demonstrated in the laboratory by placing one microelectrode inside a neuron and a second microelectrode very close to the first electrode but just outside of the neuron's cell membrane. The two microelectrodes are connected to a volt-meter. The voltmeter confirms that there is an electrical potential difference of -70 millivolts across the neuron's cell membrane.

The neuron is said to be "polarized" because it has a potential electrical difference across its cell membrane. This 70-millivolt transmembrane potential corresponds to the "resting" potential of the neuron.

Do not confuse this concept with the term *bipolar neuron*. Bipolar neurons do not have a positive pole and a negative pole - that's an electrical definition. Bipolar, for neurons, is an anatomical definition. The two poles refer to the one end (or pole) of the neuron that is composed of dendrites and the opposite end (or pole) of the neuron, the axon.

Active Transport and Transmembrane Sodium Ion Pumps

How does the neuron create this transmembrane potential? The neuron cell membrane is covered with transmembrane structures called *ion pumps*. These structures transport ions across the cell membrane against the transmembrane concentration gradient of the ion.

An example of this type of transport occurs with the positively charged sodium ion, $Na+$. Cell membranes are semipermeable, some particles can freely cross cell membranes and others cannot. Ions have difficulty crossing cell membranes. Some leakage of ions does occur across cell membranes, but in general, cell membranes are considered to be impermeable to charged particles. Some ion pumps transport sodium ions from the inside of the cell to the outside of the cell. This transportation process reduces the concentration of sodium ions inside the cell. As the process continues, the concentration of sodium ions inside the cell is a progressively lower compared to the concentration of sodium ions outside the cell.

The difference between these two sodium ion concentrations is called the sodium ion transmembrane gradient. There is a greater concentration of positively charged sodium ions outside the cell than inside the cell. The result contributes to the creation of a transmembrane electrical potential. As the sodium gradient increases, the transmembrane electrical potential increases and the neuron becomes more polarized.

NOTE: Several other ion concentrations are regulated by cells. The most important of these are the potassium ion (K+). The chloride ion (Cl-) and the calcium ion (Ca ++). All of these ion concentrations contribute to the neuron's transmembrane electrical potential.

Transporting charged ions from a region of low concentration to a region of high concentration requires energy. This type of transport is called active transport. The neuron's active transport ion pumps use energy derived from intracellular ATP molecules to power this process.

Active transport requires a lot of energy. The average human brain weighs three pounds but it uses 20 percent of the total energy required by the human body. Most of this energy is required to maintain the transmembrane electrical potential of the brain's neurons.

NOTE: The sodium ion pump is actually much more complicated than we have described. In reality it is called the *sodium/potassium ATPase ion-exchange transporter*. Neurons and other electrically excitable cells have many types of transmembrane pumps or transporters. The explanation provided here is accurate, but simplified. The AP Psychology exam will not expect you to understanding this topic in any greater detail.

Ligand-Gated Sodium Ion Channels

Neuron membranes have surface receptors for molecules called *neurotransmitters*. Neurotransmitter receptors are most abundant in the dendritic regions of the neuron, but they can be found anywhere along the outer membrane surface of the neuron. When a neurotransmitter molecule binds to one of these receptors, the transmembrane electrical potential of the local membrane region surrounding the receptor can change.

In many instances, this process occurs because the neuron's cell membrane also contains transmembrane structures called "ion pores" or "ion channels". Ion channels that are activated by the binding of specific molecules to membrane receptors are called ligand-gated ion channels. The *ligand* is the molecule that binds to the membrane receptor.

In neurons, the binding of a neurotransmitter molecule to one type of receptor on the neuron's membrane triggers the opening of nearby ligand-gated sodium ion channels. The ligand is this case is the neurotransmitter molecule. When these channels open, sodium ions from the outside rush through the channel to the inside of the neuron.

In contrast to the active transport of sodium ions, this process does not require energy. The sodium ions are moving from a region of high concentration to a region of low concentration, which according to physical laws, is what they want to do. This type of movement is called passive transport or simple diffusion because it does not require the cell to use any energy for it to occur.

Membrane Depolarization

When ligand-gated sodium ion channels open and positively charged sodium ions rush into the cell, the transmembrane electrical potential near the channel changes. The transmembrane sodium ion gradient decreases because lots of sodium ions are entering the cell, thereby increasing the sodium ion concentration inside the cell. Consequently, there is now a smaller difference between the sodium ion concentration inside the neuron compared to the sodium ion concentration outside of the neuron.

This local region of the neuron's cell membrane becomes less polarized. Typically, the binding of a small number of neurotransmitter molecules to a local group of membrane receptor results in a localized 0.5 millivolt decreased depolarization of the neuron's membrane, from -70 millivolts to -69.5 millivolts. By itself, such a small change as this will not have much effect on the neuron.

But here is a key fact, these individual small depolarizations, which are called excitatory end plate potentials (EEPPs), can combine or "sum up" and produce a much larger local membrane depolarization. If the depolarization reaches a critical threshold, usually around -55 millivolts, something truly amazing will happen.

Voltage-Gated Sodium Ion Channels

When a sufficient amount of neurotransmitter molecules bind to their receptors at a small region of a neuron's outer cell membrane, their combined effect can depolarize a local transmembrane region from -70 millivolts to a critical threshold level, usually around -55 millivolts. When this threshold is reached, it triggers the activation of a new type of transmembrane ion channel, the voltage-gated sodium channel.

Voltage-gated sodium channels function in a similar manner to the ligand-gated sodium channels. The difference between the two is that ligand-gated sodium channels open in response to the binding of a neurotransmitter to a membrane-bound receptor. In contrast, voltage-gated sodium ion channels are activated by electric currents. It is the electrical current generated by changing localized transmembrane electrical potentials that triggers the voltage-channel to open, not the binding of a neurotransmitter to a membrane-bound receptor.

NOTE: Other mechanisms can cause membrane depolarization resulting in voltage-gated sodium channel activation in electrically excitable cells. Most importantly, in sensory receptor cells, such as light striking photoreceptor cells in the retina, or sound vibrations stimulating hair cells in the cochlea of the middle ear.

Action Potentials

Voltage-gated sodium channels allow so many sodium ions to rush in so quickly that there is a sudden, very large change in the local membrane potential. In fact, the potential actually reverses. The local potential spikes upward from -55 millivolts to +40 millivolts in less than 1 millisecond. The activated voltage-gated sodium channels slam shut about 1 millisecond later. Then, other types of ion gates are activated resulting in a second reversal of the local membrane to about -90 millivolts within another millisecond.

About five milliseconds after this process beg, the local membrane is restored to its resting potential of -70 millivolts and the voltage-gated sodium channels are ready to fire again.

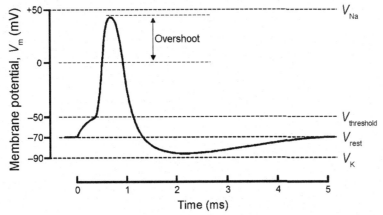

© *PhysiologyWeb* at www.physiologyweb.com

This incredibly fast electrical spike is called an action potential and it is one the the most important phenomena in biology, Action potentials are the fundamental units of information required for all neurological processes.

Two key concepts regarding *action potentials* are: 1) The voltage-gated sodium channel requires about 1-2 milliseconds to reset after it generates an action potential. This is called the channel's refractory period. During the refractory period, the channel cannot generate another action potential. 2) Action potentials are an "all or none" phenomenon. They either happen or they don't. There are no partial action potentials.

NOTE: Neurotransmitters do not always cause membrane depolarization when they bind to membrane-bound receptors on a neuron. Many types of neuron membrane-bound receptors do not activate ligand-gated sodium channels. It is common for neurotransmitter binding to inhibit rather than trigger the generation of action potentials.

You are expected to know that neurotransmitter inhibition occurs and you are expected to know several of the important circumstances where certain specific neurotransmitters have an inhibitory effect. You are not expected to know any details of the biochemical mechanisms underlying these inhibitory effects.

Propagation of an Action Potential

So what is the "action" in an action potential? To begin, it is important to restate that once voltage-gated sodium channels close, they will not reopen during the refractory period of the sodium channel.

Next, consider that a neuron's axon contains the highest concentration of voltage-gated sodium channels. The most easily triggered sodium channels on the axon are located at the axon hillock, the region where the axon emerges from the neuron's main body (soma). Consequently, action potentials almost always begin at the origin of the axon hillock.

Finally, be aware that there is nothing more likely to trigger voltage-gated sodium channels than an action potential. The entire length of the axon is loaded with voltage-gated sodium channels, which are all primed and ready to fire. A good analogy is to think of these sodium channels as a line of upright dominoes.

The initial action potential at the axon hillock activate adjacent voltage-gated sodium channels. This generates another action potential right next to the first action potential, which is already dying off. This second action potential triggers another potential a bit further down the axon. The process continues like a cascade of falling dominoes. The action potential appears to flash down the length of the axon, beginning at the axon hillock, and proceeding to the terminal end of the axon.

The propagation of the action potential does not move backward because the sodium channels in the reverse direction have recently fired and cannot be refired while they are in their refractory period. An action potential can travel down an axon at velocities as high as 220 miles per hour. That is how is how electrical signals are transmitted along a nerve fiber.

Action Potentials and the Myelin Sheath

Many axons are wrapped in a myelin *sheath*. The myelin is actually an extension of the cell membrane of another type of cell, called a Schwann cell or an oligodendrocyte. The myelin wraps around the axon several times in short segments. There are small gaps of bare axon between the myelin segments called nodes of Ranvier. Myelinated nerve fibers conduct action potentials much faster and more efficiently than unmyelinated nerve fibers. Tissues containing a high percentage of myelinated nerve fibers appear white - this is the "white matter' of the brain and spinal cord. Grey matter is composed mostly of the main bodies (or somas) of neurons.

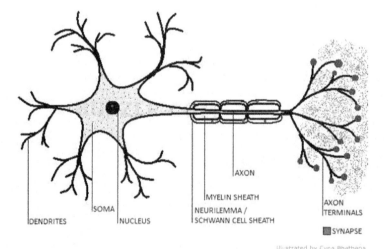

Illustrated by Cyna Bhathena

Neurotransmitters

Neurotransmitters are small molecules that are able to bind to membrane-bound receptors on other cells. The target cell is usually another neuron, a muscle cell, or an endocrine cell. As their name implies, neurotransmitters are involved in the transmission of signals throughout the nervous system.

Neurotransmitters are synthesized by all neurons including sensory receptor cell, which are actually highly specialized neurons. An individual neuron can synthesize more than one type of neurotransmitter and an individual neuron can have many receptors for many different types of neurotransmitters.

Synapses

We have discussed how an action potential transmits signals down a nerve fiber, but how are these signals sent beyond an individual neuron? The far end of an axon is called the axon terminal. An axon often has several collateral branches, with each branch possessing a terminal segment. At the terminal segment, the axon forms clusters of smaller terminal branches. The tips of the terminal branches are somewhat enlarged. These terminal swellings are called *synaptic bulbs* or *terminal boutons* or *axon terminals*.

Terminal boutons are almost always located adjacent to another cell called a target cell. Usually the target cell is another neuron or a muscle cell. This junction is called a synapse. The gap separating the bouton and the target cell membrane is called a synaptic cleft. When an action potential reaches a terminal segment, it triggers the release of neurotransmitter molecules from the terminal boutons into the synaptic gap.

The neurotransmitters diffuse across the synaptic gap and bind to receptors on the target cell membrane. If enough of the neurotransmitter molecules bind, the neurotransmitter will have a physiological effect on the target cell. One way to classify neurotransmitter effects on target cells is as excitatory or inhibitory.

Recall in the discussion of action potentials how neurotransmitter binding can produce localized depolarization of a target cell membrane called excitatory end plate potentials. These small depolarizations can combine and possibly trigger an action potential. In this case, the neurotransmitter is classified as *excitatory*, and the presynaptic neuron is classified as an excitatory neuron.

In contrast, neurotransmitter binding can produce localized increased polarization (hyperpolarization) of a target cell membrane called inhibitory end plate potentials. These small depolarizations can cancel out excitatory end plate potentials. They decrease the likelihood that the postsynaptic target cell will fire an action potential. In this case, the neurotransmitter is classified as inhibitory, and the presynaptic neuron is classified as an inhibitory neuron.

NOTE: There are many other mechanisms by which neurons and neurotransmitters can have excitatory or inhibitory effects on postsynaptic target cells. you are not expected to know the details of these other mechanisms, but you are expected to know that they exist and to know where certain neurons and neurotransmitters have excitatory or inhibitory effects on more complex neurological regions and interconnected neural pathways.

Acetylcholine and the Parasympathetic Nervous System

All of the motor neural pathways of the parasympathetic nervous system begin with *parasympathetic neurons* located either in the brainstem region of the brain or in the spinal cord. These neurons are called preganglionic parasympathetic neurons. All preganglionic parasympathetic neurons send their axons via parasympathetic nerves to various parasympathetic ganglia located close to organs, glands and other structures throughout the body.

In a *parasympathetic ganglion*, a synapse always occurs between preganglionic parasympathetic axons and a second parasympathetic neuron. The first neuron fires an action potential resulting in the release the neurotransmitter acetylcholine (ACh) from a terminal bouton into the synaptic cleft. The ACh molecules diffuse across the synaptic cleft and bind to ACh receptors on the membrane of a dendrite of the second parasympathetic neuron.

If enough Ach molecules bind to receptors on the second parasympathetic neuron, the second parasympathetic neuron's membrane will depolarize to its threshold level and it will fire another action potential. Let's follow this second action potential as it travels down the axon to the next synapse.

This second neuron, which is called the *postganglionic neuron*, does not synapse with another neuron, instead it synapses with a different type of target cell. For instance, it may travel to and synapse with a smooth muscle cell located in the stomach.

Most biologists do not refer to this as a synapse. They call it a neuromuscular junction, but for our purposes they are basically the same thing. The second action potential triggers the release of ACh molecules into the synaptic cleft. The smooth muscle has membrane receptors for ACh molecules.

The Ach molecules diffuse across and bind to their receptors on the smooth muscle cell. Depending on what type of Ach receptor this is, this binding may trigger the smooth muscle to relax or to contract. Recall that the parasympathetic nervous system tends to increase the process of digestion. The parasympathetic neural pathway we have just described is an example of how this occurs.

Acetylcholine and the Parasympathetic Nervous System	Acetylcholine and the Somatic Nervous System
motor neural pathway starts in brainstem or spinal cord with the *preganglionic parasympathetic neuron* releases….	Begin with *upper motor neurons* in the *postcentral gyrus* of the cerebral cortex (primary motor cortex)
↓ ACh into synaptic gap of next neuron	Send *action potentials* down axons through spinal cord
Postganglionic neuron receives ACh threshold for depolarization is met or not	Synapse with other motor neurons located within *somatic motor ganglia* (cluster of motor neurons)
Depolarization ↓ releases ACh into *neuromuscular junction*	ACh into *neuromuscular junction*
Neuromuscular junction is attached to the smooth muscle of an organ called a *smooth muscle cell*	Postsynaptic motor neurons are called *lower-motor neurons*
Muscle *relaxes or contracts*	Muscle *relaxes or contracts*

Key facts to emphasize include: 1) all parasympathetic motor pathways begin with parasympathetic neurons located either in the brainstem or the spinal cord 2) the first motor neuron in a parasympathetic motor pathway always sends its axon to a parasympathetic ganglia where it synapses with a second parasympathetic neuron 3) the second neuron in a parasympathetic motor pathways does not synapse with another neuron, instead it synapses with a different type of target cell, usually a smooth muscle cell 4) the neurotransmitter for all parasympathetic motor neurons is acetylcholine (ACh).

Acetylcholine, in addition to being the major neurotransmitter for all neurons of the parasympathetic motor system, has several other important roles within the central and peripheral nervous systems

Acetylcholine and the Sympathetic Nervous System

The sympathetic motor pathways begin in sympathetic ganglia mostly located along either side of the vertebrae of the spine. Acetylcholine is the neurotransmitter within the sympathetic ganglia. Acetylcholine has an excitatory effect on the postsynaptic neurons located in the sympathetic ganglia.

Acetylcholine and the Somatic Nervous System

The motor neural pathways of the *somatic nervous system*, which control all the voluntary muscular systems of the body, begin with upper motor neurons located in the postcentral gyrus of the cerebral cortex. This is basically the same region as the primary motor cortex. These neurons are called upper motor neurons.

Voluntary decisions to carry out physical movements are transmitted to *upper motor neurons*, which send action potentials down their axons through the spinal cord or through bones in the skull to synapse with other motor neurons located within somatic motor ganglia. Postsynaptic motor neurons located in the ganglia are called *lower-motor neurons*. Acetylcholine is the neurotransmitter within these ganglia.

Spinal and Cranial Nerves

The upper motor neuron axons that pass down the spinal cord synapse in ganglia located in the vertebrae of the spine. Acetylcholine triggers action potentials in the postsynaptic motor neurons. These neurons are called lower motor neurons. Axons from lower motor neurons of the spinal motor ganglia emerge from the vertebrae and form the spinal *motor nerve tracts* of the spinal nerves. The spinal motor nerve tracts innervate voluntary muscles located below the neck.

The axons from upper motor neurons that pass through other openings in the skull synapse in ganglia with lower motor neurons whose axons arrange themselves into the twelve cranial motor nerve tracts. These nerve tracts innervate the voluntary muscles of the head and neck. Sympathetic and parasympathetic nerves of the head and neck often travel alongside many of the cranial nerves.

NOTE: The *sensory nerve tracts* of the somatic nervous system transmit information from sensory receptor cells to higher centers of the central nervous system. Somatic sensory and motor nerve tracts that innervate the same body regions travel together as mixed somatic nerves. There are 12 pairs of somatic cranial nerves and 31 pairs of somatic spinal nerves.

Acetylcholine and the Neuromuscular Junction

Lower motor neurons of the somatic nervous system almost always synapse with skeletal muscle fibers. Skeletal muscle fibers are voluntary muscles fibers. They are also called *striated* muscle fibers. The "synapses" are called *neuromuscular junctions*. At the neuromuscular junctions, acetylcholine is released and binds to receptors on the muscle fiber membrane. This results in the generation of action potentials that are conducted into the muscle fibers and trigger muscular contraction. The neurotransmitter of all somatic neuromuscular junctions is acetylcholine.

The other types of muscles in the body are *smooth muscle* and *cardiac muscle*. Smooth muscle is composed of individual smooth muscle cells, but cardiac and skeletal/striated muscle are composed of muscle cells that are partially fused together by open cytoplasmic connections among the muscle cells called *gap junctions*. This interconnected arrangement of cells is called a *syncytium*.

Sympathetic and parasympathetic "synapses" with muscle cells are also neuromuscular junctions. Neurotransmitters at these junctions are not always excitatory; often they promote relaxation of the muscle.

An important overall feature of the peripheral nervous system is that acetylcholine is the neurotransmitter at ALL motor neuron and target junctions except for one. *Norepinephrine* is the neurotransmitter at the sympathetic-target cell junction.

Acetylcholine and the Central Nervous System

Acetylcholine is also a major neurotransmitter within the central nervous system, particularly cortical regions of the brain associated with arousal, REM sleep, and memory consolidation. Acetylcholine deficits in the brain are thought to be a major cause of memory loss in patients with Alzheimer's disease.

Norepinephrine and the Sympathetic Nervous System

Another important neurotransmitter is norepinephrine. In the peripheral nervous system, it is released only by *postsynaptic sympathetic* motor neurons. Postsynaptic sympathetic motor neurons release norepinephrine at target cell junctions. Target cells of the sympathetic motor system are usually muscle cells or glandular cells.

Norepinephrine Receptors

There are four major types of norepinephrine receptors in the sympathetic nervous system, they are alpha-1, alpha-2, beta-1 and beta-2 receptors. You are not required to know which specific type of norepinephrine receptors are present at the various target regions of the body but you should be able to predict what their effects are based on the concept that the sympathetic nervous system generates a high state of arousal and prepares the body for intense physical activity referred to as the fight **or** *flight response*.

Two very important targets of sympathetic motor neurons are *cardiac muscle* and smooth muscle located in the *bronchial air passages* of the lungs The effect of norepinephrine at beta-1 receptors on cardiac tissues is to increase the heart rate and the force of contraction of the ventricles. The effect of norepinephrine at beta-2 receptors on smooth muscle in the bronchial air passages of the lungs is to dilate (expand) the bronchial air passages.

Norepinephrine and the Heart

Beta-1-blocker drugs are commonly used in the treatment of angina pectoris, cardiac arrhythmia and for the long-term treatment of patients who survive myocardial infarction. These drugs block the beta-1 receptors located on cardiac muscle fibers, preventing the binding of norepinephrine released from nerve terminals of the sympathetic nervous system. Therefore, beta-blockers are *beta-1 antagonists*. By diminishing the effect of the sympathetic nervous system on the cardiovascular system, beta-blockers reduce the workload of the heart.

Norepinephrine and the lungs

Within the walls of the bronchi of the lungs there are smooth muscle fibers that have receptors for norepinephrine. These receptors are *beta-2 receptors*. Postganglionic nerve fibers of the sympathetic nervous system terminate at neuromuscular junctions with the smooth muscles fibers and release norepinephrine. The effect of norepinephrine at the neuromuscular junction is *inhibitory*, resulting in relaxation of the smooth muscle fibers. The result is that the bronchial airways *dilate*. When bronchial airways dilate, it is easier to breath.

Beta-2-receptor *agonists* like the *albuterol* in asthma inhalers mimic the effect of norepinephrine and improve asthma symptoms by causing bronchodilation. The use of Beta-2-receptor agonists in severe asthma attacks has saved the lives of tens of thousands of asthma sufferers.

Norepinephrine and Arteries

Most of us have probably used a norepinephrine *alpha-1 receptor agonist* in the form of Afrine or similar nasal sprays to relieve nasal congestion. Nasal congestion occurs due to swelling of small arteries in the nose. Arteries usually have alpha-1 receptors on smooth muscle in their artery walls. Norepinephrine causes the muscles to contract. This is one of the mechanisms for *decreasing blood flow* to various regions of the body such as the *digestive system* and *increasing blood pressure* during fight or flight reactions of the sympathetic nervous system.

Norepinephrine can also cause blood vessels to dilate. This occurs at arteries that provide blood flow to the skeletal muscles. In this manner we see how most of the features of the fight or flight response is accomplished by a single neurotransmitter namely, increased blood pressure, increased heart rate and force of contraction of the heart, easier breathing and redistribution of blood flow from the digestive system to the skeletal muscles.

Norepinephrine and the Central Nervous System

The effects of norepinephrine in the central nervous system are related regions of the brain involved in maintaining *general activation*, alertness, drive and emotional processes.

The Alpha-2 Receptor

The *norepinephrine alpha-2 receptor* acts as modulators and inhibitor of the actions of other neurons. They feed back on sympathetic neurons and are involved in central nervous system areas associated with drug addiction and alcoholism. Alpha-2 agonist drugs act on centers in the brainstem to reduce CNS activation resulting in sedation and reduces blood pressure. They are also used to treat opiate dependence and alcohol withdrawal symptoms.

Dopamine

Dopamine is an important neurotransmitter of the central nervous system. It modulates widespread neural pathways throughout the CNS including motor control and reward-motivated behavior pathways. Most addictive drugs increase dopamine activity in the brain. *Parkinson's disease* results from degeneration of the *substantia nigra*, a midbrain area that is a critical motor control brain region of the midbrain that produces and distributes dopamine to other motor control regions. Altered levels of dopamine are also a feature of *schizophrenia*. Most antipsychotic drugs reduce dopamine activity in the brain. The highest percentage of dopamine receptors in the central nervous system are located in the *frontal lobes* of the cerebral cortex.

Serotonin

Serotonin is another major CNS neurotransmitter. Serotonin is involved in the regulation of sleep, mood and appetite. Most of the serotonin in the CNS is produced in the *Raphe nuclei* in the brainstem. Neural pathways from the Raphe system connect to nearly every important functional region of the CNS. Serotonin is involved in the cognitive functions of learning and memory. Low serotonin levels are associated with obsessive-compulsive disorder, anxiety and depression. Some studies have shown altered serotonin levels in persons who have recently fallen in love. Most of the modern antidepressants are modulators of serotonin at synapses in the CNS. Most of the effects of hallucinogenic drugs appear to be related to alterations at serotonin synapses in the brain.

GABA

The primary inhibitory neurotransmitter in the CNS is *GABA (gamma amino butyric acid)*. Throughout the nervous system, GABA acts to reduce the excitability of neurons and is directly involved in the regulation of muscle tone. Benzodiazepines, such as Valium, are perhaps the safest and most effective drugs for reduction of anxiety and for muscle relaxation. Benzodiazepines are GABA receptor agonists.

Endorphins

Endorphins are neurotransmitters that are involved in inhibition of the sensation of pain. They are similar in structure to opium derivatives such as morphine and heroin. Endorphins seem to play a central role in *depersonalization disorder*. Drugs that block endorphin receptors, such as naloxone, have been shown to substantially reduce the severity of, and sometimes eliminate, depersonalization disorder in patients.

Neurotransmitter Agonists and Antagonists

Many important drugs are designed to bind to neurotransmitter receptors. If the drug binding mimics the effect of the neurotransmitter is called an agonist. If it blocks the receptor so that the receptor cannot function, it is called an *antagonist*. It is important not to confuse the terms with excitatory and inhibitory. For instance, if an agonist acts at a site where the neurotransmitter has an inhibitory effect, the agonist will also have an inhibitory effect. If an antagonist acts at the same site, it will have an opposite effect, in this case, an excitatory effect. Therefore, agonists and antagonists can each have excitatory or inhibitory effects.

Neurotransmitter Release and Reuptake

Neurotransmitters are synthesized and stored in neurons then released to target cells. Drugs that affect neurotransmitter actions can use several different means to accomplish this. One of the ways is to change how much and for how long neurotransmitters are present in a synapse or neuromuscular junction. In addition to direct agonist or antagonist action at neurotransmitter receptors, drugs may stimulate or block the release of neurotransmitters. They may also block the *reuptake* of neurotransmitters by the neurons that released the neurotransmitter. An example of this is the class of drugs called selective serotonin reuptake inhibitors (SSRIs) that are used to treat many psychological and psychiatric disorders. Another means is to block the action of enzymes whose function is to deactivate neurotransmitters at a synapse. The neurotransmitter acetylcholine is inactivated at synapses and neuromuscular junctions by the enzyme *acetylcholine esterase*. Inhibitors of this enzyme prolong the presence of ACh at neuromuscular junctions. This effect can be fatal. The deadliest substances ever created are the nerve gas poisons such as *sarin*, which are acetylcholine esterase inhibitors.

1. The end of each terminal button is almost connected to the next neuron, and contains sacks of chemicals called *neurotransmitters*. An electrical charge traveling down the terminal fiber releases the neurotransmitters into the *synaptic gap*.

2. The neurotransmitters fill receptors of the receiving neuron. That neuron then calculates the input from thousands of receptors, resulting in either an *excitatory* or *inhibitory* response.

3. After the transmitters fill the receptors, they are taken back up by the releasing neuron. This process is called *reuptake*. After reuptake neurotransmitters are recycled to function again

The Endocrine System

The endocrine system, in conjunction with the nervous system, integrate control and regulation over metabolic and cognitive function of the body. Together with the nervous system, the endocrine system allows the human mind to emerge and interact with the body so that it is able to achieve the extraordinary capacities of consciousness and physical adaptability that uniquely characterize our species.

The endocrine system is composed of glands that secrete hormones. Hormones are chemical substances that have regulatory effects on other cells and organs in the body. The definitional difference between a neurotransmitter and a hormone is that hormones are secreted into the bloodstream whereas neurotransmitters are released at neural junctions such as synapses and neuromuscular junctions. In fact, several hormones are also neurotransmitters, an example is norepinephrine, which is released as a neurotransmitter within the nervous system and is also released by cells in the adrenal medulla directly into the bloodstream. Therefore, by definition, norepinephrine is also a hormone.

There is a constant interaction between the endocrine system and the nervous system. Hormone levels can have a profound effect on mood and cognition. Voluntary actions such as substance abuse, poor nutrition and risk taking behaviors can have effects on hormone levels. At the unconscious level, the hypothalamus and the pituitary gland orchestrate the metabolic activities of the body by secreting hormones that regulate the actions of the other endocrine glands of the body.

A central distinction between the endocrine and nervous systems is that the actions of most hormones occur slowly, from a few hours to days, weeks and even years. One effective way to organize and understand the endocrine system is literally from the top down, beginning with the hypothalamus and pituitary gland, which are adjacent to each at the base of the skull.

The Hypothalamus

The *hypothalamus* is a region of the brain mainly concerned with regulatory processes necessary for survival. For instance, the hypothalamus regulates feeding, drinking, sleep, stress responses, thermoregulation, and reproduction.

The hypothalamus receives information both from the nervous system and directly through the bloodstream, Based on this information, the hypothalamus delivers hormones into the general circulation and through veins that connect directly to the pituitary gland. This type of local circulation is called a *portal vein system*. Hormones sent to the pituitary gland from the hypothalamus are called releasing hormones. Many of the hormones of the pituitary gland are secreted into the bloodstream in response to these releasing hormone. Important hormones of the hypothalamus include growth-hormone releasing hormone (GHRH), thyrotropin-releasing hormone (TRH), gonadotropin-releasing hormone (GnRH), corticotropin-releasing hormone (CRH), somatostatin and dopamine.

The Pituitary Gland

The hormones synthesized by cells in *the pituitary gland* generally are hormones that affect the other endocrine glands, most notably the thyroid gland the adrenal gland. The interaction between the hypothalamus, pituitary gland and the adrenal gland is called the hypothalamic-pituitary-adrenal axis. This axis regulates a large number of developmental and metabolic activities of the body including kidney functions, growth and sexual maturation, female fertility cycles, immune system activity and adaptation to stress. Important hormones of the pituitary gland are *prolactin, thyroid-stimulating hormone (TSH), luteinizing hormone (LH)* and *follicle stimulating hormone (FSH)*.

The Thyroid Gland

The pituitary gland, located in the neck as two lobes on either side of the trachea, produces *thyroid hormone* that increases the metabolic activity of the body. Thyroid hormone levels are controlled by the pituitary hormone, *thyroid-stimulating hormone (TSH)*. Levels of TSH are controlled by the hypothalamic hormone *thyrotropin-releasing hormone (TRH)*.

Abnormal levels of thyroid hormone have major effects on mood and cognition. Low thyroid level cause *hypothyroidism* that leads to depression, fatigue, lethargy and weight gain. Severe hypothyroidism can result in *myxedema madness*, a potentially fatal condition that may be misdiagnosed as severe psychosis. High thyroid levels can cause *hyperthyroidism*, resulting in severe anxiety, weight loss, confusion and mania. The most severe form of hyperthyroidism is a *thyroid storm*, which is rapidly fatal if not treated. Conversely, thyroid disease needs to be ruled out in cases of suspected clinical depression, psychosis, mania, schizophrenia and cocaine and methamphetamine overdose.

A historically important condition in western civilization and a continuing problem in underdeveloped countries is hypothyroidism due to inadequate dietary iodine intake. Iodine is required by the thyroid to synthesize thyroid hormone. In the United States, government regulations require iodine supplementation to table salt, as a result this type of hypothyroidism has been virtually eliminated. The driving force behind this requirement was that hypothyroidism in pregnant women often caused severe mental retardation in the mother's offspring. This condition is called *cretinism*.

The Parathyroid Glands

The *parathyroid glands*, which are located within the thyroid glands, produce *calcitonin*. Calcitonin regulates the level of *calcium ions* in the blood. Calcium ions play critical roles in neurotransmission, the electrical activity of the heart and many other vitally important enzyme and cellular metabolic processes. The symptoms of hypercalcemia and hypocalcemia can frequently be misdiagnosed as psychological disorders or psychiatric diseases and vice versa.

The Pancreas

The pancreas is both an endocrine gland and an exocrine gland. Exocrine glands secrete substances through tubes called ducts onto the surface of the skin or organs. Most people do not realize the inside of the intestines are actually outside of the body. Until material inside of the intestines is absorbed, it has not actually entered the interior of the body. The pancreas secretes digestive enzymes into the intestine so this is an exocrine gland function. Other exocrine glands are under control of the nervous system, including sweat glands, salivary glands and tear duct glands.

In its role as an endocrine gland, the pancreas produces *insulin* and *glucagon*. Both are required to maintain proper levels of glucose in the blood. There is direct innervation of the pancreas by the autonomic nervous system. The *parasympathetic system* stimulates insulin secretion and the *sympathetic system* inhibits insulin secretion.

Insulin is absolutely required by most cells in order to absorb glucose. The major exception is the brain. Neurons in the brain can absorb glucose in the absence of insulin. This is believed to be an evolutionary protective mechanism that ensures that the brain always has priority to the glucose it requires. Without an adequate glucose supply, neurons in the brain begin to die within five minutes.

Abnormal levels of glucose can also mimic psychological and psychiatric disorders. High blood glucose levels (hyperglycemia) can cause and headache fatigue and coma. Low blood glucose levels (hypoglycemia) produce symptoms of anxiety, confusion, Irritability and delirium.

The Adrenal Gland

The adrenal gland, after the hypothalamus and the pituitary gland, is the next most important regulatory endocrine gland in the body. The adrenal gland is separated into two regions, the adrenal cortex and the adrenal medulla.

The Adrenal Medulla

The adrenal medulla is considered a *modified sympathetic ganglion*. Cells in the adrenal medulla are innervated by *sympathetic preganglionic neurons*. Like the postganglionic neurons of the sympathetic ganglia, cells in the adrenal medulla release *norepinephrine* (they also release *epinephrine*). In this case, epinephrine and norepinephrine are considered hormones because they are released to the circulation. However, they both bind to *adrenergic receptors*, and thus have similar physiological effects as sympathetic neural stimulation.

The Adrenal Cortex

The adrenal cortex produces and distributes adrenal cortical hormones cortisol and aldosterone. It is also crucial for its role in producing testosterone and the precursors for the other hormones of the gonads. The adrenal gland is regulated by the hypothalamus through secretion of gonadotropin releasing hormone (GnRH) and by the pituitary gland through secretion of adrenocorticotropic hormone (ACTH).

As with many hormones, abnormal levels of cortisol have many effects on mood and cognition. Low levels of cortisol are the cause of *Addison's disease*, which can often be mistaken for severe psychiatric illnesses such as anorexia nervosa. Addison's disease is fatal if untreated, Cortisol is essential to maintain the body's ability to respond to stress and it plays a critical role in the immune system. Excess cortisol levels are common because cortisol drugs are used to treat many illnesses *Cushing's disease* results from excessive cortisol levels and is usually associated with mood swings and depression.

The Gonads

The *testes* in men and the *ovaries* in women both secrete hormones, *testosterone* in men and *estrogen* in women. Gonadotropin releasing hormone (GnRH) from the hypothalamus and follicle stimulating hormone (FSH) and luteinizing hormone (LH) from the pituitary interact at the gonads to direct the maturation of egg and sperm cells and to maintain ovulatory cycles. Abnormal levels of estrogen and testosterone occur in both men and women. Often the first signs of these conditions are changes in mood and cognition.

Functional Regions of the Cerebral Cortex

We have discussed the anatomical organization of the central nervous system and described the general functions of the spinal cord, brainstem and cerebellum as well as some of the higher brain centers, including the hypothalamus, amygdala and the hippocampus. For the AP Psychology exam, you are expected to know more detail regarding higher brain functions such as neurological regions and systems involved in mood, emotion, motivation, and cognition as well as mechanisms of learning, memory, language acquisition, sensory perception and executive function. These functions are primarily functions of the *cerebral cortex*.

As described in the neuroanatomy section, the *cerebral cortex* has a right and a left hemisphere. Each hemisphere is subdivided into lobes. The frontal lobes are positioned behind the forehead of the skull. Further back, immediately behind the frontal lobes are the centrally positioned parietal lobes. The temporal lobes are position alongside the parietal lobes, corresponding to the positions of the temples of the skull and the ears. The occipital lobes are behind the parietal and temporal lobes at the very back of the cranial cavity.

Left and Right Hemisphere Functions

It is a common misconception that there is a large amount of brain function that is localized to the right or the left hemispheres, even to the point that entire modes of thinking and personality are characterized as "left brain" or "right brain" modes. The term for this is hemispheric lateralization or hemispheric specialization. In fact, most of the functions of the cortex are distributed roughly equally between the two hemispheres. The notable exceptions are the language processing centers on the left hemisphere and the motor and somatosensory cortices of the frontal and parietal lobes.

Hemispheric Lateralization

Hemispheric Lateralization of Language Functions

Wernicke's area and Broca's area are located in the temporal and frontal lobes respectively of the left hemisphere in over 95% of people. These areas are involved in the construction of words and statements both in terms of fluency of speech and in the meaning or sensibility of verbal speech.

Broca's area is thought to be responsible for the ability to generate ease and fluency of speech. Persons with injuries to Broca's area can convey meaning in sentences, but sentences are difficult to enunciate and lack much of the grammatical content of normal speech.

Wernicke's area is considered to be a localized region devoted to producing meaningful or *sensible* verbal statements, Patients with injuries to Wernicke's area can easily produce well-spoken strings of words, but the statements do not seem to make any sense.

It seems these distinctions are somewhat oversimplified and that other areas of the brain are involved in the language processing tasks described for both Wernicke's and Broca's areas, but there is obviously a substantial amount of this processing that is localized and lateralized to the left hemisphere

Hemispheric Lateralization of Sensory and Voluntary Motor Function

There is also reasonably good evidence that in most people, analytical thought and abstract thinking involves processing that occurs more on the left hemisphere, and visual and spatial relations and musical abilities involves processing that occurs more on the right hemisphere.

There is absolutely a partitioning of motor control and somatosensory (touch, vibration, heat and cold sensation) perception in the motor and sensory cortices of the left and right frontal and parietal lobes. Motor control of the left side of the body occurs in the right motor cortex and vice versa and somatosensory information from the left side of the body is processed in the right sensory cortex and vice versa.

In the visual cortices of the occipital lobes, the right visual field information is processed in the left visual cortex and left visual field information is processed in the right visual cortex.

The crossing of the nerve tracts from the left to the right is called *decussation*. It is unclear why this form of organization evolved, but it is a typical theme in the higher brain centers.

NOTE: The major neural interconnection between left and right cerebral hemispheres is the *corpus callosum*. Much of the information that supports the concept of hemispheric lateralization is based on accounts of injuries to that resulted in a severing of the corpus callosum in humans, cases where humans were born without a corpus callosum and cases where surgeons intentionally severed the corpus callosum. These are referred to as split-brain studies. The AP Psychology exam expects you to know that the most important investigators who conducted split-brain studies were Roger Sperry and Michael Gazzaniga.

The Frontal Lobes

The frontal lobes reach their highest level of relative size and complexity in species that are considered to be the most intelligent. This is particularly true for humans. Many researchers believe that the cognitive abilities that sets the human species at the apex of intelligence are largely due to the superior functional capacities of human frontal lobes.

In general, the frontal lobes may be considered to be the controlling authority over the structure and expression of personality and executive function. Emotional character, problem solving, language, judgement and sexual behavior appear to emerge from processes that occur in the frontal lobes.

The frontal lobes are central to the ability to predict and plan for future consequences of actions and to consideration of the morality of actions. They provide mechanisms to override basic emotional and primal drive states and to suppress socially unacceptable behavior.

The frontal lobes have complex interaction with the limbic system, which is a primary center concerned with mood and instinctive behavior. Hunger and dominance and instinctive nurturing of offspring are perceptions that emerge within the limbic system The long-term memory functions of the frontal lobes are often closely associated with perceptions derived from the limbic system. Finally, voluntary motor functions the primary motor cortices and Broca's area, important in language function are located in the frontal cortex.

There are two ways to organize the other functions of the cerebral cortex. One is to list the other lobes, the parietal, temporal and occipital lobes and identify the functional roles found in each. A more useful and efficient method is to organize cortical function as motor and sensory. This method makes it easier to understand higher functions that involve more than one lobe of the brain or include important contributions from regions that are not part of the cerebral cortex. This is the method used here.

NOTE: As in the case of split-brain studies and for functions of other regions of the brain, much of the initial evidence for the function of regions of the brain was obtained from accounts of injuries or maldevelopment of certain anatomical regions of the brain, or from surgeries that involved certain anatomical regions of the brain. You should be able to answer questions on the AP Psychology exam that are based on hypothetical injury to these brain regions and then ask you to draw conclusions based on your knowledge of what the normal function of the region is. In the case of the frontal lobes, you should be familiar with the specific historical account of the injury suffered by *Phineas Gage* to his frontal lobe and to the surgeons who notoriously pioneered the *prefrontal lobotomy*, Walter Freedman and António Egas Moniz, as well as the effects of prefrontal lobotomy surgery.

The Primary Motor Cortex (PMC)

The primary motor cortices are located in the frontal lobes, adjacent to the parietal lobes. Upper motor neurons of the PMC initiate voluntary muscle movements. The neurons are arranged to correspond to their anatomical target muscles, essentially the PMCs reproduce **anatomical** *maps* of the left and right sides of the human body. This type of mapping also occurs in the primary sensory cortex, the visual cortex and the auditory cortex. The phenomena of a representation of a human body within the nervous system is referred to as a *homunculus*.

Additional motor processing occurs in the parietal and subcortical motor regions. Axons from upper motor neurons travel to the brainstem. At the brainstem, axons from the left and right motor cortices cross to opposite sides and continue through the lateral corticospinal tracts of the spinal cord to target muscles. This crossing over or decussation of nerve fibers means that the left motor cortex controls movement on the right side of the body and the right motor cortex controls movement on the left side of the body.

The Sensory Cortices

The perception of sensations occurs in the sensory cortices of the cerebrum. The primary sensory cortices are the visual cortex, the auditory cortex, the olfactory cortex and the primary and secondary somatosensory cortices.

The Somatosensory Cortex

The sensation of what most people refer to as touch actually consists of several different sensations. There is the vibration sense, the sense of light touch, the sensation of heavy touch or pressure, there is also the sensations of temperature and pain. Finally, there is a sense of the positions of the body, referred to as kinesthetic sensation. Together, these various types of sensations combine to form the somatosensory sense.

Each of these sensations are detected by *specialized sensory receptors* cells located not just in the skin but also throughout the entire body. Sensory receptors send signals to neurons located in the spinal cord or brainstem. From there, the signals are relayed to opposite sides of the nervous system and then to higher brain structures including the thalamus, the cerebellum and the primary somatosensory cortices. The somatosensory cortices are interconnected with visual centers for planning movements.

The primary somatosensory cortices are located in the parietal lobes and adjacent to the motor cortices of the frontal lobe. The sensations of touch and some types of pain are perceived through the primary sensory cortices. Sensations on the right side of the body are processed in the left primary sensory cortex and vice versa. These sensations are also mapped in the primary sensory cortices as a homunculus as we described for the primary motor cortex.

The Visual Cortex

The *visual cortices* are located in the occipital lobes. It is also called the striate cortex, due to its unique staining pattern on microscopic slides. Visual information is passed from the retinae of the eyes, through the thalamus to the visual cortex. Information from the left and right visual fields are separately directed to the opposite left and right visual cortices. There are at least six subdivisions of the visual cortices, V_1 - V_6. The *primary visual cortex*, V-1, is the best studied division and is involved in processing pattern recognition. The other visual subdivision have other specialized functions but all are highly interconnected with each other and numerous other brain regions.

The details of visual processing are beyond the scope of the AP Psychology exam, but you should know that the left and right visual fields are sensed by both eyes, images on the left side of the head are focused on the right side of both left and right retinae and images on the right side of the head are focused on the left side of both left and right retinae. left and right optic nerve fibers are combined into left and right visual fields and cross at the intersection of the left and right optic nerves at the optic chiasm near the thalamus, In the visual cortices, visual information is arranged in a map that reproduces the image of the outside world, again like the mapping that occurs in the somatosensory and motor cortices. Also, there are critical periods associated with the development of visual abilities in children, and the ability of the visual pathways to change over time is an important topic in the *theories of brain plasticity*. This plasticity allows the visual cortices to rapidly reprogram and adapt to maintain an accurate visual perception that reflects changes in the environment.

The Auditory Cortex

The primary auditory cortex is located in the temporal lobe. There is also a secondary and tertiary auditory cortex, also located in the temporal lobe *alongside the primary auditory cortex*. There is equally important auditory processing that occurs in the frontal and parietal lobes. Auditory information is passed from sensory cells called hair cells located in the middle ear to the thalamus. Then to the right and left auditory cortices.

Input from both ears is transmitted to both left and right auditory cortices. Along with the visual system, the neural pathways and information processing that occur in the brain are incredibly complex and scientists are still struggling to understand how these systems produce the perceptions of sight and sound. In fact, some mathematicians and computer scientists believe that that it is theoretically impossible for us to ever fully understand how these systems work.

The Olfactory (Smell) Cortices

The primary olfactory cortices are located in the temporal lobes. Olfaction, or the sense of smell, is deeply connected to primitive brain structures. In fact, olfactory receptors, called *olfactory bulbs*, are not receptors connected to the brain; they are literally bulbous extensions of the brain. Some olfactory receptors connect directly to the limbic system, including the hypothalamus and the amygdala of the brain. These direct connections are a unique feature compared to other sensory inputs to the central nervous system. Other olfactory information is sent directly to the frontal lobe where the actual perception of smell occurs. The direct connections to the limbic system may explain why certain smells are able to evoke strong emotions and memories associated with these smells.

Brain Plasticity

The philosopher William Blake was the first to propose that the human brain is not a permanent anatomical structure, but an organ that is able to physically change and adapt to its environment. This seems today to be an obvious necessity, otherwise how is one to explain how the brain is able to learn new skills and create and store new memories? The first scientific evidence for this view was provided by the work of *Karl Lashley* who showed that the neurons of rhesus monkeys made new synaptic connections that correlated with new learning situations. The studies of *Eric Kandel* later showed neural adaptation to *classical conditioning* in the invertebrate worm Aplysia.

Construction of new neural pathways and elimination of other pathways was well demonstrated by the work of *Hubel and Wiesel*, where they showed that *neuronal pruning* occurs in the visual cortices of newborn *kittens* and that development of functional pathways can be altered by altering visual input during critical periods.

Subsequently, there have been studies showing changes in the *neural mapping* in motor cortices of monkeys after limb amputations and that actual regeneration of neurons can occur in some parts of the brain following injury. A comparison of brain scans of medical students in 2005 showed increased grey matter (corresponding to neuron bodies) in students after a course of medical studies compared to before they began their studies.

Historical accounts, most notably in the case of Phineas Gage, report recovery of personality deficits following traumatic injury to the frontal lobes. This implies that the most complex neural functions may be able to be able to be reconstituted in other areas of the brain. Documented recovery of function following stroke and the ability of neural implants such as cochlear implants to function are believed to require physical remodeling of the nervous system and reprograming of neurons. Other phenomena including phantom limb pain and the possible ability of some blind persons to "see" by echolocation are difficult to understand without assuming that extensive restructuring of the brain is possible.

There is an enormous amount of current research into neuroplasticity of the human brain. The evidence is mounting that the human brain is capable of undergoing remarkable changes to compensate for lost functions due to injury and that sensory stimulation can result in reprogramming of neural pathways and even transfer of functions from one region of the brain to another.

Evolutionary Theories of Psychology

So far, we have discussed the hard biological science that underlies the basic function of the nervous system and the more complex neurological systems and higher brain functions that are involved in many aspects of psychology. Among these are the basic drive states such as hunger, and sexual reproduction, basic emotions and moods, levels of general arousal and awareness as well as higher functions including perceptual and cognitive abilities such as memory, pattern recognition, language and learning.

Evolutionary psychology encompasses all areas of psychology and there is a wide gap between the well-established biological science of the mind and most of the comprehensive evolutionary theories of psychology. Some aspects of evolutionary psychology have good support based on biological research but large generalizations are more difficult to pin down as clearly due to specific neural pathways or programmed behaviors residing within the brain that are genetically coded for and can be passed to one's offspring. That is not to say that there are not powerful arguments and very intriguing data to support evolutionary theories in all areas of psychology.

We do have some suggestive evidence that there may indeed be a "shyness" gene. The demonstration of universal emotions such as disgust, anger, fear, happiness, sadness and surprise strongly suggest they are evolutionary based emotions and we do know roughly how these emotions are elicited by the central nervous system. The existence of critical periods for various stages of learning and social development are also difficult to explain without an evolutionary context.

The field is far too broad to summarize in a few paragraphs or pages, but in general, you should be able to recognize questions that have an *evolutionary theme* and be able to reason in an evolutionary psychology mode. This is based on the general principles that human psychological traits are evolved adaptations to the ancestral human environment. For instance, much of the apparently harmful individual and group social behaviors are difficult to explain except as behaviors that were adaptive in past societies but are maladaptive in modern societies. The persistence of such behaviors is due to the insufficient time that evolution has not had to select them out and to evolve more functional behaviors.

One fundamentally new concept that has emerged from evolutionary psychology is that of quasi-inheritable behavior that is not genetically coded. These ideas, behaviors and patterns of behavior may have an independent evolution that is not necessarily beneficial to their human hosts.

These informational units, called *memes*, appear in human psychology as traits or behaviors that tend to persist and expand once they are established. In essence, they are psychological parasites or viruses, pursuing their own evolutionary course. They are under different selection pressures than those of human organisms and societies. There is very good evidence for a similar type of coevolution in biology. The human genome and all vertebrate genomes are largely non-functional. This apparently useless DNA is often described as "junk" DNA. Apparently, we have in some sense evolved as a survival mechanism for DNA rather than the other way around. Perhaps the same may be said of the informational memes that contribute to our psychological nature.

NOTE: For purposes of the AP Psychology Exam, The person most notable for developing the meme concept was *Noam Chomski*.

Twin Studies

Perhaps the most scientifically rigorous and convincing form of arguments that particular psychological traits are inherited are those based on studies that compare identical (monozygotic) twins who are raised in the same household with identical twins who are raised in separate households. In these studies, the two groups can serve as their own control groups, but if the studies also include non-identical twins raised together and separately, the studies are very well controlled. When the data show little difference in the expression of a psychological trait between identical twins raised together compared to apart and where there is a greater occurrence in identical vs non-identical twins, there is strong evidence that the trait has a significant genetic character. There are only a few of these studies that do not show at least a significant genetic component to a full spectrum of psychological traits. Often the biological component is much greater than the environmental component of the trait.

The criticism of twin studies is that perhaps people interact in the same way with persons who have nearly the same physical appearance. There is some evidence this is somewhat true in some cases, but also evidence that this is not true in many other cases. The criticism also logically suggests that people in general have a universal social interaction pattern with respect to the physical appearance of others. That is evidence of genetically programmed behavior, since it must occur in all households where twins are raised. That would be a very broad and powerful argument for evolutionary psychology theories.

NOTE: The AP Psychology exam expects you to know that *Thomas Bouchard* is the most significant researcher in twin studies.

Genetics

With the exception of memes, evolutionary theories require that psychological traits can be passed to offspring through the parents' genes. Here is a brief review of how genetic traits are passed from one generation to the next.

The human genome consists of 23 pairs of chromosomes, 22 pairs of autosomes and 1 pair of sex chromosomes (XX for females and XY for males). There are at least one pair of genes for every specific hereditary trait, for example, eye color. The genes that code for a specific type of trait may be different, i.e. one may code for blue eyes and the other may code for brown eyes. Different genes that code for the same type of trait are called *alleles*.

Male and female *gametes*, sperm cells and eggs (ova) respectively, have one of the alleles for every gene from each of the parents. During fertilization, the male and female gametes combine to form a hybrid cell called a *zygote* that has a full complement of DNA, 23 pairs of chromosomes composed of half of the male alleles and half of the female alleles. The complete set of genes is called the *genotype*. The zygote develops into a new human being.

When a pair of alleles are different, and one is dominant and one is recessive, certain traits may or may not be expressed. For instance, the blue eye allele may not be expressed because there is also a brown eye allele present, which is dominant. The set of all alleles that are expressed is called the *phenotype* of the individual.

In many cases, certain traits may not be present at birth, but do appear in response to *environmental influences*. Therefore, many or most psychological traits may appear in individuals to variable degrees based on the particular environment an individual is exposed to during his or her lifetime. The strong evolutionary psychology theories suggest that **ALL** psychological traits have a genetic component.

Chromosome Abnormalities and Impaired Neurological Functions

There are several abnormalities of chromosomes that result is conditions where impairment of cognition, emotional temperament and social functioning are major features of the condition. Impairments of these types are often defined as *mental retardation*.

Down's syndrome (Trisomy 21)

Down's syndrome patients have cells with three pairs of chromosome 21, rather than the normal 2 pairs of chromosome 21. Persons with Down 's syndrome have an average IQ of 50 and represent approximately 30% of the intellectually disabled in the U.S. Developmental milestones are delayed and 30% of sufferers have autism. There is higher occurrence of mood disorders including depression and anxiety and a much higher incidence of Alzheimer's disease in persons with Down's syndrome.

Turner's syndrome (XO)

The cells of women with Turner's syndrome have only one X chromosome rather than the normal number of two X chromosomes. Women with Turner's syndrome usually have normal intelligence but also have a high incidence of learning disabilities related to perception of spatial and mathematical relationships.

Klinefelter's Syndrome (XXY)

Males with Klinefelter's syndrome have cells containing more than one X chromosome. They usually have normal intelligence but have a higher incidence of reading and speech difficulties.

Fragile X syndrome

Fragile X syndrome results from an inherited defect in the X chromosome. Approximately 50% of persons with the syndrome have autism. It is a major cause of intellectual disability, in particular in boys, where the average IQ is 40. There are mild to severe behavior and social disabilities associated with the disorder, including social anxiety and stereotypical movements such as hand flapping.

Viruses and infectious organisms

Fetal exposure to viruses and infectious organisms is historically and currently a major cause of birth defects. They often cause a constellation of injuries (syndromes) where impairment of neurological function is prominent and severe, including intellectual and social disabilities.

Rubella, the German Measles virus, is an extremely dangerous threat to unborn children and it is the reason that vaccination against the virus is mandatory in school children. Pregnant women who contract German measles often elect to abort their pregnancy due to the risk of delivering a profoundly and permanently disabled child.

Other common viral and infectious agents that present risks of this nature include the syphilis spirochete, the viruses that cause herpes and the parasite toxoplasmosis that is found in domestic cat feces. The risk to the fetus from toxoplasmosis is the reason many authorities advise that pregnant women and those trying to become pregnant avoid contact with feline litter boxes.

Substance Abuse

The risks to unborn children from cigarette smoking, drug and alcohol abuse are well documented. There is good evidence that behavioral problems in children whose mothers abused cocaine during pregnancy may have permanent learning and social disabilities. By far the most significant neurological damage however, results from heavy alcohol use during pregnancy.

Fetal Alcohol Syndrome

Heavy alcohol use during pregnancy can result in fetal alcohol syndrome. One of the most prominent features of the syndrome is intellectual and functional social impairment. The average IQ of children born with fetal alcoholism is 70. The world Health Organizations classifies fetal alcoholism as the number one cause of preventable mental retardation.

Methods of Investigating the Brain

The AP Psychology Exam expects you to be familiar with the following types of studies that can provide information on the structure and function of the nervous system. All of these studies are imaging studies except for the EEG, which is a recording of the electrical activity of the brain.

Computerized Tomography (CT) Scanning

CT scans take continuous rotary X-rays of the body which are recombined in a computer to provide 2 dimensional or 3 dimensional images of the internal body structures, CT scans provide excellent images of the bony structures and good images of general features of soft tissue structures. Earlier CT machines subjected patients to a possibly harmful dose of radiation, but current CT technology has reduced this dosage far below levels that are considered safe.

Magnetic Resonance Imaging (MRI)

MRI scans also provide 2D and 3D images of the internal body structures. The MRI machine produces very powerful (1.5 Tesla) magnetic field pulses that are absorbed by certain atoms, usually hydrogen, in the human body. In between pulses, the atoms release the magnetic energy, which is then recorded and processed by computer to produce the internal body images. The images show much better detail of soft tissue structures compared to CT scans. There is no X-ray risk with MRI scans , but patients with metal instrumentation inside their bodies, such as pacemakers, may not be able to safely undergo MRI scanning.

Positron Emission Tomography (PET) Scanning

Positrons are positively charged electrons, they are in fact antimatter. PET scans can image areas of the brain and determine how much glucose various regions are utilizing. This correlates with the metabolic activity of the regions and therefore provides information on which areas of the brain are most or least active when patients are engaged in various physical or mental tasks. This helps to determine which areas of the brain are involved in the specific neurological functions under investigation.

Functional Magnetic Resonance Imaging (fMRI)

fMRI combines MRI and PET scan technology to provide images of the blood flow rates to various regions of the brain. The results give information on the function roles of regions of the nervous system based on the correlation between neural activity and blood flow rates, fMRI is unique in that it can provide real time imaging (movies) of this activity.

Electroencephalography (EEG)

Electroencephalography uses electrodes applied to the surface of the skull to record brain waves, a group of general electrical patterns resulting from electrical activity of the brain, There are several major patterns of brainwaves; delta, theta, alpha and beta waves. One of the uses of EEGs is to determine the presence of the rapid eye movement (REM) sleep stage in patients with sleep disorders.

Chapter 4: Sensation and Perception

Sensation and Perception

Our discussion begins with the first step in perception, the collection, detection and transduction of sensory information by the peripheral components of the specific sensory system.

Vision

Within the eye, there are two types of visual receptors, *rod cells* and *cone cells*. Both types are specialized neurons that *absorb electromagnetic energy* in the form of *photons* and both are located in the *retina* of the eye. Both cell types contain light-sensitive receptor proteins called *opsins*. When photons strike rod or cone cells, the photons are absorbed by the opsin proteins. This triggers a set of intercellular processes that hyperpolarizes the cells. This is the first step in a very different type of signal transmission process compared to the typical process that occurs in the nervous system.

Usually, signal transmission begins with the depolarization of a neuron resulting in the generation of an action potential. The action potential is conducted down the neuron's axon and triggers the release of neurotransmitters at a synaptic cleft or a neuromuscular junction. In contrast, rod and cone cells continuously release their neurotransmitter, *glutamate*, at their single synapse with a bipolar cell, which is a signal processing cell in the middle layer of the retina. The hyperpolarization of rod and cone cells in response to photon absorption causes inhibition of glutamate release at their synapses. It is the decrease in neurotransmitters at the synaptic cleft that results in either an inhibitory or an excitatory effect on the bipolar cell.

Rod cells and cone cells have different thresholds. A threshold in a sensory receptor cell refers to the level or intensity of stimulation that is required to cause the receptor cell to generate a signal at its synapses. All sensory receptor cells and all neurons in general, have thresholds. The absolute threshold is the minimum level of stimuli required for a generation of a response by the cells. This is also referred to as the sensitivity of the receptor cell. Rod cells are adapted to provide visual information in dim or low light conditions. They have a very low threshold and very high sensitivity to photons. Under certain conditions, some rod cells can detect one single photon, and in repose, they can transmit that information to postsynaptic cells. It is literally impossible for such rod cells to have a lower threshold or a higher sensitivity to photons. In contrast, cone cells have a relatively higher threshold and a relatively lower sensitivity to photons. A cone cell requires the absorption of 50-100 photons to generate a signal at its synapse.

Rod cells and cone cells have different specializations of function and different distributions in the retina. As we mentioned, rod cells are specialized for dim light or low intensity light conditions. This is also called *night vision*. Persons with poor functionality of their rod cells have *night blindness*. Rod cells are also specialized to provide peripheral vision information. Rod cells are most abundant in the peripheral regions of the retina and become progressively less abundant in regions closer to the center of the retina. Cone cells are adapted to provide information under bright light or high intensity light conditions. They are designed for, and so distributed on the retina to provide, central vision and to detect fine visual details. This is called *high acuity vision*. Cone cell distribution on the retina is the opposite of rod cell distribution. Cone cells are densely packed and most abundant at the central portion of the retina and are progressively less so in regions further away from the center of the retina. The fibers of the optic nerve pass through a small channel in the center of the retina. This area is a *blind spot* in the retina's visual field.

Rod and cone cells are tuned to respond to different frequency or wavelength ranges of photons. Photons are packets of electromagnetic energy. In some ways, they behave like solid particles, but at the same time, they also appear to be waves of electromagnetic energy. This is a quantum mechanical phenomenon called *wave-particle duality*. It is the wave like properties of photons that are relevant in vision. When we say a photon is a wave, we do not mean it is one single wave. We mean (a photon) it is a continuous series of waves or a *wavetrain* of electromagnetic energy that is moving through space at the speed of light. The length of a single wave in this wavetrain is the *wavelength* of the photon. The total number of waves in the photon's wave train that travels past a given point in one second is the *frequency* of a photon. A photon's or any wavetrain's frequency is always inversely proportional to its wavelength. The shorter a photon's wavelength the higher a photon's frequency and the higher the electromagnetic energy of the photon. Rods and cones can only absorb photons within a very narrow range of energies or wavelengths.

This narrow range of absorbable wavelengths is called the *visible light spectrume* of the electromagnetic energy spectrum. Within the visible light spectrum, the photons with the longest visible wavelengths, and therefore the lowest energies, are perceived as the color red. The photons with the shortest visible wavelengths, and therefore the highest energies, are perceived as the color violet. As photon wavelengths progressively decrease from the red wavelengths towards the violet wavelengths, they are perceived as the color changes of the rainbow. The mnemonic for this color progression is *"ROY G. BIV"* - red, orange, yellow, green, blue, indigo, violet. Photon wavelengths that are just above the visible are the ultraviolet wavelengths and those just below the visible are the infrared wavelengths. Electromagnetic waves with longer wavelengths and less energy than the infrared include microwaves and radio waves. Those with shorter wavelengths and higher energies than the ultraviolet are called x-rays and gamma rays.

A continuous stream of photons is called a *beam of light* or a *light ray*. A light ray is usually composed of photons with different energies. sometimes light rays, such as those emitted by the sun or a light bulb, contain an almost of the entire visible spectrum of photon energies. This type of light is perceived as the color white. White light passing through a prism can be separated out into all the corresponding colors of the spectrum of visible light. When light is comprised of photons that have about the same energy they are perceived as individual colors. Laser light or *coherent light* is composed of photons that all have the same frequency. Objects may selectively absorb and reflect light of differing wavelengths. The wavelengths reflected off an object are the wavelengths that correspond the objects perceived colorations. If an object only absorbs and does not reflect any of the visible wavelengths of light, it is perceived to be the color black, If an object is reflecting a full spectrum of wavelengths of light, it is perceived as the color white.

Visible light (photons) pass either directly from visible-light-emitting objects such as the sun, a campfire, a video monitor, etc. or indirectly, by reflecting off object in one's *visual field* through the *cornea* of the eye, then through the *iris* via the pupil, then through the *lens* of the eye, where the light rays are focused onto the *retina*. The retina is located on the inner surface of the back of the eye. Rod cells and cone cells, located in the retina, then absorb the photons of the visible light spectrum. All rod cells best absorb photons within the same narrow blue-violet wavelength range. This range is usually perceived as shades of grey or a *grey scale* in peripheral vision and in night vision. In the late afternoon, near sunset, when light intensity is low, rod cell vision predominates and the blue-green light they respond to results in the perception that brightly colored object appear to darken and develop a greenish-blue tinge or hue. This is called the *purkinje effect.* Rod cells are completely insensitive to red wavelengths. This is why persons who work under conditions where they may unexpectedly require immediate night vision (military personnel in particular) use only red light to illuminate their workspace environment. On the other hand, cone cells come in three varieties of wavelength range sensitivities: those with a red range, those with a blue range and those with a green range. We will discuss the theories of color vision a bit later, but the three-color range sensitivities of cone cells clearly play a vital role in the perception of color.

Hearing

The sensory receptor cells of the auditory and vestibular systems are called hair cells. Hair cells (and rod and cone cells as well) are *bipolar* sensory cells. The sensory cellular apparatus is located at one end of the cells and the axon terminal is located at the opposite end of the cells. The sensory end of hair cells includes thread-like extensions of the cell membrane ("hairs") called *stereocilia*. When a mechanical force causes the stereocilia to bend, intracellular processes are triggered that eventually lead to the release of neurotransmitters at the hair cell synapse. Hair cells of the auditory system are located in a structure called the *organ of Corti.* The organ of Corti is an elongated strip of tissues that rests upon a flexible membrane called the *basilar membrane.* The basilar membrane is the membrane that longitudinally (lengthwise) divides a lower fluid filled chamber called the *scala tympani* from a middle fluid filled chamber and an upper fluid filled chamber called the *scala media* or *cochlear duct* and the *scala vestibuli* respectively. These middle and upper chambers are separated from each other by another membrane called *Reissner's membrane.*

Reissner's membrane forms the roof and walls of the middle chamber and the basilar membrane forms the floor of the middle chamber. The Organ of Corti extends along the entire length of the basilar membrane. The middle chamber (scala media/cochlear duct) is completely sealed off from the upper and lower chambers (scala vestibuli and scala tympani). The fluid that fills the upper and lower chambers is called *perilymph*. The fluid that fills the middle chamber is called e*ndolymph*. Finally, there is another structure, the *tectorial membrane* that emerges from the inner surface of the scala media just above the top of the organ of Corti. The tectorial membrane arches over the organ of corti, forming a shelf or awning just above and for the entire length of the organ of Corti. Hair cells of the organ of corti are arranged in four rows that run along the entire length of the organ. The hair cells of the three outer rows are called *outer hair cells*. Hair cells of the fourth/innermost row are called inner hair cells. The Hair cells' stereocilia are physically attached to the underside of the tectorial membrane. Outer hair cells are not sensory receptor cells. They are *electrically motile* cells. Fluid pressure waves in the surrounding endolymph cause outer hair cells to contract, somewhat like a muscle cell. This contraction draws the tectorial membrane back and forth across the inner hair cells. This motion bends the inner hair cells' stereocilia and cause the inner hair cells to release neurotransmitter *glutamate* that stimulate action potentials in interneurons located in the *spiral ganglion* of the organ of Corti. It is therefore the inner hair cells that are the sensory receptor cells of the auditory system.

This three-chamber complex, consisting of the scala vestibuli, scala media and the scala tympani occupies the central region of a structure known as the *cochlea*. The cochlea is a thick walled hollow spiral coil or tube that is located in a bony cavity of the temporal regions of the skull called the inner ear. The cochlea's shape resembles a snail's shell (a conch shell actually - hence the name "cochlea"). The three-chamber complex follows a spiral pathway down the center of the cochlea beginning at the base of the cochlea and continues toward the far end or *apex* of the cochlea. The base of the cochlea is directly adjacent to the *middle ear*. There are two openings in the bony wall that separates the base of the cochlea from the cavity of the middle ear. These openings are called the *oval window* and the *round window*. The oval window is continuous with the scala vestibuli and the round window is continuous with the scala tympani. Both openings, the oval window and the round window, are sealed by thin flexible membranes. If this were not so, the perilymph contained inside the scalae vestibuli and tympani could flow freely into the middle ear cavity.

The basilar membrane forms the floor of the scala media and the roof of the scala tympani. The basilar membrane is attached or anchored to the base of the cochlea and to both sides of the scala media chamber. It extends towards to a point just short of the apex of the cochlea. The terminal end of the basilar membrane is unattached. This allows the membrane to move up and down or vibrate like a reed in a saxophone or clarinet. At the free end of the basilar membrane, the scala vestibuli, and the lower canal, the scala tympani, are connected by the gap at the free end of the basilar membrane. This means the scala vestibuli and the scala tympani are actually one continuous canal that begins as the scala vestibuli at the oval window membrane, then bends around the free end of the scala media, and ends as the scala tympani at the round window membrane.

The basilar membrane is thickest and stiffest (least flexible) at its anchorage to the cochlear base and becomes progressively thinner and more flexible as it extends further toward the apex of the cochlea. The result is that different local regions of the membrane vibrate in response to different specific sound wave frequencies. The frequency that causes vibration of a specific region of the basilar membrane is called the *resonate frequency* of that membrane region. The highest perceptible frequencies are detected at the base of the membrane. Progressively lower frequencies are detected further down the membrane, with detection of the lowest perceptible tone occurring at the apex of the membrane. Only hair cells at the specific region of vibration on the basilar membrane are stimulated, and this correlates with a specific sound frequency. This is how the basilar membrane and organ of corti function as a *frequency analyzer*. The hair cell outputs and their relative positions on the basilar membrane are recreated as a tonotopic map in the auditory cortex of the temporal lobe of the brain. This allows for the perception of the full range of tonal sound patterns, particularly the perception of music.

The basilar membrane and the organ of corti indirectly collect information that arrives through the external ear canals in the form of rhythmic patterns of variations of atmospheric pressure called *acoustic or sound waves*. The energy of sound waves is the transferable kinetic or mechanical energy of motion of air molecules. The level of energy of sound waves is the sound wave height or *amplitude*, which is perceived as the *volume or intensity* (loudness) of a sound. The number of sound waves detected per second is the *sound frequency* and is perceived as tone or pitch of a sound. Low frequency sound waves are perceived as low-pitched and high frequency as high pitched. Sound frequencies that are lower than the lowest frequency that can be perceived are perceived not as sound tones, but as individual repeating sounds (beats or rhythms), that correspond to the detection of each individual sound wave.

Sound waves enter the *outer ear* through the external *auditory meatus*, the entryway to the *external auditory canal*. The sound waves travel through the external canal to its terminus at the *tympanic membrane* (eardrum). The energy of these sound waves is absorbed over the relatively large surface area of the tympanic membrane and causes the membrane to vibrate at the same frequencies as the sound waves. The vibrations of the tympanic membrane are mechanically transferred by three interconnecting bones or ossicles of the *middle ear*, the incus, the *malleus* and the *stapes* (commonly called the hammer, the anvil and the stirrup) to the much smaller membrane located at the oval window. So, the middle ear structures are converting sound wave energy in the air at the external auditory canal of the outer ear into pressure wave energy within the endolymph in the scala media. This mechanical transfer of vibrational sound wave energy in air from one membrane to pressure wave energy in a fluid like the perilymph fluid in the scala vestibuli on the other side of the oval window membrane is an example of *coupling*. The coupling process between the much larger tympanic membrane and the much smaller oval window membrane concentrates the sound wave energy and allows the middle ear bones to generate a much higher (20x higher) force at the oval window and to regenerate the sound frequency waves as pressure wave of identical frequencies within the perilymph of the scala vestibuli on the other side of the oval window. This is a form of mechanical *force amplification*. It requires a much larger force to produce pressure waves in liquids (including endolymph) than the corresponding sound waves in air. This is why the amplification of force is necessary. This air to liquid force amplification/energy transfer process is called *impedance matching*. When the middle ear ossicles transfer energy to the oval window, the pressure waves they generate in the perilymph travel through the scala vestibuli and around the bend at the tip of the cochlea at the gap between the ends of the basilar membrane. The pressure waves are now in the scala tympani section of their pathway. They continue to the base of the scala tympani and force the membrane at the round window to bulge outward. This is necessary because fluid cannot be compressed so the displacement of the pressure waves must be accommodated by the bulging of the membrane. During this journey, the pressure waves are also transmitted to the endolymph of the scala media and to the basilar membrane resulting in specific vibrations on the basilar membrane and the stimulation of inner hair cells as we have discussed. These directly induced vibrations of the basilar and tectorial membranes are usually not energetic enough to directly stimulate inner hair cells. They are sufficient to stimulate outer hair cell to contract in response and increase the movement of the tectorial membrane so that the inner hair cells are stimulated. This is how the auditory input is amplified within the cochlea. Direct synaptic connections between higher brain centers and outer hair cells allows signals from the higher brain centers to alter or modulate the sensitivity of outer hair cells to pressure waves and the force of contraction of outer hair cells in response to pressure waves This is another example of *rapid adaptation*, where the sensory systems and other neural process can change or adapt to the environment over a short period of time. By this process, the brain is able to increase sensitivity to very low intensity or soft sounds and decrease sensitivity to very high intensity or loud sounds. Inner hair cells then transmit signals to the spiral ganglia of the *cochlear nerve* where they are relayed to the auditory cortex and other higher processing centers in the brain.

The Vestibular Sense

The vestibular sense is the perception of two categories of information. The first is the fixed or *static* (unchanging) position or tilt of the head in all three dimensions relative to the ground (technically the center of the earth) and the bodies overall spatial orientation. The second category is the *dynamic* (changing) perception of *acceleration*. Acceleration is the direction and magnitude of changes in speed (velocity), in other words, how quickly, and in what directions your body is speeding up or slowing down in a straight line (*translational or linear acceleration*) and if it is turning (changing direction), how quickly those changes are occurring (*angular acceleration*). Notice that for angular acceleration, your body does not have to be moving from one spatial location to another (*translational motion*). It can, instead, be spinning around one or more of the three axes of your body. The spinning or pirouetting of a figure skate is rotation around the long or *vertical plane axis* of the body. In other sports, such as gymnastics and diving, performers can also execute maneuvers that involve rotation around *sagittal plane axis* - front and back flips or somersaults and of the frontal plane axis - cartwheels. Spinning or rotational motion even at a constant speed requires a constant force and always has a *continuous angular acceleration*. In addition to these perceptions, this information is vital input for numerous subconscious automatic motor processes of the central nervous system. One example is the complex coordinated eye movements as occurs in the *vestibulo-ocular reflex*. A second example is the automatic motor system that continuously generates complexly choreographed movements and subtle shifts in the body's center of gravity that are required to maintain one's balance. This requires constant communications among the vestibular system, the kinesthetic sensory system and the cerebellum. Dysfunctions of the vestibular system produce nausea, an unsteady stumbling gait and sensation of spinning dizziness, known as *vertigo*.

The *semicircular canals* and the *otolith organs* are the primary anatomical structures of the peripheral vestibular system. They are anatomical substructures of the complete inner ear structure that includes the cochlea. In general, their anatomical features are designed so that deflection (bending) of the stereocilia of their hair cells correlates with the type of motion they are intended to detect. The hair cells of the vestibular system are located in canals contained within three types of structures; the utricles, the saccules and the semicircular canals. Hair cells in the semicircular canals detect *rotational movement* (angular acceleration). The otolith organs, the *saccule* and *utricle*, detect *linear acceleration*. The saccule detects vertical linear acceleration and the utricle detects horizontal linear acceleration. On either side of the head there are three semicircular canals, each is oriented at 90 degrees (orthogonally) to the other two semicircular canals. When rotation of the body occurs, the combined sensory input of the semicircular canals allows one to perceive the precise direction of such rotation in three-dimensional space.

Smell

The olfactory and the gustatory sensory systems directly detect chemicals in the substances we place in our mouths and in the air that we breathe. These taste and smell senses are called chemosensory *senses* because they both transduce chemical signals into neural signals that result in the sensory perceptions of either smell or taste. The olfactory sensory receptor cells are neurons specialized to directly detect a huge variety of individual types of airborne or volatile chemicals. They are located on airway surfaces, primarily in the nasal passages. Individual olfactory receptor cells are maximally sensitive to only a few of these types of chemicals, so there are literally thousands of functional subtypes of olfactory receptor cells each of which generates a perception of a different type of odor. In 2004, *Linda Buck* and *Richard Axel* won the Nobel Prize in Physiology for their work on olfactory receptors. These receptors are considered to be central nervous system neurons so they are literally a direct anatomical extension of the brain.

When olfactory receptor cells bind to their preferred types of chemicals, they generate action potentials that travel along their axons, which, as a group, are the *olfactory nerve*. The olfactory nerve terminates at the *olfactory bulb*. Olfactory information is transmitted from the olfactory bulb to several other regions of the brain, most notably to the *piriform cortex* where the identification of specific odors are perceived, the *amygdala* where it is used to process social functioning behaviors such as mating and recognizing other members of our species, and to the *entorhinal cortex* where there is a fundamental matching of odors with memories of the environmental and emotional circumstances under which these odors were perceived. This is believed to an important neurological process that may explain why certain odors are often able to evoke vibrant and emotionally charged memories.

Taste

The gustatory or taste sense results in perception of one or a combination of five primary taste categories; *sweet, salty, bitter, sour,* and *umami* (delicious). These taste attributes are the result of chemicals that are dissolved in saliva or other liquids binding to receptor molecules on the microvilli at the apical (top) surface of *taste receptor cells*. Taste receptor cells are contained in the *taste buds*, raised papillae found primarily on the surface of the tongue. The purpose of the taste sense is to evaluate the carbohydrate and salt content of substances and the potential risks of infectious or poisonous content of substances before they are swallowed. The sweet taste perception is due to high carbohydrate content, and is presumably evolved to be pleasant based on the historical human environment where the relatively rapid conversion of carbohydrates into energy made them highly desirable from a survival perspective. Not all animals are fond of sweets; cats in particular seem to avoid them. The bitter taste is perceived as unpleasant initially but it can be overcome as evidenced by the acquired appreciation of coffee. Nitrogenous organic molecules are perceived as bitter tasting and many of these molecules are poisonous to humans. Salty tastes are critical to survival, as the salt we require is sodium chloride and the sodium levels of our blood and inside our cells must remain within a very narrow concentration range. Levels just slightly above or below this range are fatal if not rapidly corrected. For most land animals including humans, a craving for salt has evolved due to the frequent difficulty in obtaining enough salt from the environment. Too much salt however causes an unpleasant taste reaction. Small amounts of sour tastes are somewhat pleasant but generally, we avoid sour tasting foods, particularly if we do not expect them to be sour. This is likely because the sour taste indicates high acidity, and this is often associated with spoiled or rotten substances. There is not a lot of information on the nature of the umami sense, but whatever it is, it is delicious.

Somatic Senses and Kinesthetic Sense

The sense of touch actually consists of several different types of perceptions and these as a group are called the somatic senses. They include proprioception and mechanoreception, the senses of the relative position of parts of the body and mechanical forces acting on the body such as stress, strain, pressure and displacement, the rmoreception, the perception of temperature and nociception, the perception of pain. Touch, in general terms, involves the combined perceptions of pressure, skin stretch, vibration and temperature. There are specialized sensory cells for all of these perceptual stimuli that are distributed in the skin and surfaces of the digestive tract, muscles, bones, joints and internal organs, the heart and lungs in particular. Somatic sensations are processed in the somatosensory cortex of the parietal lobes. The spatial locations of sensations in the sensory cortex corresponds to the location of the peripheral receptors on the body. This mapping results in an anatomical reproduction or cartoon of the body within the sensory cortex called a *homunculus*. Mapping of this type also occurs in the visual and auditory cortices. The *kinesthetic sense* is the least well-defined of the senses. It involves the integration of sensory information from proprioceptors and the vestibular system to produce a sophisticated awareness of the body and its capabilities within a dynamic physical environment. A superior kinesthetic sense is considered to be a distinguishing characteristic of elite athletes.

Transduction

We have seen how the visual and auditory systems convert two forms of energy, electromagnetic energy in the form of photons and kinetic or mechanical energy in the form of sound waves into neurochemical signals that can then be processed at higher levels of the sensory systems. Similarly, the olfactory and gustatory systems transduce chemical information about specific molecules that enter the body and the vestibular, somatic sensory and kinesthetic senses transduce information about physical properties of objects and mechanical and gravitational forces that are interacting with our bodies.

Thresholds

A general feature of all of these transduction processes is the concept of *thresholds*. At the level of sensory receptor cells, an *absolute threshold* is the minimum level of stimuli required for signal detection. We define signal detection as the generation of a transmissible neural signal by a sensory receptor cell in response to the stimuli it is designed to detect. At a level of perception, an absolute threshold is the minimum level of stimuli we are a capable of perceiving. A rod cell may have an absolute threshold of one photon and a cone cell an absolute threshold of 50 photons for signal detection, but that does not mean we are capable of perceiving the signal generated by the rod or cone cell. Just as every sensory receptor cell has an absolute threshold, there are absolute thresholds at every subsequent level of signal processing including the final processing stage that actually generates a conscious perception. In conditions we perceive as total darkness or absolute silence, photons and sound waves are being detected by receptor cells, but at a level below our absolute perceptive threshold.

Difference Thresholds

At the perceptive level, there is another type of threshold, the difference threshold. This threshold is the minimum or just right amount of change in sensory input required to be a perceived change. This depends on the initial intensity level of the perception. Consider a situation where the background or *ambient* sound level perceived is very soft compared to when it is very loud. It requires a smaller increase in sound intensity to be perceived as an increase in loudness for soft ambient sound levels than for loud ones. *Ernst Weber's* research on difference thresholds led to his development of *Weber's Law* which states that the that the minimum or just right difference threshold to be perceived as a change in an of the perception must be a specific fractional change of the initial intensity level. The specific fractional change, or *Weber's constant* for perceived changes depends on the specific sensory modality. In the visual system, the Weber's constant for a perceived change in brightness is about 8% or 8 in 100. There are different Weber's constants for other types of perceptions as well. For instance, there is a Weber's constant for the minimum fractional change in the number of a group of objects that is required to be perceived as a larger or smaller group of objects. Weber's law does not apply to perceived changes in light or sound wave frequency such as color changes or changes in auditory tone or pitch. *Gustav Fechner* extended Weber's work by transforming Weber's principles into a more precise and detailed mathematical model. *Fechner's law*, or *Fechner's scale*, states that a subjective change in sensation is proportional to the logarithm of the stimulus intensity.

Adaptation

Sensory adaptation occurs when sensory receptors or other processes alter stimulus thresholds. This phenomenon occurs in all senses, with the possible exception of the sense of pain. As we mentioned earlier, adaptation occurs in the visual system in the form of decreased rod and cone thresholds for photon absorption. These are features of *dark adaptation,* or adaptation to reduced light intensity in the visual system. Specifically, this involves an immediate dilation of the pupil, which allows more light to enter the eye to stimulate rod and cone cells. Rods and cones increase their sensitivity in low-light conditions by increasing their opsin concentrations, which increases the probability of photon absorption. Dark adaptation is a type of *slow adaptation*. Cones become completely dark-adapted within about five to ten minutes, but this adaptation is not sufficient to allow cones to contribute to night vision. Rods become fully dark-adapted after about 20-30 minutes.

The opposite also occurs in the visual system, namely *light adaptation*. Light adaptation occurs by an immediate pupil constriction and as a consequence of the rapid destruction or photolysis of opsins by photons under increased intensity levels. Light adaptation is a type of *rapid adaptation* because it occurs in seconds, rather than the minutes required for dark adaptation. *Accommodation* is a neuromuscular rapid adaptive process under control of the central nervous system that focuses images on the retinal by adjusting the tone of muscles attached to the lens of the eye. We also discussed how the central nervous system can functionally decrease the threshold for detection of soft sounds and increase the threshold for the response to very loud sounds by signaling outer hair cells to alter their force of contraction in response to fluid pressure waves at the tectorial membrane. This is an *electromechanical adaptation* that amplifies or dampens the motions of the tectorial membrane. The *protective adaptation* against injury due to persistently loud ambient noise levels also occurs by reflex contraction of muscles of the middle ear ossicles that decrease the force transmitted during air-fluid wave coupling between the tympanic membrane and the oval window membrane.

Higher-level Perceptual Processes

There is little doubt that perceptive experience in humans at the highest level is a process of sensory integration to produce an awareness of the external environment as stable, with physical properties and dynamic interactions that are fundamental and predictable. To that end, our minds have the tendency to fill in gaps in what is actually detected by sensory receptors and to ascribe meaning in terms of the mind's own global internal model of the nature of reality. Therefore, the mind tends to search for patterns and relationships based on various parameters even when such patterns or relationships may not actually exist. The mind is constantly generating a perceived reality that is based on assumptions about and conclusions derived from incomplete information or too much irrelevant information. Essentially the mind assumes and anticipates that the external world is and behaves as the internal model of the world that it has created through genetic evolved neural circuitry and refined by reprogramming based on past experiences or learning. We see this best exemplified through perceptual phenomena that occurs in the visual system.

Visual Fields and Receptive Fields

One's full field of vision, or the totality of everything you can see at a given moment in time can be divided into two visual fields. Beginning at the midline of your face, everything to the right is the *right visual field* and everything to the left is the *left visual field*. Most Light rays from each field can reach the retinae of both eyes. Some rays from the extreme periphery of the visual fields car blocked from entering the opposite eye by the contour of the nose. Light from the right visual field shines upon the central or left half of the right retina and on the outer or left half of the left retina. The reverse is true for the left visual field. Information from each visual field is relayed from rods and cones to signal processing cells in a second layer of the retina. Left visual field information is sent from both eyes to the right visual cortex and vice versa. These cells are bipolar, horizontal and amacrine cells. Information is first relayed to bipolar cells. Each bipolar cell receives information directly through synapses from photoreceptor cells located within a precise anatomical region of the retina. This region is different for each bipolar cell and is called the *receptive field* of the bipolar cell. The size of the region occupied by the photoreceptor cells is the size of the bipolar cell's receptive field. For some bipolar cells, the receptive field is one single cone cell. This occurs in corresponding locations of the central region of the retina called the *fovea*. Cone cells are most densely distributed at the fovea. Since cone cells are adapted to respond rapidly to changing light and have three different types of color sensitivities and since they are so numerous at the fovea and since the corresponding bipolar receptive fields are so small and densely correlated to the fovea, the fovea produces extremely high *acuity vision*. Visual acuity refers to the resolution capacity of vision. *Resolution* is defined as the minimum distance required between two small dots such that they can still be perceived as two separate dots. Persons with 20/20 vision can distinguish a separation between objects as small as 1/1000 of a meter (1 millimeter). If you had the visual acuity of an eagle, you could see an ant crawling on the ground from the roof of a 10-story building. At the center of the cornea, the tracts of the optic nerve pass into the retina. There are no photoreceptors at this location and it is therefore a *blind spot*. Photoreceptor cells' signals are relayed within a complex network of horizontal bipolar and amacrine signal processing cells in the middle layer of the retina. They all have individual receptive fields and these fields overlap. Through ingenious and often previously completely unknown and unsuspected principles and circuit wiring patterns, these cells as a system operate as a small version of the visual cortex, a sort of mini visual peripheral brain. This allows for complex reflex-like reactions to the visual environment, such as instantly jerking away from a threat signal or instantly pouncing on a moving prey item. This heavy level of processing converts raw visual data into very complexly pre analyzed and pre organized categories of information before it is sent to the brain. For example, there is, in amphibians, and probably in humans as well, a retinal "bug detector" that can operate without much participation of the visual cortex. In humans, this may be transmitted from the retina as the immediate perception: "Hey that's a bug! Kill it!"

Objects, Backgrounds and Perceived Motion

Program of the bug-detector type are possible at the retinal level because basic photoreceptor cell sensations are processed into higher-level sensation categories. The overlapping receptive fields of the midlevel retinal processing cells are interactive. For static or unmoving visual features, the contrast between light and dark fields can be enhanced by changing the total receptive field of adjacent regions to completely on or completely off. This establishes the contours or outlines of objects, and identifies which regions represent an object and which represent the visual background. This is a basic element of visual perception called the *figure-ground relationship*. Contrast contours and color content within these contours also establish the visual details or individual features of objects and backgrounds. Once these concepts are fixed, the processing cells can combine objects and backgrounds into larger categories of receptive fields and follow them as they change position on the retina over time to produce *perceptions of motion.*

Optical Illusions

Static optical illusions can occur when the figure-ground relationship is ambiguous, such as images where the white central region can be perceived as an object and the surrounding black region as the background or vice versa. A famous example is an image where perceptions rapidly switch back and forth between of a white, long stemmed class surrounded by a black background and two facing black silhouette profiles separated by a central white space. A string of lights with a precisely timed sequential blinking pattern can produce a *dynamic optical illusion* of motion. This is called the *phi phenomenon.* More complex optical illusions seem to involve higher levels of processing that occur in the brain.

Visual Pathways in the Brain

The receptive field information of retinal visual processing cells is transmitted via the optic nerves through the optic chiasm, the intersection of the left and right optic nerve. At this junction, left and right visual field information of the opposite retinal origin cross over so that all right visual field information travels to the left visual cortex and vice versa. The fibers of the optic nerve do not travel directly to the visual cortex. Instead they synapse in one of four locations, the *lateral geniculate nucleus* of the *thalamus* where visual perception appears to begin to occur, the *superior colliculus* of the midbrain which is a center for complex automatic and voluntary control of eye movements; the *pretectum* of the *midbrain,* for control of the pupillary light reflex; and the *suprachiasmatic nucleus* of the hypothalamus, for control of *diurnal rhythms* and hormonal changes. Most of the optic nerve fibers terminate in the lateral geniculate nucleus where their information is further process then relayed to the visual cortex, perceived motion, and depth cues.

Gestalt

The brain appears to have evolved programs that preprocess sensory input into perceptual categories or concepts. *The gestalt principles of visual perception* are based on observations that there are general categories of fundamental visual phenomena. These include the principles of *proximity*, which describes the tendency to perceive objects as belonging to the same group based on their closer proximity to each other compared to other objects in the visual field. *Similarity*, where perceived grouping is based on shared features of objects such as shape, color and shading patterns and *closure*, where our mind fills in the visual gaps with images such as shapes, symbols and even entire sceneries that are missing parts so that they are perceived as being intact.

Constancy

Another remarkable perceptual visual phenomena is *subjective constancy*, the perception that physical attributes of objects such as their size, shape, brightness (or lightness) and color are not really changing even though the actual sensory information reports that they absolutely are changing. The orientation of an object relative to the eyes can change and this is accurately reported by the visual receptor systems as a change in shape. An example of the alteration of shape due to a changed perspective is a donut. The top view of a donut is detected as a completely different shape compared to the side view of a donut. As objects move closer or farther away from the eyes their size increases or decreases relative to the visual background. The true brightness of an intrinsically brightly colored object is less bright in dimmer light. Except for very low light conditions, the object is not perceived to have changed color or brightness. Instead, the brain matches these changes with its instinctive recognition of the laws of physics in action. The result is that we perceive not that an object's shape is actually changing but, instead, that the object has a rotational or linear motion and that an object is not changing it brightness or color, but that the ambient light levels are changing. Sometimes, however, subjective constancy can create an optical illusion. *Distance* constancy uses visual reference features that include the relative sizes of apparently nearby objects. In the case of the moon, this results in the perception that the size of the moon is much larger when it is close to the horizon than when it is high in the sky where it is apparently without nearby objects for comparison.

Depth Perception

The overall perception of depth involves the principle of size constancy and binocular and monocular cues to estimate the absolute and relative size and distances of objects from the eyes. When you focus directly on an object, the spatial separation between the pupils of your eye requires each eye to move inward by a precise angle to converge on an object. The closer the object to your eyes the larger the angle the eyes must turn inward to converge on the object. This is called a *parallax* or *parallax angle*. The brain uses a basic trigonometry calculation based on its estimate of the parallax angle and the distance between your eyes to automatically and almost instantly perceive how far away the object is. The brain estimates the parallax by using two cues. One is the comparative disparity between the left and right images. The closer the object, the greater the difference in the image relative to the visual background. This cue is called *stereopsis*. The second cue is provided by the kinesthetic sense of the amount of stretching of extraocular muscles that occurs when the eyes turn inward. The greater the stretch the closer the object. This cue is called *convergence*. Both stereopsis and convergence require input from both eyes, so they are called *binocular cues*.

Monocular cues require information from only one view. These are the clues that create an illusion of the 3-dimensional perception of depth on a 2-dimensional surface, such as a painting, drawing or photograph. *Linear perspective* is the appearance that parallel lines are converging. *Relative size cues* occur from differences in objects' positions that are suggested by linear perspective (bigger is closer and smaller is farther away). Objects that are closer obscure overlapping regions of objects that are farther away. Objects that are closer have more detail than those further away and different shading features of objects suggest their relative positions with respect to a single light source. These are the *interposition*, *gradient* and *shadowing cues*, respectively.

Signal Detection Theory

Signal detection theory deals with more complex situations where a person's perceptions are also altered by past experience, learned knowledge and awareness of overall integrated perceptive reality. An example is the perception of a streetlight during foggy conditions. If you had never been in fog before and knew nothing about it from anything you had read or heard and made no conscious intellectual effort to analyze the potential perceptual distortion caused by fog, you would greatly under perceive the true brightness of the streetlight and over perceive the distance to the streetlight. Through past experience, formal learning and general situational awareness, persons can not only intellectually know the streetlight is actually brighter and closer than it appears, but their actual perceptions of the brightness and distance changes and becomes closer to reality. This demonstrates the mind's ability to reprogram or adapt the perceptual process and to increase the ability to separate relevant information from irrelevant information or distortions of information. Information theorists call this the ability to discriminate between *signal and noise*. Computer programs are written to improve signal processing so that radar, television and radio transmissions can be more effectively separate signal from noise to provide more detailed and accurate sounds and images. The mind possesses similar types of signal processing programming.

Attention

Another aspect of signal detection theory is the alteration of perceptual thresholds based on the context and expectations of the perceiver. In high-noise perceptual environments, there are many competing stimuli or noise during one's search for a specific signal or patterns of signals. This requires the attention of the perceiver and that attention depends, in part, on the motivation level of the person who wishes to receive or perceptually detect a signal. More specifically, it depends on how strongly they desire to receive a perception. It also depends on how strongly the receiver expects to receive a perception. These factors can result in *false perceptions*, when expectations and/or motivations are high, such as mistaking an incorrect number for a correct number on one's lottery ticket. When motivation and/or expectations are low, missed perceptions are more likely to occur. Researchers have found that most people, when shown a picture of a crowd where a certain percentage of the crowd have had their heads photo-shopped off, fail to notice this fact. That's because most people have very low expectations that people would be walking about without their heads, and most people are really not motivated, in general, to see headless persons. In other words, they are not paying attention to the state of existence or nonexistence of people's heads. These types of influences on one's perceptions are known as *receiver criteria* or *receiver operating characteristics*. In research, false perceptions are called *false positives* and missed perceptions are called *false negatives*. Researchers can quantify and statistically analyze these characteristics in controlled studies to extend our understanding of the mechanisms of perception.

Top-Down and Bottom-Up Processing

In 1970 psychologist *Richard Gregory*, in his Perception as Hypothesis theory, argued that top down visual processing is required due to the heavy filtering of visual information. Specifically, that at least 90% of the information is lost before it reaches the higher brain centers. This requires that visual perceptions begin with a best guess of what the visual stimuli represent based on memories and related past experience. In part, he supported this view by citing various forms of optical illusions that presumably represent incorrect guesses or wrong hypotheses about what is really being visually perceived. In general, this suggests perceptions that occur through top-down processing are rapid but prone to error. Top-down processing or *conceptually-driven processing*, is perceptual pattern recognition that relies on contextual information. Expectations, beliefs and intellectual thinking capacities allows us to first consider a general or big-picture concept and based on our impressions, using both unconscious and conscious processes, such as logic and reasoning, we are able to rapidly, sometimes almost instantaneously, perceive a detailed perception of the larger concept. In other words, we begin with the general and work toward the specific. The brain knows what it expects to perceive based on its cognitive awareness of how the world works and on its past experiences, then it fills in the blanks. We have all experienced this when we have seen a neon sign with burned out letters. Using top down processing, usually we are automatically able to fill in the missing letters and create a perception of the specific message. If there are a lot of missing letters, we need to apply intense concentration to get the message. Wheel-of-fortune champions are apparently great top-down processors.

Psychologist *Eleanor Gibson* was the most notable early contributor to the *bottom-up theory* of visual perception. Based on her research studies with infants and a "visual cliff," she argued that perception is not initiated by a hypotheses. Instead, perception is a bottom-up, direct, "you see exactly what you see" phenomenon. In her studies, Gibson showed that infants almost always refused to crawl out over the cliff edge, even when enthusiastically coaxed to do so by their mothers. This showed an intrinsic ability to perceive a detailed accurate visual concept without any top-down expectations to see a cliff or motivation to see a cliff. True, it wasn't a real cliff, but it appeared as one. The infants were presumably using their inborn ability to perceive depth and their past painful experiences of falling from "too high" places to build up a more general perception of "stop! that's a cliff!"

Bottom up reasoning begins with all the details and a big perceptual picture is built up from there. A top down process might predict a different outcome to this experiment, where the infants begin processing their perception of the situation as a big picture such as "I trust mom, she would not try to harm me" and the detail that is filled in is "it must therefore be possible for me to crawl across thin air." Bottom up processing requires many small incremental steps of learning from past experience so the bottom up process occurs more slowly compared to top down processing, but the perceptions are much less prone to error. Dr.Gibson summarized bottom-up processing, as exemplified in her visual cliff studies, thusly: "*We perceive to learn, as well as learn to perceive.*"

Gregory and others proposed top down processing based primarily on the phenomena of various types of optical illusions. Bottom up theory, they argued, could not account for many features of these false perceptions. Gibson and colleagues rebutted that these illusions did not exist in the natural world. They were artificial abstractions that did not require an initial hypothesis about their true nature, nor were they due to the brain's attempt to complete an incomplete perception, because there was nothing real to perceive. Rather, it was just how the brain perceived relative aspects of contours, contrasts and depth cues in patterns that had no meaning in the external world. Nevertheless, there is no reason to think that we do not use both types of processing and the AP Examination presumes both processes do occur.

Culture and Perception

Both top-down and bottom-processes propose that there are intrinsic capabilities for perceptive processes. Recent cross-cultural research has shown evidence that these may not be inborn abilities but to some extent learned or conditioned perceptual processes. Evidence for this is seen in studies showing cultural differences in the perception of certain types of optical illusions. *Richard Nisbett's* theory of culture and perception cites psychological experiments that compared perceptual and attentional differences between Westerners and Asians. These studies showed large differences in *change blindness* between Westerners and Asians. Change blindness refers to the failure to detect large differences between two pictures shown in succession. The evidence from these studies suggests that visual perception in Americans is more analytical and in Asians it is more holistic. Americans examine objects in isolation and are more likely to pay more attention to, perceive and remember the specific distinguishing features of objects. Asians are more sensitive to context and are inclined to pay more attention to, perceive and remember contexts and relationships.

Paranormal Phenomena

We conclude this chapter with the following advisory: regardless of your personal beliefs, the professional psychological community and the science community in general take a very dim view of the subject of paranormal phenomena such as extra sensory perception and cast a jaundiced eye upon those who claim there is scientific evidence for such phenomena. The law of physics provides no hypothesis to explain such phenomena. At least for the duration of the AP examination we strongly suggest you adopt this position as well.

Chapter 5: States of Consciousness

States of Consciousness

Consciousness is so fundamental it defies description in more fundamental terms. Perhaps it is best to define your consciousness as what you are. In addition, since you are you, you cannot really ever know exactly what you are. There are very compelling theories in physics, math and computer science that argue it is theoretically impossible for any system to ever completely understand itself.

Historically and conceptually, attempts to define the nature of consciousness began with two towering intellects, the philosopher *William James* and the founder of psychoanalytic theory, *Sigmund Freud*. James developed the philosophy of pragmatism and is considered to be the founder of American psychology. His concept of consciousness is found in his *theory of self*, which describes two defining elements of the self: the *"me" self* and the *"I" self*. The "me" self has three elements: (1) the *material self*, consisting of what belongs to us, our body our material and financial assets and what we belong to such as our family, our church our nation (2) the *social self*, a highly adaptable persona tailored to integrate with the features of an ever changing social milieu and (3) a spiritual self that embodies our core values. The "me" self is not fundamental. It emerges from experience. The "I" self is the thinking self that James equated with the soul or the mind, which he called this the *pure ego*. James considered the "I" self or the soul to be outside the realm of the physical universe and therefore impossible to examine using scientific methods. This philosophy is known as *dualism*. James' theory set the stage for the two major debates regarding consciousness. The first is whether our consciousness or at least a core consciousness is, as James believed, separate from our brain or, as *reductionist* or *monist* philosophy contends, it is entirely a product of neurological processes occurring in the brain. The second is whether we have *free will* or, as *determinist* philosophy contends, everything that occurs in our lives and within our minds, including what we perceive to be the freedom to choose how to behave, is actually predetermined inevitable outcomes based solely upon previous events and the laws of physics.

Freud proposed that consciousness is of three internal mental realms: the *preconscious*, the *conscious*, and the *unconscious*. These are the arenas for complex and often conflicting interactions of primal psychological forces that generate an individual's personality and behavior. These three mental realms constitute different levels of awareness. James called the essence of what we are the "I" self or the pure ego or the soul. He implies that consciousness is either absolutely the soul or an indivisible element of the soul. For Freud, consciousness is a backdrop for the fundamental essence of what we are. Freud considered it not the essence of ourselves but an indispensable process that we require in order to generate a perception of emotion, to acquire the traits of our personality and to behave or to interact with our environment. Others describe different definitions of the preconscious level as well as the additional nonconscious and subconscious levels. Clearly, there are thought processes or at least complex levels of neurological processing that serve critical functions within the brain, and, in the physical world, we could not achieve consciousness without them.

Awake and Fully Conscious

The two primary, normal conscious states are the *awake state* and the *sleep state*. In the fully conscious awake state, we are receiving and perceiving sensory information accurately. We are processing perceptions and integrating them with memory, emotion and drive states such as hunger thirst reproductive and other survival urges. This produces an overall state of mind that executive functions act upon to produce strategies and initiate actions and behaviors to operate as a normal human being is expected to act in the external environment. In the fully conscious state, you appear to be able to make choices and to have voluntary control over your actions. It is clear based on very well-conducted research that many unconscious processes are contributing to your ability to maintain a conscious state and are even perhaps creating illusions that you are actually making choices to act voluntarily.

This view that free will, that you have any ability to voluntarily choose what actions you take in the physical world, is an illusion known as *epiphenomenalism*. This view states that consciousness is an *epiphenomenon*, a byproduct of neurological processes, a sort of weird accidental side effect. Although it is real, it has no ability to influence any events in the real world because it (consciousness) possesses no physical tools to alter the physical processes occurring in the material universe. Essentially, we are literally mere observers in our own lives. It is a scary thought but if true, for most of us it is a very convincing illusion and an utterly engrossing observational experience.

Levels of Consciousness

The *preconscious level* is a sort of repository of readily accessible information or potential elements of our consciousness that we are currently not specifically aware of but are aware of their availability. They are additions, substitutions or accessories that we can, if we so desire, switch on or integrate into our overall conscious state level to produce a different character or content to our overall conscious state. Examples include details such as names, dates, etc. stored in memories that you could call up if you wished or perhaps even very complex programs or algorithms such as switching from a state of artistic appreciation to a state of analytical suspicion and acute awareness of potential threats in the environment.

The *nonconscious level* is the processing that controls automatic functions such as breathing, heart rate, temperature regulation and so forth. These are primarily the functions of the autonomic nervous system but there are many other types of nonconscious processes that occur continuously, cyclically, or on an as-needed basis. We are generally completely unaware of nonconscious process and as long as they are functioning properly, they have no influence over our conscious state.

The *Subconscious level* is a level of which we have little conscious awareness or access. In contrast, this level is aware of us (the conscious level) and does have, to some extent at least, access to or even control over conscious processes. Here are two examples that illustrate this concept of the nature of the subconscious level. There are two phenomena that researchers have identified that provide very strong evidence that the subconscious level as we have described actually does exist. One is mere-exposure effect and the other is the priming phenomenon

The *mere-exposure effect* is also known as the *familiarity principle*. It describes a favorability or previous-exposure bias. The bias is the tendency for persons to react in a more positive or favorable manner to things that they have been previously exposed to as compared to their reactions to *novel stimuli,* meaning stimuli that they have not yet been previously exposed . The favorability of the individual's reaction is measured by various means such as likeability or pleasantness rating scales. Another method to measure the positive bias of the mere-exposure effect is through the use of forced choice. Individuals have, when forced to choose, a preference for or bias towards a stimuli they have been previously exposed to over novel stimuli.

The key aspect of the mere-exposure effect is that research shows it occurs even without the conscious memory of the exposure. Even more significantly, it also occurs when there is no initial conscious awareness of the exposure. Most importantly, the effect is often stronger when the exposure is not consciously perceived compared to when it is consciously recognized or remembered as a previous exposure.

Priming is a very general effect involving several types of cognitive processes including memory retrieval abilities and other performance criteria. The effects of priming are those that occur when a previous exposure to one stimulus influences the subsequent response to another stimulus. An example is the *word-stem completion test* where a subject is shown a list of words that may include the word "carton." Later the subject is asked to complete a word that starts with the stem "car" The probability that the subject will complete the stem as "carton" is much higher than if the priming did not occur. Research shows priming effects can affect word choice on a word-stem completion test long after the words have been forgotten. Other research protocols showed the effect is at least as strong when the subjects are never aware of a previous exposure.

The mere exposure effect and the priming phenomena shows that there is a complex neurological mechanism that can among other things perceive information that the conscious mind may be completely unaware of, convert it to memory and reprogram the mind so that it can be more efficiently recalled and then cognitively processed at an enhanced performance level. We call this the *unconscious level of consciousness* or perhaps more correctly, the subconscious level of the mind.

The unconscious level is like a dark closet where events and/or feelings that are unacceptable to the conscious mind are repressed. The concept of an unconscious level is basically a concept of Freudian psychodynamic theory. In contrast to the preconscious, there is little if any solid research to support the existence of nonconscious and subconscious levels..

Sleep

Sleep is one of the two naturally occurring periodic states of the sleep-wake cycle. The sleep state is characterized by decreased or suspended wakeful consciousness and muscular activity and reduced responsiveness to outside stimuli. The state of sleep is easily and immediately reversible in contrast to other states of diminished or absent wakefulness, including hibernation and coma.

The Sleep-Wake Cycle

The sleep wake cycles are generated by two independent mechanisms. One is *circadian rhythms* and the other is *sleep-wake homeos*tasis. Circadian rhythms are 24-hour day-night light cycles that oscillate between neurological and other biological activities that correspond to wakeful and sleep associated schedules. In addition to sleep patterns, circadian rhythms regulate feeding patterns, core body temperature, cell regeneration and repair activity, hormone production and brain wave activity. Wakeful process are most active during the day and sleep process during the night. The cycle is regulated by the hypothalamus through the secretion of the hormone melatonin. Increasing melatonin levels lead to greater activation of sleep processes and decreasing levels lead to greater activation of wakeful processes.

Sleep-wake homeostasis occurs by the steady buildup of sleep inducing chemical in the body while one is awake. The longer one is awake the higher the levels of sleep inducing chemicals and the greater the urge to sleep. During sleep, the sleep-inducing chemicals decrease to their lowest levels. The maximum benefit of sleep occurs when sleep-wake homeostasis and the circadian rhythm cycle are in sync. The circadian rhythm is independent of how much a persons has recently slept or when a person last slept. If the sleep-wake homeostatic mechanisms forces one to sleep at a wakeful period of the circadian cycle, much or even all of the benefits of sleep during this time will be lost.

The Sleep Cycle

There are two main types of sleep. *REM* and *non-REM* sleep. Non-REM sleep consists of stages 1, 2 and 3. A typical adult sleep period is 8 hours. For infants in may be as long as 18 hours and total sleep time decreases as persons enter their elderly years. During a sleep period, sleep cycles through these four stages over a 60-120 minute periods usually for a total of five cycles per sleep period. Rem sleep and each stage of non-REM sleep have unique characteristic patterns of brain wave activity.

Brain waves

Brain waves are patterns of electrical activity that are detected through the use of *electroencephalography (EEG)*. The EEG uses multiple electrodes placed on or near the scalp surface to record this surface electrical activity. There are five basic categories of brain waves; *gamma waves* are the highest frequency waves and are associated with formation of ideas, language and memory processing. *Beta waves* are high frequency waves that are the most prominent during the wakeful state and indicate high levels of brain activity. *Alpha waves* are slower frequency waves that correspond to relaxed wakeful states and are the waves that are most prominent just before the onset of sleep. *Theta waves* are high frequency low amplitude waves that occur during states of light sleep and extreme relaxation. Theta waves become slower and higher as sleep deepens from stage 1 to stage 2. *Delta waves* are the lowest frequency waves and are associated with the deepest levels of sleep. A specific type of brainwave pattern is the *sleep spindle,* which is a short burst of high frequency waves that are typical of stage 2 sleep.

Stage 1 sleep is the stage between wakefulness and sleep brainwaves transition from erratic or unsynchronized gamma and alpha waves of the awake state to slower more synchronized alpha waves and increasing theta waves as sleep deepens. Breathing rates become more regular and heart rate slows. Dreaming is rare in stage 1 and the stage lasts only about 10 minutes. Persons awakened from stage 1 sleep often do not feel that they were actually asleep. Only about 5% of total sleep time is spent in stage 1 sleep.

In *stage 2* sleep, muscle activity decrease and the responsiveness to and awareness of the outside world is almost completely lost. Theta waves dominate stage 2 sleep but there is also the appearance of sleep spindles and K-complexes - very short wave forms that together are believed to suppress the response to outside stimuli and aid in information processing "housekeeping chores" and in the consolidation of memories. In adults, 40-50% of total sleep time is spent in stage 2 sleep.

Stage 3 sleep is also known as delta or slow wave sleep, it is the deepest level of sleep. Delta waves are the dominant wave pattern and some spindles occur during stage 3 sleep. Persons in stage 3 sleep are completely unresponsive to normal stimuli and are very difficult to arouse. The stage is longest during the first 2 phases of the sleep cycle and is often absent for the final cycles of sleep before waking. Core body and brain temperature, breathing and heart rate are lowest during this stage. Dreaming is infrequent but not rare. The *parasomnias* (sleepwalking, sleep talking, night terrors and bedwetting) occur almost exclusively during stage 3 sleep. Information processing and memory consolidation are occurring during this stage. Children and young adults spend more time in stage 3 sleep and elderly persons often do not have any stage 3 sleep.

REM (rapid eye movement) sleep is associated with rapid side-to-side closed eye movements believed to reflect the events occurring during dreams. REM sleep occurs in each sleep cycle during a sleep period and increases with each cycle. It is the longest portion of the cycle before waking. REM sleep is longest in infants, where it may constitute 80% of total sleep time. Adults spend 20% of sleep in REM sleep. Brain activity is very high during REM sleep with mixed frequency brain wave patterns including theta, alpha, and beta waves that are very similar to wakeful state brain patterns. For this reason, REM is also called paradoxical sleep. Breathing becomes rapid and irregular and heart rate and blood pressure increase to waking levels. Voluntary muscles are completely paralyzed in a state called *atonia* during REM sleep. The majority of the vivid memorable dreams occur during REM sleep. REM sleep is probably very important during early neurological development and appears to play a role along with stage 3 sleep in memory consolidation. *REM rebound* is a phenomena where interruption or shortening of REM sleep in made up for by increased time spent in REM sleep during subsequent sleep periods.

The Purpose of Sleep

There is very little if any conclusive data to show why we actually need to sleep but there is good evidence that sleep is a consolidation and recuperation phase where memories of the wakeful day are primed for encoding and information obtained during the day is organized and synthesized into more useful form. There is also a restorative effect that provides for better functioning under stressful circumstances and enhancements that are made to the immune system that increase our resistance to illness during stressful periods.

Sleep Disorders

Sleep disorders include insomnia a common problem affecting up to 10% of the population that is a recurrent difficulty is falling and/or staying asleep. Persons with *insomnia* often resort to sleep inducing medications, but this is often counterproductive since these medications tend to disrupt the normal sleep cycle and result in the loss of many of the benefits of normal sleep. *Narcolepsy* is a much rarer condition, affecting only 1 in 100,000 persons. It is characterized by sudden unpredictable lapses into deep or REM sleep during period of complete wakefulness. Obviously, this can be extremely hazardous particularly when driving or operating heavy machinery. *Sleep apnea* is another common disorder where persons wake up multiple times due to airway obstruction during a sleep period. Sleep apnea often prevents deep sleep stages from occurring. This results in not only chronic daytime weariness, memory impairment and difficulty concentrating but also, if undiagnosed and untreated, can cause severe health problems including congestive heart failure due to persistently low oxygen levels during sleep. Persons with sleep apnea are often unaware that they have the condition and due not remember the multiple awakenings that occur throughout the night. Treatment of the condition often requires the use of CPAP (continuous positive airway pressure) breathing devices during sleep periods. Men who are overweight are at highest risk for sleep apnea. *Somnambulism* (sleepwalking) and *night terrors* are closely related conditions that occur during deep sleep or Stage 3 sleep. Night terrors occur mostly in children beginning at the age of three and cause the child to awaken abruptly is a confused inconsolable state of panic. The child is often sweating profusely and has an elevated heart rate and blood pressure. The child is usually unable to recall any details of the night terror experience and generally does not recall that the episode even happened upon awakening in the morning.

Dreams

Dreams are involuntary, strangely distorted sequences of images, ideas, and emotions that are experienced as a theme or storyline where the dreamer is the principal character but has little or no control over the subject matter or events that occur within the dream sequence. Except for lucid dreams, the dreamer has no awareness that the experience is a dream. The most vividly recollected dreams occur in REM stage sleep but they do occur in other stages, most often stage 3 sleep. The urge to dream is so strong that dreams or dream-like states often can intrude upon a wakeful state particularly in persons with severe sleep deprivation. So yes, it is possible to dream while you are awake.

Theories of Dreams

For historical interest and for possible AP Psychology questions, *Freud's psychoanalytic explanation* for the nature of dreams contends that dreams are a window into information that is stored on the unconscious mind and that dreams could undergo analysis or interpretation to uncover this otherwise secret information. He defined dreams as *wish fulfillment* where we act out our unconscious desires. Dreams are so bizarre because the ego is protecting us from the *latent content* or true meaning of the dream by transposing it like a cipher or code into a *manifest content* or the literal storyline of the dream.

Information processing theory holds that dreams are a result of the REM stage bases processing of information into memory. Support for this theory includes the hypothesis that high stress environments are associated with higher and more complex information inputs and that this is supported by the observation that that stress increases the number and intensity or our dreams There is also the observation that dream content is often related to daily concerns and that infants spend more time in REM sleep, presumably because they have a lot more novel stimuli to process.

Freud's theory has no neurological basis and information processing has a general neurological principle for explanation of dreams but no actual mechanism for the occurrence of dreams. The other major theories of dreams are based on neurological principles. There are three major theories, all of which have their strengths and weaknesses. As research continues, a more fully developed understanding of the dreaming process is emerging. The *activation synthesis model* of J. Allan Hobson and Robert McClarley suggest that REM sleep activates specific REM circuits that then activate other circuits in the limbic system that are involved in emotions, sensations and memories. The purpose of this activation is not to create a dream, but to carry out the memory and information processing tasks that are best accomplished during the sleep state. Dreams are just the sleep conscious mind trying to make sense out of these processes that are, at a conscious level, no more meaningful than random signals - in other words dreams don't occur for any real purpose and they simply do not mean anything.

Eugene Tarnow's *long-term excitation theory* explains dreams as a manifestation of the brain's continuous internal excitation of long-term memories. During the waking state, the executive function of the brain performs fact-checking of these excitations and suppresses them as conscious perceptions because the executive function judges them not to be real. During sleep, the executive function is suspended and the sleep conscious mind doesn't make a distinction between the reality or unreality of perceptions, it simply runs the perceptions as scenarios where the excited or elicited long-term memory units are interpreted in as logical a fashion as possible which is usually pretty not logical at all.

Jie Zhang's *continual activation theory* argues that dreams are a feature of the neurological processes required to consolidate working or declarative memories into long term or procedural memories. During REM sleep, presumably the conscious and nonconscious systems for working memory need to always be on or activated. If this activation level falls too low, the brain generates a data stream from memory storage to maintain a sufficiently activated working memory program. According to this theory, dreaming is the incidental perception of these data streams, and, once again, dreams are just an accident and do not mean anything.

Hypnosis

Hypnosis is an interesting phenomenon and certainly appears to be an altered state of consciousness. Before we go further, it should be noted that there are no discernable differences between the brainwaves of a normal waking state and a purported hypnotic state. We will assume it may be a true altered conscious state and the AP Psychology exam expects you to be able to familiar with several features and theories of the hypnotic state.

Hypnosis is an artificially induced state where the hypnotized subject seems to be in a heightened state of suggestibility and to have a decreased awareness of the peripheral environment. The process of hypnosis begins with *hypnotic induction*, where a practitioner or hypnotist focuses a series of stylistically monotonous rhythmically delivered verbal instructions or suggestions on the person of hypnotic intent.

Historically hypnotism was practiced as stage hypnosis by entertainers who were able to make suggestions that caused normal appearing people and even entire audiences to behave is very peculiar manners, which one would not expect that they would voluntarily engage in especially in public unless they were under some sort of hypnotic compulsion to do so. This is the highly suggestible state of hypnosis. There are also two other effects of hypnosis that practitioners appeared to be able to induce in subjects. One is the *post hypnotic* suggestion, where after the subject is released from the hypnotic state they engage in some unusual and often embarrassing acts or behaviors when they encounter a cue, often in the form a specific word or gesture that was suggested during the hypnotic state.. The second effect is *post hypnotic amnesia* where the subject appears to have no recollection of any aspect of their hypnotic state or even that they were in a hypnotic state. Often the first reaction upon emerging from a hypnotic state is one of surprise, presumably from the perception that they have passed from one time and place to another instantaneously.

State theories contend that hypnosis is an altered state of consciousness. For support of their view state theorists, cite the success of hypnotherapy in the reduction of the perception of pain and other somatic symptoms in various real injury and disease states and for the reduction of cravings or urges in smoking and other addictions.

Ernest Hilgard's *neodissociation theory* hypothesizes that the hypnotic state is not an alteration of a state of consciousness but occurs to be due a voluntary division of consciousness into 2 simultaneous streams, one which responds to the hypnotist and the other that retains an awareness of reality. This effect is demonstrated in the ice water bath experiment where the hypnotists suggests that there is no pain that results from dipping one's arm into an ice water bath. Although the subjects reported that they felt no pain the subjects did raise a finger when asked to raise a finger if any parts (interpreted by the researchers as other parts of consciousness) of the subjects were experiencing pain.

Role theory claims the hypnotic state is not a neurologically based alteration or division of consciousness but it is a social phenomenon where the hypnotized persons who are playing out a role and that they are more likely to do so do so based on their level of suggestibility. Those with higher suggestibility tended to have richer fantasy lives, are particularly good at following directions and could focus intensely on a single task for long periods of time. The concept that this is a social phenomenon is based on the assumption that persons with highly suggestible characteristics gain positive reinforcement or rewards from playing a hypnotized role within a social context. An analogy would be persons with a high financial motivation who would act is the same hypnotized fashion if you paid them enough to do so. The difference being that the financial reward would be clearly apparent to the actor and there could be no confusion that the behavior was an act on the actor's part. The suggestible persons may not however be so aware of the rewards they are receiving and may actually be convinced they are under hypnotic control.

Our final topic for this chapter is the consciousness altering effects of drugs these alterations are primarily abnormally altered or diminished states of consciousness. To discuss these, we need to provide the terminology for the levels and types of abnormal consciousness. The least severe is the *clouding of consciousness,* a very mild form of altered mental status characterized by inattention and reduced wakefulness. Next is the *confusional state,* a more serious state that includes disorientation, bewilderment, and difficulty following commands. Individuals with lethargy have severe drowsiness. They require moderate stimuli to become briefly more alert but then drift rapidly back to sleep. *Obtundation* is a state similar to lethargy in which the Individual has a lessened interest in the environment, slowed responses to stimulation, and tends to sleep more than normal with drowsiness in between sleep states. *Stupor* means that only vigorous and repeated stimuli will arouse the individual, and when left undisturbed, the individual will immediately lapse back to the unresponsive state. *Coma* is a state of unarousable unresponsiveness.

There are other forms of abnormal consciousness or abnormal features of consciousness that are discussed in detail in the abnormal psychology chapter, they are noted here as the abnormal moods of mania and depression the perception of dissociation the states of delirium, dementia and the features of psychosis including delusions, hallucinations, catalepsy, and other catatonic phenomena

Psychoactive Drugs

Psychoactive drugs are drugs that are able to alter the neurological functioning of the brain resulting in altered state of consciousness. to achieve their effects, they must be able to pass from the bloodstream into the brain and eventually to specific brain regions and alter the normal synaptic activity of the neurons. This alteration of synaptic function may be a direct or indirect effect. The brain is protected from a large majority of potentially harmful substance in the bloodstream by the blood-brain barrier.

The Blood-Brain Barrier

The blood brain barrier is created by modifications of the capillaries and the substances and tissues that surround capillaries in the brain. Capillaries in the brain differ from those found elsewhere in the body because in the brain, endothelial cells, the cells that create the capillary walls, have tight junctions. These are what they sound like -tight junctions or seams between endothelial cells, tight junctions prevent molecules that are above a certain size and molecules that are polar, charged or lyophobic (dissolve in water but not in oil or fatty solutions) from passing out of the capillaries and into the brain. The material surrounding the outside of the capillary walls - the basement membrane is also denser than basement membranes of other capillaries. Finally, astrocytes -specialized cells in the brain - form foot processes that unsheathe the capillaries, creating an additional barrier layer. Consequently, the psychoactive drugs are almost all small molecules that are soluble in oil but not in water since these are the types of molecules that can cross the blood-brain barrier.

Mechanisms of Psychoactive Drug Effects

Psychoactive drugs can exert their effect directly or indirectly. Direct effects are caused by drug binding to postsynaptic receptors on neurons. If the drug binding has the same effect that the neurotransmitter that normally binds to the receptor has, the psychoactive drug is called an *agonist*. If the drug blocks the receptor but does not induce an effect that the normal neurotransmitter at the synapse would have, then the drug is called an *antagonist*. Psychoactive drugs can have indirect antagonist and agonist actions by several mechanisms. The drug can change the levels of neurotransmitter at the synaptic gap by blocking the release of the neurotransmitter by the presynaptic cell or by stimulating or otherwise increasing the release the release of neurotransmitters by the presynaptic cell. Psychoactive drugs may also interfere with the processes that normally remove the neurotransmitter from the synaptic junction by altering the reuptake of the neurotransmitter or interfering with enzymes at the synaptic junction that normally breakdown or inactivate the neurotransmitter. There are much more complicated series of events by which psychoactive drugs exert their effects but the primary immediate effects are due to their actions as neurotransmitter agonists or antagonists.

Tolerance

Whether a psychoactive drug is used for legitimate medical purposes or for illicit purposes as a drug of abuse, there is a desired effect of the drug. In pharmacology efficacy relates the desired effect of a drug to the dose of the drug that is required to produce the desired effect. The efficacy or ED_{50} is the dose of the drug that will produce the desired effect 50% of the time it is administered. The efficacy of a drug decreases as the dosage required to achieve the effect increases. Tolerance is a phenomenon where the efficacy of a drug decreases with repeated usage over time. Tolerance occurs for most of the psychoactive drugs. Particularly for drugs of abuse, tolerance is the most important feature of the drug because there is also a lethality for nearly all drugs. Lethality or the LD_{50} is the dose of a drug that will result in death 50% of the time. As the efficacy of a drug decrease through tolerance, users will increase their dosage of the drug in order to achieve the desired effect. The lethality of the drug generally remains the same. At some point, the dosage required for the desired effect approaches the lethal dose and overdose occurs. If the dosage reaches the lethal dosage the results is a fatal overdose. This is most likely to occur with *barbiturates*, whose lethal dose is very close to their effective dose.

Dependency and Withdrawal

The factors that influence whether or not one begins to abuse psychoactive drugs are complex and even sometimes accidental, inadvertent or, in the case of management of chronic severe pain conditions, unavoidable. Dependency is a drive or urge to continue the use of a drug. The causes of dependency are also complex but they are due to a combination of psychological and physiological effects. One of the physiological effects is *feedback inhibition*. Drugs that mimic the effects of neurotransmitters often cause the neurons that normally release those neurotransmitters to decrease or even stop releasing the neurotransmitter entirely. If users attempt to stop using a drug, there will be a lack of the normal levels of the neurotransmitter at the areas where the drug was acting as an agonist and this can cause various unpleasant and potentially dangerous psychological and physiological consequences. These effects as a group constitute the *withdrawal* symptoms for a given drug. Dependency to a large extent occurs due to an overwhelming desire by the user to avoided these effects. The severity of withdrawal depends on the particular drug. Opiate withdrawal, such as heroin withdrawal is well featured in many films and other media forums. It is a very unpleasant experience but it is almost never permanently harmful or fatal. Lesser-known types of withdrawal such as valium or other benzodiazepine withdrawal are well documented to often be fatal. *Reverse tolerance* is a term for a phenomena where subsequent doses of a drug have a greater effect than that of the first or earlier doses of the drug. This is also known as the *kindling effect*. The kindling effect also refers to the phenomena when subsequent withdrawal effects from a drug are increasing more severe compared to earlier withdrawal effects.

Categories of Psychoactive Drugs

Stimulants

Stimulants are drugs such as caffeine, nicotine, cocaine and amphetamines that increase the metabolic activities of the body, increase the arousal state of the central nervous system and generate an elevated mood, often excited and even euphoric but particularly with continued or heavy use, irritable, agitated and increasingly manic moods. Stimulants increase heart rate and blood pressure, interfere with sleep processes decrease appetite. In addition to mania, stimulants can cause anxiety including panic attacks and can generate a psychosis that includes severe paranoid delusions, and hallucinations. Hallucinations occurring from stimulant abuse is often a somatic hallucination called formication where the sufferer perceives that insects are crawling beneath the surface of the skin. The psychosis induced by methamphetamine overdose in particular is often indistinguishable from schizophrenia. Tolerance to cocaine and amphetamines occurs rapidly and dependency is the very common. Some authorities are convinced that dependence or addiction to cocaine and methamphetamine can occur with the first use of the drugs. Withdrawals are extremely unpleasant and "crashes" after binges of drug use can cause severe depression. Withdrawals are otherwise not usually harmful. The physiological effects of stimulant overuse can result in heart attack and permanent brain damage including fatal strokes.

Depressants

Depressants include alcohol, barbiturates and anxiolytics such as antidepressants and antianxiety medications. Depressants lower the arousal level of the central nervous system and interfere with cognitive thinking, judgement and reaction time. They tend to reduce heart rate and breathing, blood pressure. Depressants can produce euphoria and dream-like states but also can cause depression. With increasing dosage, depressant produce progressive diminishment of wakeful consciousness from clouding of consciousness to confusional states, lethargy, obtundation stupor coma and death. Alcohol intoxication in particular is notable for the impairment of judgment and of motor coordination and response time but the effects of barbiturate overdose is virtually the same as that of alcohol intoxication. Barbiturate overdose is particularly dangerous because the drugs depress breathing al relatively low dosages and tolerance to barbiturates occurs rapidly and continuously. Overdose of alcohol can also be fatal, consumption of a pint of 80 proof liquor in under an hour can be sufficient to result in death. Tolerance also occurs with alcohol and withdrawal from alcohol can be fatal. Prolonged abuse of alcohol can also result in acute hallucinatory states called alcoholic hallucinosis and in permanent psychosis and dementia.

Hallucinogens

Hallucinogens or psychedelics such as LSD MDMA psilocybin, mescaline and sometimes marijuana are drugs that have a consciousness altering quality that is characterized by a range of alterations and distortions of one's sense of reality and the nature of the environment. Often there is a perception of the loss of individuality or identity. These hallucinogenic states usually feature a variety of primarily visual hallucinations and alterations of perceptions and thinking in ways that are difficult to describe. Many user describe a heightened or expanded sensory capabilities and a general sense of wonder and amazement. Visual hallucinations are often described as vivid complex and dynamic. Physiological effects are unpredictable but usually not severe or dangerous. The misperceptions of reality can be dangerous and result in injury and even death. Misperceptions of reality can become frightening and can cause anxiety and panic attacks. Brief psychotic episodes may occur. Tolerance and withdrawal are not nearly as significant compared to the other psychoactive drug categories. There is some good evidence for tolerance and withdrawal in heavy marijuana users. These drugs often have very long half-lives and repeated doses can build up to produce larger effects than would be anticipated from a single dose. This is sometimes classified as a type of reverse tolerance. There is reliable evidence that prolonged use can result in permanent personality changes including psychotic changes.

Opiates

Opiates are a class of drug that is either derived from or synthesized to resemble and mimic the effects of morphine which is a produced by opium poppies. The drugs are agonists at endorphin receptors, which are involved in pain regulation in the central nervous system. They are very important for pain management in medical conditions but they produce a euphoric state that has led to their illicit use for centuries. Opiates are very physically addicting and tolerance to their effects develops rapidly. They suppress breathing and overdose deaths are the result of this depression of breathing. Withdrawals are very unpleasant but not dangerous and can be managed with methadone treatment. The effects of opiates can be immediately reversed by the administration of the drug naloxone, which is an endorphin receptor blocker,

Chapter 6: Learning

Key Terms, Concepts, and People

Key People: Sigmund Freud; Karen Horney; Nancy Chodorow; Carl Jung; Alfred; Adler; Hans Eysenck; Abraham Maslow; Carl Rogers; Raymond Cattell; Paul Costa; Albert Bandura; Robert McCrae; Gordon Allport; Julian Rotter; Walter Mischel; George Kelly; Mary Rothbart; Jerome Kagan; B.F. Skinner

Overview

Learning can be defined as long-lasting changes in behavior resulting from experience or study. The changes in behavior are acquired through knowledge or skills, and are not based on biological factors, such as entering puberty. Several different types of learning exist: non-associative learning, associative learning, and social learning.

Non-Associative Learning

Non-associative learning occurs when an individual or animal changes its response to repeated exposure to an environmental stimulus apart from receiving reinforcement. There are two types of non-associative learning: habituation and sensitization. When a response to a stimulus is diminished without any type of reinforcement, *habituation* has occurred. These responses are unconditioned or are reflexive. *Sensitization* refers to the progressive strengthening of a response when repeatedly exposed to a stimulus. When the original response to a stimulus reappears, this is known as *dishabituation*.

Associative Learning

Associative learning is a learning process through with a stimulus becomes associated with another stimulus or behavior. There are two types of associative learning: classical conditioning and operant conditioning.

Classical Conditioning

Classical conditioning was introduced by **Ivan Pavlov**, a Russian physiologist. In classical conditioning, a neutral stimulus is paired with a natural stimulus to elicit a certain response. There are four concepts related to classical conditioning. The stimulus that evokes the response is the unconditioned stimulus (US). It is unconditioned because the response it elicits occurs naturally or reflexively. The response elicited by the unconditioned stimulus is the unconditioned response (UR). In other words, the response does not have to be learned (conditioned); it occurs naturally. When the neutral stimulus (NS) is paired with the unconditional stimulus, the result is the conditioned stimulus (CS). The response that is elicited by the conditioned stimulus is the conditioned response (CR). The response is learned by associating the two stimuli.

Let's examine Pavlov's experiment in order to understand these four concepts. While observing dogs, Pavlov noticed that food (the US) caused the dogs to salivate (UR). Pavlov repeatedly paired the food with the sound of a bell (NS) to elicit salivation. After repeated pairing of the stimuli, the dogs began to associate the sound of the bell (NS) with the food (US). Once the sound of the bell (NS) caused the dogs to salivate, the sound of the bell became the conditioned stimulus (CS). When the dogs heard the bell, even when food was not present, they salivated. Since the salivation was in response to the sound of the bell (CS), the response was conditioned (CR).

In classical conditioning, the stimuli can be paired in different ways. During *forward conditioning*, the CS precedes the US. There are two types of forward conditioning: delay conditioning and trace conditioning. *Delay conditioning* involves presenting the CS and letting it overlap with the presentation of the US. To use Pavlov' experiment as an example, the ringing of the bell will continue while the dogs are given food (US). The second type of forward conditioning is *trace conditioning,* in which the CS begins and ends, and, after a short interval of time, the US is presented. For example, the bell rings, stops ringing, a short length of time passes, and the food is presented. Learning occurs faster with forward conditioning.

There are a few other types of conditioning. During *simultaneous conditioning*, the CS and US are presented at the same time and end at the same time (begin and end simultaneously). In *backward conditioning*, the CS immediately follows the US. Backward conditioning is not very effective because the presentation of the US before the CS may interfere with an association being made between the US and CS. The animal may not pay attention to the CS because the US is already present.

John Watson and his assistant, **Rosalie Rayner** conducted a very controversial and most probably unethical experiment with a boy known as **Little Albert**. Watson wanted to use classical conditioning to demonstrate the emotions, such as fear, are unconditioned responses. Before the experiment, Albert had no fear of rats, but he did have a fear of loud noises. Albert was repeatedly allowed to play with a rat (NS), but every time he touched it, Watson and Rayner would make a loud noise (US). The loud noise scared Little Albert and made him cry (UR). After repeated pairings of the white rat with the loud noise, Albert was shown the rat (CS). Even though there was no loud noise accompanying the presentation of the rat, Albert became very upset and cried and acted afraid every time he saw the rat (CR). Further, Little Albert's fear of the white rat generalized to other white, furry things, like white rabbits, white furry dogs, and white beards. This concept is referred to as generalization. Little Albert was not able to the tell a difference between the rat and other similar stimuli, a concept known as discrimination.

Using Little Albert as an example, other concepts related to classical conditioning can be understood. Acquisition occurs when the repeated pairing of the CS (white rat) with the US (loud noise) elicits the same response (fear) as the US (loud noise), without the US being present. However, just as things can be learned, they can also be unlearned. This concept is referred to as extinction. Extinction occurs when the CS (white rat) is presented without the US (loud noise) repeatedly until the CS no longer elicits the CR (fear). However, one process that is hard to explain is spontaneous recovery. Spontaneous recovery refers to the brief reappearance of the conditioned response (fear) when the conditioned stimulus (white rat) is presented after a period of time has passed. The response is not as strong as it was before extinction. Spontaneous recovery illustrates that extinction does not eliminate the learned association between the conditioned stimulus and the conditioned response.

Another type of classical conditioning is *second-order conditioning* (sometimes called higher-order conditioning). Second-order conditioning refers to a process of learning in which a previously neutral stimulus is paired with a conditioned stimulus to elicit the same conditioned response as the conditioned stimulus. Using the example of Pavlov's experiment, the sound of the bell is associated with food (first-order conditioning). The sound of the bell may then be paired repeatedly with a light (neutral stimulus) until the light is associated with food (second-order conditioning). Once the dog makes the association between the light and food, the light will cause the dog to salivate. The conditioning happens because the animal makes an association between the neutral stimulus and a stimulus that has already been conditioned to elicit a response.

Two reasons have been offered to explain why classical conditioning works. The first reason is the *contiguity approach*, which refers to how frequently the natural stimulus and the neutral stimulus are paired. The greater the number of times the two stimuli are paired, the stronger the association between the two stimuli. For example, the more frequently the sound of the bell is paired with food, the stronger an association the dog will make between the two. The second plausible reason, the contingency approach, was proposed by **Robert Rescorla**. The contingency approach states the two stimuli become associated because the conditioned stimulus predicts the presentation of the unconditioned stimulus. The two conditions are contingent upon each other. For instance, when the dog hears the bell, he will expect food. Rescorla and others have demonstrated through experiments that it is possible for two stimuli to possess contiguity without conditioning occurring. In order for conditioning to occur, the animal must associate the presence of one stimulus with the presence of the other. *An easy way to remember the difference between contiguity and contingency is to associate contiguity with time and contingency with predictability.*

Operant Conditioning

Operant conditioning (also called instrumental conditioning) is defined as a process of learning in which behavior is changed or controlled through the use of positive and negative reinforcement. Unlike classical conditioning, in which an association is made between stimuli, operant conditioning is based on associating behaviors with consequences. **B.F. Skinner** coined the term operant conditioning. Skinner's theory of operant conditioning was based on the work of **Edward Thorndike**, who proposed the theory referred to as

"Law of Effect." The *Law of Effect* states that any behavior that is reinforced has a greater likelihood of recurring. More specifically, behavior that produces desirable consequences will be repeated, but behavior that has undesirable consequences is not likely to be repeated.

Skinner conducted many experiments to develop his theory of operant conditioning. Skinner used a special box he created, the Skinner Box, in his research with animal learning. The box had a lever and a hole through which food was delivered to a rat inside the box when the rat pressed the lever. Skinner used a process called *shaping* to train the rats to press the lever. In shaping, small, successive steps (also referred to as successive approximations) toward the behavior are rewarded until the animal engages in the desired behavior. The rat in the box was rewarded for going near the lever, then for accidentally touching the lever, until the rat purposefully touched the lever in order to receive a reward (food).

In operant conditioning, the purposeful action or response is called the operant because it operates on (effects) the environment to produce consequences. *Reinforcement* is anything that strengthens a behavior, thereby making it more likely to be repeated. A reinforcer is anything that increases the probability that a behavior will be repeated. There are different kinds of reinforcers. A primary reinforcer is anything that provides reinforcement without the need for learning. Examples of primary reinforcers are sex and food. Secondary reinforcers are those that are reinforcing because of their association with a primary reinforcer. Money is an example of a secondary reinforcer. It has no value in and of itself but it can be used to get other items that serve as strong reinforcement.

There are two types of reinforcement: positive and negative. *Positive reinforcement* is anything rewarding that increases the probability that a behavior will be repeated. In Skinner's experiment with rats, the food served as positive reinforcement. The food increased the chances that the rat would press the lever again. *Negative reinforcement* is the removal of an unpleasant stimulus or event that increases the likelihood the behavior will occur again. If the rats in Skinner's experiment learn to press the lever to avoid a loud noise, negative reinforcement is being used. Both positive and negative reinforcement lead to an increase in the likelihood of the behavior occurring; the difference is that positive reinforcement adds something rewarding, whereas negative reinforcements removes something aversive. Closely related to positive and negative reinforcement are two other concepts: escape learning and avoidance learning. *Escape learning* occurs when an unpleasant stimulus can be terminated by the animal or individual. *Avoidance learning* occurs when an aversive stimulus can be avoided altogether. For example, if Molly dislikes an activity in class and acts out and is asked to not participate in the activity, she is engaging in escape learning. But, if Molly knows an activity she hates is planned for a certain day, she may avoid going to class that day or for that period of time. This is an example of avoidance learning.

Just as behavior can be shaped by receiving desirable consequences, it can also be affected by receiving undesirable consequences. Unlike reinforcement, which strengthens a response or makes it more likely to be repeated, *punishment* weakens or eliminates a response. Punishment is any aversive stimulus or event that decreases the likelihood the behavior will occur again. Just as there are two types of reinforcement, there are two types of punishment. *Positive punishment* involves applying an unpleasant stimulus in order to eliminate a behavior; *omission training* (sometimes called negative punishment) occurs when a rewarding or pleasant stimulus is removed in order to weaken or eliminate the behavior. If a student receives a bad mark every time he engages in a particular behavior, positive punishment is being applied, but if the student loses a token every time he engages in a certain behavior, omission training is being used. In general, punishment is not as effective as reinforcement. Punishment, if not used carefully, may result in aggressive or fearful behavior. It also only suppresses negative behavior; it does not eliminate it. Once punishment is no longer being administered, the behavior will return. Also, punishment does not provide the person with guidance as to what needs to be done; instead, it only shows the person what does not need to be done. Reinforcement is more effective at changing undesirable behaviors. Furthermore, many of the concepts of classical conditioning, such as acquisition, extinction, spontaneous recovery, generalization and discrimination, apply to operant conditioning.

Sometimes people or animals come to believe that they cannot avoid or escape certain situations. This concept is referred to as *learned helplessness*. Learned helplessness occurs when a person or animal is repeatedly exposed to painful or aversive stimuli, which they are unable to avoid or escape. If the exposure continues, the person or animal learns that the situation cannot be controlled, and stops trying to avoid the aversive stimulus, even if the situation is escapable. This theory demonstrates that prior learning can cause significant changes in behavior resulting from negative expectations. These negative expectations may lead to passivity, chronic sadness, low self-esteem, and chronic failure. Learned helplessness has been linked to such conditions as depression, poverty, drug abuse and alcoholism.

Principles of operant conditioning are applied in many different settings, such as prisons or schools. Many times, teachers will use what is referred to as a *token economy* to help modify a student's behavior. With a token economy, every time the student engages in a desired behavior, the student receives a token. Tokens serve as secondary reinforcers that can be exchanged for a reward. Token economies have proven to be effective in increasing positive behaviors.

When choosing which reinforcers to use, it is important to remember that different people find different things rewarding. Some children may be motivated by candy, but other children may prefer to spend 10 extra minutes on a desired activity. This idea is expressed by the *Premack Principle,* which states that the opportunity to engage in a more rewarding and pleasant activity or behavior can be used to reinforce less rewarding activities or behavior. For example, if Carol likes to play a certain video game but hates to clean her room, Carol's mother can use the video game to reinforce Carol cleaning her room.

In conditioning, different *schedules of reinforcement* have different effects on the speed of learning and on the rate of extinction. Schedules of reinforcement determine how often reinforcement for a given response will be administered. When a behavior is being learned, the most effective type of reinforcement to use to reward the behavior every time it occurs is *continuous reinforcement*. A continuous reinforcement schedules results in fast learning and in fast extinction.

Partial reinforcement schedules (sometimes called intermittent schedules) are those in which all responses are not reinforced. Partial reinforcement schedules can either be based on the number of responses (ratio) or on intervals of time, and the rate of reinforcement is either fixed or changing (variable).

Fixed-ratio schedule: reward is administered after a certain number of responses. Example: A student may have to engage in a certain behavior 3 times before receiving a reward. With a fixed-ratio schedule, learning occurs quickly and the extinction rate is medium.

Variable-ratio schedule: response is rewarded after an unpredictable and variable number of times. Example: A student may have to engage in a certain behavior 3 times, 5 times, or 7 times before receiving a reward. Gambling is also a great example of a variable-ratio schedule. Learning occurs relatively quickly but the behavior is very hard to extinguish because of the unpredictability of when the behavior will be rewarded.

Fixed-interval schedule: response is rewarded after a set period of time provided at least one response has been made. Example: A child receives an allowance every week so long as the necessary tasks are being completed.

Variable-interval schedule: Reinforcement is given at varying intervals of time provided at least one response has been made. Example: A self-employed person is paid at variable intervals of time.

Because of the unpredictable nature of variable schedules, extinction is more difficult.

Cognitive Processes

Behaviorists argue that learning occurs because of an association made between a stimulus and a response; they believe learning is a relatively passive and unconscious process. However, psychologists in other fields have proposed other views. Cognitive psychologists believe learning is much more active. In their view, the person (or animal) realizes that his responses will produce certain outcomes.

Experiments with pigeons suggest that animals have the ability to develop concepts that help them sort stimuli into categories. As the animal is presented with new stimuli, the animal has already formed a general concept that enables it to place similar stimuli in the same category. An example of this type of abstract learning was evidenced in experiments with pigeons in which pigeons would peck pictures of trees they had never seen because the trees were similar to other pictures of trees for which the pigeons had been rewarded for pecking. These studies suggest that learning is far more complex than just pairing a stimulus with a response.

Latent Learning

Edward Tolman used experiments with rats to study *latent learning*. Latent learning is learning that may not be outwardly evidenced until the appropriate situation develops. In Tolman's experiments, three groups of rats were placed in mazes. One group of rats received a reward after successfully navigating the maze. One group of rats were never rewarded for completing the maze. The third group was rewarded only during the second half of the experiment. The rats that received reinforcement demonstrated consistent improvement in the time it took them to complete the maze. Once the group that received no reinforcement during the first half of the trials began to get rewarded for completing the maze, the time it took to complete the maze decreased significantly. The group of rats that received no reinforcement demonstrated only slight improvement. These experiments illustrate that reinforcement is a motivating factor in learning. Also, Tolman asserted that the rats learned how to navigate the maze because they developed a *cognitive map,* or mental representation, of locations within the maze. Once the rats began receiving reinforcement for completing the maze, their knowledge of how to complete the maze became evident.

Insight Learning

Insight learning is sudden or clear learning or understanding in which people are able to make associations that aid them in solving problems. **Wolfgang Kohler** conducted studies with chimpanzees. Kohler placed a banana outside the reach of the chimpanzees and observed them. Kohler also had numerous boxes spread throughout the room, but none of the boxes alone were high enough to reach the banana. The chimpanzees wasted much time trying to figure out how to get to the banana. Suddenly, they realized they could stack the boxes on top of one another to reach the banana. Kohler theorized that until the chimpanzees developed cognitive insight into how to solve the problem, they could not find a solution.

Social Learning

Social learning is also called observational learning. Social learning is learning that occurs by observing others. In this type of learning, which is sometimes called vicarious learning, a person observes another and tries to imitate the behavior modeled by the person.

Albert Bandura developed a social learning theory, which focused on observational learning, modeling and imitation. Bandura believed that learning does not occur simply because a behavior is reinforced. In his Bobo Doll experiments, children were shown a film in which an adult beat up a Bobo doll and used aggressive language. Later, the children were placed in a room with a Bobo doll. Those children who witnessed the violent and aggressive behavior were more likely to act violently toward the doll, whereas those children who did not watch the film with the violent and aggressive model were far less likely to beat up the Bobo doll. The children received no rewards for beating up the doll; they simply imitated the behavior that had been modeled. Bandura's experiment demonstrates that violent and aggressive behavior can be learned by watching violent shows or films or by observing aggressive and violent adults.

Effective observational learning requires four elements. First, the observer must pay *attention* to the particular behavior. Then, the observer must remember the behavior (*retention*). Third, the observer must reciprocate the action, which means the observer must demonstrate the action at a later time (*reciprocation*), and lastly, a *motivation* for the observer to engage in the behavior in the future must exist.

Bandura's social learning theory can be applied to motivation for learning and to the important role of self-regulation and self-control in addressing behavioral issues. When students have confidence that they can perform a certain task, they are more motivated to set goals and direct their behavior to fulfill those goals. Successfully completing one goal will motivate the student to engage in more of those behaviors that contribute to meeting the goal. Children learn self-control and self-regulatory behaviors from seeing those characteristics modeled by adults. Self-control and self-regulation help a child manage and direct his own behavior.

Practice Questions

1. **Amelia is angry with her boss for adding a new project to her tasks. When Amelia arrives home, she argues with her children, gets mad at them, and sends them to bed early. Which defense mechanism is Amelia using?**
    (Lower order)

    (A) reaction formation
    (B) sublimation
    (C) rationalization
    (D) compensation
    (E) displacement

The correct answer is E. Displacement.
Amelia is taking her unwanted feelings towards her boss out on people who are less threatening, her children. In reaction formation, the person acts the opposite of how she feels. Sublimation is redirecting one's sexual and aggressive drives to more socially acceptable goals. Rationalization involves creating excuses in order to justify one's actions or feelings. Compensation is used when a person who fails in one area directs energy to succeeding in another area.

2. **Which of the following statements best describes incongruence?**
    (Higher order)

    (A) Ken's marriage is ending so he throws himself into his work.
    (B) Marcy sees one group of her classmates as "cool" and the other group as "uncool."
    (C) Henry believes in having a good work ethic but he steals from his boss.
    (D) Candi makes a high score on her SAT and attributes her success to her intelligence.
    (E) Adam distances himself from his son when his son fails to make the football team.

The correct answer is C.
Henry believes in having a good work ethic but he steals from his boss.
Incongruence refers to the gap that exists between who one wishes to be and who one actually is. Henry may wish to have a good work ethic, but he actually does not have a

good work ethic, as evidenced by stealing from his boss. Choice A is an example of the defense mechanism of compensation. Choice B describes a personal construct. Choice D is an example of an internal locus-of-control, and Choice E illustrates the concept of conditions of worth.

Challenge Question:

3. **Max is known across many settings for being dishonest, grouchy, funny, intelligent, overly emotional, and ambitious. Which of the following statements is true?**

    (A) These characteristics indicate that Max needs to work on self-actualization.
    (B) These characteristics probably show that Max has a mental disorder.
    (C) These characteristics show that Max has a high level of self-esteem.
    (D) These characteristics describe Max's central dispositions.
    (E) These characteristics can change if Max explores his unconscious.

The correct answer is D. These characteristics describe Max's central disposition. Central dispositions are those that stand out the most in an individual. Since Max demonstrates these traits across different settings and is known for these traits, these are the traits that people associate with Max. It will not hurt Max to work on self-actualization, but the type of traits someone has does not make achieving self-actualization any more or less important for them. There is no evidence that Max has a mental disorder. Some of his central dispositions are good and some are bad, but that does not indicate a mental disorder since all humans have good and bad personality traits. These traits also do not support the idea that Max has high self-esteem, and there is not enough information to make that assumption. Most likely, these characteristics will not change significantly, regardless of what type of therapy Max receives, especially that of exploring his unconscious mind.

Chapter 7: Cognition and Learning

Cognition

Cognition concerns memory processes; language acquisition, development and usage; attention and information processing; problem solving strategies and characteristics of creative thinking.

Memory

Memory is a fundamental cognitive process. A fully functional memory requires neurological architecture that allows for: 1) memory acquisition, 2) memory formation, 3) memory storage and 4) memory retrieval. A memory may be defined as a unit of learning. To learn is to first acquire and then to know something new. In this sense, a memory may be defined as any indication that learning has occurred.

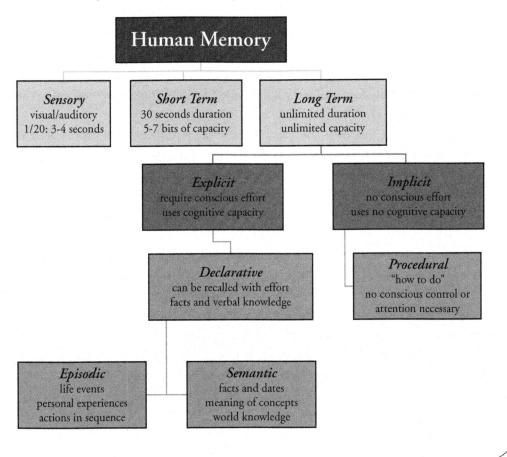

Human Memory

- **Sensory**
  visual/auditory
  1/20: 3-4 seconds

- **Short Term**
  30 seconds duration
  5-7 bits of capacity

- **Long Term**
  unlimited duration
  unlimited capacity

  - **Explicit**
    require conscious effort
    uses cognitive capacity

    - **Declarative**
      can be recalled with effort
      facts and verbal knowledge

      - **Episodic**
        life events
        personal experiences
        actions in sequence

      - **Semantic**
        facts and dates
        meaning of concepts
        world knowledge

  - **Implicit**
    no conscious effort
    uses no cognitive capacity

    - **Procedural**
      "how to do"
      no conscious control or
      attention necessary

The Multi-Store Model of Memory

In 1968, **Richard Atkinson** and **Richard Shiffrin** proposed the *multi-store* or *modal model* for memory. This is also known as *the three box model of memory* because the theory proposes that there are three fundamental components to human memory; 1) the sensory register where sensory information enters the memory process 2) the short term store -also known as working or short-term memory that receives sensory register information and also receives information from the third memory component 3) long term store where information from short term memory is permanently stored. We refer to these for the remainder of the chapter as sensory memory, short-term memory and long-term memory

Sensory Memory (the sensory registry)

In the three-box model, the sensory memory is the entryway for sensory information into the memory processing system. There are actually separate sensory memories or specific sensory registries for each type of sensory stimuli. The best studied of these are the iconic memories of the visual system and the echoic memories of the auditory system. This information is held as complete individual sensory information packages of all the specific sensory information that occurs over very brief sequential time intervals. The complete content of the visual fields in the form of iconic memory can be as short as 1/20 of a second. For the auditory system, the echoic memories can be every sound that is heard over a 3-4 second timespan. There is an immense amount of raw information detected by sensory systems at a given point in time. The three-box model proposes that there is a filtering or buffering mechanism that selects a small amount of this information for packaging and transfer to short term memory. This selection process requires the active attention of the perceiver. In other words, you remember the information that attracts your attention or that you are actively searching for. This is known as *selective attention*. The vast majority of sensory information does not gain your attention and therefore rapidly disappears and is forgotten.

Evidence for the existence and capabilities of sensory memory is provided by the **George Sperling's** *iconic memory tests* where he showed support for his hypothesis that human beings store a perfect image of the visual world for a brief moment, before it is discarded from memory. Sperling's *cued recall* experiments first showed that when subjects were shown a 3x3 grid of differently colored lights for 1/20th of a second and were then immediately given an auditory cue in the form of a tone they could accurately recall the light pattern that corresponded to the tone. Subjects were highly accurate in their response although not perfect as has been incorrectly reported in other published review sources. Next, Sperling introduced a five millisecond (5/1000 of a second) delay between the disappearance of the visual light grid and the cue tone. The ability of subjects to correctly recall the cued light pattern decreased sharply compared to the instantaneous cue. This demonstrated that visual information that is not transferred to short-term memory is forgotten less than five milliseconds after it disappears from the visual field.

Short-Term Memory

The process of transforming sensory memory to short term memory is known as *memory encoding*. Encoding is a key concept in the process of memory formation. In the three-box model, memories that pass through the filter of sensory memory via the selective attention and encoding processes are held in short term memory for short periods of time, usually 10 -30 seconds. Memories can also be transferred out of long-term memory into short-term memory. Your short-term memory encompasses everything you are currently aware of. If you actively don't think about these items, in other words if you just let them sit there, they fade away. If they are newly arrived from sensory memory they are forgotten. If they were transferred from long-term memory they disappear but may be retrieved from long-term memory at a later time.

The research of **George Miller** showed that the capacity of short-term memory is limited to on average 5 to 7 specific new or random items such as individual digits of a phone number. Much larger amounts of memory can be held in short term memory by various memory enhancement techniques. *Chunking* is a technique where specific units of information, names, dates really any type of specific knowledge or perception are grouped into larger conceptual units. An example of chunking is a *mnemonic*, where a group of items is remembered by the first letter of their names a single word such as the mnemonic "HOMES" for the five great lakes; H-Huron, O-Ontario, M-Michigan. E-Erie and S-Superior.

Mnemonic and other chunking techniques can be used to facilitate the conversion of short-term memory items into long-term memory and to enhance retrieval from long-term memory. Whether short-term memory items are raw bits of information or assembled into individual groups by mnemonic or other chunking techniques, they are encoded for long-term memory with increasing strength by the process of *rehearsal* or actively repeating them over and over. The longer that items are stored in short-term memory the more strongly they are encoded for long term memory. The hypothesis is that rehearsal throws short-term information back into sensory memory where it is again immediately retrieved into short-term memory. This resets the clock for the information in short term memory. The total time that information spends in short term memory can be extended for as long as one wishes by continuing the rehearsal process and thereby continually resetting the short-term memory clock.

Long Term Memory

In the three-box model, long-term store is the equivalent of long-term memory. While the storage capacity of sensory memory is practically unlimited but of very short duration and short-term memory storage capacity is very limited and of short duration, long-term memory capacity is, at least for the needs of a human over a lifetime, unlimited. In terms of duration, memories are permanent with certainty for some memories and perhaps for all memories. In other words, you will never fill-up your long-term memory and it is possible that you will never really truly forget anything that makes it into your long-term memory storage. As time passes, however, you will most certainly experience increasing difficulty retrieving a large portion of these long-term memories.

Memory Formation

How do new short-term memories become long-term memories? The process of memory formation presumably requires encoding just as the transfer of memory from sensory memory to short-term memory requires encoding. In sensory-to-short term memory transfer, selective attention is required for encoding. In short-term-to-long-term memory transfer, encoding is believed to depend in large part on how long new memories are held in short term memory and on how intensely you concentrate or focus your attention on the memories while they are in short term storage. This is the principle of rehearsal or repeating new information over and over.

Memory Retrieval

In terms of long term memories being permanent we mean they are always in storage but they may be, in a sense, forgotten because the process required to retrieve them or to take them out of long term storage and back into short term memory are no longer adequate. It is as if you have lost the connection to forgotten long-term memories. They are still there; you just can't get to them. We will discuss theories of memory retrieval in more detail later in this chapter.

Categories of Long Term Memory

There are two major subdivisions of long-term memory: 1) explicit memory and 2) implicit memory. You require your conscious intent or desire to form and to recall or retrieve *explicit memories* (also called declarative memories) Examples of this are remembering your daily schedule, the names of sea-going mammals or the events of a high school reunion party from several years ago. Since explicit memories are memories that require a conscious effort, you have to pay attention to the information you intend to memorize then actively try to memorize it by rehearsing it either through rote memorization it or by using other a mnemonic or other chunking or association memory techniques. This is defined as *effortful processing*. Rehearsal also requires that one's attention is focused attention, or attention that entirely devoted to a single task. Attention that alternates or switches between two or more task is divided attention. Information processing tasks that require focused attention are disrupted or terminated by divided attention.

Implicit memories (also called non-declarative memories) include those that are used to perform a task such as tying your shoes. Not explicitly displayed in your mind while you perform the activity, in fact, you may not ever have explicitly analyzed what those precise movements actually consist of. In addition, you may have implicit memories you are completely unaware of and which you have never used. You may have observed your mother peeling a potato when you were younger. Even if you have never actually held a potato peeler you likely would be able to peel a potato on your first attempt without explicitly picturing how to accomplish the task. Instead, you would automatically use your implicit memories acquired during your youth to perform the task.

Research strongly indicates that completely different neurological processes are occurring during implicit vs explicit memory activities. Damage to the hypothalamus can cause anterograde amnesia where explicit new memories cannot be formed but implicit procedural memories such as new skill can be. Animal research indicates procedural memories seem to be localized to the cerebellum.

They key feature of implicit memories is that they are often formed subconsciously. Some theorists believe that all implicit memories are formed subconsciously. Tying shoes and riding a bike are one type of implicit memory, which is called *procedural memory*, but implicit memories are involved in many other cognitive processes. For instance, implicit memories are the memories that are believed to be formed during the mere-exposure and priming effect phenomena that we discussed in the sensation and perception chapter. Explicit memory functions require focused attention. This is a type of *effortful processing*. In Contrast, implicit memory processes do not require effort or attention so they are a type of *automatic processing*. Implicit memory processes can occur simultaneously with explicit memory functioning. This simultaneous processing ability also indicates that the two memory functions are generated by two separate processing mechanisms.

Memories are also categorized as one of three types or formats of memory: 1) episodic memory, 2) semantic memory, and 3) procedural memory. *Episodic memories* are memories of autobiographical events that are stored as a sequence. We are able to reintegrate the details of episodic events such as dates, locations events and their emotional context into a complete episode that we can re-experience. In a sense, we travel backward in time. The episodes may be recent but some of our most remote or longest-term memories are retrieved as episodic memories.

Semantic memory is not autobiographical or acquired from personal experience. Semantic memories constitute the body of knowledge that we acquire over our lifetimes. They are general world knowledge or common knowledge usually in the form of facts, meanings and categories - the names of the planets, the foods that you like, the sounds of letters or the dates of events, etc. You should rely on semantic memory while playing trivial pursuit. Jeopardy champions have great semantic memories.

We have already described procedural memory in detail in the discussion of implicit memories. To review, they are often difficult to describe with words, but in general, they are sequentially stored memories of skills and how to perform them.

Finally, there is the photographic or *eidetic memory*. Eidetic memory usually occurs in the form of powerful and persistent visual images. At its highest level, an eidetic memory provides the ability to perfectly recall every detail of information one is exposed to. Usually eidetic memory is not perfect, but typically, persons with excellent eidetic memory can recall any information from a book they have read by generating, in visual memory, a photographically accurate image of the page of the book containing the specific information they wish to retrieve. The phenomenon of eidetic memory is most notably associated with **Alexander Luria**'s case study of an individual with an exceptional ability to almost instantly memorize lists of random letters or digits up to 70 items long and to perfectly recall these as long as 15 years later. Eidetic memory actually is surprisingly common, particularly during childhood. As many as 10% of children have eidetic memory. Usually this ability partially or completely disappears as one grows older.

The Levels of Processing Model of Memory

The levels of processing model of memory of Fergus Craik and **Robert Lockhart** offers an alternative to several central concepts of the three-box model. The principles of the levels of processing model contends that memories are neither long term or short term but that the there is a range of depth to memory processing, from shallow processing to deep processing., *Shallow or maintenance processing* results in memories that are easily forgotten. *Deep or elaborative processing* results in memories are more likely to be retained and remembered. The levels of processing model denies that there is a complex neurological architecture specifically devoted to creating memories. Instead, memories are an inevitable natural phenomenon resulting from the manner in which information processing occurs in the brain.

There are two components of shallow processing. One is *structural* or orthographic processing, which encodes information based on the physical qualities or appearance of information. For example, the typeface of a word or if the word is in italics are features of structural processing and encoding of that word. The other component is *phonemic* processing, which encodes information based on how information sounds. Information that is encoded with shallow processing involves only maintenance rehearsal, the simple repeating of information described in the three-box theory. It is easily forgotten. Deep processing is more specifically known as *semantic processing*. Semantic processing encodes information in complex relationships within conceptual categories and with previously learned knowledge. This type of processing requires much more complex forms of rehearsal than simple repetition. This type of rehearsal is called *elaboration rehearsal*. Encoding information by semantic processing forms stronger memories than shallow processing.

Support for shallow and deep processing is shown in a key study by Fergus **Craik** and **Ernst Tulving.** In their study, participants were presented with a series of 60 words about which they had to answer one of three questions. One question required structural or visual processing such as "Is the word italicized or not italicized?" A second question required phonemic or auditory processing, such as "What does the word rhyme with?" The third question required semantic processing, such as "Does this word make sense in this sentence?" The participants were then asked to pick the 60 words out of a list of 180 words. The results showed that participants recalled more words that were semantically processed compared to phonemically and visually processed words.

Real life examples of semantic processing can be used to more effectively study for the AP Psychology exam. You may, for instance, explain the concept of semantic processing by putting it in your own word then describing it to your study partners. This is called *reworking.* You may enhance your recall of a list of items by linking each item with a familiar location. This is called the *method of loci.* There are many other semantic memorization techniques and in terms of your academic career in general, it would be a very good idea for you to learn all you can about these techniques.

Memory Storage and Retrieval

Memory retrieval is remembering and most of us think that memories we cannot remember are forgotten memories. The question is, if we believe have forgotten something, how do we know it was ever there? Somehow we are aware that we were exposed to the memory are in some way convinced that we were exposed to the information. Therefore, we should be able to remembered it. According to the three-box model, the first part of The correct answer is that information we were exposed to in sensory memory is lost if it is not encoded by our selective attention and transferred to short-term memory. Therefore, those were never memories to begin with. Short-term memories that were never encoded for long-term memory by the rehearsal process are also lost forever. They were actual memories-short term memories, and they are truly forgotten. Once memories are transferred to long-term storage, they are presumably stored indefinitely, so they are permanent. When we say we have forgotten a long-term memory we actually mean we are unable to retrieve the memory. We have the information that constitutes the long-term memory but we can't get it out so that we can use it. Semantic network theory, which we shall discuss shortly, explains retrieval as a process that is based on the strength of memory traces. The strength of memory traces, or the strength and number of connections to a memory is determined first by how deeply the memory was first encoded i.e. by structural, phonemic or semantic processing as described in the levels of processing memory model.

Memory retrieval is often described as one of two types. *Recognition* is the of linking a current event or fact with one that is already in memory. *Recall* is the retrieval of a memory using an external cue. The factors that affect the ability to retrieve information include the order in which information is initially perceived and context under which the information was initially perceived. Experiments by **Hermann Ebbinghaus** identified three specific order effects: 1) the primacy effect where items presented at the beginning of a list are more easily recalled: 2) the recency effect where the most recent items on a list (the items nearest to the end of the list) are more easily recalled and 3) the serial position effect which is a fusion of the primacy and recency effects. It is the tendency to recall the first and last items in a series best, and the middle items worst. Therefore, in this list, the recency effect would be the most difficult for you to retrieve. Order effects are explained by and are used as evidence to support semantic network theory.

Semantic network theory proposes that new memories are formed by linking their meanings and the context under which they were acquired with the context and meanings of items already in memory. These interconnected memories form a network or web. *Memory traces* are connection pathways or networks among the neurons that are specifically associated with a particular memory and between other specific neural memory local and then progressively to larger regions of an overall complexly interconnected, diffusely distributed memory network. The strength and number of connections to the memory may be enhanced or may degraded over time. The ability to retrieve these memories depends on how strongly encoded and complexly interconnected a memory is with other memories. All the memories in a local network are more easily retrieved as the local network is reinforced.

Reinforcement occurs when the local network is activated for conscious purposes and by the addition of new memories. At a microscopic level, reinforcement occurs when the neurons in a memory network increase their responsiveness to connected neurons and make new connections to other neurons. The increased responsivity of neurons that occurs due to continuing activation of their synaptic network is known as *long-term potentiation.*

Over time, local regions of the network can degraded through lack of use. Neurons responsiveness decreases and synaptic connections are possibly lost. The *tip of the tongue phenomenon* is a temporary inability to recall information. One possible explanation is that the memory is almost complete but requires slight reinforcement of its memory local memory network. Once this happens, the memory pops into consciousness. Memories that have degraded below the tip of the tongue threshold may seem to be completely lost but evidence that their memory traces persist is shown by the *relearning effect.* The relearning effect is the well-demonstrated phenomenon that it takes longer to learn new knowledge that it does to relearn the knowledge after it has been forgotten. Two other mechanisms that affect memory recall are *retroactive interference,* where the learning of new information interferes with recall of older information and *proactive interference* where previously learned information interferes with the learning of newer information. In other words, it's more difficult to remember things when you are learning new things - retroactive interference; and it's more difficult to learn new things when you have just learned something else - proactive interference.

Memories, according to all theories, are more strongly encoded by the intensity of their perception. Exceptionally intense experiences can result in the *flashbulb effect.* For those of us old enough to have experienced it, the Kennedy assassination is such a flashbulb effect. Other famous examples are the first moon landing and the 9-11 attack on the twin towers. These memories are indelible or unforgettable because of their context or importance to the perceiver.

In addition to the specific memories of the event, we vividly recall many details of what we were doing, thinking and what was happening around us at the time of the event. This tends to support the semantic network theory of memory retrieval since these items of memory are strongly and densely interconnected to the flashbulb event. Enhanced recall based on context is also demonstrated by emotional context as *mood congruent memory.* If you are in a certain mood - happy, sad etc., you are more likely to remember events that were formed in the same mood - you recall happy memories more easily and frequently when you are happy and sad memories more so when you are sad. Enhanced recall also occurs based on similarities in context of one's state of awareness. Memories formed while excited, drowsy, under the influence of mind-altering substances, etc. are more easily and frequently recalled under the same state of consciousness. This is called *state dependent memory.*

Repressed and Constructed Memories

The topic of repressed and constructed memories is one the most important issues in the professional psychology and legal communities. We cannot possibly review this topic in detail but in general, *repressed memories* are presented as real, recently recalled memories of events that usually occurred in distant past. They often are memories of severe abuse or other criminal activity including murder. They are frequently extracted using various memory recovery techniques and are therefore described as recovered memories. **Elizabeth Loftus'** research has shown that memories are highly malleable and vulnerable to suggestion. This has provided powerful evidence that any recovered memories are likely to be false or *constructed memories*. Her earliest studies showed that the manner in which questions are worded such as leading questions could and often did alter the memories that subjects reported. Her subsequent research demonstrated the misinformation effect where eyewitness' actual memories were changed when they were exposed to false information after the event occurred. Her later research used the lost in the mall technique where she and her assistants were able to implant a false memory of being lost in a mall as a child in 25% of the research subjects. Further research showed that utterly convincing, highly traumatic yet impossible memories could be implanted in 30% of research subjects. Today in a legal context, all recovered memories must be corroborated by other physical evidence and many states have prohibit prosecutions based on recovered memories.

Language

We begin our discussion of language with a description of the structure of language. Verbal language begins with the smallest individual unique sound elements that are used to enunciate a word, these are called *phonemes*. A phoneme can be any one of the entire range of unique vocal sounds that can be produced by the human vocal apparatus. Each language creates every word of the language using a specific set of phonemes. Many languages share phonemes but there are almost always phonemes used in one language that are not used in another. The total number of phonemes used in a given language also varies. In English there are 44 phonemes; in the language spoken by the Kung people of Africa, there are 141 phonemes. Phonemes are combined to produce the smallest individual unique elements of meaning. These are called *morphemes*. Morphemes are combined to form words. Words are combined in a specific order to convey higher levels of meaning in the form of statements and sentences. This word order is called *syntax*. The rules for this word order and the types of words - nouns, verbs, adjectives etc. - that are included within the word order are called *grammar*. At the highest levels of language, a thought or a statement may be expressed in a grammatically correct fashion, but may have different or ambiguous interpretations that require consideration of broader context in which the idea or statement is made. An example is the statement "I saw the room with a telescope." The ambiguity in the statement is that either "The room was seen through a telescope." or "The room was seen to contain a telescope." The study of the meaning of language at this level is called *semantics*.

Language Acquisition

All infants pass through the same early stages of language acquisition. Infants must pass through both a *receptive language* learning phase where they learn to understand a spoken language and an *expressive language* learning phase where they develop the ability to speak a native language. Both receptive and expressive language learning stages begin around ages 4-6 months. All infants have an innate ability to hear the differences between any phoneme that is spoken in any language and an innate ability to later physically vocalize any phoneme that is spoken in any language. The receptive learning phase begins typically when infants respond to the word "no". At birth, newborn infants "coo" and grunt and make a few other utterances. The actual expressive language development stage begins with vocal play that consists or gurgling sounds that occur while infants are playing or otherwise happily occupying themselves. Infants' vocal sound inventories rapidly expand into a babbling stage. Babbling begins around 6 months of age when the vocal anatomy is sufficiently developed to produce individual recognizable sounds. The babbling becomes progressively more complex and is considered normal up to the age of 1 year. Most review forums indicate that babbling is the stage where infants are perfecting the ability to verbalize phonemes. This is the *continuity hypothesis,* that states babbling is the stage that leads to the next stage of expressive language acquisition. There is an alternate theory, the *discontinuity hypothesis* that states the babbling stage does not lead to language acquisition and in some sense actually inhibits language acquisition. The discontinuity hypothesis states that the next phase of expressive speech begins at 7-12 months where the infant's speech begins to include more consonants, as well as long and short vowels. It is probably true that during the babbling stage infants are able to reproduce any phoneme. It is unquestionably true that as infants begin to form actual words they are able to reproduce any phoneme that they hear.

The first phase of actual word usage is the *holophrastic phase* where infants speak in single words to express more complex concepts such as "down!" when an infant wishes to be released from a loving embrace. The next phase is *telegraphic speech,* which normally occurs between ages 18-36 months. Telegraphic speech begins as a two-word noun-verb type of speech that is stated in a laconic or matter-of-fact fashion but is very efficient. Even though they lack any additional syntax or grammatical content, the meaning of the two-word phrases are nevertheless very clear. An example is: "kitty mad" to indicate that the cat is angry. Telegraphic speech progresses to three or more words that include one noun and one verb that are used with correct syntax. In subsequent stages of language acquisition the grammar and syntax of statements improves but passes through a stage characterized by incomplete mastery of syntax and grammar rules. Typical types of errors during this phase are *overgeneralization* (also called over regularization) where a regular grammar rule is used when an irregular change is correct. Examples include saying "swimmed" in place of swam or swum or "gooses" in place of geese. *Overextension* is using one more specific word to encompass large concepts or categories. For instance, all furry four-legged creatures are referred to as cats. *Underextension* is the overly restrictive use of a word or concept. An example being that the family cat is a cat but other cats are not cats.

Theories of Language Acquisition_____

We have described the phases of early language acquisition in infants and toddlers but we have not explained how they accomplish the task of proceeding from the ability to recognize and enunciate phonemes to the stage where they are able to fluidly construct normal language with correct semantic and grammatical structure. There is no debate that there is an innate ability in infants to recognize and then physically vocalize any phoneme spoken in any language. There is also solid research that shows that this ability is limited to an absolute sensitive period - a window of time or age range where the child has this ability. After a certain age, children completely lose the ability to recognize and reproduce any phoneme. Past this point a second language may be learned but the non-native speaker will never perfect the precise enunciation of a phoneme in the second language that does not exist is the native language.

Behaviorist Theory of Language Acquisition

Advocates of **B.F. Skinner**'s behaviorist model of learning propose that all that is required for children to proceed from the ability to produce all the phonemes of their native language to the mastery of syntax and grammar is conditioning and reinforcement. This is a trial and error process that does not require any additional innate or inborn neurological mechanisms that are specialized for language acquisition. As children begin to use phonemes to form words and then words to construct meaningful statements they are rewarded. These rewards may be smiles, encouragement and physical rewards for progressively improved use of syntax and grammar. For example, when children first correctly speak the word "cookie" they may receive a cookie as a reward. When they continue to use incorrect grammar, such as "me want a cookie" they may be punished with increasing looks of disapproval or admonishment from caregivers. When they use the correct grammatical form "I want a cookie", they are rewarded again with smiles. Praise and hopefully, a cookie. This continuous refinement of language skills through conditioning is an example of behaviorist concept referred to as *shaping*.

Nativist Theory of Language Acquisition

The renowned linguist **Noam Chomsky** rejected the behaviorist theory of language acquisition and proposed an alternate theory, the nativist theory of language acquisition. Chomsky and supporters insisted that due to the sheer immensity of specific syntax and grammar rules that apply to an unlimited number of possible expressions of language, there simply is not enough time available to acquire a language through classical or operant conditioning. There are too many possible incorrect ways to express language. Classical or operant conditioning could not correct all of these even over the lifetime of an individual, let alone the few years that children requires to accomplish mastery of basic speech. There must be, therefore, an innate linguistic ability or language acquisition devices in all human children that explains how children are able to learn to speak their native language so rapidly. More specifically, one of these language acquisition devices must be a universal grammar ability that is built into the neural circuitry of the brain specifically for the purpose of language acquisition. Chomsky's theory proposes that there are inborn neurological mechanisms that assign words into categories, such as a noun category, and adjective category and so on. The neural circuitry of universal grammar is preprogrammed to combine these word categories into phrases. Once children have learned to speak the words of their native language, they can instinctively combine them to produce meaningful and grammatically correct phrases. Furthermore, the theory proposes that this universal grammar ability functions most efficiently during critical periods of language acquisition. There is an order to these critical periods, in other words children must successfully pass through a more basic critical period before they can successfully proceed to the next critical period. If children are in a linguistically impoverished environment or faced with other conditions that interfere with their language development during these critical periods, their language abilities may be impaired, perhaps permanently.

This debate between the two theories of language acquisition in early childhood continues to the present day and there have been many refinements to both theories. As research continues there is mounting evidence that is redefining the debate, but most authorities agree that many aspects of both theories are true and this is the position you should assume for purposes of the AP Psychology examination.

The Linguistic Relativity Hypothesis

Edward Sapir and **Benjamin Whorf**'s linguistic relativity hypothesis (the Sapir-Whorf Hypothesis) proposes that the unique patterns of one's native language result in thought patterns that are unique to native speakers of a particular language. The hypothesis contends that the perception of the structure of the world is determined by the structure of the perceiver's native language. It's difficult to explain but basically the hypothesis say certain native speakers of certain languages have no words for concepts that are expressed in the words of another language. For instance, Hopi language speakers are claimed by supporters of the hypothesis to have some concepts of time that are impossible for non-native Hopi speakers grasp because there are no words in their language for these concepts. There is little scientific support for the hypothesis.

Thinking and Problem Solving

Units of Thought

We already have addressed two indispensable elements of thought - memory and language. It is safe to say one cannot think in any but the most primitive or rudimentary fashion if one cannot form memories and retrieve them. It is difficult to imagine how one might conceive thoughts within one's mind in any other form than language. When we are actively or purposefully thinking about things, there are building blocks or fundamental units of that thinking.

Mental Images

Perhaps the most fundamental unit of thought is an image. Images are commonly defined as visual but in the context of thinking, images are mental images that we create to represent aspects of the external environment. They can be purely visual, but they are often a more complete combined image that includes any or all types of sensory content. Your mental image of your pet cat, for instance, may include how the cat looks , how it's fur feels, what its vocalizations and purring sound like and how it smells (which is usually a pleasant smell but sometime anything but pleasant). Under no circumstances should this mental image ever include how your pet cat tastes.

Concepts

Concepts are units of thought that are mental representations or idealizations of things including physical entities such as objects, people and places or physical processes or actions They may be purely mental concepts such as ideas or mathematical theorems. They are useful as a means of grouping items into categories based on their similarities. "A concept" is a central element of philosophical debate. Entire books are devoted to the precise nature of "the concept."

Prototypes

Prototypes are generalizations of groups of individual things, The prototype of the group is a conceptualized typical example of a member of the group. The prototype features characteristics of the objects that are most typical for member of that group. Once again, your pet cat can be used to illustrate what a prototype is. The concept of "The Cat" is idealized because there is no "the cat" walking around in real life, but a thing that one sees may be perceived as sufficiently similar to "the cat" concept to then be identified as "a cat" or at least categorized as a cat-like entity. Prototypes can have an almost unlimited set of defining elements. In other words, they represent what a member of a group is and a group can be defined by any parameters that you can imagine.

Thinking

There are two general types of thinking. Effortful thinking requires conscious focused attention so it is *explicit thinking*. It is slow but more likely to be highly accurate thinking. It is often carefully crafted to solve a problem and to avoid error so it is often strategic thinking. The purpose of strategic thinking is often to achieve a reward for solving a problem so it is often reward based thinking. This is the type of thinking that defines goal oriented or directed research. Intuitive thinking is often not based on obtaining a reward other than the reward of the satisfaction of achieving a goal. For intuitive insights, solving a problem is the goal of this goal-based thinking.

Heuristics in Judgment and Decision-making

Problem Solving

Evolutionary theorists convincingly argue that thinking evolved as a problem solving ability. The capacity to solve problems provides an enormous survival advantage for any species. There are two distinctly different types of thinking used in problem solving. Analytical thinking and intuitive thinking. *Analytical* problem solving requires slow careful precise thinking that strives to avoid possible sources of error such a cognitive biases. *Intuitive* problem solving is rapid, spontaneous effortless and often completely subconscious thinking. Intuitive problem solving uses mental shortcuts that are often accurate but subject to many types of cognitive biases and other forms of irrational thinking. For the AP Psychology exam analytical problem solving is exemplified by algorithms and intuitive problem solving is exemplified by heuristics.

Algorithms

An *algorithm* is a method to solve problems or arrive at answers that begins with an initial query:" is this problem either on thing or one of these other things?" depending of what you think the correct answer choice is there is a second question for each choice, so if it is one choice then there is another either- or set of questions to answer. The process continues as the initial problem is narrowed down to one of all of the possible answers or solutions to the initial problem. Two types of algorithms are the flowchart and the decision tree. Computer languages and computer programs are mostly composed of or based on algorithms. They are basically automatic problem solving methods that do not require much in terms of higher cognitive thinking but they do require continuous focused attention and are therefore effortful problem solving methods. They are designed to be a fool-proof problem solving method that guarantees a correct solution. It is best to use an algorithm when the consequences of a wrong decision are severe. If you are operating a nuclear power plant you really want to rely on algorithms to make decisions.

Heuristics

In our daily lives, it is completely impractical to use algorithms to make the hundreds or even thousands of decisions that we are faced with. Instead, we usually rely on heuristic based problem solving strategies. *Heuristics* are methods of approximation or rules-of-thumb that allow for rapid problem solving and quick judgements (snap judgments). In contrast to effortful thinking that requires focused attention such as analytical thinking or a strategy-based thinking, heuristic thinking is a form of often subconscious effortless intuitive thinking. They allow us to function without constantly engaging in over analytical attempts to deal with normal everyday situations. Without heuristic thinking, our lives would basically grind to an indecisive halt. Heuristic thinking is however prone to error and is a primary source of cognitive biases. Where one overlooks or misjudges the significance or relevant explicit information or evidence. Two of most widely utilized and most well studied heuristics are the availability heuristics and representative heuristics.

The Availability Heuristic

Availability Heuristics allow us to make quick decisions based on how easy it is to bring something to mind. Typically, things are easier to bring to mind if you were exposed to accounts of these things how frequent, how recent and if they were highly unusual or had a powerful emotional effect upon you. Availability heuristics are often used to determine that a situation or behavior may be dangerous. You may not venture out across a frozen lake because you easily recall many stories of persons falling through thin ice and drowning. You may not venture into a particular neighborhood because you easily recall numerous recent news reports of muggings that have occurred in that neighborhood.

Errors of this heuristic can result in false and negative stereotyping, Hypothetically, you may learn that a person who you just met lives in the neighborhood we just described. You assume they are more likely to mug you. Upon further analysis however, It turns out the neighborhood is near to a subway exit that criminals use to quickly enter and escape from the neighborhood. This makes the neighborhood a prime target for individuals who do not live in the neighborhood. Furthermore, citywide statistics show that residents of the neighborhood actually have fewer records of criminal activity on average than the average for residents of most other neighborhoods in the city.

The Representative Heuristic

The *representative heuristic* is based not on how easily it is to bring to mind examples of certain events. Instead, you use your personal past experiences or the model or prototypes of things that are the consensus of other people's past experiences. You make generalizations about things because they share similarities with other things you have experienced in the past or because they have similarities to models or prototypes of things that you assume are true.

Faulty representative heuristic thinking can lead you to greatly exaggerate or underestimate the risk of certain situation. In the walking on thin ice example, if you rely on a representative heuristic based on the fact that you have seen persons on frozen lakes many times in the past and conclude the ice conditions before you seems similar so decide to venture across the ice. Hypothetically, what you may have failed to understand is that those persons that you saw on the ice were ice fishermen and most ice fishermen would never venture out on the ice unless they or others have confirmed the ice is at least a minimum thickness by drilling ice core samples. In general, it is extremely dangerous to step upon the surface of any unfamiliar frozen body of water.

Faulty representative heuristic thinking can create negative stereotypes of people in the same fashion as we described for the availability heuristic. In the representative heuristic, you may have a prototype of surfers based on your past personal experiences with surfers during your years of living in a beachside community. Your experiences were that almost all of the surfers you met were surly, under the influence of drugs and were likely to break into your car if anything of value was in plain sight. Now when you first meet someone and discover that he or she is an avid surfer, you suspect they are likely to be drug users and petty criminals. Your prototype for a surfer is based on a non-representative set of surfers, very likely a quasi criminal gang that defends it local surfing spot. This a well-recognized sub culture in the surfing community but the community in general has a code of conduct that abhors violence and this subculture you experienced is ostracized from the larger surfing community. You have overgeneralized negative aspects of past experiences with a non-representative sample of surfers to create a faulty negative prototype to all surfers. Hence is a negative stereotype born.

Creativity and Suboptimal Thinking

For purposes of the AP Psychology exam you should categorize the following as cognitive biases and as impediments to thought. You may also think of these things in different way. *Cognitive biases* are basically the downside of heuristic thinking. As we mentioned in the introduction, cognitive biases are usually biases that cause one to overlook or misjudge the significance of relevant explicit information or evidence. They are however, often essential parts of heuristic thinking and are often very useful. They can be viewed as biases but under typical or normal circumstances they can be either good approximations of the truth or they may provide a basis to think efficiently and rapidly with conviction and confidence. Several of these concepts are typical of the average or the norm so they are normal. In particular, many obstacles or impediments to thought are by definition normal thought. These normal or average thought patterns may be suboptimal or not the best way to think. If you restate these concepts in a slightly different way, they become definitions of characteristics or types of creative thinking.

The overconfidence bias seems to be an almost universal bias. Most people are overconfident in their basic ability to make correct judgements. While it may be true that your judgments are usually correct you probably overestimate how likely it is that your judgements are correct. Research has consistently shown that when subjects are given questions to answer or problems to solve a large majority of the subjects greatly overestimate how well they scored on the tasks. For example, a typical study may show that on a true or false, ten question quiz. On average subjects believed they answered at least 80% of questions correctly but in fact on average subject's scores were 60% correct. The actual percentages vary depending on the particular study but there is a strikingly consistent overall tendency for subject to greatly overestimate how accurate their judgements are. Most of us tend to overestimate our true abilities and expertise. This is the basis for the *overconfidence effect* and powerful arguments identify this effect as the most important cause of the most devastating errors of judgement in human history. Wars, famines, engineering disasters and ecological disasters usually can be traced to decisions that were errors of overconfidence.

The *belief bias* is one of the most difficult biases to define. It is the bias to make illogical judgements because of your belief system. To understand belief bias you must realize that the definition of an illogical judgement is extremely precise and specific. It is impractical to review the explanations of all types of errors of formal logical arguments in this forum. We can say a formal logical argument can be either true or false and the premises and conclusions of a formal argument can be true or false. Logical statements can be any of one of all of the possible combinations of true and false premises and conclusions. Belief bias can result in an incorrect evaluation of any logical statement. Here is unfortunately one of the most well known examples of belief-bias-generated logical error: "All mafia members are Italian. My boss is Italian, therefore my boss is a member of the mafia." Yes, it's an offensive, false ethnic argument. Millions of Americans once believed this argument was true. Many still do.

Belief perseverance is the bias where one's belief continues despite convincing or even irrefutable evidence that the belief is flawed or wrong. It is a form of irrational overconfidence is one's belief because it has been shown that belief results in wrong conclusions or solutions to problems. Nevertheless, the person continues to use the same belief to arrive at conclusions or solutions for similar problems. The belief perseveres as a truth despite all evidence to the contrary. It is a significant bias because most other biases only increase the likelihood that you will be wrong. Belief perseverance almost guarantees you will be wrong.

Confirmation bias occurs when one has a preconceived expectation of what is true or not true. One tends to ignore or at least undervalue or underestimate the significance of evidence that tends to contradict what you already believe to be so. That is ignoring evidence and that is basically what most if not all cognitive biases have in common. The confirmation bias goes a step further. One actively searches for evidence to support one's belief.

The illusion of correlation effect is the belief that because there is a correlation between two things there is a connection between those things. This is not a bias per se but a misunderstanding of principle that degrades the quality of judgement. This effect is addressed in detail in the methods and testing chapters. The *normalcy bias* refers to people's tendency to not prepare for a disaster because they (disasters) are not normal or have never happened before. The death toll from Hurricane Katrina shows that the normalcy bias is the worst of all possible biases in certain circumstances.

Framing is an impediment to problem solving when defined as an inability to see problems in a new perspective. We may restate this definition as reframing which is a way to enhance the normal ways of solving problems: "reframing is the ability to see problems from a new perspective or to state things in a different way." Restating or reframing question can be a characteristic of creative thought. It can drastically change the way we view a problem. Mental set includes two concepts: *functional fixedness* and *rigidity*. Functional fixedness is the tendency to think that things can only be used for what they were originally designed to do. But is that bad thinking? Its normal thinking. If there is a better single sentence definition for a type of creative thought process than, "thinking of ways that things might be used for something other than they were originally designed to do" I have not heard of it. Rigidity is the propensity to rely on established thought patterns, "established thought patterns" is literally a synonym for normal thinking. In particular, creative thought is new and unique therefore not the norm or normal. If you refuse to think creatively then you are being rigid. Not breaking a problem down into parts is an impediment to normal thinking. However, this is another way of saying that you are only thinking about a problem in one way. The creative process of thinking about a problem in a different way would be to think about problems in two ways, one is by breaking a problem down into parts; the second is to think about the problem as perhaps being larger than the sum of its parts.

BE ADVISED: Until recently there has not been a strong consensus on the how to describe specific common elements of creative thought and creative persons. Over the past 18 months very well received research papers have changed this and a consensus has emerged. The consensus conclusions are likely to be reflected in future AP Psychology Examinations. So don't rely on older material for preparation. Here are the conclusions as summarized by this author:

The first conclusion is that creativity correlates with high levels of dopamine in the brain.

The second conclusion is that There are three independent categories of personality traits that predict high creativity in people: 1) Plasticity, which consisting of high energy, extroversion, inspiration, eagerness for new experiences, and a thirst for exploration; 2) Divergence, which includes the traits that are often dominant in personalities of highly independent thinkers. These are impulsiveness, disagreeability, non-conformity and low conscientiousness. This is in contrast to persons with high conscientiousness. Persons with high conscientiousness are self-disciplined, well- organized, purposeful and driven to achieve 3) Convergence - convergence personalities are highly conscientious, precise, persistent, and have an excellent critical sense (critical eye).

The third conclusion is that the most creative thinkers are high energy, flexible and adaptive. They can rapidly assume any of the personality traits among the plasticity, convergent and divergent categories. As they engage in creative thinking they will effortlessly recombine traits and assume whatever combination of traits works best for a particular stage of creative thinking.

The fourth conclusion is that high creativity requires two critical stages of cognitive processing. These are 1) the Generation stage- during the generation stage possibilities are considered and ideas are produced. Creativity increases as the quantity of original idea increase so the newer ideas the better. The generation stage functions best when self-critical judgments of ideas are suspended so there should be no such thing as a bad idea during the generation phase. The generation phase produces ideas that are new but to achieve high creativity, the second stage, 2) selection must follow this stage screens generation stage ideas and shepherds them through a course of critical evaluation formalization and elaboration into their final forms.

Chapter 8: Motivation and Emotion

Explaining Motivation

There is heavy overlap with this chapter and the biological basis of behavior chapter. We encourage you to review the biological basis of behavior chapter at this time or immediately following this chapter. This will enhance your understanding of both chapters.

Homeostasis, Needs, Drives and Instincts

At the very most fundamental level, behaviors emerge from the principles of *homeostasis*. All life, including one-celled life forms and at the level of individual cells in our body must maintain a stable internal cellular environment that is separate from the external environment. For the human body, this requires an ability to sense the primary needs of the body's cells Homeostatic mechanisms can determine if the body has sufficient amounts of oxygen and sources of chemical energy in the form of glucose and fats and proteins that are the macronutrients required to construct and maintain the physical body itself. They are able to measure and maintain correct concentration of ions such as sodium, potassium and calcium both inside and outside of the cells of the body. Finally, they can monitor for an optimal temperature range including a core body temperature that must be regulated for survival.

Needs at the most basic biological level are the absolute critical requirements to sustain homeostasis and therefore to preserve life. These are the physical needs for oxygen, water, food and the slightly more abstract need to obtain shelter when necessary in order maintain an optimal temperature range including a core body temperature. The nervous system generates irresistible urges to satisfy these basic biological needs. These are the *primitive drives* that are experienced as hunger, thirst, life-threatening cold and excessive heat. Oxygen is the most critical of all needs. In the most extreme cases of oxygen deprivation, the most strongly motivating sensation of all occurs - the sensation of suffocation.

Instincts are precise and predictable genetic behavior programs. They are programs one could literally write for a computer. These specific instincts can be grouped into an overall instinctive theme. The instinctive theme of self-preservation and an instinctive theme to preserve the species. Instincts are behaviors that require no motivation. In general, they are optimum genetically scripted behavior patterns designed to satisfy evolutionary needs. There are specific drives or motivations required to generate instinctive behaviors. In a sense they are automatically driven and automatically motivated

The Biological Basis

At the most basic level we have very detailed understanding of survival and self-preservation mechanisms. These are the behaviors that deal with things that are a threat to the individual survival that require an instantaneous response. The deep tendon reflexes respond to mechanical stress that threatens crippling injury to bones and joints. The pain reflexes are similarly response to external forces of extreme heat, chemical reactions and mechanical force that are capable of inflicting instantaneous injury or death.

These reflexes are the reflex arcs that consist of sensory receptor cells and one or two neurons that activate a skeletal muscle response. There is no participation of the higher nervous systems require for these responses, but even at this most basic level there can be conflict and there is some ability of the higher nervous systems to influence these reflex responses. Individuals may find themselves in circumstances where deep tendon reflex triggers a competing pain reflex. At the most basic decision level this may be is it preferable to destroy a knee ligament or to extend ones was face into a blowtorch. One reflex action could be instantaneously tied to the other. The decision will be too fast for the higher nervous system to consider, but a huge conflict exists and it is resolved at a level of two to three neuron complexity. The conflict can extend from reflex to the highest levels of cognition. If you have a gun to your head or if the life of your child depends on it you may be able to voluntarily overwhelm these reflexes and choose to suffer the resulting injury, perhaps even a fatal injury. There will be a reflex response; you will not be able to overcome these reflexes for long, and in the end, sufficient pain will make anybody do anything.

The nervous systems likely evolved to calculate all the costs and benefits of behaviors in an external environment filled with risks and opportunities. Better decisions require more neurological complexity. Beyond the reflex arcs are the next level of complexity. Behaviors that are tied to things that may not be instantaneously harmful, but that are imminent threats to survival or can evolve into imminent threats to survival. The very earliest evolved structures of the central nervous system is the hind brain or *brainstem* and the critical functions of the regulation of heart rate, blood pressure breathing sleeping and eating pain sensitivity alertness awareness and consciousness are managed by the brainstem region known as the medulla oblongata.

The next evolved levels of the brain including the *limbic system* and the *hypothalamus* in large measure evolved to serve the needs of the medulla with their ability to provide more precise monitoring and regulation of homeostasis and higher levels of behavior to increase the ability to survive at a basic needs level higher, namely drive states, which we have discussed. The hypothalamus is most notable in that it is capable of directly or indirectly sensing the levels of glucose water and sodium ion concentrations in the body and can exert a wide range of control over the body systems at many levels through the production and release of releasing hormones (hormones that control the release of other hormones) it is a proven center for sensations of hunger and thirst and participates in the production of emotions in concert with the other structures of the limbic system, It is also an important element of the bodies systems for dealing with external stress.

The Sympathetic Nervous System

The autonomic nervous system is described as a peripheral nervous system but it originates in the central nervous system and is deeply integrated with all neurological functions of the central nervous system. The *sympathetic nervous system* is one arm of the autonomic nervous system; the parasympathetic nervous system is the other arm. The sympathetic nervous system responds to situations that the central nervous system judges to require potentially rapid and vigorous physical responsiveness. This is commonly referred to as a fight or flight response. Situations that are likely to require running and/or fighting are not the only things that can trigger the sympathetic nervous system. In general anything that is highly interesting can trigger the response. The sympathetic nervous system is fast and it causes rapid adaptations by direct innervation of a multitude of targets throughout the body, Blood flow is redirected to the skeletal muscles, digestion processes are dampened pupils dilate and heart rate and blood pressure increase. There is also a higher level emotional response of fear and excitement. The entire body, is at an elevated state of activation, alert a ready for action.

The fight or flight response can be triggered as a nearly automatic reflex; by an unexpected noise or a sudden movement. There is, however, a continuum of motivational and emotional interactions and processes that can trigger the fight or flight response. It is not necessarily an all or none response. It can gradually be turned up as a situation becomes increasingly of concern. This is the dramatic principle of suspense a steady growing level of excitement. Depending on the context of this excitement it can manifest and emotions of fear or exhilaration and progress from mild unease to absolute terror and from a mere piqued interest to states of mesmerized fascination, manic enthusiasm and ecstatic exhilaration. The most memorable moments of one's lives are very often connected to these moments of maximal stimulation of the sympathetic nervous system.

The Parasympathetic Nervous System

The other arm of the autonomic nervous system, the parasympathetic nervous system, acts to balance the actions of the sympathetic nervous system. It encourages a restoration to a state of calmness. At the most basic physical level, it redirects blood flow to the digestive system, lowers heart rate and blood pressure and encourages restful functioning. Within the central nervous system, it lowers the overall state of arousal. At the highest levels of emotion and motivation, it encourages a sense of relaxation and peacefulness. At the motivation level it depresses the primal urges and drive states.

Internal vs External Psychological Factors

For the AP Psychology exam, the terms internal and external are interchangeable with the terms *intrinsic* and *extrinsic*. We have a good model for the types of *external stress* that can interact to generate and influence a person's emotions and motivations and even their physical well-being. It is important as we proceed to note that we have discussed external stress but there can be *internal stress* as well. Stress that is not a directly or even an indirectly related to external factors, they are stressors that results from one's abstract higher level cognitive functions. these can be difficult to define and to measure but some examples include the concept of higher ideals of religion, morality, good and evil; concepts of an existence on a higher or nonphysical plane; concepts of nobility, righteousness, justice and artistic sensibility. By the same definition of internal and external related psychological processes, there are levels of internal and external drives and internal and external motivations. When these psychological factors are incompatible with each other the mind must resolve this incompatibility or conflict. So there is a critical element of conflict resolution that must occur to generate an overall state of mind which determines how we behave. These conflicts can also be internal conflicts or external conflicts.

Emotions

Stress and the General Adaptation Syndrome

Hans Selye developed the general adaptation syndrome stress model that describes physiological process that occur in persons subjected to stress. Selye observed that patients with a general set of physical signs and symptoms often had no specific identifiable medical cause for their condition. They appeared to be fatigued with difficulty concentrating and some dulling of memory process and often with signs of a depressed immune system. Selye in earlier research had investigated lab animals that showed similar physical states. The suspicion was that an undiscovered hormone was involved in producing this syndrome of physical impairment.

Selye's subsequent studies were key to identifying the *hypothalamic-pituitary-adrenal (HPA) axis*, a neuroendocrine system that is responsible for the body's response to stress, and ultimately for the physical effects that occur in the general adaptation syndrome. The HPA axis is triggered by stressful events. These are not only what is normally considered to be stressful events in the sense that they are unpleasant and psychologically distressing. They can also be very positive and exciting events. Selye categorized positive stress triggering stimuli as eustress. What all stress stimuli had in common was that they triggered the HPA axis. The HPA axis begins with an interaction of stimuli that trigger the sympathetic nervous system. The hypothalamus plays a key role in initiating and the generation and maintenance of the sympathetic state it releases - releasing hormone to the pituitary which release ACTH hormone that stimulates the adrenal gland to release the steroid hormone cortisol

The Three-Phase Response to Stress

The three-phase response to stress describes the body's attempts to respond to environmental stress. The body does not necessarily proceed through all three phases for any single stressful event. A short low intensity stressor may require only a phase 1 response. As the stress events become stronger more numerous and more persistent over time the body responses with progression to phase 2 and eventually phase 3 responses.

- Phase 1 - *the alarm stage*, begins with a rapid stress response by activation of the sympathetic nervous system by the hypothalamus. This results in the release of epinephrine by the adrenal gland, which raise the activity levels of tissues and organs throughout the body. It is a high-energy state and increases the workload of the heart and increases the demands upon the all the bodies systems that are needed to maintain this state of high physical and psychological arousal. For routine occasional stress events the alarm phase is quickly resolved once the stress event passes, the parasympathetic system is activated and the body is restored to homeostatic balance

As persons are subjected to more frequent stress events and to stress events that a more powerful and more persistent the stage 1 phase is prolonged, but this high energy high arousal state cannot be maintained for long. The energy reserves of the body are depleted and the physical demands on the body begin to exceed the body's capacity to function at the higher demands placed on it by the stage one level. The individual progresses to phase 2 - the Resistance stage.

- Phase 2 - *resistance stage*, there is a partial reduction in the level of sympathetic activation but the overall arousal state of the body is still abnormally high and the organ systems of the body are operating at levels that increase their vulnerability to injury. The energy demands of the body are straining the systems that are producing the energy and the hypothalamus is stimulating the pituitary to release steroid releasing hormones that in turn stimulate the adrenal gland to produce increased amounts of the steroid hormone cortisol. This hormone is critical to maintain overall body homeostasis. Without cortisol the body cannot respond to stress and in the absence of cortisol death will occur within weeks or months. At homeostatic levels this is fine but at increased levels of the phase two stage. The effects of cortisol are increasingly harmful. It interferes with the body's ability to heal and impairs the body's immune system, rendering it more susceptible to infectious diseases.

- Phase 3 - *the exhaustion stage,* results from prolonged and excessive episodes of the stage 2 phase. The body has been so compromised by the excessive demands of the phase 2 stress response it is no longer able to maintain the phase 2 levels of arousal. The effects of the phase 2 state have compromised the capacity of body systems to function at a normal level. The effects of abnormally high cortisol levels have begun to exert long lasting and more severe impairments of the bodies repair and restoration capacities and the immune system is significantly suppressed and dysfunctional. If the stage 3 stress response persists there will be the potential for a burnout phase. In a burnout phase, individuals where they become ineffective in their normal daily functions and perhaps incapable of continuing to function in their jobs and in their relationships with others. The stage 3 stress response episodes can become an abnormal baseline state. People in this baseline state are unhappy apathetic and are generally more prone to disease and more likely to suffer from the effects of aging processes. Unfortunately this stage is also more vulnerable to external stressors so there is a vicious cycle of increasing external stress which worsens the stage 3 condition.

Stress Measurement Scales

The general adaptation syndrome has identified a physiological basis for harmful effects of stress. researcher who are continuing to determine what specific illnesses may be stress related need to actually measure stress levels and identify which external events generate stress in individuals and how powerful the stressful events are .An example of this measurement or quantification of stress is the *social readjustment rating scale (SRRS)* that was developed by **Thomas Holmes** and **Richard Rae.**

The researchers used a questionnaire to identify major stressful events in people's lives. The questionnaire respondents rated this events in terms of how traumatic the events were perceived to be. Based on the results they assigned relative stress values to the events. The severity of the perceived trauma was converted into units of stress called *Life Change units*. A total of 43 of these stressful life events were identified and ranked based on their assigned values in life change units. Individuals may now calculate their total life stress by comparing their life experiences with the events of the SRRS ranking. The life change unit value of events that match an individual's current or recent life experience over the past 12 months are then added together to give a total life stress value. The stressful events in the SRRS are all life changing events.

The top eight are:
1. death of a spouse (100 LC units)
2. divorce (73 LC units), marital separation (65 LC units)
3. imprisonment (63 LC units)
4. death of a close family member (63 LC units)
5. personal injury or major illness (53 LC units)
6. marriage (50 LC units)
7. being fired or laid off from work (47 LC units)

Although we all have stress the total life stress value identifies when this stress is generating true suffering. Persons suffering from stress are at increased risk of the type of damage that is described in the general adaptation syndrome. Persons with 150 life change units they have a 30% chance of suffering from stress. those with 150 - 299 life change units a 50% chance of suffering from stress and those with 300 life units have an 80% chance of developing a stress related illness,

There are no illnesses cause by stress alone but an individual's susceptibility or their probability of developing certain diseases does correlate with the total value of their SRRS score. . In particular these are illnesses related to persistent elevated high blood pressure (hypertension) such as heart disease and stroke. Gastric ulcers and increased susceptibility to infectious disease are also clearly stress related. Research is ongoing to further define what the actual stress related illness are.

Theories of Emotion

Research has identified seven basic emotions that are universally experienced and expressed in the same way regardless of cultural factors. The most famous researcher in this field is Psychologist Paul Eckman. The Facial Action Coding System (FACS) is a taxonomy that measures the movements of the face's 42 muscles as well as the movements of the head and eyes. Eckman and other researchers others have identified six facial expressions universal to people all over the world, (later a seventh emotion was added): happiness, sadness, surprise, fear, anger, and disgust, then contempt.

Theories of Emotion can be divided into arousal/physiological theories, or cognitive appraisal theories.

An Important Advisory: The most recent guidelines for the AP psychology Examination indicate you should compare and contrast major theories of emotion. The historical and current range of theories regarding emotion is quite large and the research into the nature of emotions is rapidly evolving. In particular advanced neuroimaging techniques are providing very detailed and complex data that is allowing researchers to test the premises of the major theories of emotion and to develop highly complex modern theories that are beyond the scope of the AP Psychology Examination. The AP guidelines only identify three specific emotion theory as expected knowledge for the exam. These are the James–Lange, Cannon– Bard and Schachter two-factor theories.

The guidelines indicate these are examples of the emotional theories. For the AP examination, we consider the expected knowledge to represent an introduction to this very complex and rapidly evolving field of psychology. As an introduction to emotion theories, for the AP exam, we feel that there are several other theories that you may be responsible for. Finally, we feel that earlier interpretations of the relevancy of James-Lange theory for the AP Psychology exam is no longer correct. The James-Lange theory was one of the earliest emotion theories and until recently was considered to be of historical interest but not particularly relevant otherwise. Most current researchers and theorists have revised this opinion and reinstalled central elements of the theory as very relevant. It serves as an important conceptual basis for many modern emotional theories and as a guidepost for continuing research into the neurobiology of emotion.

Arousal Theories

The James-Lange Theory

In the mid-1800s, **William James** and **Carl Lange** proposed independent but very similar interpretations of emotions that have been combined into the James-Lange theory of emotion. The Theory states that the emotions that we experience are interpretations by the mind of the body's physiological state. In other words, that the bodies physiological state causes emotions. For instance, when we "feel" fear, this feeling or emotion is how the mind interprets the physiological state of high arousal that includes sudden alertness, increased heart, increased breathing and increased muscle tone and trembling. Today we know this is primarily due to activation of the sympathetic nervous system. The emotion of sadness is felt as the mind's interpretation of, in part, the physiological process of crying. Research shows that fear can be induced in subjects simply by elevating their heart rate and without any other fear-inducing stimuli. Also if the activation of the sympathetic nervous system is blocked, subjects in situations that would be expected to cause fear often report they do not feel fear. This is an important element of the theory. It implies that one can learn to ignore physiological states and thereby not experience an unwanted emotion. If you do not pay attention to your fearful physical state you actually will not experience fear.

The Cannon-Bard Theory

Walter Cannon contributed to the *Cannon-Bard theory* by first criticizing the James-Lange Theory. He noted that emotional responses can happen very quickly and that physiological responses related to these rapid emotional responses are often too slow to be the cause of the response. Cannon Also noted that emotional responses are often too complex and rapidly evolving to be caused by the corresponding physiological states and that the changes in emotion would correspond to changes in the physiological states that would be too small to be detected. (Note that the facial expression model can account for Cannon's criticisms). Therefor there is no cause and effect relationship between a physiological state and the concurrent perception of an emotion. The connection between the two is that events that cause emotional reactions are events that are interesting or exciting so they also activate the sympathetic nervous system resulting in the fight or flight response. **Philip Bard** backed up Cannon's position by conducting animal experiments that showed that the sensory signals that correspond to a physiological state must travel through the diencephalon before they reach the cerebral cortex, since the emotions are presumed to be generated in the cerebral cortex. They are occurring while the sensory stimuli is still in transit to the cerebral cortex. Modern research indicates Bard's conclusions were not entirely accurate and that there are neural pathways and processing that can integrate sensory information and emotional processes at the same time.

The Opponent-Process Theory

This theory by Richard Solomon and John Corbit explains emotions in relation to its opposites. Emotion disrupts the body's state of balance and basic emotions typically have opposing counterparts. When one emotion is activated its opposite counterpart is suppressed. That suppressive state remains until the initial emotion has subsided. Then the opposite emotion is intensified and experienced, as a counterbalance type of reaction.

Cognitive Appraisal Theories

Cognitive appraisal theories are theories that address emotional experiences that involve more than a more or less simple rapid evolution of a random stimuli that causes arousal. These emotional reactions do occur but there are much more complex contexts of appraisal that can drastically alter how an individual experiences emotions. In real life much of our emotional response to our environment is an ongoing continuous process. It requires a higher level appraisal of the life we are leading. This Includes events in the past and what we anticipate will be events in the future. It is not sufficient to simply recognize that circumstances around you are causing an increased state of arousal. It is also not sufficient to simply make a basic analysis to determine what is causing your state of arousal. The emotional experience may include this as an initial emotion i.e. "Hmm- this is strange. Something has piqued my interest.-strange how? Oh! This is a dangerous situation, I feel fear". As you progress from this initial fear you begin to appraise the situation. What in the past has caused you fear? Is it similar to this situation? How did things work out afterwards? Is that likely to be the case her? You begin to develop a fuller, richer emotional experience. The experience can suggest future possibilities each with their own emotional content. These are the modern theories of emotion. As we said the details of these theories are quite complex and research is providing new information to improve these theories. The details may be beyond the scope of the AP exam, but they could be provided to you in the form of a higher level AP question. You should be aware of the general features of cognitive appraisal theories as we have just described.

Emotions do not exist in a psychological vacuum. They are essential elements of the dynamic overall experience of life. For our final topic we discuss a major feature of human psychology that is deeply tied to emotions. That topic is motivation. Motivation is the desire to do things, to engage in actions that have a purpose. Emotions play a central role in motivation but there are many other aspects of motivation that are addressed in the following theories.

The Schachter-Singer (two-factor) Theory

Stanley Schachter and **Jerome Singer** proposes that emotion is based on two factors: physiological arousal and cognitive assessment of the external context or environment of the arousal. The result of the interaction of these two factors a sudden state of arousal and then the brain's interpretation of the state of arousal results in an emotional perception. This theory addresses a problem with the James-Lange theory. The same state of arousal can produce completely different emotional experiences. Theorists have generally agreed that emotions correlate with events that generate high arousal. This arousal is associated with the stimulation of the sympathetic nervous system. The sympathetic nervous system generates the aroused physical state by releasing epinephrine and norepinephrine. In experiments subjects have received injections of epinephrine in neutral controlled environments. The subjects report that they sense the increased arousal that the epinephrine produces but they do not have any particular emotional experience that occurs with this sensation. Schachter and Singer conducted experiments with epinephrine injections in subjects. They provide two different environments for the subjects. In one environment subjects found the experience to be funny as in amusing. In the other environment subjects found that the experience made them angry. These results tend to support the two-factor theory that emotions are the result of an aroused state produced by the environment and a subsequent cognitive assessment of the aroused state to determine the nature of the stimuli that caused the arousal. First, you recognize that you are aroused by something in the environment. Then, you try to determine what that something is. Based on what you find you have an appropriate emotional experience. If it is a bear, then you feel fear, if it's a long lost friend, you feel surprise and joy and so forth. There is modern research that questions this conclusion but it is beyond the scope of the AP exam.

The Facial Feedback Theory

The Facial Feedback Theory is a more modern theory of emotion. It is very similar to the James-Lange Theory but it addresses a problem with the James Lange Theory. There seems to be a huge range and of complexity and subtlety of two emotional states. They are usually not single raw emotions of anger, joy, sadness, surprise, fear or disgust. There seems to be a very limited range of different physiological states that can be felt as individual emotional states. There is one extraordinarily complex and rapidly variable physiologically produced phenomenon that the brain could monitor continuously and in incredible detail. There are 33 pairs of muscles beneath the surface of the human face. These muscles produce individual facial expressions. Research has shown there are thousands, perhaps millions of different facial expression and that very specific facial expressions correspond to an enormous variety of very specific but very complex and subtle emotional states or moods. If the brain can sense these specific facial expressions (and it can) it could produce a specific flavor of emotional feeling corresponding to any specific facial feature. As these features change over time the brain can produce an even richer emotional experience; not as a single picture or moment in time, but as a dynamically evolving emotional storyline within one's own mind.

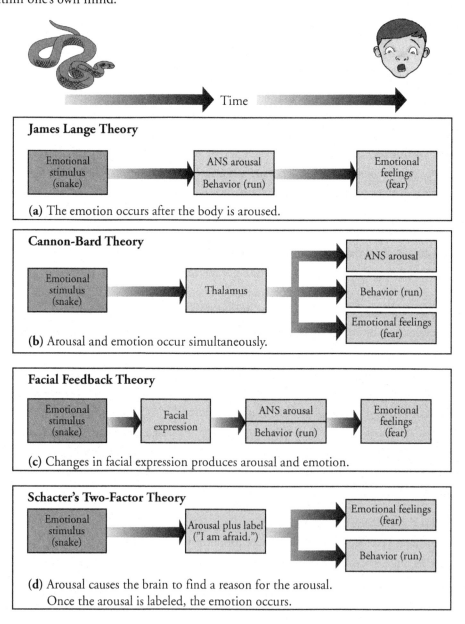

James Lange Theory

(a) The emotion occurs after the body is aroused.

Cannon-Bard Theory

(b) Arousal and emotion occur simultaneously.

Facial Feedback Theory

(c) Changes in facial expression produces arousal and emotion.

Schacter's Two-Factor Theory

(d) Arousal causes the brain to find a reason for the arousal.
Once the arousal is labeled, the emotion occurs.

Theories of Motivation_____

Drive Theory of Motivation

The Drive Theory, or as some call it, the drive reduction theory proposes that persons are motivated to behave in ways that they perceive will reduce a general internal state of unease or **tension**. In general the body is not in a desirable homeostatic state and desires to reestablish a proper homeostatic balance. This internal tension is comprised of basic drives or urges. Those drives are triggered by a biological needs, a need for water, a need for food, a need to be at the optimal temperature. The resulting drives motivate behaviors to satisfy these needs. Warmth, thirst, and hunger drives motivate individuals to take actions to satisfy these biological needs. There is but also needs to rest to regenerate as well' so there can be a motivation to suspend activity as well. The primary drives can motivate actions that directly result in satisfaction of of biological needs. You may have to physically drag yourself to a watering hole in a desert for instance. But often actions can not directly satisfy needs. There is often an intervening obstacle to the goal of the primary drive. For instance, you may not be allowed any water unless you can pay for it. This establishes a secondary drive and a secondary need - a need to obtain money. There is then a resulting motivation to work to attain the money. These secondary drives are not fundamental; there is no primary biological need for money, and no neurological mechanism that directly generates a specific drive to obtain money. For this reason these secondary drives are called *learned drives.*

We can place drive theories on a continuum close to motivation of a largely biological nature but moving toward more abstract desires and motivations such as the desires for wealth and behaviors designed to obtain valuable resources. Drive theories are less successful at accounting for behaviors that do not seem to directly or indirectly fulfill a basic biological need. Behaviors are not always clearly motivated by physiological needs. For example, people often eat or drink when they are not really hungry or thirsty. The advocates of the drive theory can argue that all such behaviors can be perhaps not secondary but instead three or more times removed from the biological need. Critics object to this increasingly vague and tenuous connection to basic biological needs. They insist that other theories of motivation are required to account for more complicated needs. We can also observe there is a higher level progression of motivations towards something that is not precisely a motivation of need but rather a motivation of desire.

The Incentive Theory of Motivation

The incentive theory of motivation proposes an individual's behavior is motivated by a desire for reinforcement or incentives. Incentive theory is a close relative of operant conditioning theory of learning. In incentive theory, an incentive is an external reward that is learned by behaviors of the individual. The individual has learned by past experience that certain behaviors will result in these rewards through positive reinforcement. The individual has also learned that certain behaviors are punished through negative reinforcement. This knowledge is used to convert the reward into an incentive and the punishments into disincentives. The conversion being that rather being behaviors that are simply reinforced by the rewards as operant conditioned learning, the individual actively seeks these rewards. It is no longer a welcome reward for behavior, it is now specifically identified as a reward the individual covets. There is not a specific behavior that has been reinforced, now any potential behavior is reinforced if is perceived to be helpful in attaining the reward. That is why they are incentives, they motivate behavior that is designed to attain them. Similarly, the punishments that occurred in response to certain behaviors become disincentives for those behaviors and individuals avoid those behaviors in the future, and also are motivated to behave in ways that actively avoid these disincentives. What actually constitutes an incentive or disincentive depends on the nature of an individual's personal desires and on how much personal value he or she places on the incentive. Everyone can have different incentives for the exact same types of behaviors. That accounts for why it is difficult to predict what will motivate any one particular person and why it is hard to predict how any one person will behave in a specific situation.

The Arousal Theory of Motivation

Arousal Theory of Motivation is seen as another theory that relies heavily on the autonomic state of the body and seems to imply there is a drive toward the sympathetic state or the parasympathetic state. This is based on an individual's preferred state of arousal. The desire to attain this desired level of arousal is analogous to a biological drive state, but there clearly is a higher cognitive character to this preferred level of arousal. It also seems likely that there are genetic factors that predispose an individual towards a preference for a higher or lower relative baseline level of arousal. This can also be thought of as a fundamental feature of an individual's personality. Where an individual's personality falls on the continuum from meek to bold from or from careful to reckless defines that person's preferred state of arousal. There is likely learned experiences that can change this preferred level of arousal. A thrill seeking person at heart may become less so as the consequences of being a high arousal personality result in negative consequences. This is not an intellectual decision to rein in one's natural urges but a literal modification of natural urges a lowering or raising of the preferred state of arousal that may be entirely subconscious. This shows a different type of drive compared to other theories that link motivations to the purely biological drives such as hunger thirst procreation and nurturing. This is an existential drive, in other words a drive to exist in a certain state for no more important reason that it is a preferred state of existence, There is a new type of fundamental need, a need for a certain state of arousal and the motivation is to behave in ways that maintain or reestablish this particular level of arousal.

The Yerkes-Dodson Law

An important element of arousal theory is that one's' level of arousal has an influence on one's performance. There is an individual level of arousal that will be optimal for a peak performance. This level depends on the individual and it does not guarantee peak performance, but it is the most desirable arousal level for the occurrence of peak performance. As one's arousal levels diverge from the optimal level, performance tends to progressively decrease. The classic example of this is a student's performance on a test, the AP Psychology exam for instance.

You have almost certainly experienced test anxiety. This anxiety is a state of high arousal. In arousal theory performance is related to arousal levels by the *Yerkes-Dodson Law*. This law states that one's performance will increase as one's level of arousal increases, but only to a certain point. After that point, increasing levels of arousal will progressively impair performance. This increase in arousal begins from a level of basically no arousal. Obviously you will perform poorly on a test if you are at zero level of arousal meaning you are asleep. But as you progress from asleep to barely awake to merely groggy to somewhat alert you are in progressively better shape to take a test.

When you are at a neutral state of arousal, calm but alert, you will feel little if any anxiety. For most of us this is not the optimal level to take a test. As we anticipate the test looming in the near future, our level of arousal increase and we begin to feel anxiety. There is an optimum level of this test anxiety; it keeps our energy up and our attention focused. If you have too much test anxiety your performance begins to falter. Anxiety begins to generate incapacitating fear and higher anxiety states also make it more difficult to concentrate in general. When test anxiety becomes severe, one's performance can be so impaired that failure is almost guaranteed. It may become impossible to even attempt to take the exam.

The Opponent-Process Theory

Richard Solomon's *Opponent-Process Theory* states that that emotions exist as opposing pairs beginning at one extreme to the other, for instance the fear is one end and relief is the other. When fear is generated by a set of circumstances (stimuli). The theory indicates that a fearful situation is initially purely fearful but that as it continues to persist the fear emotion is less able to suppress the relief emotion relief is suppressed. In other words you cannot experience both fear and relief simultaneously. The theory proposes that individuals prefer a baseline emotional state and that when one extreme of an emotional opponent pair is present the individual is motivated to behave in ways that tends to restore the individual to the baseline state. If the situation continue it is less fearful either because decreased suppression of relief results in more relief that balances out the fear. This is an odd way to view things however what is the stimulus to generate the relief? And obviously fear and relief can be experienced simultaneously otherwise how does one cancel out the other and how is a less fearful state not a combination of pure fear and a lesser amount of pure relief.

One response to this criticism is that the situation becomes intrinsically less fearful as time passes. The fearful threat persists, but the fearful consequence of the situation do not occur. So someone points a gun to your head and you are instantly fearful. As time passes, the gunman does not pull the trigger so it is in one's mind less likely he actually will pull the trigger. Critics point out this is at least as well explained by the operant conditioning principle of habituation. So relief is emerging because the situation is not as dangerous as it first appear. There is a removal of some fear and this disappearance of fear causes an appearance of relief.

That is the second principle of the opponent process theory; that once the stimuli that caused one emotion is removed, the opposite of that emotion is suddenly fully expressed. This is used to explain thrill seeking behavior and perhaps a mechanism to explain drug addiction including the withdrawal effect of drug addiction.

For the thrill seeker, the bungee jump off a cliff is immediately terrifying but when the bungee cord (usually) prevents the splattering of the jumper's body on the rocks below the fear disappears and is replaced with intense pure relief. After a while, the bungee jumps just become fun, so the fear relief cycle kind of morphs into a general sensation of joy. That does not obviously explain why thrill seekers tend to progress to even more risky activities. The addictive process for drugs is even less clear the proponents of the theory suggest this is a pleasure pain cycle. Initial pleasant effects replaced by unpleasant effects when the drug is removed, if as proponents claim the theory accounts for the drive to seek increasingly risky behavior and to in drug addiction to increase drug use to over time and for the cravings for drugs to increase over time the opponent emotions that are generating and amplifying these behaviors are awkward to describe and the emotions are difficult to describe.

There are clear physiological explanations to explain many aspects of drug addiction and withdrawal that do not involve opponent emotion processes. Risk seeking behavior is often described in the form of a person who is an adrenaline junkie. Indeed, the arousal theory of motivation does a much better job of explaining what the opponent theory attempts to explain and also provides a very specific physiological mechanism for addiction including addiction in the sense of the adrenalin junkie. So it is an odd theory and not well supported by research, as a theory of motivation it is difficult to explain the emotion-motivation connection and as a theory of emotion it is not helpful because it really only describes emotional processes but does not explain much about the nature of the emotions themselves.

Humanistic Theories of Motivation

The *humanistic theories of motivation* introduces the concept that individuals have needs that extend beyond basic biological needs. These needs are generated at the level of cognitive thought. The most notable example of humanistic motivational theories is **Abraham Maslow's** hierarchy of needs.

Maslow's Hierarchy of Needs

Abraham Maslow's theory proposes that there is a hierarchy or pyramid of needs the lowest level of this pyramid consists of basic biological needs, food shelter etc. the next level consists of needs for safety or security, love and esteem. At the top of the pyramid are the highest level needs of self-actualization. The lower level of needs must be fulfilled before an individual may begin to pursue higher-level needs. Although the higher level needs are not basic biological needs, Maslow assert that they are independent inborn and fundamental, not secondary needs connected to basic biological needs or motivated by processes that are connected to basic biological needs. They are generated at the cognitive level and the motivation to pursue these needs is a motivation to fulfill one's full personal potential. Fulfillment of these highest-level needs are an individual's ultimate goal, and the

Self-
Actualization
higher-order goal
attainment

Self-esteem Needs
sense of achievement,
respect from others

Social Needs
friendship, family, relationships,
sense of belonging

Safety Needs
sense of security of body, resources,
health

Basic Physiological Needs
breathing, food, water, air

motivation to achieve these goals is the motivation to be happy. In order to achieve this ultimate goal, lower level needs, however, must be fulfilled first.

Needs are also categorized as *deficiency needs* or *"d" needs* and the lack of these needs causes discomfort and other negative consequences. At the highest level, there are *being* or *"B" needs*. These type of needs are not perceived as a deficiency or lack of something, but as a desire to achieve a higher level of personal development. A desire that is well stated in military recruitment advertising as "to be all that you can be"

The critics of Maslow's theory point out that research shows that across cultures people often have not fulfilled lower level needs but still seek to fulfill higher level needs and in fact do attain higher level objectives. Furthermore, the specifics of the theory do not lend themselves well to scientific investigation and what has been investigated seems to show that individuals just do not think of their needs in terms of a hierarchy.

The Expectancy Theory of Motivation

The Expectancy Theory of Motivation focuses on motivation in terms of what individuals believe may occur in the future. When individuals perceive pathways that lead to desirable or undesirable outcomes they are motivated to behave in ways that are intended to bring about the desirable outcomes and to avoid the undesirable outcomes. The theory proposes that motivations consists of three key elements: valence, instrumentality, and expectancy. *Valence* refers to the value with place on the potential outcome. Things that seem unlikely to produce personal benefit have a low valence, while those that offer immediate personal rewards have a much higher valence.

Instrumentality refers to whether people believe that they have a role to play in the predicted outcome. If the event seems random or outside of the individual's control, people will feel less motivated to pursue that course of action. If people believe they may play a major role in the success of the endeavor, people well feel more motivated to engage in the process.

Expectancy is the belief that one has the capabilities to produce the outcome. If people feel like they lack the skills or knowledge to achieve the desired outcome, they will be less motivated to try. People who feel capable, on the other hand, will be more likely to try to reach that goal.

Hunger Motivation

What motivates persons to eat begins at the physiological level in the brain; specifically in the hypothalamus. Research has determined that the lateral hypothalamus triggers the desire to eat. Here then we have precisely identified the region of the brain where a fundamental biological drive begins as a motivation for specific behavior. This is where hunger begins, Research has also identified that the ventromedial hypothalamus generates the signal to stop eating. This is perceived as satiety -the sense of fullness. This is where the sense of satiety begins. It is a subtle point but this is not simply a loss of the desire to eat. It is a separate sensation. A person does not stop eating just because the lateral hypothalamus is no longer generating a desire to eat. The ventromedial hypothalamus is generating a different desire, a different drive that motivates one to stop eating. .That is an important point. We usually think of motivations as motivation to engage is certain behaviors, but motivations are perhaps as important or more important when they are suppressing certain behaviors. As we have just described, there are aspects of biological drive states that motivate one to avoid certain behaviors and to terminate certain behaviors.

Set Point Theory

Set Point Theory is based on the research that established the hypothalamus is the origin of hunger and satiety signal and on research showing the hypothalamus can monitor the total energy state and overall weight of individuals. The hypothalamus has also been shown to regulate the metabolic state of the body, it can increase the overall metabolic state so that energy is utilized freely and storage of energy in the form of fat is minimized. Alternatively, the hypothalamus can decrease the overall metabolic rate of the body so that energy is utilized sparingly and as efficiently as possible. This state favors the storage of energy in the form of fat. There is strong support for the hypothesis that the hypothalamus can establish a set point or target weight and target fat storage level for an individual. It can do this by raising and lowering metabolic rates and by triggering hunger and satiety signals to motivate eating behavior to achieve and maintain this set point. There is strong evidence that there is a genetically determined set point. Pima Indians have been shown to have a very high susceptibility for severe obesity. There is also good evidence that eating behaviors and other behaviors can change this set point. One theory with good scientific support is that the act of dieting is interpreted by the hypothalamus as an environment of starvation. In response, the hypothalamus sets a higher weight set point and higher fat storage set point in anticipation of future starvation periods. This is seen in the effect where weight lost by dieting is almost always gained back and additional weight is gained. By repeated dieting cycles this can result in a vicious cycle of increased set points and increasing obesity.

The Garcia Effect

The *Garcia effect*, is when an extreme aversion to a stimulus results from a single pairing. It usually occurs in the context of eating when a one-time instance of eating something that makes you violently ill, will create an aversion to that food for a long time, perhaps years and decades. For purposes of the AP Psychology exam, consider the Garcia effect to be an example of classical conditioning where the unconditioned stimulus is and illness that causes nausea *on a single trial*. The conditioned stimulus is the food associated in time with the illness and the conditioned response is to feel nausea or to vomit.

Psychological Factors in Hunger Motivation

Research has shown that there are *external food cues* that motivate persons to eat, these include the attractiveness of food - it sure looks tasty; and the availability of food - it's right in front of you, so eat it. This suggests you may learn to modify eating behavior by learning how to ignore the appearance of food or not be in the presence of food or do things so that food is not so tasty looking or not so easily attainable. There are also *internal cues* such as the obvious hypothalamus hunger signal but others as well, stomach growling and more specific signal of low blood sugar - weakness and vague nausea for instance. You may learn to ignore these cues. There are also theories that eating becomes associated with pleasure and pleasure can cancel out our bad feelings like sadness and anxiety. This is the comfort food notion, and we learn bad eating habits by this association process. We also perhaps have learned from our childhood to prefer foods that we raised with and often these foods that are more likely to result in weight gain.

Eating Disorders

A few words of caution: we see no evidence that the topic of severe life threatening obesity and other eating disorders is to be specifically addressed in terms of motivation and emotions by the AP Psychology exam. These are properly the subject of abnormal psychology and are well covered in that chapter in this manual. Emphasizing a motivation or emotion basis for these disorders is unfair to those who suffer from these conditions and this attitude can frankly be dangerous if it suggests other than the medically recognized forms of treatment for these disorders.

Severe bulimia can indirectly result in death but in particular, anorexia nervosa involves behaviors that seem to override all motivations as described in the motivational theories. Too often anorexia turns out to be a form of mindless suicide. The ability to literally starve one's self to death is about as abnormal as things get. There is some evidence that anorexia begins with a routine attempt to diet. This may even begin with the first attempt in a young person's life to diet. There is specifically evidence this dieting somehow causes a critical impairment of the survival mechanisms concerned with maintaining a proper body weight. The crucial concept is that these severe eating disorders may involve actual physical brain damage. In essence, the higher cognitive functions are sticking their noses where they don't belong and indirectly cause unintentional but irreparable damage to lower level survival programs that can have lethal consequences.

Sexual Motivation

There is a basic drive to reproduce in all species of life and humans are no exception. There are physiological and psychological factors that generate and sustain sexual behavior. The physiology of sexual behavior is most notably described in the research of **William Masters** and **Virginia Johnson** This research identified four stages of the *human sexual response cycle.*

- Stage 1 is *initial excitement,* where there is an increase in heart and breathing rate and increased blood pressure. Often there is dilation of blood vessels in the skin that results in a reddening of the skin that is called the sexual flush. Heavy drenching sweats are also common during this phase.
- Stage 2 is the *plateau phase*, where heart rate and blood flow increase and sexual pleasure sensations steadily increase muscle tension increases and involuntary vocalizations often occur.
- Stage 3 is the *orgasm phase*, where male ejaculation occurs. There are strong involuntary muscle contractions and involuntary vocalizations that peak in an experience of intense pleasure and euphoria.
- Stage 4 is the *resolution phase* ,where arousal diminishes at a physiological level and for males there usually is an absolute refractory period or recovery time that is required before the cycle can be repeated

The evidence that there are well developed and specific psychological and physical systems involved is sexual behavior are illustrated by the research that shows the two aspects of sexual behavior can function separately from one another. When there is injury or disease that renders an individual incapable of generating physical sexual responses there is commonly still a well-developed sexual interest and sexual desire that remains. In cases where individuals are unable to perform the physical act of sex, there is often, in men in particular, a physical sexual response to erotic material. This shows that the male is fully functional to perform the act of sex, but that there are psychological factors that are interfering with the normal sexual behavior that occurs in a sexual response cycle.

Motivation Conflicts

There are four categories of motive conflict. The first is the *approach-approach* conflict where there are two attractive outcomes and one must decide which to pursue. The conflict is if you pursue one you by definition cannot pursue the other. In high school an athlete may excel at two sports that are played at the same time of year, volleyball and tennis perhaps. There are potential rewards that will occur from playing either sport. The athlete must evaluate and compare the personal value the rewards of playing each sport at a personal level. There is also the issue of probability to consider, how likely for instance that the athlete will start for the team or in the end be singled out for post season awards and possible athletic scholarships. *Avoidance-Avoidance* conflicts involve choices between to potentially bad outcomes, *approach-avoidance* involves an assessment of a single outcome that has both good and bad elements to the outcome. In *multiple approach -avoidance* conflicts the decision are between two or more outcomes each with its own good and bad aspects.

Social Motivation

Our final discussion features the motivations of individuals at the level of interactions as members of society. *Social motivation theories* features the concept of intrinsic or extrinsic motivations. One type of prosed motivation is *achievement motivation*. Persons who are achievement motivated have an intrinsic desire to acquire knowledge, develop new skills, and to set and then achieve various goals. In this sense achievement is as intrinsic a need as is food or water. They are not motivated by rewards that result from achievement except for the satisfaction of achievement itself. An achievement motivated person would perhaps be driven to climb Mount Everest and focus all of his or her efforts for years upon this desire. The key to this being a purely achievement motivation is that the person would have the same motivation even if no one ever knew that that they desired to climb the mountain or if they ever in fact attempted or succeeded to climb the mountain. This is exemplified to the classic response to the question "why did you climb that mountain?" the achievement motivated climbers response is "Because it was there."

Management Theory

In *Management Theory* the most commonly discussed theory comes from McGregor's description of management styles: *Theory X* describes a management style in which employees are assumed to be lazy, irresponsible, not good decision-makers, and in need of strict orders and discipline. *Theory Y* describes a management style in which employees are assumed to be hard-working, eager for responsibility, good problem-solvers, and in need of occasional guidance and support. Research consistently shows that the management Y style is more effective and that employees sustain their motivations over a longer period of time when those motivations are intrinsic rather than extrinsic.

Most recently a Theory Z has emerged from Ouchi. In this theory the manager sees the employees and the organization as a family. Employees are given responsibility and respect but also can expect very slow promotion and a long term commitment to the company. This management styles is said to foster employee loyalty and satisfaction.

Chapter 9: Developmental Psychology

Developmental Psychology
Key Terms, Concepts, and People

Developmental psychology

Normative development

Longitudinal research

Nature

Nature-Nurture debate

Continuous development

Critical period

Collectivist

Stages

Life-span psychologists

Cross-sectional research

Plasticity

Nurture

Maturation

Discontinuous development

Culture

Individualist

Physical Development

Key Terms:

Germinal stage

Fetal stage

Fetal Alcohol Syndrome (FAS)

Reflex/reflexive movement

Palmar reflex

Head-turning/rooting reflex

Orienting reflex

Rudimentary movement

Specialized movement

Application substage

Embryonic stage

Teratogens

Neonate

Sucking reflex

Babinski reflex

Moro reflex

Stereotyped response

Fundamental movement

Transitional stage

Environmental interaction

Cognitive Development

Key People: Jean Piaget; Lev Vygotsky

Jean Piaget's cognitive development theory: Key Concepts

Equilibration

Assimilation

Sensorimotor stage

Preoperational stage

Egocentrism

Artificialism

Static reasoning

Schemas

Accommodation

Object permanence

Symbolic thinking

Centration

Animism

Concrete operational stage

| Reversibility | Conservation |
| Formal operational stage | Metacognition |

Lev Vygotsky's cognitive development theory: Key Concepts

Internalization	Guided participation
Zone of proximal development (ZPD)	Scaffolding
Actual development level	Potential development level
Fluid intelligence	Crystallized intelligence

Other Key Concepts: information processing approach; theory of mind (TOM)

Social Development

Key People: Erik Erikson; Harry Harlow; John Bowlby; Mary Ainsworth; Konrad Lorenz; Diana Baumrind

Key Terms and Concepts:

Social development	Psychosocial theory
Generativity	Attachment
"Strange situation"	Imprinting

Attachment Patterns:

| Secure attachment | Insecure/anxious-resistant attachment |
| Avoidant/anxious-avoidant attachment | Disorganized attachment |

Parenting Styles:

| Authoritarian parents | Authoritative parents |
| Permissive parents | |

Moral Development

Key People: Lawrence Kohlberg; Carol Gilligan
Key Concepts:

| Preconventional moral reasoning | Conventional moral reasoning |
| Postconventional moral reasoning | |

Sexual & Gender Development

Key Person: Sigmund Freud
Key Tems and Concepts:

Gender identity	Gender differences
Gender typing	Gender constancy
Androgyny	

Psychosexual development theory:

Oral stage	Anal stage
Phallic stage	Latency stage
Genital stage	Fixation
Oedipal complex	Electra complex

Overview

Developmental psychology is the study of how behaviors, thoughts, abilities and interactions change as people age, beginning with conception and ending with death. Developmental psychology studies both *how* and *why* people change over time. It recognizes that development occurs in multiple contexts, and that one domain of development affects all other domains of development. Because of the broad scope of developmental psychology, many topics and concepts overlap with other areas of psychology. For example, concepts in personality development are important in developmental psychology. One area that demonstrates this common study is Sigmund Freud's psychosexual stages. Personality theorists and developmental psychologists both apply concepts of Freud's theory to their respective fields. Developmental psychologists use research from other areas of psychology and apply it to topics regarding development, maturation and change over the course of our lifetimes. Developmental psychology studies the following dimensions of development: physical, cognitive, social, moral, and sexual and gender development.

Lifespan Approach

Life-span psychologists study how development occurs throughout life. Psychologists in this area may focus on changes and challenges for individuals in different phases of life. For example, child psychologists are interested in how and why children change as they grow, and geriatric psychologists focus on studying how elderly individuals change. Developmental psychology also examines how people change or remain stable over the course of the lifespan. The term *plasticity* refers to the idea that individuals can be changed, or molded, by factors influencing their development, throughout the lifespan.

Research Methods

When studying development, two kinds of research are most helpful. *Cross-sectional research* compares individuals of different ages to one another to determine which factors may change over the course of time. For instance, researchers who want to know how memory changes over time may use participants from groups of 6 year-olds, 10 year-olds and 15 year-olds, and compare results across each age group. Results from cross-sectional research are helpful in determining *normative development*, which is the normal progression of development among different age groups. Cross-sectional research can help developmental psychologists recognize when certain skills, tasks, or processes occur. Although cross-sectional research produces results quickly, there are a few drawbacks to this method. One disadvantage is that cross-sectional studies do not reveal much about the development of a single individual, but rather provides information about a certain group. Further, when using cross-sectional research, researchers must be careful to account for effects resulting from cultural or historical trends. Individuals of different cultures and historical periods may not have the same experiences as others outside of their age group or cultural group. As a result, the researcher may not know which other factors may have affected the results of the study. With cross-sectional research, the researcher may assume that any differences are a result of age. For example, millennials may have different educational experiences than those of their parents and grandparents.

Unlike cross-sectional research, which deals with differences among various age groups, *longitudinal research* examines the same group of individuals over a long period of time. The researcher will assess the participants at set intervals (ex. every 5 years) to see which changes have occurred. Longitudinal research, however, is more difficult and challenging, as well as expensive, because it involves acquiring data over several decades. Some advantages of longitudinal research are that specific aspects of development can be measured, and differences between participants (i.e. cultural or historical differences) can be eliminated. Longitudinal research presumes that any changes are the result of time. One easy way to remember the difference between cross-sectional research and longitudinal research is to associate cross-sectional with *across ages* and longitudinal with *long time*.

Developmental Issues

Concepts and theories of development focus on explaining human development in terms of the influence of *nature* (genetic factors) and *nurture* (environmental factors). The nature versus nurture debate asks the question: How much development is a result of genetic factors and how much is a result of environmental factors? While most developmental psychologists acknowledge an interaction between nature and nurture, the issue of debate is how much each factor affects development. A person's genetic makeup will elicit different kinds of nurture, and that nurture will influence the nature of a person. For example, a child with a fussy temperament may elicit a parental response of anger or frustration, and that response will reinforce the child's fussy nature.

Maturation is the process of development that culminates in the individual fully maturing. Maturation includes cognitive development that occurs as a result of biological processes and environmental factors and learning. As individuals learn and interact with their environments, cognitive processes and behaviors become more complex and multifaceted.

Genetics also play an important role in development. Much about an individual is determined by genes that are passed down from parents to their children. Some individual traits are more likely to be passed down to other generations than other traits. Temperament is an example of a trait that is largely determined by hereditary factors. Many of the abilities someone is born with are a direct result of heredity. For instance, a parent who has quick reflexes may pass this propensity down to his child, or a mother who easily grasps language may pass this ability down to her child.

Just as the issue of nature versus nurture is important to developmental psychology, so is the issue of whether development occurs gradually or occurs in stages. Development that occurs gradually is called *continuous*, or stable, development, and development that happens in stages is referred to as *discontinuous* development. Each stage of development has a critical period, or a time in which new abilities or processes must occur. If certain aspects of development do not occur during the critical period, the individual will not develop normally and will be at a disadvantage in cognitive or social functioning.

In studying development, the effects of culture must be considered. Culture is defined as the values, practices, customs, and behaviors that set one group apart from other groups. Cultures can be categorized by gender, socioeconomic status, age group, ethnicity, and race, among other things. A person's culture will create the environment (nurture) in which development must occur. Some societies or cultures value individual needs over the needs of the entire group. Cultures who place more emphasis on individual needs are *individualist*, whereas cultures who promote the needs of the group over the needs of the individual are *collectivist*. The individual's development will be influenced by his cultural environment, just as his culture and environment will be affected by his development.

Developmental Theories

Development is categorized into physical development, cognitive development, and social development. Some developmental psychologists may approach the study of development from the theoretical perspective that development is a continuous and stable process, whereas other developmental psychologists believe that development is discontinuous and occurs in sequential stages. A *stage* is a set of behaviors or processes that happen in a fixed progression. Even though development can be divided into stages, each stage affects the other stages. Dimensions of development also happen simultaneously in each individual, but there may be overlap among different domains of a stage. Each stage of development builds on the skills, abilities, and cognitive processes from earlier stages and introduces new challenges.

Physical Development

Conception to Birth: Physical development begins at conception. A fertilized egg is called a *zygote*. During the period of gestation, a zygote goes through three periods. In the germinal phase, which lasts for two weeks, the zygote undergoes cell division and is implanted into the uterine wall. During the next stage, the *embryonic stage*, organs begin to form. This stage lasts about eight weeks. The final period is the *fetal stage*, which begins in the ninth week and ends with birth. During this phase, sexual organs differentiate, and the fetus develops greater ability to move. In the fetal stage, growth happens quickly as organs begin to fully function and other body structures fully develop.

While in the womb, the environment can have harmful effects on the developing baby. Many harmful chemicals or other agents, which are called *teratogens*, can have a profound effect on the developing fetus. Some examples of teratogens are drugs, alcohol, and tobacco. Certain diseases and conditions of the mother are also considered teratogens. If the mother has a disease, such as rubella, or suffers from malnutrition, the developing fetus can be negatively impacted.

It is important to know that the timing at which a developing fetus is exposed to a teratogen can impact the effects of the teratogen. During fetal development, there are critical periods of time in which a teratogen may do more damage. For example, during weeks three to sixteen of gestation, the central nervous system is forming. Exposure to teratogens during this period can result in neural tube defects or mental retardation. One of the most common forms of neural tube defects is spinal bifida. Spinal bifida is a condition in which the backbone that encloses the spinal cord fails to close or develop properly, which causes defects in the spinal cord and nerves. This condition may result in physical and mental disability; the extent of the damage is determined by the location and size of the defect and which parts of the spinal cord and nerves are affected.

Teratogens do not just affect development in the womb; these agents also affect development after a child is born. Teratogens can cause physical impairments, learning problems, difficulties regulating emotions, and behavior problems. These types of problems can also influence the growing child's social interactions. Problems resulting from exposure to teratogens are a great illustration of how one area of development affects all other areas of development.

One of the most common teratogens is alcohol. When a mother drinks alcohol during pregnancy, the baby may be born with *fetal alcohol syndrome (FAS)*. Babies with fetal alcohol syndrome have physical abnormalities marked by distorted faces, small eyes and thick upper lips. These babies may also have cognitive impairments and emotional and behavioral problems. *Fetal alcohol effect* (FAE) is a milder condition in which children may have cognitive deficiencies and emotional problems. In both instances, children may have learning disabilities and other cognitive defects that negatively affect their social interactions and relationships.

A newborn baby is called a *neonate.* Although babies are relatively helpless, they are born with reflexes that contribute to their ability to survive and grow. A *reflex* (sometimes called a reflexive movement) is an involuntary response to a stimulus. These are the most basic of reflexes and set the stage for the development of more specialized movement. When an object is placed in a baby's mouth, the baby will suck on it—this is the *sucking reflex.* The *rooting reflex* (also called the head-turning reflex) causes the baby to turn his mouth in the direction of anything that touches his cheek. The sucking reflex and the rooting reflex are reflexes that enable feeding. When an object is placed in a baby's hand, the *palmar reflex* causes the baby to grip the object tightly. When an infant's feet are stroked, his toes bend and splay upward. This is the *Babinski reflex.* The *Moro reflex* is when infants fling their arms and legs outward and then bring them to their chests as if holding on to something in response to being startled. When a baby hears a loud noise, he will turn his head toward the noise; this is an example of the *orienting reflex.* These reflexes are not necessary for survival, but they are indications that the baby is developing normally. The orienting reflex continues into adulthood, but the other reflexes disappear as the baby continues to develop normally.

Babies are born with the same sensory apparatus as adults. Before they are born, infants are able to hear in the womb. They learn to recognize their mother's voice and may have preferences for some sounds over others. They have similar preferences in taste and smell as adults do. If someone places something sweet or sugary in an infant's mouth, the infant will begin to suck and smack his lips. This reaction, also called a *stereotyped response*, is unlearned and reflexive. It is an adaptive mechanism that occurs in response to an environmental stimulus. Like adults, infants do not like sour tastes, such as that of lemons. Many taste and smell preferences may change as babies grow.

At birth, vision is the least developed sense. Newborns are born "legally blind." They cannot see objects that are more than a foot away. By the time a baby reaches four months of age, he is able to focus both eyes on the same object. At twelve months of age, a baby has normal vision, unless there is a vision problem. The sense of touch also develops rapidly after birth. Babies learn to distinguish their caregivers' touch from the touch of others. This ability aids the adult in being able to soothe and comfort the infant and aids in the bonding process.

Development of motor skills is one example of sequential development. Gross motor skills initially develop from reflexes. As the brain grows and develops, babies develop better motor control. Rudimentary reflexes and movements develop first. *Rudimentary movements* are voluntary movements that develop in sequential order. Examples of rudimentary movements are rolling, crawling, and standing. These movements develop in stages from birth until the age of two. Before a baby is able to walk, he must first be able to stand. This is an illustration of how some skills build upon other skills.

From the ages of two to seven, a child develops *fundamental movement*. In this period, the child increasingly learns how to control his body and initiate more complex movements, such as running, throwing and jumping. These movements require greater motor control. Movements in this stage are initially uncoordinated and uncontrolled. By the end of this stage, the child engages in movements that progressively become more controlled, coordinated, and organized.

As children develop the ability to combine fundamental movements, they enter the phase of *specialized movement*. In this stage, children can apply their movements to specific tasks. This period can be divided into two stages: the *transitional* substage and the *application* substage. In the transitional substage, the child develops the ability to combine movements. During the application substage, the child learns how to apply skills to specific activities and tasks. For example, a child may decide to apply specific skills to dancing, whereas another child may use the same skill set to take gymnastics. Not only are children able to apply certain skills to accomplish a given task, they are also able to determine the best way to achieve their desired goal.

The skills and abilities children develop continue to become more coordinated and controlled as they move into adulthood. As the person progresses throughout life, he learns to apply the skill sets from earlier periods of life to other situations and other skills.

From birth through adolescence, the brain continues to develop and new neural connections are made. As a result, motor development becomes increasingly complex and refined. Even though the development of motor skills occurs in a sequential order, the developing child must interact with his environment. *Environmental interaction* fosters brain development, which in turn provides the child with a greater ability to control, refine, and coordinate movement. If a child is in an environment that restricts movement, he may experience an impairment in his motor skills. Also, lack of adequate stimulation hinders perception. These examples provide greater insight into the importance of recognizing critical periods in development and illustrate the complementary interaction between nature and nurture.

This same principal applies to brain development. In order for the brain to develop normally, individuals must receive adequate stimulation, as well as opportunities to engage in activities that build upon earlier skills and teach new skills. When one part of the brain is underdeveloped, another part of the brain may take over the function of the underdeveloped part of the brain. This adaptation demonstrates the plasticity of the brain. Just as humans can change throughout their lifespan, the brain can change the way it functions.

During puberty, the body undergoes many changes. This period is usually associated with growth spurts and the development of secondary sex characteristics. In puberty, girls begin their menstrual cycles, and boys may experience nocturnal emissions. While these physical changes are occurring, pubescent teenagers are also experiencing changes in their social relationships and in their cognitive abilities.

By the time a person enters their thirties, their bodies have already reached their physical peak. Throughout adulthood, men and women gradually undergo physical changes that result in a decrease of physical abilities. Although a good diet and regular exercise can slow the aging process, it cannot be avoided. Women enter into menopause, which is the cessation of the menstrual cycle, in their fifties, but there are variations in this time frame. Some women may enter menopause earlier than their fifties, whereas other women may not go through menopause until their sixties. While the timing of the change may be different, the sequence of the events does not change.

The elderly also begin to experience drastic changes in their cognitive abilities, and they undergo changes in their senses. For example, their vision and hearing may become worse. Their movement also slows down, and the speed of their reflexes significantly lessens. Many elderly individuals develop health conditions that affect their quality of health and overall quality of life. Diseases, such as Alzheimer's or Parkinson's, greatly impact the personality and cognitive abilities of the elderly. The effects of these changes not only present new challenges for the older adult, they are often complicated by stressful life events, such as the death of a spouse. Just as in the other stages of life, the physical, cognitive and social domains of development and change interact with and influence the others.

Cognitive Development

Cognitive development involves intellectual and learning processes. This area focuses on learning, reasoning, problem solving, and memory processes. *Three main theories: Piaget's theory of cognitive development; Vygotsky's theory of cognitive development; and information processing theory.*

Jean Piaget

One of the most influential theories of cognitive development was formulated by **Jean Piaget**. Piaget developed his theory after observing the intellectual growth of children. Piaget's theory of cognitive development is a stage theory, which means that development occurs in a set progression, with each stage building on learning from other stages. Piaget also believed that a child could only be in one stage at time; stages could not overlap.

As children try to balance their mental processes, they are engaging in *equilibration*. Children will use both assimilation and accommodation in this process. Children's thinking operates out of *schemas*, which are mental representations of objects. In *assimilation*, children integrate new ideas into their existing schemas. For example, if a child understands that dogs are animals with four legs, when he sees another animal with four legs, he will incorporate (assimilate) this information with his existing schema of animals. Since dogs have four legs and are animals, then a lion is an animal, too, since it has four legs. The other way children attempt to understand events in their environments is through the process of accommodation. *Accommodation* happens when children are not able to fit new information into their existing schema; as a result, they must change their mental representation of an object to include the new information. If the same child as in the earlier example sees a bird, he will not categorize the bird as an animal unless he modifies his schema in order to accommodate the new information. *An easy way to remember the difference between assimilation and accommodation is to associate assimilation with integration and accommodation with change.*

According to Piaget, children go through four distinct stages of cognitive development. The first stage Piaget proposed was the *sensorimotor stage*. This stage begins at birth and ends around the second year of life. In this stage, infants use their senses and motor skills to learn. As children progress cognitively, they are also learning and using new motor skills, both of which are affected by the maturation of the brain. Children's early interactions are reflexive, but, as children grow, they develop a greater ability to direct their actions and interact with others based on past experiences. Children in this stage engage in circular reactions, which are attempts to manipulate their environment by repeating behaviors. For example, an infant who blows bubbles and gets his caregivers to laugh or smile is likely to repeat the action to continue to elicit the same response.

Object permanence develops during this stage. *Object permanence* refers to a child's awareness that objects and people continue to exist even when they cannot be seen, heard or touched. In other words, an infant understand that *objects are permanent*. During the sensorimotor stage, children's interactions progress from being reflexive to being goal-directed. As children learn about their environments, they become increasingly able to act with a specific purpose in mind. An example of goal-directed behavior can be illustrated by considering how a young child who cannot yet walk, crawling in order to get to a favorite toy. At this stage of cognitive development, children do not have the ability to engage in symbolic thinking or mental problem solving.

The second stage, which begins around of two and ends around the age of seven, is the *preoperational stage*. In the preoperational stage, children begin to develop schemas. Preoperational thinking means that children do not yet have the ability to operate with logic and reason. Children in this stage begin to use symbolic thinking. *Symbolic thinking* is the ability to replace objects with words. The development of language and imagination occur in this stage. Children in this stage are characterized by *egocentrism*, or lacking the ability to see the world through any perspective other than their own. They are self-centered. Egocentrism is one aspect of *centration*, which refers to the tendency to focus on one aspect of something and excluding all other views. In the preoperational stage, children believe that all natural objects are alive, which is called *animism*, and they think all objects are made by humans, a characteristic referred to as *artificialism*. Children in this stage also use *static reasoning*, which means they think the world does not change—it is static.

After the preoperational stage, children enter into the *concrete operational stage*. This stage typically begins around the age of seven and ends just before puberty. At this stage, children have the capacity to engage in operational (logical) thinking and reasoning. During this stage, children are able to reverse their thinking, a concept known as *reversibility*. Children's thinking in this stage is marked by the idea of *conservation*, which means they believe the amount of something stays the same (is conserved) even when the substance may change in appearance. For instance, for children in the preoperational stage, if two identical glasses contain the same amount of milk, and milk from one glass is poured into a taller and narrower glass, the child will think that the taller glass has more liquid. Children in the concrete operational stage know that the amount of milk did not change even when it was poured into a narrower container.

The last stage of Piaget's theory of cognitive development is the *formal operational* stage, which typically starts around the age of twelve. Children in this stage have the ability to think abstractly and symbolically. They also have the ability to recognize their own learning processes and change those processes if necessary; this ability is referred to as *metacognition*. Children operating in this stage can think hypothetically. They are able to offer explanations of things that might occur, if, for example, zombies attack.

Criticisms of Piaget's Theory

Many researchers disagree with Piaget's theory, claiming that cognitive development does not progress as consistently as Piaget believed. Stages of cognitive development are not as distinct as Piaget described, and cognitive processes develop more gradually than Piaget thought. Piaget's theory did not address how cognitive development is influenced by environmental and social factors. Because children's cognitive development is not solely based on genes, parents have an important role in enhancing their children's intellectual development. For example, parents can read to their children and talk about what was read, provide stimulating experiences and activities, and nurture the natural curiosity of their children.

The *information processing theory*, which is uses computers as a model, offers a different perspective for cognitive development. The information processing approach focuses on how the mind receives, retrieves, stores, and processes new information. This approach studies selective memory abilities, gradual changes in memory as children grow attention and memory storage capacity.

Theory of Mind (Tom)

Theory of mind refers to children's ability to understand others' perspectives. This important cognitive ability appears around the age of four. After children acquire TOM, they understand that thoughts do not necessarily reflect reality. Theory of mind has been tested through the "false belief task." For example, one experiment used to test TOM involved an adult showing a 3-year-old child a box of candy. The researcher asked the child what was in the box, to which the child replied, "Candy." When the child opened the box, pencils were inside instead of candy. Obviously, what the child thought was not true; it did not reflect reality. When the adult asked the child what his friend, who had not seen what was inside the box, would think was inside the box, the child responded, "Pencils."

Theory of mind supports the concepts of egocentrism and static reasoning, all of which are characteristic of children in the early preoperational stage. Theory of mind and the "false belief test" indicate that not all cognitive development occurs in distinct stages, contrary to what Piaget proposed. Theory of mind seems to suddenly appear, which demonstrates that development can occur in leaps and bounds, as well as with zig-zigs and curves. However, research has proven that maturation of the brain, rather than the age of the child, explains TOM. Studies involving children with autism have helped psychologists understand how brain development affects children's thinking and actions.

Vygotsky

Whereas Piaget attributed cognitive development to maturation of the brain, Vygotsky's theory focused on the critical role of social influences on cognitive development. According to Vygotsky, children learn by taking in knowledge to themselves through social interactions and environmental factors, a process called *internalization*. Children's cognitive growth is stimulated by their environments and guided by adults through what is called *guided participation*. Each person has skills they can perform with help from others but are not quite able to perform independently; this concept is referred to as the *zone of proximal development (ZPD)*.

Scaffolding is temporary support from parents or teachers in the child's environment that assists a child in reaching his full *potential development level*, or the ability the child has the potential to achieve, rather than just his *actual development level*, which is the ability a child demonstrates. Scaffolding progresses incrementally, with the child carefully building on earlier skills and knowledge to reach a new level of ability. If a child experiences difficulty in attaining new skills, adults and teachers need to adjust the scaffolding steps closer to the child's ability level.

Like other domains of development, cognitive development continues into adulthood. However, as individuals age, they lose brain mass and some cognitive abilities. Many elderly adults experience a significant decrease in their ability to think abstractly and symbolically—this ability is referred to as *fluid intelligence*. Also, as adults age, they experience an increase in their ability to recall specific facts; this ability is called *crystallized intelligence*.

Social Development

Social development refers to how the ability to interact with others and within various social contexts changes over the course of the lifespan. *Social development can be grouped into several categories: psychosocial development, moral development, and sexual and gender role development.* Social development also considers the importance of *attachment patterns and parenting styles.*

One of the most important theories that examines the challenges of social development was proposed by Erik Erikson. *Erikson's psychosocial theory* delineated and described a series of stages, with each stage presenting a new developmental task or crisis. In order for healthy and normal development to occur, the task of each stage must be successfully achieved. Failure to resolve the crisis of one stage could pose greater challenges in the subsequent stages. Erikson's psychosocial stage theory was the first theory that approached development as a lifelong process, beginning with birth and ending with death.

Erikson's Psychosocial Theory

Trust versus mistrust

In this stage, the infant learns if adults can be trusted to meet their needs. The infant will either come to see the world as hostile or friendly depending on how well adults meet his basic needs. If the infant learns, through interactions with those in his world, that the world can be trusted, he

The task of this stage, which occurs during the toddler years, is for toddlers to develop the ability to control their bodies and actions. In this stage, toddlers must master toilet training, walking, and other skills that contribute to autonomy. Failure to attain these skills can create feelings of shame and cause toddlers to doubt their abilities.

Initiative versus Guilt

From the ages of three to six, children are faced with the challenge of taking the initiative in learning and social interactions. In this stage, learning and acquiring new skills and knowledge fosters self-esteem. As children build self-esteem, they are more confident in their abilities and are willing to try new activities and put forth more effort in their tasks. The social interactions of children have extended beyond the home to the school environment. However, in this stage, the way parents and other adults respond to the efforts of a child is important. Parents and other adults can either encourage a child, which builds the child's self-esteem and instills a sense of pride in the child, or they can overlook a child's effort or be too critical of a child. If parents and adults respond negatively to the initiative and efforts of a child who is in this stage, the child may feel guilty about his actions. Children who do not meet the task of this stage successfully may develop a poor self-concept.

Industry versus Inferiority

This stage occurs between the ages of six and twelve. By the time children enter this stage, their social environment has expanded and they have regular interactions with adults and children in a multitude of contexts. During this stage, children actively try to master new abilities and skills. They may feel they are productive, competent and successful, or they may feel they are useless, incompetent, and a failure. Self-control and motivation are positive outcomes of this stage.

Identity versus Role Confusion

Adolescents in this stage try to understand themselves. They are searching for their identity and trying to figure out where they fit in to society. Adolescents in this stage engage in a lot of self-reflection and self-assessment as they forge an identity based on their own values. The goal of this stage is identity achievement in which the adolescent is true to himself. An adolescent who does not successful achieve an identity may demonstrate a lack of commitment and indifference to goals and values.

Intimacy versus Isolation

This stage occurs in early adulthood. Adults in this stage seek to form close and intimate relationships. The adult may form close friendships, romantic relationships and strong affiliations with others as a way to satisfy the need for intimacy. Those who commit to intimate relationships learn how to sacrifice and give of themselves in a loving way. Young adults who do not develop intimate relationships with others may experience feelings of loneliness and isolation.

Generativity versus Stagnation

People in middle adulthood struggle to find meaning and productivity in their careers and home. As adults in this stage attempt to be productive, they may have children or find other ways to positively contribute to society, including the next generation. This type of productivity is called **generativity.** Adults in this stage may question the type of legacy they want to leave for the next generation. Unsuccessful resolution of this stage may result in feelings of isolation and stagnation, or in great dissatisfaction.

Integrity versus Despair

The last stage of Erikson's psychosocial theory occurs in late adulthood or old age. Individuals in this stage reflect on their lives and come to terms with the choices they made. They must accept their successes and failures. Those adults who successfully meet the task of this stage will gain wisdom. Those who do not achieve integrity may feel angry, bitter, and discontent.

Harry Harlow

Harry Harlow was a psychologist who conducted a study using infant monkeys. Harlow separated the monkeys from their mothers not long after birth. The monkeys were bottle. One group was fed from a bottle that was attached to a wire surrogate mother, and the other was fed from a bottle attached to a cloth surrogate mother. Both groups of monkeys preferred the cloth mother. The monkeys fed by the wire mother only went to that mother when they were hungry. When Harlow put an unfamiliar object in the cage with the baby monkeys fed by the cloth mother, they ran to the cloth mother to be comforted. When the object was put in the cage of the monkeys fed by the wire mother, the babies were frightened. As a result of the study, Harlow concluded that love and comforting touch are essential for healthy attachment and development. Harlow's research changed the way sick or motherless children are treated.

Attachment Theory and Parenting Styles

Throughout this content review, you have learned how development in any area affects development in other areas. You now understand that development is affected by a multitude of factors and across many different contexts. You know that both nature (genetics) and nurture (environment) contribute to development. With the exception of Erikson's psychosocial theory and Vygotsky's cognitive social learning theory, there has been little discussion about the reciprocal interaction between a child's temperament and parenting. Parents or caregivers are without a doubt one of the strongest influences on how a child develops. The way parents respond to a child will determine the quality of the child's relationships later in life. Since the first relationship children have is with their parents or caregivers, it is essential for children to have an environment that fosters healthy development.

Attachment refers to loving bonds that infants form with their caregivers. This bond may cause the infant to prefer familiar people over those with whom they are unfamiliar.

John Bowlby

Bowlby is the father of attachment theory. Bowlby's theory focused on the importance of early childhood experiences. He viewed attachment as being critical for healthy development. Attachment is a relationship between the caregiver and an infant, with each one responding to and influencing the behavior of the other. The first attachment relationship, according to Bowlby, is the most crucial. From this relationship, the child will develop a mental model that will affect later relationships. For the child is to feel confident and secure, the mother must be responsive. If a caregiver is not responsive to the needs of the infant, the child will experience difficulty, both in short-term development and in later relationships.

Mary Ainsworth

Mary Ainsworth was another attachment theorist. Ainsworth studied human infant attachment using a technique referred to as the *"strange situation."* In this study, a caregiver leaves a child alone with a stranger for a short period of time and then returns. The most important indicator of the attachment bond between the mother and the child was how the infant responded once the caregiver returned. From this information, Ainsworth determined *four attachment style patterns.*

Secure Attachment

When a secure attachment exists, the infant is happy when the caregiver returns, and the infant will initiate some type of contact with the caregiver. The infant is confident that the caregiver will be responsive to his needs. This attachment style is the most common.

Insecure Attachment

This attachment style can also be referred to as anxious-resistant. In this attachment style, the infant is ambivalent when the caregiver returns. Infants with this kind of attachment style seek contact with their caregiver when she returns, but also resist the caregiver. The infant is not sure that the caregiver will be responsive, and the infant demonstrates feelings of discomfort if held by a stranger. This type of attachment affects between 7 to 15 percent of the population.

Avoidant Attachment

Avoidant attachment, which can also be referred to as anxious-avoidant attachment, is rare. Infants with this attachment style remain calm when the caregiver leaves, and they accept the stranger. When the caregiver returns, these infants avoid her. In this type of attachment, the infant is not secure and does not feel that the caregiver will be responsive.

Disorganized Attachment

This style of attachment is common for infants who are being abused. The infant's behavior is erratic and unpredictable.

Konrad Lorenz's Imprinting Theory

Lorenz used the term *imprinting* to describe the instinctual, innate, and adaptive phenomenon that is necessary for survival. Lorenz developed his theory after conducting an experiment with geese. He separated goose eggs into two groups. The first group of eggs remained with their mother, and the second group of eggs were incubated until they hatched. Immediately upon hatching, the geese who stayed with their mother followed their mother, and the geese kept in incubation followed Lorenz even after the baby geese were no longer separated. Lorenz's research demonstrated that within hours after birth, babies attach to whoever is present. It also supported the idea that a critical period exists for attachment.

Parenting Styles

Diana Baumrind studied the interactions between parents and their children. From her research, Baumrind categorized parenting into *three distinct styles.*

Authoritarian parents set very high behavioral standards for their children. They are rigid and controlling. They provide strict discipline and do not like to be questioned. These parents punish their children for disobedience and other undesirable behaviors; they are more likely than other parenting styles to use physical punishment, such as spanking. These parents typically are not affectionate, supportive, or nurturing, and communication about feelings is discouraged, if not altogether absent.

Children with authoritarian parents often have difficulty forming relationships. They are used to having decisions made for them, so they lack the ability to make their own decisions. Since they are not allowed to freely speak their minds and express themselves, they typically do not develop the ability to be creative. They may have difficulty trusting people.

Authoritative parents set rules and behavior expectations for their children, but the rules are not unreasonable. These parents are flexible and they care about the feelings and thoughts of their children; as such, they will discuss the rules and the rationale behind the rules with their children. Authoritative parents use both praise and punishment to direct the actions of their children. They give their children some responsibility for making their own choices. These parents are nurturing, supportive and affectionate, but they also guide and discipline their children. The authoritative parenting style provides the best environment for healthy development.

Children of authoritative parents are able to make choices and solve problems. They take responsibility for their actions. They are confident and have good communication skills.

Permissive parents have few rules or standards for their children. If there are rules, the parents typically do not enforce them. These parents seem more concerned with being their child's friend than parent. There may an attitude of anything goes in the home. These parents are warm and nurturing but they let their children get away with too much. They may buy expensive things for their child and give their children whatever they want.

Children of permissive parents lack the ability to control themselves. They are used to getting their own way, so they do not accept blame for their actions. These children may have an attitude of entitlement and may not appreciate the thing they have. Because their parents have given them almost anything they wanted, they may not develop independence.

Moral Development

Just as parents have a significant impact on their children's development, they also contribute to the moral development of their children. The home is the first place children experience rules and behavioral expectations. Parents or caregivers are the main people who teach children right from wrong.

The most influential theory of moral development was presented by **Lawrence Kohlberg**. Kohlberg used some of Piaget's work to develop his theory. Kohlberg sought to describe and understand how moral reasoning changes throughout the lifespan. Kohlberg's theory of moral developed is divided into three levels, and each level consists of two stages.

The first level is *preconventional moral reasoning*. The moral reasoning of children in stage one of this level is guided by their desire to avoid punishment and to get rewards. Children in this stage are fearful of being punished, so they obey the rules. Children in the second stage are still very self-centered and will act accordingly. Out of their self-interest, children will be nice to others so that others will be nice to them.

The second level is *conventional moral reasoning*. The moral reasoning of children in stage one of this level are focused on social rules and what society views as right or wrong, good or bad. The child's actions have shifted from being self-centered to being community-centered. Good behavior will please others. Children in this stage care more about social approval than they do about being rewarded. The next stage of moral reasoning is characterized by the individual's desire to be a good citizen by obeying laws. The individual feels that he or she has an obligation to society. Individuals in this stage often make choices about right or wrong out of the dictates of their conscience.

At the third level, *postconventional moral reasoning*, individuals focus on moral principles and ideals. In the first stage of this level, individuals enter into a social contract with others. They obey rules and laws because they benefit all members of society. Individual rights and values may sometimes conflict with societal laws. If societal rules are no longer beneficial, individuals may feel they no longer have an obligation to the moral principles of the society. Individuals in this stage may think it is moral to disobey the law under certain circumstances. The last stage of Kohlberg's theory represents the highest level of moral reasoning. Few individuals reach this stage. This stage focuses on universal moral principles, not on the needs of the individual or the community. Universal principles of justice determine what is right or wrong.

Criticisms of Kohlberg's Theory

Carol Gilligan criticized Kohlberg's theory because she thought Kohlberg's theory did not consider gender differences. Gilligan presented the idea that gender development affects moral reasoning. In Gilligan's opinion, boys have a more rigid view of what is moral, whereas girls consider relationships and want to know the situational context. Gilligan's criticism highlighted the importance of studying gender differences.

Sex and Gender Development

Developmental psychology also explores sexual and gender development. Gender roles are often defined by the culture in which one lives. Each society determines which behaviors are proper for males and females.

At birth, there are distinct sexual differences between males and females. Gender differences can be partly explained by biological factors. They are also influenced by social and cognitive factors.

Sexual and gender development involves becoming aware of one's sexuality and what it means to be a male or female. *Gender identity* refers to a person's awareness of and acceptance of the roles and behaviors that society expects of biological males and females. *Gender differences* are differences in the roles and behaviors of males and females as defined by their culture. By the time children are three years old, they identify as a male or female. When children assume roles based on their gender and sexuality, which is referred to as *gender typing*, they become aware that gender is unchangeable. That is, they recognize *gender constancy*. When an individual has a balance of masculine and feminine characteristics, they are considered to be *androgynous*.

Sigmund Freud's Psychosexual Theory

Freud's theory is one of the most influential theories regarding sexual development. Like other stage theories, Freud's theory is based on the assumption that development occurs in a series of sequential stages. Freud's *psychosexual theory* proposed that individuals are driven by unconscious pleasure seeking desires. In each stage, the developing individual derives pleasure from different things. Problems in one stage can hinder healthy development. *Fixation* refers to a persistent focus of pleasure seeking energy upon objects associated with a psychosexual stage of development. Fixation makes it difficult for the person to move forward and develop normally.

Freud's psychosexual theory is divided into five stages. Each stage focuses on a different area of the body. The first stage is the *oral stage*, which begins at birth and ends around the age of one. In this stage, infants' libidinal energy is focused on the mouth. Infants derive pleasure from putting objects in their mouths. The focus of activities pertain to the mouth (sucking, swallowing, biting).

After the first year of life, the infant enters the *anal stage*. The focus of pleasure in this stage is the anus, and the child derives great pleasure from defecating.

Between the ages of three to six, children are in the *phallic stage*. In this stage, the child gets a lot of pleasure from genital stimulation. During this stage, children develop an awareness of their anatomy, which results in conflictual feelings. Boys in this stage experience the *Oedipus complex.* They develop sexual desires for their mothers and begin to fear their fathers. In order to resolve this conflict, boys begin to identify with their fathers and adopt masculine roles. Females develop the *Electra complex.* The Electra complex is milder than the Oedipus complex. Girls desire their fathers and fear their mothers. To resolve this conflict, the girls identify with their mothers and take on feminine gender roles.

The next stage is the *latency stage*. This stage begins in middle childhood and ends with puberty. In this stage, the child's libidinal desires are dormant. No psychosexual development occurs during this stage. Much of the child's energy is focused on school, friendships and acquiring new skills and abilities.

The last stage, which begins with puberty and lasts throughout adulthood, is the *genital stage.* The individual derives sexual pleasure from the genitals through sexual experimentation and relationships. In this stage, the individual desires to form a loving, sexually satisfying relationship with another person.

Sexual development, proper gender roles, and normal sexual behavior are all products of the culture in which an individual lives. Different cultures view sexuality and its expression in different ways. Although sexual and gender development are largely affected by biological factors, like other domains of development, they act upon and are acted upon by social, cognitive, and environmental influences.

Practice Questions

1. **The idea that cognitive development is impacted by both biological and environmental factors best represents the theoretical perspective of which person?**
   (Lower order)

   (A) Jean Piaget
   (B) Sigmund Freud
   (C) Lawrence Kohlberg
   (D) Konrad Lorenz
   (E) Lev Vygotsky

The correct answer is E. Lev Vygotsky.
Vygotsky believed that social factors greatly affect a child's cognitive development. He was critical of Piaget's cognitive development theory because it did not consider social factors. Sigmund Freud's theory focused on psychosexual development, and Kohlberg's theory centered on moral development. Konrad Lorenz contributed to attachment theory with his concept of imprinting.

2. Alicia's curfew is 10:00. When she arrives home 30 minutes late, her parents express concern and frustration. They remind Alicia about the importance of rules and the reason for the rule. They let Alicia know that there will be consequences for her actions, but they first want to know why Alicia was out past her curfew. Which type of parenting style do Alicia's parents have? *(Higher order)*

(A) Permissive

(B) Insecure

(C) Authoritative

(D) Authoritarian

(E) Indulgent

The correct answer is C: Authoritative.

Authoritative parents set clear and reasonable behavioral standards, and they consistently enforce the rules. However, they also care about the thoughts of their children and allow their children to have some role in setting the rules. They discuss the rationale for the rules. These parents are warm and nurturing and communicate with their children. Permissive parents are warm and nurturing but they have few, if any rules. Insecure refers to an attachment pattern, not a parenting style. Authoritarian parents have strict rules and high behavioral expectations. They do not discuss the reason for the rules, and they are rigid and inflexible. They are not very nurturing or supportive. The term indulgent is often used to describe permissive parents.

Challenge Question:

3. **Analyze and discuss Freud's and Erikson's theories of development. In what ways are the theories similar? In what ways do they differ? Provide clear and specific examples in your analysis and discussion. In your opinion, which theory is more relevant and useful in understanding development? Support your argument by clearly stating your reasons and providing specific examples.**

Chapter 10: Personality

Personality
Key Terms, Concepts, and People

Personality

Conscious mind

Id

Superego

Reality principle

Repression

Reaction formation

Rationalization

Denial

Basic anxiety

Neo-Freudian

Shadow

Animus

Personal unconscious

Complexes

Inferiority complex

Social interest

Self-actualization

Self-concept

ncongruence

Unconditional positive regard

Triadic reciprocality/reciprocal determinism

Self-efficacy

Internal locus of control

Personal-construct theory

Nomothetic traits

Factor analysis

Cardinal dispositions

Secondary dispositions

Self-concept

Self-understanding

Psychoanalytic theory

Unconscious mind

Pleasure principle

Ego

Defense mechanisms

Displacement

Compensation

Regression

Sublimation

Psychodynamic

Persona

Anima

Self

Collective unconscious

Archetypes

Superiority complex

Humanistic theories

Self-esteem

Conditions of worth

Social-cognitive theories

Locus of control theory

External locus of control

Trait theories

Idiographic traits

Big Five trait theory

Central dispositions

Temperament

Self-esteem

Me-self

I-self	Physical self
Active self	Social self
Psychological self	Halo effect
Reliability	Validity
Barnum effect	

Personality Assessments:

Eysenck Personality Inventory

Rorschach inkblot test; Thematic Apperception Test (TAT)

Minnesota Multiphasic Personality Inventory (MMPI);

16 PF (Personality Factor) Questionnaire

Key People: Sigmund Freud; Karen Horney; Nancy Chodorow; Carl Jung; Alfred Adler; Hans Eysenck; Abraham Maslow; Carl Rogers; Raymond Cattell; Paul Costa; Albert Bandura; Robert McCrae; Gordon Allport; Julian Rotter; Walter Mischel; George Kelly; Mary Rothbart; Jerome Kagan; B.F. Skinner

Overview

Personality is a pattern of relatively enduring traits and characteristics of a person. Psychologists from many different approaches explain the formation, growth, and adjustment of personality in different ways. Theories of personality can be divided into five general categories: psychoanalytic, humanistic, social-cognitive, behavioral, and trait theories.

Personality Theories and Approaches

Psychoanalytic Theories

Sigmund Freud developed one of the most famous of personality theories, that of the *psychoanalytic approach*. Freud divided the mind into two levels, the conscious and unconscious. The *conscious mind* contains everything we are aware of at any point in a given day. The *unconscious mind*, on the other hand, consists of ideas and thoughts of which we are unaware and to which we do not have easy access. According to Freud, the unconscious mind has a major motivating influence on behavior.

The mind is further divided into three parts: the id, the ego, and the superego. The id is the most basic, primal part of the unconscious, and it exists at birth. The *id* is the core of the personality; it is the part of the unconscious that seeks to immediately satisfy basic pleasant desires through the *pleasure principle*. The id is contained solely in the unconscious mind and has no sense of reality. The *ego* operates partly in the conscious and partly in the unconscious mind. It develops from the id during infancy, and it acts as a mediator between the id and reality. It is the part of the mind that enable the person to make decisions, think logically, and function in the environment by satisfying the drives and desires of the id only when it is feasible to do so; this principle is known as the *reality principle.* The *superego* is that part of the mind that develops last. Like the ego, the superego operates partly in the conscious and partly in the unconscious mind. The superego is comparable to a conscience. It represents ideas of right and wrong, social rules and mores, and morality. It is the complete opposite of the id.

Part of the job of the ego is to protect the conscious mind from threats of the unconscious mind and to relieve the tension between the id and superego by using defense mechanisms.

Repression: Blocking threatening feelings or thoughts from coming to conscious awareness and pushing these thoughts into the unconscious. For example, a child who was abused may force those memories into her unconscious and have no memory of the abuse.

Denial: Not accepting the truth or threatening beliefs or actions. For example, a teenage girl whose boyfriend just broke up with her may tell her friends that they are still dating.

Displacement: Redirecting unwanted feelings away from the source of the feelings to an object or person that is less threatening. A boy who is angry with his mother may take his frustration out on a favorite toy.

Reaction formation: When a person acts the opposite of how he truly feels, but does so in an exaggerated way. For example, a young girl whose boyfriend broke up with her may tell her friends that she cannot stand the ex-boyfriend and her expressions of hatred toward him are exaggerated.

Rationalization: Coming up with valid excuses for unacceptable feelings or actions. A person who steals money may attempt to justify his behavior by telling himself that the owner has plenty of money and that he needs the money in order to buy food.

Regression: Returning to an earlier and more infantile stage. For example, a woman who is going through a divorce may revert back to an earlier stage and react to the anxiety by staying in bed all day and burying her head in the blanket.

Sublimation: Redirecting sexual or aggressive desires into a more socially acceptable goal. According to Freud, sublimation is healthy and beneficial to both the individual and the social group. For example, a sculptor may redirect his sexual desires toward creating another sculpture that can be enjoyed by a large social group.

Compensation: Making up for failures in one area by succeeding in another area. For example, a man with a failed marriage may throw himself into his work, where he is very successful.

Criticisms of Freud

Karen Horney and **Nancy Chodorow** viewed much of Freud's theory to be biased against women. Horney developed her own theory of personality that focused on the innate need for security. She presented the idea that social and cultural experiences, especially those of childhood, strongly influence personality development. If children do not have their need for love satisfactorily met, they will experience *basic anxiety*. Basic anxiety is described as feelings of being alone, isolated, and helpless in a world that seems unfamiliar and hostile. In order to experience security in adult relationships, children must have their needs for security and love met during childhood. Children who do not have these needs met will suffer from feelings of insecurity and mistrust as adults, resulting in unhealthy relationships and problematic personality styles.

Freud's theory was not based on empirical study, but rather on *case studies and observation*. Some of Freud's ideas have been supported by research, but others have not. Further, Freud's focus on the unconscious has been controversial. Also, many psychologists believe that Freud put too much emphasis on sex, sexual motivation and early childhood; research does not support Freud's belief that personality has basically been formed and set by the age of five.

Psychodynamic Theories

Those who based much of their theory on Freud's ideas also are considered to be psychoanalytic theorists. Theories that took some of Freud's basic ideas and built upon them are considered as *psychodynamic* or *Neo-Freudian*. Two of the most well-known followers of Freud who later went on to develop their own psychodynamic theories are Carl Jung and Alfred Adler.

Carl Jung asserted that the mind consists of a conscious level and an unconscious level. Jung divided the unconscious into two parts: the collective unconscious and the personal unconscious. The *personal unconscious* contains all the repressed thoughts and experiences of the person. The personal unconscious contains *complexes,* which are thoughts, feelings, and memories that carry with them strong, and often threatening or painful, emotions. The *collective unconscious,* which is the part of the unconscious mind that consists of ancestral knowledge and experiences that are passed down from generation to generation, is more important than an individual's personal experiences. The collective unconscious contains memories, images, thoughts and behaviors that are common to all people. These are called *archetypes*. Archetypes are two opposing forces within the same person. There are several archetypes conceptualized by Jung. The *persona* is the side of the personality that the person shows to others. The *shadow*, in contrast, is the person's dark side. The shadow consists of characteristics and tendencies we do not want to acknowledge, yet we try to hide these characteristics from ourselves and those around us. Two other opposite archetypes are the *anima* (a female side) and an *animus* (a male side). Jung called the largely unconscious core portion of the personality the *Self.*

Alfred Adler viewed childhood as being the most important period for personality development. Unlike Freud, Adler emphasized the role of the conscious. According to Adler, all children are born with some sort of physical deficiency that creates feelings of inferiority. These feelings of inferiority will motivate the child to strive either for superiority or success. Individuals with an *inferiority complex* strive for superiority and have little to no concern for others, whereas individuals with a *superiority complex* strive for success and are motivated by *social interest*. Individuals motivated by social interest are concerned with helping others and with setting goals that will benefit all of society. Adler also was interested in how birth order affects personality development.

Humanistic Theories

Humanistic theories view humans as being innately good. They are more concerned with the whole of a person, rather than the parts of a person (ex. unconscious, id, ego). Humanistic theories focus on the subjective thoughts and experiences of a person. Humanistic theory believes each individual can take control over his destiny by using free will. The view holds that people can overcome their past. Concepts important to humanistic theories are self-esteem and self-concept. The main purpose of living, according to the humanist approach, is to achieve *self-actualization*. Self-actualization is the process of becoming all one can be in a manner that is psychologically healthy. It can also be described as attaining one's full potential.

Abraham Maslow and Carl Rogers are the theorists whose names are synonymous with humanistic psychology.

Abraham Maslow's theory focuses on a hierarchy of needs. The assumption of this hierarchy was that lower level needs must be met before higher level needs can be satisfied. Each of the five needs serve motivational purposes. The need at the top of the hierarchy is self-actualization. According to Maslow, self-actualization can only be achieved after esteem needs are met. *Self-esteem* is not dependent on what others think, but is based on the person's feelings of confidence, competence, and worth.

Carl Rogers' person-centered theory is based on the assumption that all people move toward self-actualization. The self, as proposed by Rogers, is the most important part of personality. Each individual develops a *self-concept*, which includes all aspects of how we see ourselves. When a gap exists between how one wishes to be and how one actually is, *incongruence* occurs. In order for healthy personality development to occur, individuals must receive certain things from their interactions with others. One thing all individuals, especially children, need from others is unconditional positive regard. *Unconditional positive regard* means to love and accept people without any conditions. Unfortunately, many people do not receive unconditional positive regard; instead, they perceive that others accept and love them only if certain expectations are met, a concept referred to as *conditions of worth*. In other words, the acceptance and love of the person are conditional. For example, a parent who makes her child feel like she will only be accepted if she makes the cheerleading squad is placing a condition of worth on the child. When individuals receive unconditional positive regard, they can begin to work towards self-actualization.

Criticisms of Humanistic Theory

One of most common criticisms of humanistic theory is that the theories are not supported by empirical evidence. Another common criticism is that humanistic theories are overly optimistic about human nature.

Social-Cognitive Theories

Social-cognitive theories focus on both the environment and the thoughts of the individual. Through our environments, we learn, observe, develop and alter our thoughts and other cognitive constructs, which form the basis of personality.

Albert Bandura's theory assumes an interaction between behaviors, environment, and personal factors. This assumption is based on the concept of *triadic reciprocality*, also referred to as *reciprocal determinism*. The interaction between these three factors is ongoing, which each factor affecting the other two. The personal factors Bandura focused on were mostly cognitive—anticipation, planning, and memory, for example.

One strong influence on personality is a person's sense of self-efficacy. *Self-efficacy* refers to an individual's expectations and beliefs about his ability to achieve a certain task in a given situation. If someone has a high level of self-efficacy for a certain task, the greater the likelihood the person will actually be able to do the task.

The *locus-of-control theory*, which was proposed by **Julian Rotter**, is another important social-cognitive theory. Each person has either an internal or external locus-of-control. A person with an *internal locus-of-control* attributes success or failure to his own efforts, whereas a person with *external locus-of-control* will attribute success or failure to external factors, or even luck or chance.

George Kelly developed the *personal-construct theory*. People give meanings and interpretations to events; these are called constructs. These constructs are unique to each individual and can change or be replaced over time. People's behavior is affected by these constructions because these constructs help people understand their world. It is the person's constructs that make up their reality, and their constructs may or may not be an accurate reflection of the world. Personal constructs tell someone how things/people are similar and different. The similarities and differences must occur along the same dimension. For example, two people may be seen as being ugly or pretty when compared, but for the interpretation to be a personal construct, one person cannot be pretty and the other smart. Attractiveness and intelligence are two different dimensions. Ugly/pretty and smart/dumb would be accurate examples of personal constructs.

Criticisms of Social-Cognitive Theories

In general, social-cognitive theories do not consider the impact of biological factors and inherited traits on personality formation and development. These theories also do not address how affective and emotional processes affect personality or behavior.

Behaviorist Theories

The most influential behaviorist theory was that of **B.F. Skinner**. Skinner believed that one's environment determines one's personality. As such, Skinner would say that personality can only be defined in terms of behavior. He emphasized the importance of reinforcement contingencies that occur within one's environment on shaping and changing behavior. Since behavior can be changed, so can personality.

Criticisms of Behaviorist Theories

One of the most common and significant criticisms of behaviorist theories is that they do not consider how cognitive processes influence behavior, social interactions, and personality. Many of the social-cognitive theorists discussed in the above section combined both behaviorist theory and cognitive theory to form their own social-cognitive theories.

Trait Theories

Trait theories focus on understanding the traits (characteristics) that describe people's personalities. In general, trait theorists view personality traits as being inherited, with little focus on how the environment may influence personality development. Rather, it is someone's traits that determine how they will interact with their environment and will create personal experiences. *Nomothetic traits* are those that are common to all personalities, or universal, and *idiographic traits* are those that are not universal; that is, they are unique for each individual. An example of an idiographic trait is trusting. One person may be very trusting of others while another person is much more suspicious of others. Trait theories are based on *factor analysis* procedures that use correlational studies to measure personality factors and group them into clusters.

Hans Eysenck developed a biologically based trait factor theory. He believed that biology and hereditary factors have a large role in determining one's personality traits. The three dimensions of personality Eysenck described are extraversion/introversion, neuroticism (instability)/stability, and psychoticism/superego. According to Eysenck, all people fall somewhere within each of these three dimensions. The uniqueness of each person's personality can be understood in how much of each trait in each of the three dimensions that person exhibits. Eysenck's three factor theory is an example of a nomothetic theory because all people have some degree of these traits.

Paul Costa and **Robert McCrae** developed the *Big Five trait theory*. The five stable traits of this theory are extraversion, neuroticism, openness, agreeableness, and conscientiousness. Costa and McCrae saw these traits as basic tendencies or core components of the personality, but they also viewed them as being influenced by the environment, experiences, and psychological and cognitive processes, as well as biological processes. **Raymond Cattell** believed in common traits shared by many humans and unique traits, those specific for each individual. Traits were also divided into source traits and surface traits. Cattell described sixteen source traits, which are found on his *16 Personality Factors Questionnaire (16 PF Scales)*.

Gordon Allport placed much emphasis on the uniqueness of each person. His study of the individual is referred to as *idiographic approach*, Allport proposed the concept of personal dispositions, which are specific to each individual. Allport categorized three levels of personal dispositions. *Cardinal dispositions* are those that are dominant in the person. *Central dispositions* are those that stand out the most in an individual and are the traits around which someone's life is focused. *Secondary dispositions* are not central to the individual's personality, but they are more numerous than central dispositions and account for much of a person's behaviors.

Walter Mischel presented the view that situations affect behavior. He believed that a person's traits are not consistent across all situations. The person and situations interact, with both affecting the person's behavior. Some traits are more consistent than others. A person's behavior is affected by personal traits and by cognitive and affective processes.

Criticisms of Trait Theories

A couple of criticisms of trait theories need to be noted. Many traits theories do not consider the impact of situations or the environment on one's behavior. Further, trait theories are unable to explain exactly how one's personality forms, develops and changes. Also, not all traits described by these theories take cultural differences into account. For example, many of the traits described in the Big Five trait model do not explain aspects of the personalities of Asian people.

Growth and Adjustment

Self-Concept and Self-Esteem

Personality growth and development is affected by self-concept and self-esteem. *Self-concept* can be described as how we perceive ourselves; it is our beliefs about our nature, qualities and behaviors, whereas *self-esteem* describes our overall sense of self-worth and value. Both of these terms relate to *self-understanding*, or an awareness of oneself, including understanding your attitudes, motives, strengths and weaknesses, among other things. Self-understanding consists of two parts: the *I-self*, or subjective knower, and the *Me-self*, or the object that is known. The *Me-self* consists of internalized knowledge of oneself based on what has been learned through interactions with others, including their attitudes of and perceptions of ourselves, and our environments. It consists of four parts: the physical self, the active self (behavior), the social self (social interactions) and the psychological self (personality, feelings). The *I-self* represents the way the individual responds to the attitudes of culture or society.

Self-esteem is affected by our interactions with others and by how we compare ourselves with others. When our interactions with others are positive and our comparison of ourselves to others are positive, our self-esteem is likely to be higher than if either of those factors is negative. The *Halo effect* occurs when someone has an inflated self-concept across different domains, such as social, physical, academic, or family relationships. Self-esteem begins to develop in early toddlerhood and continues throughout life. As children mature, they are able to form and change their opinions about their physical, social, cognitive, and behavioral domains. With maturity, children also begin to evaluate themselves across more domains, and they begin to describe themselves based on their innate psychological traits. Self-esteem and self-concept are both affected by cultural factors and social roles. Some societies value certain traits over others and actively encourage and promote those traits. Social roles, which are also largely dictated by the society in which one lives, also affect self-esteem and self-concept. If someone is acceptably fulfilling the social roles prescribed by their culture, they will view themselves more positively, as well as be viewed more positively by others.

Temperament is described as stable patterns of relating to others and the environment that are present at birth. Differences in temperament can explain differences in people's personality. **Mary Rothbart** proposed three dimensions of temperament: surgency/extraversion, negative affect, and effortful control. Surgency includes positive anticipation and increased activity levels. Negative affect refers to anger, frustration, fear, and sadness, and effortful control refers to a person's ability to regulate impulses, ability to focus and direct attention, and to regulate their emotions.

Jerome Kagan conducted research on a temperamental category known as "reactivity." Children with high levels of reactivity demonstrated high levels of distress, frustration, and anxiety. They elicited a high level of fear of unfamiliar or new situations, which Kagan labeled as inhibited. Children with high levels of reactivity experienced increased levels of physiological arousal, as indicated by increased heart rate and greater muscle tension.

Assessment Techniques

When discussing psychological assessment techniques, one must understand the importance of validity and reliability. *Reliability* refers to consistency and stability across multiple applications and clinical trials, whereas *validity* means that the test measures what it is intended to measure. A test can be reliable but not valid, but a test cannot be valid without also being reliable.

Projective assessments

Psychoanalytic assessments are usually subjective and not based on empirical research. These types of assessments may be broadly interpreted by the therapist so as to support the therapist's hypothesis with little evidence. Frequently, psychoanalytic assessment techniques are based on case studies, interviews, and observation. Examples of assessments used in psychoanalytic approaches are free association and dream analysis/recall. In *free association*, the patient relaxes and gets calm and begins to report things that come into his mind while the therapist listens. The therapist looks for themes that may help him determine the root cause of the patient's problems. In *dream analysis*, the therapist analyzes the patient's dreams to look for *Freudian symbols* that may represent items or events in the unconscious. For example, a knife may represent male genitalia, and ships may represent female genitalia.

The *Rorschach inkblot test* asks the client to look at a series of ambiguous inkblots then describe what they see. This test is highly subjective.

With the *Thematic Apperception Test*, the client is shown a neutral but ambiguous picture and is asked to devise a story to tell what is going on in the picture.

These tests are thought to give the therapist insight into the unconscious mind of the patient. However, because of the ambiguous nature of these types of assessments, reliability is an issue of concern because the therapist can interpret the client's answers very broadly.

Self-report Inventories

Humanistic theorists, trait theorists and cognitive-behavioral theorists often use self-report inventories or questionnaires and interviews. Self-report questionnaires offer some objectivity in interpreting results, but interviews can be more subjective and left to the interpretation of the therapist.

Examples of common trait theory self-report inventories are the Minnesota Multiphasic Personality Inventory (MMPI), the Eysenck Personality Inventory, and the

16 PF (Personality Factor) Questionnaire. The *Minnesota Multiphasic Personality Inventory* is one of the most commonly used assessment tools for measuring personality traits. The MMPI is also used to evaluate for mental disorders. The *Eysenck Personality Inventory* examine each of the three dimensions of personality proposed by Hans Eysenck. The 16 Personality Factor Questionnaire measures and describes the 16 source personality factors proposed by Robert Cattell.

Many self-report questionnaires and surveys rely on the honesty of participants. However, many participants may not be totally honest when responding to these types of inventories, so many of the assessments have built in methods of detecting and controlling for dishonest answers. Also, many individuals who fill out these types of assessments are curious about the results; as a result, many people have been deceived by dishonest individuals who want to make an easy profit. Psychics and astrologers are two examples of those who use people's natural curiosity in order to deceive them. The reason these types of individuals can so easily deceive people is based on the *Barnum effect*, which is the propensity people have to perceive themselves and their personality characteristics in vague, ill-defined ways.

Practice Questions

1. **Amelia is angry with her boss for adding a new project to her tasks. When Amelia arrives home, she argues with her children, gets mad at them, and sends them to bed early. Which defense mechanism is Amelia using?**
   (Lower order)

   (A) reaction formation
   (B) sublimation
   (C) rationalization
   (D) compensation
   (E) displacement

The correct answer is E. Displacement.
Amelia is taking her unwanted feelings towards her boss out on people who are less threatening, her children. In reaction formation, the person acts the opposite of how she feels. Sublimation is redirecting one's sexual and aggressive drives to more socially acceptable goals. Rationalization involves creating excuses in order to justify one's actions or feelings. Compensation is used when a person who fails in one area directs energy to succeeding in another area.

2. **Which of the following statements best describes incongruence?**
    (Higher order)

    (A) Ken's marriage is ending so he throws himself into his work.
    (B) Marcy sees one group of her classmates as "cool" and the other group as "uncool."
    (C) Henry believes in having a good work ethic but he steals from his boss.
    (D) Candi makes a high score on her SAT and attributes her success to her intelligence.
    (E) Adam distances himself from his son when his son fails to make the football team.

The correct answer is C. Henry believes in having a good work ethic but he steals from his boss.

Incongruence refers to the gap that exists between who one wishes to be and who one actually is. Henry may wish to have a good work ethic, but he actually does not have a good work ethic, as evidenced by stealing from his boss. Choice A is an example of the defense mechanism of compensation. Choice B describes a personal construct. Choice D is an example of an internal locus-of-control, and Choice E illustrates the concept of conditions of worth.

Challenge Question:

3. **Max is known across many settings for being dishonest, grouchy, funny, intelligent, overly emotional, and ambitious. Which of the following statements is true?**

    (A) These characteristics indicate that Max needs to work on self-actualization.
    (B) These characteristics probably show that Max has a mental disorder.
    (C) These characteristics show that Max has a high level of self-esteem.
    (D) These characteristics describe Max's central dispositions.
    (E) These characteristics can change if Max explores his unconscious.

The correct answer is D. These characteristics describe Max's central disposition.

Central dispositions are those that stand out the most in an individual. Since Max demonstrates these traits across different settings and is known for these traits, these are the traits that people associate with Max. It will not hurt Max to work on self-actualization, but the type of traits someone has does not make achieving self-actualization any more or less important for them. There is no evidence that Max has a mental disorder. Some of his central dispositions are good and some are bad, but that does not indicate a mental disorder since all humans have good and bad personality traits. These traits also do not support the idea that Max has high self-esteem, and there is not enough information to make that assumption. Most likely, these characteristics will not change significantly, regardless of what type of therapy Max receives, especially that of exploring his unconscious mind.

Chapter 11: Testing and Individual Differences

Standardized Testing

For the AP Psychology Examination, testing refers in this chapter almost exclusively to standardized testing. In this chapter, we discuss standardized testing that is used for the purpose of measuring individual differences. In particular, we focus on standardized testing that is designed to measure intelligence. For an individual a standardized test of intelligence results in a specific score such as an IQ score for that individual. We also discuss the topic of intelligence in general. Intelligence is a slippery topic; how it is defined, who has it, who doesn't and what it should be used for. There is a highly political element associated with the nature of intelligence, and with the topic of standardized testing. In the end, these are much bigger discussions than what is required to answer AP Psychology questions on the subjects. We will focus on specifics in this chapter. We will address larger issues to the extent that they are relevant in terms of the AP Psychology exam

There is heavy overlap with the subject matter of this chapter and the methods chapter. We recommend you review the methods chapter before you tackle this chapter or that you review the methods chapter after reading this chapter. The two will reinforce each other and enhance you understanding of both chapters.

A broad distinction between types of testing is whether the test is administered to a group of people or to a single individual. Testing groups is (historically) less expensive and there is less interaction between the subjects and the test administrators so there is less source of error related to administrator subject interaction. The question then is why ever use individual testing at all when there is an option for group testing? The answer was that usually there was no reason. Sometimes the test is constructed such that it requires a one-on -one interaction between the subject and the test administrator. In other words, sometimes what is being tested does not lend itself to group testing. A historical example is the Rorschach inkblot test. This test required that the administer show the inkblot to the subject and that the subject explain to the administrator what the inkblot looks like. Really, you could automate this test but you get the idea. Other times it is just very important to determine a specific individual's overall abilities. An example is the individual oral examination that is required of every candidate for a PhD degree. With the advent of computerized administration of standardized tests, many of the factors that made group testing more desirable than individual testing have become less relevant.

In general, and historically, a standardized test is used to test individuals in a group setting. the questions on a standardized test are most commonly multiple choice format but they may also be true-false questions, short-answer questions, essay questions, or a mix of question types. It is becoming more common that an individual may be administered a computerized version of a standardized test and that the test candidate may have a choice of dates, times and locations, including locations that may be a single person environment, for the administration of the examination. What remains the same is that the standardized test is designed to produce a consistent, reliable normal distribution of scores for a particular population of interest. This begins with the process of test design and development where questions are constructed to measure what the test is intended to measure and to ensure full coverage of the entire range of what is intended to be measured. This results in a repository or test bank of questions that are used to construct the test itself. The test generally consists of more than one version and this is a key concept. There is a misconception that a standardized test should be exactly the same questions for everyone who takes the test. In other words, there should be one and only one version of a standardized examination. If this were the case, the test would rapidly become useless as test takers reported the test content to others. The goal of standardization is to be able to generate equivalent exams. The details of how test bank questions are used to create different versions of a test are beyond the scope of the AP examination but the result is that equivalent questions or groups of questions can be switched in and out to create equivalent versions of the exam.

The next stage of development is to establish that any one version of the exam will measure what it is intended to measure when it is administered to the population that it is intended to evaluate. For instance, the law school admission test (LSAT) intends to evaluate all the candidates for admission to law school. To make these determinations experiments are conducted. These experiments are test runs or pilot programs where a subpopulation of subjects are selected to be a true random sample of the of the tests target population. If the selection of a true random sample is impractical then every practical effort is made to ensure that the test group is fairly representative of the overall population. Test versions of the exam are generated and administered to the test subject groups and the results are analyzed to estimate the validity and reliability of the test. As we have mentioned, one of the possible fundamental objectives of a standardized test is to create a basis to compare an individual's performance to the performance profile of all members of a population. That performance profile is the normal scoring distribution curve for the examination. It is intended to represent the distribution that would occur if every single member of the population took the examination. As we discussed in the methods chapter if the sample population is selected with proper randomized selection procedures and if the population is of sufficient size then researchers or test designers can calculate p values that demonstrates the test scoring distribution curve is probably a very accurate representation of the overall populations scoring distribution. Once that is established the test can establish population scoring norms including a mean score and other measures of variance from the mean score including standard deviation scores from the mean. This allows for the testing of individual differences within a group and also for differences between groups.

Psychometric Testing

When we test a human being, we are performing research. In the methods chapter we identified a standardized testing as a form of observational research. In this chapter the issue is what is being tested for and how is it being tested? In psychology, we are testing for psychological (or neurological) things that subjects possess. Testing that attempts to quantify or measure how much of a psychological thing a person has is known as *psychometric testing*. Persons who design psychometric tests are called psychometricians. If we really are accurate in defining what is actually observed or what data is obtained when subjects engage in psychometric testing, we are usually observing what bubbles a person fills in on pieces of paper when they are in a specific environment. Therefore, we are never directly observing the psychological thing we want to measure. That is the fundamental problem with psychometric testing.

This is not an esoteric philosophical issue. When a person sits for the medical college admission test, there are huge issues at stake, for the test taker it his or her life as a physician vs life as not a physician. For the rest of society, it is the consequences of allowing a particular person to be a physician. That is just about as important as things get at a personal level and at the level of potential impact to the members of a society. Now the MCAT is not a psychometric test but many medical schools also require a psychometric test such as the *Minnesota Multiphasic Personality Inventory (MMPI)* to determine if they will accept or reject an applicant for their MD training programs. In a legal context, whether or not an individual is sent to jail or perhaps even executed for a crime he or she is convicted of can depend on the results of court ordered psychometric testing. In particular, the US and other national and international courts have addressed whether the *IQ score* of an individual can be an absolute standard to prohibit the application of the *death penalty*. Specifically, these courts have already ruled or are actively considering that individuals with an IQ score that is below a certain level cannot be sentenced to death under any circumstances.

Reliability

A test is reliable to the extent that an individual receives the same score on the test regardless of when or what versions of the test he or she takes. At a statistical level the scoring distribution curve for a given population should not change or be influenced by other factors. However, of course, other factors absolutely will change test performance particularly what time and under what external circumstances the test is administered. That is why a well-constructed standardized testing of groups of test takers includes not just a well-constructed test but also a well-controlled environment. The time of day and the conditions of the test taking facility should be as consistent and uniform as possible. It is not covered in the AP exam but one element of an examinations reliability is durability — that they are resistant to the environment in which they are administered so that equivalent scores tend to occur regardless of the conditions under which they are administered. Still even the largest and best-controlled tests have shown different score distribution curves depending on what time of year they are administered and in what particular year they are administered and in what geographical region they are administered. Sometimes these differences are surprisingly large. The testing authorities will compensate or renormalize scores so that they are consistent with historical overall averages up to a certain point. Sometimes these scoring discrepancies require further investigation to determine what precisely is causing them - sometimes its widespread cheating. Sometimes that cheating is at a nationwide level.

The AP exam expects you to know three specific types of methods to assess the reliability of standardized tests; 1) the *test-retest* method involves the administration of the exact same test to individuals on two separate occasions. The two separate test scores are statistically analyzed and a correlation coefficient can be calculated. A perfect test-retest correlation coefficient is a positive +1 coefficient (it is also a highly suspicious correlation coefficient). 2) *Split-half* methods of estimating reliability divide it into two halves. The two halves can be administered to the same individuals or groups or to different individuals or groups. Again, the scores of the two halves of the test can be compared and a correlation coefficient calculated just as it is for a test -retest correlation. Sophisticated split-half methodologies can generate any possible versions of the two halves of an examination. 3) *Alternate forms* methods give two separate complete versions of the test to the same persons or groups on two separate occasions. Correlation coefficients are calculated as described for the previous two methods.

Types of Reliability

Split-half Reliability

Does half of the test correlate with the other half?
Based on the correlation between two halves of the same test.
The closer to +1 the better the reliability.

Test-retest Reliability

Does the test correlate with itself if given twice to participants at different times?
Based on the correlation between the first scores and the second scores at a later date.
The closer the correlation is to +1 the higher the reliability.

Alternate Forms Reliability

Does the test show a relationship with another version of the same test?
Based on the correlation between the two versions of the same test.
The closer the correlation is to +1 the higher the reliability.

Validity

It is virtually impossible to prove that a psychometric standardized test is valid. Theoretically, it is impossible to prove anything but if you want to split hairs, we cannot ever have anywhere near the confidence that we are accurately testing for a psychological thing compared to the confidence that we are accurately testing for a physical quantity like temperature or mass. There always must be an assumption that correct answers to questions are an indication of the amount of a psychological thing that a person possesses. That is a built in fundamental uncertainty in the validity of any psychometric testing.

Types of Validity

Face Validity

Does the test "appear" to measure what it is designed to measure?

Based on a logical or rational look at the test

Criterion-related Validity

Does the test show a real relationship with variables it should be related to?

Based on the correlation between test scores and a criterion variable or behavior

Content-related Validity

Does the content of the test match theoretically with the concept being tested?

Based on a panel of experts' opinion

Concurrent Validity

Is there a strong relationship between scores on the test and scores on similar tests?

Based on the correlation between the test scores of similar tests

Construct Validity

Is the operational definition of the test consistent with the concept being tested?

Based on empirical studies using different methods to prove

Predictive Validity

Is there a relationship between scores on the test and performance at a later date?

Based on the correlation between the test score and a future criterion variable

Face/Content Validity

Content or face validity is sometimes described as a superficial type of validity. It is literally validity on its face or how it appears to persons who decides if a test's content is actually testing what it is supposed to be testing. This does not mean it is a crude or trivial measure of validity. It usually does require an opinion of an expert to determine if test questions are actually testing what they are supposed to test for and that the questions cover the full range of what is being tested for. If there are no other sources to judge this validity, such as other types of tests, previous versions of the test or theories about the test subject, the expert judgment of the face validity of an exam is the only validity of the test. At the most imprecise level, face validity may be that the best that an expert can say about the matter is "well, I have no specific basis to say this is valid except that it feels about right to me."

A distinction may sometimes be made between general face validity and content validity. *Content validity* is based on expert opinion of completeness - that the content fairly and proportionately tests for the full range of the thing that is being tested for and appropriateness - that the content is focused on this thing and does not include content that is extraneous or unrelated to what is being tested for. For the AP Psychology exam, think of face or content validity as an expert's general opinion about how clear or obvious it is that the material will test for what it is intended to test for. If the expert says this is obviously not material that will measure what one wishes to measure, then there is no face validity to the test. If the expert conclusion is that, unquestionably, the material will a very accurate measure of what one wishes to measure, that is about as high as the face validity of an exam can be.

Construct validity

The expert opinion may improve if there is a theoretical basis to make a judgment about the validity of an exam. The expert may say, "There is a very well-supported theory about what we are testing for, based on this theory, this test content should accurately measure what we are testing for." This type of validity is known as construct validity. It is still a subjective judgment so it is a form of face validity but not for the AP Psychology exam (unless you choose to make the case in a free response question). In is also an expert opinion that can be designed into the new test during its construction (hence the name - construct validity). Construct validity can show a clear connection to a theory about what the test is intended to measure and the content of the test. Based on the theory, the expert can make a rational argument to explain why the content of an exam will likely measure what the test is intended to measure. Construct validity depends on the quality of the argument and the quality of the theory. Ideally, the argument is a formal logical argument and the theory is so well founded that it is considered to be a physical law of nature. In general, there are good arguments and bad arguments and good theories and bad theories; so there is a continuum for construct validity from none to practically perfect. Never theoretically perfect, the null hypothesis is that it is all due to chance and that can never be ruled out.

After trial runs or actual administration of the new test, the construct validity of the test can be assessed retroactively. For instance, the theory may predict that an overall test score should increase as the age of the test taker increases or that one type of subscore in the test should decrease as the birth order of test takers increase. These would be positive and negative correlations that are predicted by theory. After a new test is administered the test results can be analyzed and an overall correlation coefficient calculated for test results and the correlations predicted by theory. A perfect correlation coefficient of +1 shows a perfect construct validity correlation. Still, if it is a bad theory, well-then one might say the validity of the construct validity is not so good.

Criterion-Related Validity

Criterion-related measures validity by correlating a measure with a criterion or external measure. The AP psychology exam expects you to be familiar with the following two types of criterion related validities.

Concurrent Validity

Concurrent validity is the degree to which a new test correlates with older tests that are agreed to be valid for measuring what the new test is intended to measure. Again, after the new test is administered the results can be compared to the other tests and a correlation coefficient can be calculated. If there is an older test that is agreed to be (almost) perfectly valid then a new test that results in a perfect correlation with this older test has perfect concurrent validity. Often there is an older test that has shown itself to be superior to all others in measuring what it was intended to measure This is informally referred to as the gold standard of tests for the intended measurement. All definitions of concurrent validity describe them as being available right away or concurrently with collection of the test results upon the very first administration of a new examination - hence the name "concurrent". Again, in a free response question you may wish to argue that concurrent reliability may be a very restrictive definition. Some "concurrent-ish" types of validation may be subtle at the first administration of a test but can become more apparent or emerge over time and can improve as the test is administered more frequently and over longer periods of time.

Predictive Validity

The degree to which a test predicts future outcomes is called predictive validity. Content and construct validity may be established before a new test is administered and along with concurrent validity can be assessed after the first administration of a new test. Depending on how far down the line a prediction of a test takes to be measured, the first assessment of predictive validity may not occur for many years after the first administration of the test. This is the case, for example, with the SAT the ACT and the GRE. The SAT and ACT are intended to measure or predict the future performance of students in college. The GRE is used to predict the future performance of students in graduate school. With increasing time, a test may demonstrate increasingly strong predictive validity. Sometimes a formerly strongly predictive test becomes less predictive. This can be new information that something new has occurred. The test did not change but something significant has. It is usually important to conduct research to determine what that something actually is.

Achievement Tests vs. Aptitude Tests

A pristine or pure achievement test would test only for something that you currently possess and at the same time say or mean nothing or imply anything other than the simple fact that you do in fact possess this thing or these things. In physical terms, this is an inventory. We could examine or take an inventory of what items are contained in your left front pants pocket. The ideal that this inventory could be devoid of any other meaning is impossible. We could make all sorts of conclusions and assumptions about you based on that inventory, including what you may have the potential to do in the future. A pristine or pure aptitude test might be thought of as a machine that showed every one of your possible futures. That is not quite the same thing as an aptitude. An aptitude is a potential; it is a theoretical concept that is a quantifiable. We believe we can measure it with a test and say for instance that you have twice as much aptitude to be a lawyer as this other person. By aptitude we mean that under exactly similar circumstances, beginning precisely at the point in time where we measure one's aptitude, we can predict that if you do attempt something you will be more successful than others who are exactly like you in every way except they have a lower aptitude for that thing than you.

Now to the AP psychology exam - An achievement test measures something you have achieved - something that you have learned or something that you have accomplished. An example is a standardized math test. It is intended to be used for the sole purpose of assigning you a grade for a math class or another immediate purpose, but not for the purpose of predicting anything about you in the future. The math achievement test say only that you have achieved this score and in terms of achievement, you currently possess this score level of proven mathematical understanding and ability to solve problems. You can compare your score to the overall score distribution curve and see exactly how much math ability you have demonstrated compared to others who took the same exam. For the AP psychology exam an aptitude test measures ability or potential - it makes a quantified estimate of the likelihood that you will be successful at something if you decide to do so. You may not realize it but Colleges have a scale that converts your SAT or ACT score into a very precise percentage. Actually, they have many exact percentages that correspond to your score. They have a percentage that corresponds to the likelihood that you will drop out of college. They have a percentage that predicts what your GPA will be if you graduate. They have a percentage that predicts how likely you will be to go on to graduate school. An aptitude test, for the AP exam, measures your relative capacity to succeed at something if you chose to do so. However, in real life, aptitude tests can be and are used for other purposes. They do not simply measure what you are capable of doing in the future. They can actually predict what you will do in the future. Theoretically and practically there is no such thing as a pure achievement test and no aptitude test is without measurement of things one has achieved.

Regardless of whether a test is intended to be primarily an achievement test, as an aptitude test or something in between, there are two general features or qualities of cognitive function that can be measured with a high degree of accuracy. Simply stated these are: 1) how fast can one think? and 2) what is the highest level of complexity at which one can think? To measure these, a test will include question sets that are designed to function as speed tests and power tests. A speed test consists of a large number of questions or tasks that must be answered within a limited amount of time, say 100 questions in 20 minutes for instance. Ideally, the level of difficulty should be within the abilities of most or all of the testing population to solve given enough time (which is not given). Simple one or two-digit addition problems are a common type of problem used in speed tests. If the speed tests wishes to determine the absolute upper limit of the test populations' abilities, it should be impossible for any person in the population to complete all of the problems within the allotted time period.

A power test measures the upper limit of problem difficulty that an individual is capable of solving. It's an awkward thing to define in general terms, but it is simple to describe in practice. The set of problems in a power test begin with the easiest problems to solve and become progressively more difficult to solve. There should be adequate time to solve all the problems if an individual possess the cognitive power to solve them, but of course, there is a time limit. The most difficult problems generally should be solvable by some percentage of the test population but ideally there should be one or a few that are beyond anyone's abilities to solve. That's an interesting concept because should those problems actually be theoretically impossible to solve? Is there such a thing? (there actually is). There is really no need to do this; question designers can create problems that are theoretically solvable but require such extraordinary conceptual insight or raw mental computational power to solve that few if any humans have ever demonstrated an ability to do so within the time allotted by the examination.

Intelligence Testing

For the AP Psychology exam, note that **Francis Galton**, an English statistician and prominent early developer of psychometrics made the first well-documented attempt of develop a standardized method to rate an individual's intelligence, but he gave up and that's it as far as his contributions to the matter go

Is there, in every human brain, a system of neurons that are interconnected and capable of responding to each other is a way that fundamentally determines how efficiently and complexly information is processed? For purposes of this discussion, let's say there is and let's call this a fundamental thinking module. Furthermore, this fundamental thinking module will be or can be a vital element of any cognitive process or ability. Regardless of any other mental functions or any other considerations whatsoever, this thinking module will always serve to improve whatever cognitive process are occurring in the brain. It may not be the only thing that affects cognitive processes and in fact it is most certainly not the only thing affecting cognitive processes. However, it is the single most universal, most advanced and most highly specialized thinking-related thing in the human brain. Everything though related goes better with the fundamental thinking module. For purposes of this discussion, let's agree to call this fundamental thinking module general intelligence or just g intelligence. Now we have taken a position in the great intelligence debate. Let the debate begin and remember which side we are on.

Now really none of us can honestly say we do not believe that some people are just smarter than others. Not smarter in some ways but smarter in every way. If you really don't believe it, based on your experiences in life you must at least suspect that this might be true. Not only that, but that it seems that these smarter people tend to have smarter siblings and smarter parents and they all seem to just have a big advantage over everyone else in just about every facet of life. There is unfortunately the other side of the equation, that there are those who seem to be lacking normal intelligence.

The Binet-Simon Intelligence Test

The first person to develop an accepted standardized method to measure intelligence psychologist Alfred Binet, in collaboration with **Victor Henri** and **Théodore Simon** was inspired to do so by his concern and at the request of the French government that school children with low intelligence were at a severe disadvantage and if they could be identified they could receive special attention by the educational system to help compensate for their intellectual disadvantage. Binet's concerns were amplified by the countervailing opinion of others that these children were not simply deficient in intelligence but were literally ill. as in mentally ill, and should be removed from school and placed in mental institutions, in 1905 when the *Binet-Simon test* was published, these mental institutions were called insane asylums and their care and treatment of their inmates remains as one of the darkest blotches on the moral record of modern western civilization.

The Binet-Simon test introduced the concept of an age equivalent intelligence level or mental age for instance a typical 7-year-old would have intellectual capacities that exceed the typical 6-year-old but are surpassed by the typical 8-year-old. This was the first observation that intelligence increases with age. This allowed one to measure the severity of intellectual deficit in learning impaired children. For instance, a 10-year-old might score at the 6-year-old mental age level on the Binet-Simon scale. Binet's scale focused primarily on verbal abilities but he strongly believed that intelligence was multidimensional, and advocated for research to further investigate the nature of intellectual functions. Although Binet's views were that intelligence was remarkably diverse among individuals he did believe that there was a common controlling factor of practical judgement that operated at all levels or aspects of intelligence. In the intelligence debate, this is arguably comparable to Charles Spearman's concepts of a "g" intelligence and "s" intelligences.

As the intelligence debate progresses keep in mind the original standardized test for individual intelligence was born out of concern for the welfare of mentally challenged school children and that this test likely save uncounted thousands of these children from a lifelong nightmare existence in turn of the century mental institutions. It established an educational philosophy to individualized student education and provide programs to help special needs children. In that sense Binet is arguably the father the entire field of special education.

General (g) Intelligence

At the same time that Binet and and Simon were developing their standardized intelligence test that focused on verbal abilities, **Charles Spearman,** a British psychologist, was addressing his observations that the grades school children received in individual subjects tended to be similar for individual students. Those who received a C in one subject tended to receive C's in all subjects etc. In 1904 Spearman published the first factor analysis of this correlation of grades among specific school subjects and proposed that although there were specific types of intelligence or mental abilities, called *s intelligence* there appeared to by an underlying general or *g intelligence*. He proposed that g intelligence was a general ability that enhanced performance across the range of specific mental tasks that were assessed for in intelligence tests. These s intelligence abilities included not only Binet's verbal abilities, but visual abilities as well. Spearman noted that intelligence testing included abstract reasoning, verbal skills, arithmetic skills and general knowledge skills but that the overall intelligence score represents the individual's g intelligence. Therefore, general intelligence was a single entity or factor and could be represented by a single number. He concluded that that all mental performance could be thought of as different manifestations of g intelligence and that g or general intelligence was the essential nature of human intelligence.

The Stanford-Binet Intelligence Test

The Binet-Simon test was modified by **Lewis Terman,** a psychology professor at of Stanford University in 1916. Terman's test incorporated the *numerical IQ scale,* where a child's mental age divided by his or her chronological age multiplied by 100 is their individual IQ score. For instance, a 10-year-old who scored at the mental age of an 8-year-old would be assigned an IQ score of 80. All adults are considered to be a mental age of 20 years. The new test measured verbal and nonverbal abilities with five tests that including knowledge, quantitative reasoning, spatial perception, working memory and fluid reasoning. While The Binet test was used to identify school children with intellectual deficiencies, Terman's test was also used to not only identify lower IQ schoolchildren for purposes of specialized education but also was used to identify high IQ children and low and high IQ adults . This concept of the mentally gifted and the cognitively disabled gained prominent social relevancy with a nationwide public policy movements to discourage childbearing by those who were cognitively disabled and the emphasis of an individual's mentally gifted status as a primary criteria for determination of whom to appointment to high government, private sector and academic positions. Apparently, Stanford professors' tests are not their own tests but are actually Stanford University's tests, so Terman's revision of the Binet-Simon test became known as the Stanford-Binet intelligence test. The Stanford -Binet test has been a prominent intelligence test in the U.S. ever since and is currently in its fifth revised version.

Multiple Intelligences

LL Thurstone was an important contributor to the field of factor analysis and was instrumental in the adoption of the use of the standardized mean and standard deviation in modern IQ scores. Thurston was opposed to the notion of Spearman's general intelligence concept and formulated an alternative theory, that there were seven independent primary mental abilities or intelligence factors that individuals could possess to varying degrees. Thurston stated that there was no master or general intelligence that generated these primary mental abilities or that influenced their functions. These independent intelligent factors were word fluency, verbal comprehension, spatial visualization, number facility, associative memory, reasoning, and perceptual speed. Thurston continued to make important contribution to the development of intelligence scoring through factor analysis and his concept of independent primary mental abilities is commonly incorporated into many modern intelligence tests.

Non Intellectual Factors in Intelligence

David Wechsler was a major contributor to the great intelligence debate both as a theoretician and as arguably the most important developer of the modern intelligence test. Wechsler was one of the most prominent psychologists of his day and was a student of Spearman's. While the debate was heating up over Spearman's concept of a unifying general intelligence and Thurston's opposing view of multiple primary mental abilities, Wechsler championed the concept that factors that were not intellectual factors nevertheless are involved in intelligent behavior. He further proposed that these non-intellective factors be included as a theoretical basis in the design and construction of intelligence tests. Wechsler incorporated these non-intellectual factors into his own broader definition of intelligence as an overall ability to function purposefully, rationally and effectively in the context of one's physical, social and cultural environment.

The Wechsler Intelligence Tests

Intelligence testing was gaining prominent attention in industrial societies and government, military and academic interests wanted more information about intelligence the single intelligence score of the Stanford-Binet test provided. Wechsler responded with his version of the intelligence test that incorporated his theory of non-intellectual factors into the test's structural design and construction. In the early version of his tests, ten independently scored categories of intellectual abilities were generated. These were divided into two broad categories that were separately evaluated as subtests, the *Verbal* ability scale and the *Performance* or non-verbal scale. The tests were calibrated so that the mean of the scoring distribution curve is always equal to score of 100 and 15 points was always equal to the standard deviation above or below the mean. Over the years the Wechsler tests have be modified as new research regarding intelligence emerged. Today his two major modern versions of intelligence testing are the *Wechsler Adult Intelligence Scale (WAIS)* and the *Wechsler Intelligence Scale for Children (WISC)*. They have been and remain the most popular and commonly used intelligence tests worldwide.

Fluid Intelligence and Crystallized Intelligence

Spearman's concept of a single dominant organizing general intelligence or g intelligence that could manifest in many forms was under furious assault by the multiple independent intelligences theories of Thurston, Wechsler and others. Wechsler did not deny the possibility of a g intelligence entirely but many other prominent proponents of the multiple intelligence theories vigorously denied that there was any such thing as a g intelligence. At this stage of the historical intelligence debate, **Raymond Cattell** and others began to provide new theoretical support for Spearman's g intelligence. In 1941 Cattell proposed that Spearman's general intelligence was composed of two fundamental types of intelligence; 1) *fluid intelligence* that utilized a reasoning capacity to solve novel problems or to otherwise function well in a changing external environment, and 2) *crystallized intelligence* that was adapted to utilize an individual's general fund of knowledge acquired through study and through life experience.

This was a significant refinement of the general intelligence concept because it also predicted that fluid intelligence would after reaching a peak, tend to decrease with age and that crystallized intelligence would be resistant to degradation over time and could continue to increase over the entire lifespan of an individual. Since these were considered components of general intelligence and not independent specific intelligences, fluid intelligence was also referred to as Gf and crystallized intelligence and Gc. Now we have a concept of intelligence that can be tested and that actually makes specific predictions that can also be evaluated both retrospectively and into the future.

Culture Fair Intelligence Test (CFIT)

Cattell also expanded on Wechsler's concept of non-intellectual elements of intelligence with the observations that there were obvious socio-cultural and other environmental influences that altered the nature of an individual's intelligence. He developed the *Culture Fair Intelligence Test (CFIT)* in an effort measure of cognitive abilities in a manner that was independent of sociocultural and environmental influences. This was the earliest attempt to produce a culture-blind intelligence test.

Theories of Intelligence_____

The Gf-Gc Theory of Intelligence

In 1966 a student of Cattell's, **John Horn**, retained Cattell's concepts of fluid and crystallized intelligence as primary features of general intelligence but expanded primary intelligence to include nine or ten broad abilities. This may seem like just another version of independent intelligence theories, but remember the independent theories are separate; they function as a committee of independent experts that does not have a chairman of general intelligence. Cattell and Horn are proposing there is no committee, just a general chairman with at least 2 but likely at least ten primary abilities. So perhaps a better analogy is intelligence is a lone superhero inside the brain with at least ten superpowers. Although Horn's theory of intelligence include nine or so elements, the theory nevertheless became known as fluid intelligence-crystallized intelligence, or simply Gf-Gc theory.

Hierarchical Models of Intelligence

As the intelligence debate stands in the present day, a group of theorists have reached a compromise between independent-intelligences-only theorists and general-intelligence-only theorist. Their compromise proposal is that multiple other intelligences or s intelligences may or may not existed as discrete intelligence modules in their own right but they are in a sense subservient to g intelligence. These intelligence theories are referred to as *hierarchical models* of cognitive abilities. This compromise began to emerge with John Carroll in 1993.

The Three Stratum Model of Intelligence

In 1993, John Carroll accomplished the impossible. He had collected all the published data he considered relevant on the subject of intelligence. In particular, he collected intelligence data that resulted from factor analysis. This culminated in a massive 800-page publication where he provided a stunningly complex and comprehensive mathematical factor analysis that resulted in detailed defense of the concept of general intelligence. His three-stratum model of intelligence reasserted general intelligence as the controlling authority of a three-tiered intelligence construct. At the bottom tier, there are 24 narrowly focused intellectual functions. The second tier includes fluid intelligence and crystallized intelligence as two types of broad versions or modes of general intelligence along with six other modes. Specifically, these other six modes are memory and learning, visual perception, auditory perception, retrieval ability, cognitive speediness and processing speed. Our general intelligence - "g", sits alone at the top tier of the theory.

The Cattell-Horn-Carroll (CHC) Theory of Intelligence

The Cattell, Horn and Carroll theories are encompassed in the CHC theory of intelligence. The CHC theory is a hierarchical theory that places g intelligence at the top. Fluid intelligence is described as involving the use of new information and novel methods to engage in reasoning concept formation and problem solving. Crystallized intelligence communicates knowledge and allows reasoning based on an individual's past experience and previously acquired knowledge. There are eight other broad abilities; quantitative reasoning, reading and writing ability, short-term memory, long-term storage and retrieval, visual processing, auditory processing, processing speed and decision/reaction time/speed. These ten broad abilities generate 70 highly specific abilities. The CHC model is the most modern hierarchical model of human intelligence and is heavily relied upon to construct modern IQ tests. Modern comprehensive IQ tests still give an overall score, but they also give individual scores for many of these specific 70 abilities, resulting in a detailed intelligence profile for each individual who takes these exams.

We have come a long way since our arbitrary agreement to adopt the general intelligence position in the great intelligence debate. Our position has weathered the storm of controversy over the decades. With the CHC theory of intelligence, we are on firm intellectual footing but there remains powerfully supported alternative theories of intelligence. Although the French are no longer considering throwing their cognitively disabled schoolchildren into mental institutions and The US Supreme Court has ruled that IQ scores may not be used as a general screening criteria by employers, there are many other central issues in the great intelligence debate.

When we began this discussion, we proposed that some people seem to be smarter not just in some ways but in every way. We have defended this in the context of testing for intelligence and the factor analysis that tends to support the "in every way" as general intelligence or g. However, another central element of the great intelligence debate is that perhaps we need to broaden our definition of what we mean by "intelligent in every way". In other words, there are other ways to be intelligent than to be purely cognitively intelligent as the modern intelligence tests measure. In this sense, we really do not know anyone with the possible exception of **Leonardo Da Vinci** who is truly smarter in every way imaginable. Furthermore, g as defined may not actually be the ultimate fundamental thinking module. We must account for a superior level of fundamental intelligence that is apparent in the case of **Albert Einstein** - a genius whose cognitive abilities seem to be unique in all of human history. G is perhaps a much more powerful neurological entity than any of us are aware, We may have glimpsed its true potential once and only once in the form of Einstein's cognitive abilities.

So the debate is also that there may be an even broader and more fundamental thinking module than "g" or perhaps there is in fact more than one fundamental thinking module, and again the concept of separate fundamental intelligences rears its head but in a more general manner. A detailed discussion of this element of the debate is beyond the scope of the AP Psychology exam but you are expected to be familiar with the following theorists and with the central premises of their theoretical conceptions of the nature of intelligence in the broadest possible sense.

One concept of a completely different type of intelligence than the intelligence that is measured in modern intelligence testing is the concept of *emotional intelligence.* In 1997, Peter Salovey and **John Mayer** proposed their psychological *Theory of Emotional Intelligence*, it has been described as an ability to facilitate thinking through the acute perception of emotions, and the ability to generate a particular internal emotional context and an external emotional persona that is tailored to and rapidly adapts to the external environment. As emotional intelligence increases, individuals experience enhanced interpersonal relations that promotes intellectual interaction and intellectual growth and maturation.

Howard Gardner's *Theory of multiple intelligences* proposes there are seven independent types of intelligence. Each individual has a profile of intelligences that differ in the relative and absolute strengths and in the ways they are combined to carry out cognitive tasks. These are higher-level thinking modalities that were not considered in the theoretical design of modern IQ testing. Individuals may perform particularly well or particularly poorly on standardized IQ depending on the intelligence profile. Those who do perform poorly may show exceptional real world abilities due to the strength of their individual intelligences: strengths that are not measured by IQ tests. There are slightly different versions of these intelligences but one version is the following: 1) Visual-Spatial - thinking in terms of physical space with a highly tuned awareness of the environments. 2) Bodily-kinesthetic - a sense of body awareness. 3) Musical - a sensitivity to rhythm and sound. 4) Interpersonal - thinking that features street smarts, understanding and empathy for others, interaction with others and learning through interaction. 5) Intrapersonal - thinking that features intuition, wisdom, and motivation; also thinking with a strong will, strong opinions and confidence. 6) Linguistic - thinking in words and using words effectively with a reliance on highly developed auditory skills. 7) Logical/Mathematical - thinking that involves reasoning and calculating; thinking that is conceptual, abstract and that enhances the ability to see and explore patterns and relationships.

Robert Sternberg's *Triarchic Theory* is a general theory of human intelligence. Sternberg began to develop his theory based on his earlier research in analogies and syllogism (simple logic arguments). The theory is anything but a straightforward, simple, three-part alternate definition of intelligence. It is a richly complex, deeply researched theory that challenges the theoretical framework of intelligence that underlies IQ testing at the highest levels. It is truly beyond the scope of introductory psychology courses but the extremely simplified summarized version in most definitely required by the AP Psychology examination. Unfortunately, the summaries of Sternberg's theory are often fundamentally inaccurate, namely those that identify the triarchy as three types of intelligence, the componential/analytic intelligence the experimental/creative intelligence and the contextual/practical intelligence. These are not Sternberg's three intelligences and he does not propose there are three independent individual intelligences. They are the three subtheories of the triarchic theory. These subtheories describes the mechanisms that underlie his proposed three components of intelligent behavior. These three components of intelligent behavior are 1) metacognition, 2) performance and the 3) knowledge acquisition.

The *componential* subtheory describes the mechanisms that underlie his proposed three components of intelligent behavior. It describes how a particular potential set of mental processes are selected and incorporated to generate specific types of behaviors. The *experiential* subtheory interprets intelligent behavior based on where they fall within a range of an individual's experience, beginning with most common or familiar experiences and progressing to the most uncommon, unusual or novel experiences or situations. The *contextual* subtheory describes how intelligent behavior manifests in a sociocultural context. This involves some combination of choosing the best environments whenever possible, attempting to change or reshape a presently undesirable environment to a more desirable environment and adapting to an undesirable environment by any means necessary.

The simplified summaries of the three subtheories are usually accurate. For the AP Psychology Examination: 1) the componential/analytic subtheory involves explaining, analyzing, comparing and contrasting. 2) the experimental/creative subtheory involves an individual's knowledge and experience that generate thoughtful behaviors as situations progress from the commonplace and ordinary to new and unusual. 3) the contextual/practical subtheory can be thought of as that which underlies situational awareness or thinking on one's feet. Just street smarts in general. Here is a very easy way to remember these: The componential/analytic - think Sherlock Holmes; The experimental/creative - think of a combination of Mulder and Scully from the X-Files and MacGyver; The contextual/practical - think Jesse Pinkman of *Breaking Bad*.

Before we conclude, let's deal with all of the other things the AP Psychology exam may ask about in no particular order.

The *single score IQ number*: 100 is the average. The standard deviation is 15. In percentiles one standard deviation is plus or minus 34% so a IQ of 115 or 85 is percentile score of top or bottom 16% Two standard deviations is an IQ of 130 or 60 and that is that top or bottom percentile of 2%. Three standard deviations is 145 or 45 and that's top or bottom 0.2%. The difference in IQ among groups is less than the differences in IQ within groups. IQ scores do correlate with a lot of things but not everything.

Notable IQ Correlations:

- Mortality- compared to a person with an IQ of 100, a person with an IQ of 115 is 21% more likely to live to age 76.

- Genetics- about 20-40% correlation in children but up to 80% correlation as people get older.
- Sex - no difference whether a boy or girl. S
- Socioeconomic status- yes-higher IQ if your raised rich, lower if you are raised poor.
- Music lessons in children - no proven correlation or benefit
- Maternal infections during pregnancy - lower IQs
- IQ and grade point average -50% correlation, SAT scores - about 85% correlation.
- Job performance - 0%, smart or not, it doesn't seem to impact your work as far as employers are concerned.
- Military service - you do not get in unless your IQ is over 85.
- Income - 25% correlation, the higher your IQ the more money you are likely to earn.
- Jail - for significantly low IQ there is a correlation with prison populations.
- Mental disorders - low IQ correlates with antisocial personality disorder.
- If you graduate from college on average your IQ is about 115.
- If you become a doctor, lawyer or college professor your IQ on average will be 125.

For IQs above 125 there does not seem to be much identifiable benefit to an individual. For extremely High IQs the impact of an individual to human civilization can be enormous. Military geniuses have launched wars that nearly succeed in world conquest. Other military geniuses have be required to defeat them. Scientific geniuses have created vaccines and cures for diseases that have saved countless millions. They also have already created the weapons that one day may destroy us all.

Chapter 12: Abnormal Psychology

Abnormal Psychology_____

Definition

Psychology defines abnormal in terms of behaviors or states of mind that are unusual and generally characterized to be, at the least, undesirable or disturbing. When the negative consequences of these abnormal states of minds or behaviors reaches a threshold, they are no longer considered simply odd or undesirable characteristics. Their increased severity raises them to the level of abnormal psychological conditions. As the resulting pain and suffering and incapacitation increases, these are further classified as mental disorders. The DSM-5 uses the term disorder to describe a mental abnormality that is "currently causing distress or impairment to the individual or personal harm, or risk of harm, to others". In the extreme, mental disorders can further rise to the level of severe mental illness. Evaluation of abnormal psychological states in the broadest terms depends on the individual's overall internal state of mind or mood and how the individual's general state of mind is perceived by others. These are the individual's mood and affect, respectively.

Mood

Mood is an internal condition that is closely identified with ongoing emotions. It is fair to say that the most important aspect of one's mood is that it is literally how one feels in the broadest sense, and it generally determines whether one is happy or sad. In psychology, the broadest characteristic of a mood is where it falls in a continuum between *happiness* and *sadness*. At the extreme ends of this spectrum are the highly abnormal moods of *depression* and *mania*.

Another major mood continuum is the *state of arousal*. Depression is usually associated with very low arousal states, but not always. The severest depressive states can be paradoxically highly *agitated*. On the other hand, mania is always a mood of extreme arousal. The most extreme low arousal state is *catatonia*, where there is virtually no response to stimuli. This is mostly seen in severe cases of schizophrenia.

Affect

A person's *affect* is commonly interpreted as the physical and interpersonal expression of their mood or current emotional state. Specifically, this occurs through body postures, movements and gestures and in particular, facial expressions, tone of voice and content and manner of speech.

In reality, a person's affect is a more complex phenomena reflecting all aspects of personality, intelligence and social awareness. More often than not, normal affect involves a degree of concealment or outward falsification of one's true state of mind. We all attempt to alter our affect within our social context. In fact, those who do not are often criticized for being unable to hold their emotions in check or "wearing their hearts on their sleeves."

The definition of a "normal affect" differs based on one's ethnic or cultural background and many other factors. There is not a checklist to describe a normal affect, but there is a certain level of and range of emotional content and appropriateness of response in social situations that are common and expected for persons with a normal affect. This is called *"the broad affect."* Abnormal or inappropriate affects include a *restricted affect*, with mild restriction in the intensity and range of emotional displays, the more severe *blunted affect*, with very limited intensity and range of emotional displays and the most severe, *flat affect*, with the absence of any expression of emotion. A *labile affect* describes emotional instability with sudden mood swings and inappropriate or paradoxical emotional responses such a laughing aloud in public upon hearing of a tragic occurrence. An abnormal affect is a prominent feature of many mental disorders including the schizophrenic and autistic spectrum disorders and is the defining feature of the bipolar related and depressive disorders

Abnormal Mental States

There are general abnormal mental states that occur in various combinations and levels of severity among the specific mental disorders. These general abnormal states are discussed as follows

Anxiety is a state of increased alertness and arousal, normally in response to perceived threats to one's welfare or in response to the stress factors of daily life. In persons with abnormal anxiety levels, the increased duration, intensity and frequency of anxiety interferes with a person's ability to function. Symptoms of excessive anxiety include restlessness, easily fatigued, difficulty concentrating, irritability, muscle tension and sleep disturbances. The most severe anxiety event is a panic attack.

Panic attacks are episodes of extreme anxiety that causes symptoms of heart palpitations, shakiness, blurred vision, difficulty concentrating and a sense of losing control or sometimes feeling that one is actually having a heart attack.

Elevated moods are states of increased arousal they are energetic and usually happy, but sometimes irritable or agitated. An abnormally elevated mood is manic (an adjective) or is a mania (a noun). The most severe level of mania is dangerous and requires hospitalization.

Manic episodes are characterized by a distinct period of abnormally and persistently elevated, expansive, or irritable mood, lasting at least 1 week with at least three characteristic symptoms. These may include: increased self-esteem or grandiosity, decreased need for sleep, pressure to keep talking, flight of ideas or subjective experience that thoughts are racing, distractibility, increase in goal-directed activity and excessive involvement in pleasurable activities that have a high potential for painful consequences abnormal anxiety.

Depressed moods are states of low arousal or energy and are almost always undesirable or sad. The most severe abnormally depressed mood event is a major depressive episode.

Major depressive episodes consist of a severely depressed mood and/or loss of interest or pleasure in life activities for at least 2 weeks. These episodes feature at least five of the following symptoms: serious impairment of functioning, a depressed mood most of the day, diminished interest or pleasure in all or most activities, significant unintentional weight loss or gain, insomnia, agitation or psychomotor retardation, fatigue, feelings of worthlessness or excessive guilt, difficulty concentrating and recurrent thoughts of death. Major depressive episodes are dangerous, particularly due to increased risk of suicide.

Psychosis

A *psychosis* is a radical change in personality where there is a derangement of higher cognitive functioning resulting in distortions or a total loss of all sense of reality. There are five major general phenomena or psychotic domains that can contribute to a psychotic state, including the two major abnormal misperceptions of reality, hallucinations and delusions, the disorganized thinking demonstrated by abnormal speech patterns in thought disorders, grossly disorganized or abnormal motor behavior including catalepsy and catatonia, and negative symptoms. Psychotic states or psychotic features can occur in most of the classes of mental disorders, severe bipolar disorder in particular. Psychosis can occur in previously healthy people and can disappear completely, such as psychotic episodes induced by drug abuse, medical conditions and post-partum psychosis. The five psychotic domains are discussed below.

Misperceptions of Reality

Misperceptions of reality by themselves can be abnormal conditions, and in some mental disorders, misperceptions can be profound. Our senses can mislead us and present a false reality, which we may or may not recognize. There are misperception that we all have had, where we believe we have seen or heard something that was not really there. It may be a brief glimpse of a person or a word or two that seems to come from nowhere. This is usually triggered by your particular state of mind and unexpected visual or auditory events that your mind attempts to identify based on insufficient information or too much unexpected information. Other times there is a real physical process that provides a false image, such as a mirage. These phenomena are called illusions, and in most cases, they are normal. Optical illusions can be created to give a false impression of motion or distortions of the true relative size of images.

Hallucinations

Abnormal illusions are those that occur entirely internally. They are not misperceptions but false perceptions. These false perceptions are imaginary, nothing is the real world is being mistaken for them and they can be persistent and complex. These are called *hallucinations* and they are usually an indication of a serious mental or neurological condition.

The most common hallucinations are auditory hallucinations, where in the extreme, one or more voices can carry on elaborate on monologues inside of one's head. Visual hallucinations are not as common but do occur frequently in several physical and mental disorders. Somatic hallucinations often occur as a sensation the insects are crawling underneath one's skin.

Delusions

There is a wide range of normal in persons' thought processes but as they deviate further from the norm we begin to label these thoughts and the persons who have them as quirky, odd or eccentric. The spectrum of severity for cognitive disturbances in mental disorders often begins with thinking that is no longer merely eccentric, but becomes bizarre or delusional.

A *delusion* is a strongly held or absolute belief in the existence of something that is almost certainly unreal. Many people hold what most people would consider to be outrageous or ridiculous beliefs, but delusions are beliefs that are obviously provable, in the judgement of any rational person, to be wrong. It may be silly to whimsically "believe" in Santa Claus, but someone who truly believes that he or she is the Queen of England is severely delusional (except for Her Majesty, of course).

Normal persons can have a mild form of a delusional state called magical thinking. This flawed thought process usually includes superstitious beliefs that are widely known to have been proven to be statistically false, so technically it is a very mild, but "normal" delusion.

The Queen of England delusion is an example of a delusion *of grandeur*. A persons with one or a few simple fixed delusions may be an otherwise rational person. As delusions become more complex and intrusive they rise to the level of a *delusional disorder*, a serious mental illness. Persons with *persecutory delusions* or paranoia are convinced that people are out to get them. Severe paranoia, as occurs in *paranoid delusional disorder* can involve amazingly complex and detailed delusions of vast malevolent conspiracies that dominate a person's internal perception of reality, overwhelming their lives and completely incapacitating their ability to function. *Somatic delusions* are delusions about one's own body; often they include extremely strong beliefs that one has a severe or fatal health condition when there is no medical evidence of any such a disease. When these become severe, they rise to the level of a somatic or somatic symptom disorder. The most bizarre and debilitating delusions, as is also the case with hallucinations, occur in patients with schizophrenia.

Disorganized Thinking

Bizarre and stereotypical patterns of disorganized speech are believed to represent disorganized thinking. Disorganized thinking is one of the five domains of psychosis can be a generalized global derangement of fundamental rational thought processes that loosen or severe one's connection to reality. There are at least 15 of these patterns that are well described in mental health circles including derailment, perseveration, flight of ideas and so on. We cannot discuss every type of disorganized speech pattern and the theories of what particular mechanism of cognitive function they may be caused by. They appear to be manifestations of dysfunction of the neurological process that generate internal reality and an individual's identity and existence within that reality. These processes are considered the greatest mysteries of science. When this is the primary feature of a psychotic state, it is referred to as a thought disorder.

Catatonia

Catatonia is informally thought of as a state of complete inactivity and unresponsiveness, as though one were a statue. In abnormal psychology, catatonia can have various manifestations. Often these include strikingly abnormal motor abnormalities such as catalepsy. *Catalepsy* is often characterized by a trance-like state. The person may be unresponsive to stimuli and appears to have lost voluntary motor function resulting in muscle rigidity and a fixed body posture that can be rearrange by others as they would a mannequin. This moldable fixed posturing phenomenon is called waxy flexibility. Alternatively, catatonic persons may engage in mindless and excessive or constant movement patterns called purposeless agitation and exhibit extreme negativism, a term indicating the presence of negative symptoms, which are explained below.

Negative Symptoms

Negative symptoms, in a psychosis and other conditions, are behaviors or phenomena that usually indicate severe disease and poor outcomes. The negative symptoms are:

- *Alogia-* a pattern of limited verbal response consisting of brief replies with little content and interest;
- *Anhedonia-* the inability to feel pleasure and indifference to activities that would typically be considered pleasurable, such as eating and socializing;
- *Avolition-* lack of goal directed activity or the inability to initiate and persist in activities;
- *Anergia-* no energy and flat affect. The absence or near absence of any signs of affective expression, in particular, lack of eye contact.

Negativism associated with a condition means there are significant negative type symptoms present in the condition.

DSM-5

As of 2015, all multiple choice and free response questions on the AP Psychology Exam adheres to the new fifth edition of the *Diagnostic and Statistical Manual* (DSM-5).

There are hundreds of individual mental disorders listed in the DSM-5 and each has a very precise definition. Fortunately, these definitions are no longer organized into axis 1 through 5 as they were in previous manuals. The term "disorder" in the DSM-5 is applied to indicate that the condition has (usually) persisted for a specified period of time and that it is sufficiently severe to cause mental, physical or socioeconomic distress or harm to individuals with the condition and/ or to those around them.

Comapred to previous editions of the AP Psychology exam, subclassifications of schizophrenia have been eliminated in the DSM-5. Depression and bipolar disorder are no longer in the same category. Somatic symptom disorder and other disorders with prominent somatic symptoms constitute a new category in DSM-5 called somatic symptom and related disorders. The DSM-5 chapter on anxiety disorder no longer includes obsessive-compulsive disorder, which is now included with the obsessive-compulsive and related disorders. There is now a single condition called autism spectrum disorder, which incorporates four previous separate disorders, autistic disorder (autism), Asperger's disorder, childhood disintegrative disorder, and pervasive developmental disorder not otherwise specified. Two disorders have also been combined. Chronic major depressive disorder and dysthymia are now under the heading of persistent depressive disorder. The AP Psychology exam expects you to be familiar with the following 12 categories of mental disorders.

Anxiety Disorders

Generalized anxiety disorder is excessive anxiety that occurs more days than not over a six-month period and in more than one environmental setting such as at home and at work. *Social anxiety disorder* occurs in in individuals in social situations where they may become the focus of attention of others, such as public performances. This causes immediate, sometimes paralyzing fear, and occurs over a 6-month or longer period. Specific *phobias*, such as *claustrophobia* (fear of enclosed spaces) or *acrophobia* (fear of heights) are intense persistent fears that are excessive and/or irrational. They are triggered by the presence or anticipation of a specific object or situation; causing immediate fear or anxiety; lasting for 6 months or more; and resulting in clinically significant distress. *Agoraphobia* is a specific phobia with a brooder trigger fear of the world outside of one's own home. *Panic disorder* is a condition where, for one month or longer, the individual experiences frequent unexpected panic attacks. In panic disorder the fear of additional panic attacks can trigger a panic attack, resulting in a vicious cycle of increasing disability.

Bipolar and Related Disorder

Bipolar disorder involves extreme uncontrollable mood swings between depressed and elevated (manic) moods. There are three types of bipolar disorder:
* *Bipolar 1 disorder*, the most severe of bipolar and related disorders the primary symptoms are those of extreme mania or rapid mood swings between mania and depression.
* *Bipolar 2 disorder*, features recurrent depression alternating with hypomanic episodes, a milder state of mania in which the symptoms are not severe enough to cause marked impairment or need for hospitalization.
* *Cyclothymic disorder* is a chronic state of cycling between hypomanic and depressive episodes that are less severe than those of bipolar disorders. There are detailed qualifiers for symptom severity, context, and timeframe for all three disorders.

Depressive Disorder

A depressed mood is the defining feature of theses conditions. The most severe depressive event is a major depressive episode. The important depressive disorders are *Major Depressive Disorder, Single and Recurrent Episodes*. Major Depressive Disorder single requires only one major depressive episode, while recurrent requires two or more major depressive episodes.

Disruptive Mood Dysregulation Disorder is characterized by severe and recurrent temper outbursts in children age 8 to 13 that are grossly out of proportion in intensity or duration to the situation. Children with DMDD display a persistently irritable or angry mood. The disorder also includes specific symptom context and symptom timeframe qualifications. *Persistent Depressive Disorder* (Dysthymia) is a new diagnosis that combines two earlier diagnoses: dysthymia and chronic major depressive episode. The disorder is a depressed mood that occurs for most of the day, for more days than not, for at least 2 years in an adult or at least 1 year for children and adolescents. Major depression may precede or may occur during persistent depressive disorder. During periods of depressed mood, at least two of six depressive type symptoms must be present. There are detailed qualifiers for minimum age group previous mental disorder and duration of symptoms and symptom free periods. Premenstrual Dysphoric Disorder is also included in depressive disorders category.

Dissociative Disorder

Dissociation is the mind's attempt to insulate a person from traumatic events or memories of the traumatic events such as war, natural disasters and sexual or physical abuse in childhood. There is a growing body of evidence linking the dissociative disorders to specific neural mechanisms. General symptoms of dissociation include an unclear sense of identity, depression, anxiety and suicidal thoughts or actions.

Specific types of symptoms characterized the specific dissociative disorders. *Dissociative amnesia* features a particularly severe personally relevant amnesia where no identifiable brain abnormality can be found to explain the memory loss. *Dissociative fugue* is a state of disoriented and aimless wandering. In *dissociative identity disorder,* there is a feeling of possession by another identity or that there are two or more identities or personality traits within a single person. Often there is an apparent transfer of behavioral control the particular personality that seems to have the best capacity to function in specific social situations or other sets of circumstances.

Depersonalization/derealization disorder characteristics include a sense of detachment from oneself, sometimes described as seeing one's life as if it is a movie. Frequently there is a sense that objects in the external world are changing in shape and size and/or that people are inhuman or automatons. Dissociative disorders cause significant distress and/or functioning impairment in important areas of daily life such as at school or with interpersonal relationships. Episodes of dissociation can last for a few moments or as long as a lifetime. The primary treatment for dissociation syndromes is psychotherapy. There has been little success in the use of medications to treat these conditions.

Feeding and Eating Disorders

Feeding and eating disorders feature persistent abnormalities of perception and behavior related to the normal physiological a psychological functionality of eating. These include: eating non food items such as clay, paint, etc. as occurs in pica, the regurgitation of food which is then either re-chewed, re-swallowed or spit out, as occurs in *ruminant disorder,* purposefully avoiding or exceeding the normal dietary consumption levels required to maintain a healthy weight or body mass index (BMI), as occurs in *avoidant/restrictive food intake disorder* and *binge eating disorder*, and the restrictive subtype of anorexia nervosa. Attempting to alter the consequences of eating through induced vomiting or inappropriate and/or excessive use of laxatives occurs in *bulimia nervosa* and the bulimic subtype of anorexia nervosa. Both anorexia nervosa and bulimia nervosa are associated with increased mortality.

Anorexia nervosa is the most important of all of these disorders due to its high morbidity and mortality and its exceptional and severe derangements of perception involving one's actual physical health and normal appearance. It also includes the objective concern about how significant others and society in general perceives one's behavior and how their actions cause severe distress to significant others. Specifically, severe anorexics seem to perceive food and eating as disgusting, to not know or care that their weight loss is grossly abnormal and threatens to ruin their health or even kill them, or to be concerned that their loved ones are profoundly concerned and unhappy about their behavior. Previously, anorexia diagnosis guidelines included a failure to maintain at least an 85% level of minimum healthy body weight. This is not a DSM-5 requirement, but level of severity is based on failure to maintain various minimum BMI levels. Guidelines regarding the absence of menstrual cycles are removed in part to account for anorexia in men and in postmenopausal women.

Neurodevelopmental Disorder

Neurodevelopmental disorder conditions feature early childhood developmental deficits that can disrupt emotional expression and development, limit memory abilities, and the ability to learn, socialize, and maintain self-control. They can also limit IQs and other types of intelligence. The neurodevelopmental disorders include *autism spectrum disorder, attention deficit hyperactivity disorder,* communication disorders, intellectual developmental disorder, motor disorders, and specific learning disorders. Frequently, more than one of these disorders is present in an individual.

Neurocognitive Disorder

In the DSM-5 neurocognitive disorder, (NCD) replaces the Dementia, Delirium, Amnestic, and Other Cognitive Disorders. The NCDs are conditions that cause a decline from a previously attained level of functioning. The category includes delirium, NCD due to Alzheimer's disease, Parkinson's disease; Huntington's disease, AIDS and other neurodegenerative processes. Although cognitive deficits are present in many if not all mental disorders such as schizophrenia and bipolar disorders, only disorders whose primary abnormalities are cognitive are included in the NCD category.

Obsessive-Compulsive and Related Disorder

Obsessions are recurrent and persistent thoughts, impulses, or images. Compulsions are repetitive behaviors or rituals such as hand washing, hoarding, sorting and organizing or mental activities such as counting silently or avoiding certain types of things and/or patterns or geometries in the environment.

Obsessive-Compulsive Disorder (OCD)

OCD is characterized by frequent, irrepressible and severely distressful obsessions and/or compulsions. In contrast to those with other psychotic disorders, persons with obsessive-compulsive disorder realize their behaviors are highly abnormal and not due to external forces. They often perform their rituals clandestinely, fearing reactions of disgust and ridicule if they are witnessed by others. Depression occurs frequently in persons with OCD. Neurochemical, genetic and environmental factors likely play important roles in the development of OCD. Research project have reported a relative serotonin deficiency in OCD sufferers and an increased incidence in those who have close family relatives with OCD.

Other obsessive related disorders are: *Hoarding Disorder, Trichotillomania* (Hair-Pulling), *Excoriation* (Skin-Picking), and *Body Dysmorphic Disorder,* which features a preoccupation with one or more nonexistent or slight defects or flaws in one's physical appearance that generate repetitive, compulsive behaviors in response to the appearance concerns such as constant mirror-checking.

Personality Disorder

Personality disorders are associated with ways of thinking and feeling about oneself and others that significantly and adversely affect how an individual functions in many aspects of life. An informal definition is "who you are makes other people unhappy." The ten types of personality disorders are paranoid, schizoid, schizotypal, antisocial borderline, histrionic, narcissistic, avoidant, dependent and obsessive-compulsive.

Unquestionably, the most important of these in terms of the harm they cause to themselves and others and their cost to society is the antisocial personality. Although hostility and arrogance are typical features of the disorder, antisocial personalities can often be initially charming or even charismatic in their efforts to manipulate others. By definition, they have a pervasive pattern of disregard for and violation of the rights of others beginning by age 15 years old, as indicated by three or more of the following characteristics: failure to conform to social norms with respect to lawful behaviors, irritability and aggressiveness, reckless disregard for safety of self or others, consistent irresponsibility and a lack of remorse. Both genetics and child abuse are believed to contribute to the development of this condition, but the actual cause is unknown. Persons with antisocial personality disorder rarely seek treatment and there is little evidence to determine what if any treatment methods may be effective.

Schizophrenia Spectrum and Other Psychotic Disorder

These conditions share some or all of the five psychotic features of psychosis: hallucinations, delusions, disorganized thinking demonstrated by abnormal speech patterns, grossly disorganized or abnormal motor behavior including catatonia, and negative symptoms. They represent a range of severity from brief psychotic episodes that completely resolve, to the most severe condition, schizophrenia. The discussion of schizophrenia requires special attention.

Schizophrenia

Schizophrenia is the most common psychosis and is among the most severe forms of all mental disorders. It is a profoundly disabling lifelong mental illness that requires lifelong treatment with the most powerful antipsychotic medications. Use of these medications often results in severe and permanent side effects including tardive dyskinesias, which are highly abnormal contortions of the tongue and facial muscles. Schizophrenia prominently features all five of the psychotic domains and usually appears in previously normal appearing and functioning individuals in their late teens and early twenties. Schizophrenic patients are usually plagued by relentless and often tormenting auditory hallucinations. This is often the first symptom of schizophrenia. For most mental health professionals, persons who report hearing voices inside their head are presumed to be schizophrenic until proven otherwise. Symptoms must last for at least 6 months to make a diagnosis of schizophrenia.

In previous editions of the DSM manual, this condition was subdivided into several variants. The problem with that approach was that it became increasingly apparent that we really did not know what was wrong with schizophrenic thinking except that possibly everything was wrong. Attempting to understand the proposed definitions of at least 15 different abnormal stereotypical speech patterns and other forms of strangely distorted schizophrenic behavior among at least five subcategories of schizophrenia was difficult even for trained mental health professionals

The DSM-5 has recognized this fact and has dispensed with attempts to subclassify schizophrenia based on these descriptions of variants in schizophrenic thought and speech patterns. Schizophrenia is now just schizophrenia.

Schizoaffective Disorder is an uninterrupted period of illness during which, at some time, there is either a major depressive episode, a manic episode, or a mixed episode that occur while there are schizophrenia symptoms. During the same period of illness, there have been delusions or hallucinations for at least two weeks in the absence of prominent mood symptoms and is not due to the direct physiological effects of a substance or a general medical condition.

The essential features of *Schizophreniform Disorder* are identical in type to those of schizophrenia, but are less severe and patients have a better ability to function. Symptoms must last at least 1 month but no longer than 6 months.

Schizotypal (Personality) *Disorder* patients are not disturbed enough to be diagnosed as schizophrenic They have strangeness in thinking, speech and behavior lasting at least 6 months where for at least 1 month, at least two of the five psychotic domain symptoms are continuously present.

Brief Psychotic Disorder is also known as 3-day schizophrenia. Symptoms have a sudden onset linked to a psychosocial stressor last one month or less, includes delusions, hallucination, jumbled speech and disorganized or catatonic behavior. If symptoms last longer than three days, another psychotic disorder diagnosis is required. *Delusional Disorder* features persistent delusions including persecution, infidelity, grandiosity or somatic delusions. Other disorders include *Bipolar/Depressive Type* and *Substance Induced Psychotic Disorder.*

Somatic Symptom and Related Disorder

Individuals with *somatic symptom disorder* report highly exaggerated physical symptoms occurring in multiple body regions. Additionally, they seriously overestimate, in their own minds, the degree of limitation that these symptoms impose on them in their daily lives. They have at least one somatic symptom that interferes with daily activities. Their physical or somatic symptoms have at least two out of three defining characteristics; these being a high level of health related anxiety, an excessive degree of concern over the seriousness of their symptoms for excessive periods of time during the day and spending an excessive amount of time devoted to activities generated by the perceived seriousness of their symptoms. This state of mind continues unabated for greater than 6 months. There is a reported increased incidence of the disorder in persons with depression, irritable bowel syndrome, fibromyalgia, post-traumatic stress disorder and antisocial personality disorder. There are no effective forms of drug treatment for this disorder.

Trauma- and Stressor-Related Disorder

Exposure to a traumatic or stressful event is the most important diagnostic element of Trauma- and stressor-related disorders These include *reactive attachment disorder, disinhibited social engagement disorder, posttraumatic stress disorder (PTSD), acute stress disorder,* and *adjustment disorders.* There is a close relationship between these disorders and anxiety disorders, obsessive-compulsive and related disorders, and dissociative disorders.

Posttraumatic stress disorder (PTSD) the most severe and socially significant example of these disorders. The important features of PTSD are shared by the other disorders but with lower levels of severity. These are: re-experiencing the event including spontaneous memories (flashbacks) of and recurrent dreams related to the traumatic event, it, or other intense or prolonged psychological distress; heightened arousal including aggressive, reckless or self-destructive behavior, sleep disturbances, and hypervigilance; avoidance of distressing memories, thoughts, feelings or external reminders of the event; and negative thoughts and mood or feelings such as an inability to remember key aspects of the event. A persistent and a distorted sense of blame of self or others, estrangement from friends and family members and diminished interest in normal activities.

Theories of Abnormal Behavior

With a solid understanding of the basic premises of the major types of psychological theories and using careful reasoning and analytical skills, you should be able to answer questions about the theoretical basis and treatment of mental disorders. Advocates of various psychological theories, in particular psychodynamic/psychoanalytic, behavioral, humanistic, evolutionary, cognitive and sociocultural theorists, have attempted to explain the origins of abnormal mental disorders, and to develop modes of treatment for these disorders. So far, these efforts are mostly incomplete. The effectiveness of treatment approaches based on these theories are debatable except for the well-documented success of the biomedical models with drug therapy in the treatment of many serious disorders.

There are fierce advocates for each of these models of abnormal behavior and fierce critics of most of them. In general, behaviorists propose classical and operant conditioning model to explain and treat, but critics have compelling arguments that in abnormal psychology the explanations are strained to the point of absurdity. Humanists tend to explain and propose treatment based on feelings, sociocultural theorists often propose racism and sexism as the basis for the development of mental disorders. Psychodynamic theory is notable in that Freud developed it specifically to attempt to understand and treat abnormal psychological conditions. Most explanations for mental disorders and treatment approaches of psychodynamic theory are based on unresolved issues or complexes and psychological traumas that occurred during early stages of psychological development. Critics point out that there is very little evidence to support the premises of the theory and little evidence and even contradictory evidence to support the effectiveness of the psychodynamic treatment methods for mental disorders.

There are several specific theories and persons that relate to abnormal psychology that you should know about for the AP Psychology Examination. These are:

- **Aaron Beck**, a cognitive theorist, asserts the cognitive triad of a person's negative self-image, environment and prospects for the future can result in depression.

- **Fritz Heider**, **Harold Kelley** and **Bernard Weiner**, social psychology theorists created and refined *Attribution Theory* where a person's tendency to ascribe the responsibility or explanations for the causes of events, situations and outcomes to be in general internal or external. Those who chose external explanations are regarded as optimistic personalities, those who chose internal explanations are regarded as pessimistic personalities. Persons with pessimistic personalities are alleged to be more susceptible to depression.

- **Mary Seligman** created the concept of *learned helplessness* based on her experiments with dogs receiving electrical shocks. Dogs that had no control or means to avoid electric shock often became passive and gave up any effort to avoid the shocks. This concept of learned helplessness was proposed to extend to humans who, for the same reason of perceived lack of control of their environment, develop a fatalistic attitude and become depressed.

- *Biomedical models* have support based on success with drug therapies based on the relative low serotonin levels that are associated with depression, and the abnormal dopamine functions seen in schizophrenic patients (the dopamine hypothesis).

Chapter 13: Treatment of Psychological Disorders

Treatment of Psychological Disorders
Key Terms, Concepts, and People

Psychotherapy	Insight therapies	Psychoanalysis
Insight	Hypnosis	Free association
Dream analysis	Resistance	Transference
Countertransference	Client-centered therapy	Unconditional positive regard
Active-listener	Empathic understanding	Gestalt therapy
Existential therapy	Counterconditioning	Systematic desensitization
Aversion therapy	Extinction procedures	Flooding
Implosion	Operant conditioning	Token economy
Behavioral contracting	Modeling	Cognitive therapy
Rational-emotive behavior therapy (REBT)		Cognitive triad
Psychopharmacology	Psychotropic drugs	Antipsychotic drugs
Tardive dyskinesia	Antidepressants	Tricyclic antidepressants
Monoamine oxidase inhibitors (MAOIs)	Serotonin-reuptake-inhibitors (SSRIs)	
Anxiolytics	Electroconvulsive therapy (ECT)	
Transcranial magnetic stimulation (TMS)		Psychosurgery
Group therapy	Self-help groups	Twelve-step programs
Family therapy	Couples therapy	Primary prevention
Secondary prevention	Tertiary prevention	

Key People: Aaron Beck, Albert Ellis, Sigmund Freud, Mary Cover Jones, Carl Rogers, B.F. Skinner, Joseph Wolpe, Fritz Perls

Overview

Just as there are many different theoretical perspectives about the cause of psychological disorders, there are different views about how to treat psychological disorders. Regardless of the treatment method used, all treatments are intended to offer hope and help to those suffering from mental illness. Treatment for psychological disorders is called *psychotherapy*.

Treatment Approaches_____

Psychoanalytic therapy and humanistic therapy are called *insight therapies.* Insight therapies focus on helping clients/patients understand their problems so that the patients/clients can resolve their psychological problems.

Psychoanalytic Therapy

Psychoanalytic therapy is rooted in the psychoanalytic theory of **Sigmund Freud.** Freud's approach to treating psychological disorders was *psychoanalysis.* With traditional psychoanalysis, the therapist tries to avoid becoming too emotionally involved with the patient, so therapy is typically conducted with patients lying on a couch outside of the line of sight of the therapist. The goal of therapy is to help patients develop insight into their problems, which presumably helps patients eliminate their problems. Psychoanalytic therapists believe the cause of psychological problems can be discovered by understanding the unconscious motives and conflicts of patients.

In order to access the unconscious of patients, psychoanalytic therapists use techniques such as free association, hypnosis, and dream analysis. Some psychoanalytic therapists may use *hypnosis*, or an altered state of consciousness, in order to facilitate exploring the unconscious. *Free association*, which is when patients say whatever comes to mind, may or may not be used while the patient is under hypnosis. By having patients express thoughts without thinking about them first, the therapist may begin to understand the root cause of patients' problems. Some psychoanalytic therapists may ask their patients to recount their dreams, while the therapist looks for symbolism and patterns that may indicate unconscious conflicts underlying patients' problems. This technique is known as *dream analysis.* The hidden content or meaning of the dreams is of more significance than what the patient describes (the manifest content). Based on the contents of the dreams, the therapist gains insight into the unconscious thoughts of patients and interprets the meaning of the dreams. Patients may resist the therapist's interpretations and use defense mechanisms in order to avoid confronting painful thoughts. When patients engage in this behavior, they are demonstrating *resistance.* The therapist may then help patients explore the causes of their resistance.

Another important feature of psychoanalysis is *transference,* in which patients unconsciously redirect strong emotions experienced in significant relationships toward the therapist. The nature of these feelings help the therapist determine the cause of the problem. However, in some instances, the therapist may redirect his or her emotions toward patients, a process known as *countertransference.*

Some therapists use many of Freud's ideas, while integrating other techniques into their practice. These therapists take a psychodynamic or Neo-Freudian approach in helping patients discover and resolve unconscious reasons for their problems.

Some criticisms of the psychodynamic approach are that the techniques used are very subjective and are subject to the therapist's interpretation. Further, because psychodynamic therapy focuses largely on the unconscious thoughts and motives of patients, discovering the root cause of patients' problems can require a few sessions a week and can continue for years, which makes this type of treatment expensive.

Humanistic Therapy

Although classified as an insight therapy, humanistic therapy takes a distinctly different approach to treatment. Humanistic therapy is based on the idea that people develop psychological problems because of feelings of low self-worth due to negative experiences with others and lack of support in reaching their goals. Humanistic therapy is concerned with the present, not the past, and it focuses on clients' conscious experiences. It focuses on helping clients reach their full potential and achieve self-actualization. A major emphasis is placed upon clients' ability to make their own choices and to take responsibility for their choices.

Carl Rogers developed *client-centered* (or person-centered) *therapy.* Client-centered therapy is effective when the therapist offers unconditional positive regard to clients. Unconditional positive regard helps the client achieve self-fulfillment and find self-worth. Without unconditional positive regard, according to Rogers, people cannot attain healthy development. Unlike psychodynamic therapy, in which the therapist remains detached, the humanistic therapist is genuine, open, and nurturing. The therapist is an active-listener who encourages clients to freely express their feelings and to make their own decisions. As an *active-listener*, the therapist will often seek to clarify clients' feelings and will provide empathic understanding, in which the therapist reflects the feelings of the client and attempts to understand the client's situation through the eyes of the client. This type of empathic, accepting, and non-judgmental environment fosters a strong therapeutic relationship that promotes growth and self-acceptance for clients.

Gestalt therapy, developed by **Fritz Perls**, is another type of humanistic therapy. Gestalt therapy emphasizes the totality of the person's experiences, assisting clients in realizing how thoughts, feelings, and actions interact to create the whole person. It focuses on helping clients confront and take responsibility for unconscious feelings. Gestalt therapists help clients understand the connection between body and mind and may have clients engage in physical activities that reflect psychological conflicts.

Another type of humanistic therapy is *existential therapy.* Existential therapists view clients' problems as being the result of lack of purpose and meaning. Therapy focuses on assisting clients in achieving a meaningful existence.

Behavioral Therapy

Techniques:

Since behavioral therapists take the view that all behavior is learned, they believe there is no underlying psychological cause of maladaptive behaviors. Behavioral therapists attempt to change people's behavior by using techniques of classical conditioning and operant conditioning. Behavioral therapy, unlike psychodynamic and humanistic therapy, is short-term.

One technique based on classical conditioning is *counterconditioning*, which was developed by **Mary Cover Jones**. Counterconditioning is a technique that involves replacing an undesirable response to a particular stimulus with a desirable response. For example, if Johnny is afraid of cats, Johnny's dad can take Johnny's learned response (fear) and replace it with a feeling of happiness by consistently pairing Johnny's exposure to cats with a stimulus that creates a feeling of calmness and happiness for Johnny.

One type of counterconditioning is *systematic desensitization,* a technique developed by **Joseph Wolpe**. This technique is useful in treating anxiety-disorders and phobias. Systematic desensitization involves gradually increasing exposure to a fear- evoking stimulus. However, unlike counterconditioning, with systematic desensitization, the fearful or anxious response is countered by a feeling of relaxation. The first thing the client is taught is how to relax; this can be accomplished by using such techniques as deep breathing exercises and meditation, for instance. After the client has learned how to relax, the therapist and client create a hierarchy of fear and anxiety producing situations or images and order them from least intense to most intense. The client is then asked to imagine the fear-inducing situation or object or is presented with the actual fear-inducing event or object and is instructed to practice relaxation techniques while viewing the images. The client begins practicing relaxation techniques when he first feels fear or anxiety and continues using the relaxation techniques until the fear or anxiety has passed. The therapist and client gradually move up the hierarchy until the client does not feel any fear or anxiety when presented with the event or object that causes the most intense response. The more the anxiety eliciting situation or object is paired with relaxation techniques, the stronger the association will become.

Counterconditioning can also be accomplished through *aversion therapy*. Aversion therapy involves repeatedly pairing an unpleasant stimulus with a behavior the person wants to change. For instance, a person who wants to stop drinking may be given a substance that induces nausea every time he drinks until he associates drinking with nausea, thereby reducing the likelihood the drinking will be repeated.

Behavioral therapists may also use extinction procedures in order to weaken or eliminate dysfunctional or undesirable behaviors. There are two types of extinction procedures: flooding and implosion. *Flooding* involves exposing the client to the actual event or object that causes the most intense anxiety or fear response first. Flooding, unlike systematic desensitization, is not gradual; it requires clients to confront their worst fear first. With *implosion*, the client imagines the situation or event instead of actually being exposed to it.

Operant conditioning, which was developed by **B.F. Skinner**, is another technique used by behavioral therapists. Positive and negative reinforcement, as well as punishment, can be used to change behavior. A *token economy* is an example of a behavior-modification technique that can be used in schools or mental institutions to encourage desired behaviors. Every time the person exhibits the desired behavior, a token is earned. After the person accumulates a set amount of tokens, the tokens can be exchanged for an activity or object that are rewarding for the person. One tool that a behavioral therapist may use is *behavioral contracting.* The contract specifies what the therapist and client are required to do. The contract outlines which steps the client should take and what the client must do, such as not engage in a particular behavior, and what the therapist is required to do, such as provide a particular reward, if the client lives up to the terms of the contract.

Modeling is another treatment method behavioral therapists may use. Clients observe the behavior of someone and then imitate that behavior, after which they receive a reward. Since the desired behavior is reinforced by a reward, the client is likely to repeat the behavior.

Cognitive Therapy

Since cognitive therapists believe psychological problems are caused by maladaptive thoughts, cognitive therapy focuses on changing clients' dysfunctional thought patterns. Clients are challenged to identify incorrect or irrational thinking that are contributing to their psychological problems. Cognitive therapists assert that when thinking changes, emotions change, which results in behavior changing.

One method used by cognitive therapists is *rational-emotive behavior therapy (REBT)* (sometimes referred to as rational-emotive therapy, or RET), which was developed by **Albert Ellis**. This approach is based on the idea that people's irrational or incorrect thinking impairs their ability to accurately perceive situations. Incorrect and irrational thinking result in dysfunctional emotional responses. The therapist points out incorrect or irrational thinking and points out why the thinking is wrong. The therapist helps the client to identify and develop more rational thinking and healthier emotional responses and behaviors. Because REBT address both cognitions and behaviors, this approach is also considered a cognitive-behavioral approach.

Aaron Beck developed *cognitive therapy,* which is an approach that is effective in treating depression. Cognitive therapy focuses on identifying and challenging maladaptive thoughts that lead to depression. Cognitive distortions are caused by a cognitive triad that includes people's negative beliefs about themselves, the world, and the future. The therapist challenges clients' negative and distorted thinking and asks clients to present evidence to corroborate their thinking. The therapist will point out clients' distorted thinking with evidence contrary to clients' claims. The goal of cognitive therapy is to modify distorted and dysfunctional thinking.

Biological Therapy

Biological therapy involves applying a medical approach to the treatment of psychological problems. Practitioners operating from this perspective think that psychological disorders are caused by biological factors. As such, these practitioners treat psychological disorders by using methods that effect changes in the body; these therapies may focus on balancing neurotransmitters, changing structures in the brain, or treating physical conditions that may predispose one to mental disorders. To be most effective, biological therapies should be combined with one of the other forms of treatment previously discussed in this chapter.

By far, drug therapy, or *psychopharmacology,* is the most common form of biological therapy. While drug therapy alleviates and treats many of the symptoms of psychological disorders, it does not cure mental illness. However, it is effective in helping individuals with psychological or mental disorders achieve a better quality of life, as well as personal and social functioning.

Psychotropic drugs, or drugs that affect mental states, are used to treat a variety of psychological disorders, including schizophrenia, anxiety disorders, and mood disorders. The type of psychological disorder will determine the class of psychotropic drug that should be used.

Antipsychotic drugs, such as Haldol and Clozapine, are used to treat schizophrenia. Antipsychotic drugs block dopamine neural receptor sites. Unfortunately, these drugs have numerous negative side effects, including muscle spasms, tremors, and dizziness. One of the most significant negative side effects of antipsychotic drugs is tardive dyskinesia, a permanent neurological disorder marked by jerky and uncontrollable muscle tremors.

Antidepressants are used to treat mood disorders. There are three main types of antidepressants: tricyclic antidepressants, monoamine oxidase (MAO) inhibitors, and serotonin-reuptake-inhibitors (SSRIs). *Tricyclic antidepressants,* such as Amitriptyline and Doxepin, block the reuptake of serotonin and norepinephrine, which increases the levels of these neurotransmitters in the brain. Some common side effects of these drugs are drowsiness, constipation, dry mouth, and blurred vision. *Monoamine oxidase inhibitors (MAOIs),* like Parnate and Nardil, inhibit the enzyme monoamine oxidase and increase levels of serotonin, norepinephrine, and dopamine. MAOIs can have dangerous or deadly interactions with foods and other medications, so they are often prescribed only after other antidepressants have not worked. *Serotonin-reuptake-inhibitors (SSRIs),* like Prozac and Zoloft, selectively block the reuptake of serotonin, which increases the amount of serotonin available. SSRIs have fewer side effects than MAOIs and tricyclic antidepressants and are generally safer than other antidepressants. For these reasons, SSRIs are often the first type of antidepressant a doctor may prescribe to treat depression, and they are the most commonly used class of antidepressants.

Anxiolytics reduce anxiety by depressing the central nervous system, thereby increasing feelings of calmness and relaxation. These drugs also act as sedatives and hypnotics. Xanax is a widely prescribed anxiolytic drug. Two main types of anxiolytics are barbiturates, like Amytal and Fioricet, and benzodiazepines, such as lorazepam and Valium. Barbiturates are not commonly prescribed because it is easy to become addicted to these drugs, and these drugs can have dangerous interactions when combined with other drugs.

Another type of biological therapy is *electroconvulsive therapy (ECT).* ECT is a procedure in which electric currents are passed through the brain to intentionally trigger a brief seizure. ECT can be done on only one hemisphere of the brain or on both hemispheres of the brain. Bilateral ECT is more effective than unilateral ECT, but the side effects can be more severe. In addition to causing a seizure, ECT can cause amnesia and confusion. Before ECT is administered, patients are given general anesthesia and a muscle relaxant. ECT is given to patients with severe depression and severe schizophrenic syndromes. Because of the negative side effects, ECT is used when other forms of therapy have not been effective or if a patient is suicidal and cannot wait for antidepressants to take effect. Although it is not completely understood how ECT works, ECT may cause changes in brain chemistry that can reverse symptoms of more severe mental illnesses.

Transcranial magnetic stimulation (TMS) is another method of biological therapy that may be as effective as ECT. TMS uses an insulated magnetic coil that produces short magnetic pulses that pass through the brain. TMS is safer and has less negative side effects than ECT, and it is a non-invasive method of brain stimulation. TMS is not painful and is well-tolerated. Unlike ECT, TMS does not cause memory loss or seizures. However, like ECT, TMS is used when antidepressants have not been effective in treating depression. TMS stimulates nerve cells in the pre-frontal cortex to improve symptoms of depression.

Psychosurgery is the most extreme form of biological therapy. Psychosurgery involves removing or destroying parts of the brain to improve psychological disorders. The early and most well-known form of psychosurgery is the prefrontal lobotomy in which the connections between the prefrontal cortex and the rest of the brain are destroyed. Unfortunately, this procedure left patients in a catatonic state. Because of the controversial nature of this procedure as well as the extremely negative side effects, psychosurgery is used for only the most severe cases of mental illness and only as a last resort.

Eclectic Therapy

Although there are many different types of therapy available to treat psychological disorders, most therapists use techniques from different approaches that best suit the patient and the problem. Many therapists will use psychopharmacology in addition to other types of therapy. For example, a therapist may treat a client with depression and anxiety through the use of psychotropic medication, cognitive-behavioral therapy, and relaxation techniques. The medication will help manage the symptoms of the depression and anxiety, cognitive-behavioral therapy will address the thoughts and behaviors that are contributing to the problem, and relaxation techniques will help the client learn how to reduce anxiety.

Modes of Therapy

In addition to individual therapy, a therapist may recommend that a client participate in group therapy. *Group therapy* is effective and offers some advantages over individual therapy. Group therapy, in which individuals come together to meet with a therapist, provides clients with the opportunity to share their experiences, to better understand their problems and to learn from each other. Group therapy helps clients know that they are not alone in their struggles, and it provides a supportive network for people. Members in groups can learn from each other and offer suggestions and solutions to other members. Group therapy is less expensive than individual therapy, and the therapist can treat more people at the same time. However, one disadvantage is that the therapist cannot provide one-on-one therapy to an individual in a group therapy setting, which may require the client to also receive individual counseling.

One popular form of group therapy is *self-help groups.* These groups are effective in treating substance abuse. Alcoholics Anonymous is a well-known self-help group. This group, as well as other groups that address substance abuse problems, often are called *twelve-step programs.* Although these groups are moderated trained leaders, the leaders may not be professional therapists. Self-help groups often emphasize the role of spirituality and religion in overcoming problems, while also providing support and encouragement. Members of self-help groups also receive some of the benefits of group therapy, such as education about their problem and the opportunity to learn from and with others.

Family and couples therapy are other modes of therapy that are effective and provide some advantages over individual counseling. This type of treatment is based on the idea that interactions with others may create or exacerbate problems, and a psychological disorder affects all family members, not just the one with the problem. These modes of therapy allow family members to understand the dynamics of their interactions and to talk openly and honestly with one another about their problems and feelings in the presence of a professional therapist. This type of setting may provide an environment where family members can listen to one another and try to find solutions to their problems, tasks they may not be able to do in other settings.

Community and Preventative Approaches

Communities can provide interventions and treatments relating to mental illness. Medical professionals, mental health professionals, social workers and individuals in law enforcement, educational institutions, residential homes, rehabilitation facilities, and medical establishments can work together to provide services to prevent and treat psychological disorders. One part of prevention is educating professionals across many disciplines and individuals in the community about mental illness, risk factors for mental illness, community resources to help families and individuals affected by mental illness, and programs that help people obtain mental health services. Intervention efforts should make is easier and less expensive for people to maintain a normal life despite their problems.

There are three types of prevention: primary, secondary, and tertiary. *Primary prevention* programs are designed to reduce societal problems that can lead to incidences of mental illness. These efforts often focus on finding solutions for societal issues, such as poverty and homelessness, that can lead to mental illness. Primary prevention programs often seek to educate people about proactive ways to reduce incidences of mental illness.

Secondary prevention focuses on people who are at risk for developing a mental illness. Social, economic and environmental factors can increase the chances that certain individuals will develop a mental disorder. Examples of secondary prevention include counseling people who come from abusive homes or providing job skills training to unemployed individuals.

Tertiary prevention focuses on keeping existing mental illnesses from becoming more severe. For instance, community professionals may work with individuals suffering from PTSD to keep their disorder from becoming worse.

Practice Questions

1. **Which type of psychotropic drug depresses the central nervous system?**
   (Lower order)

   (A) antipsychotic
   (B) anxiolytic
   (C) antidepressant
   (D) monoamine oxidase inhibitor
   (E) neurotransmitters

The correct answer is B: anxiolytic.

Anxiolytic drugs reduce anxiety by depressing the central nervous system. Antipsychotic drugs block dopamine neural receptor sites; these drugs are used to treat schizophrenia. Antidepressants are used to treat mood disorders and work by altering the activity level of certain neurotransmitters in the brain. Monoamine oxidase inhibitors are a class of antidepressants. Neurotransmitters are chemicals in the brain that affect mental states.

Chapter 14: Social Psychology

Social Psychology
Key Terms, Concepts, and People

Social psychology

Attribution theory

Dispositional/person attribution

situational attribution

Consistency

Distinctiveness

Consensus

Self-serving bias

Fundamental attribution error

false consensus effect

Just-world bias

Collectivist culture

Individualistic culture

Self-fulfilling prophecy

"Pygmalion in the Classroom"

Interpersonal attraction

Positive evaluation

Shared opinions

Mere exposure effect

Conformity

Compliance

Compliance strategies

Foot-in-the-door approach

Door-in-the-face approach

Norms of reciprocity

Social facilitation

Social impairment/inhibition

Social loafing

Group polarization

GRIT

Groupthink

Mindguard

Norms

Role

Deindividuation

Attitude

Obedience studies

Persuasion/persuasive messages

Elaboration likelihood model

Central route of persuasion

Peripheral route of persuasion

Cognitive dissonance

Altruism

Prosocial/helping behavior

Kitty Genovese case

Bystander effect

Bystander intervention

Diffusion of responsibility

Pluralistic ignorance

Attraction

Similarity

Proximity

Reciprocal liking	Robbers Cave study
Antisocial behavior	Prejudice
Stereotypes	Aggression
Ethnocentrism	Discrimination
In-group	Out-group
Out-group homogeneity	In-group bias
Contact theory	Hostile aggression
Instrumental aggression	Frustration-aggression hypothesis
Bobo Doll experiment	Stanford Prison experiment
Dehumanization	Stanford Prison experiment

Key People: Solomon Asch, Leon Festinger, Stanley Milgram, Philip Zimbardo, Richard LaPiere, James Carlsmith, Harold Kelley, Robert Rosenthal, Lenore Jacobson, Muzafer Sherif, John Darley, Bibb Latane, Irving Janis

Overview

Social psychology is the study of the way people relate to others. It seeks to understand how attitudes are formed and changed, the attributions people place on their behavior and the behavior of others, and the causes behind why people behave in certain ways. Social psychology also focuses on how people's behavior is affected by the presence or absence of others.

Group Dynamics

When people interact with others, there are certain phenomena occurring; these phenomena are referred to as *group dynamics*. Individuals in a group both act upon and are acted upon by other individuals in the group. All people are members of many different groups. The rules that dictate how group members should behave are called *norms*. Each member in a group has a particular role, like employees of a corporation each have a specific responsibility or set of duties. When an improvement in someone's performance of an easy task occurs because of the presence of others, which is called *social facilitation*. An example of social facilitation is how the performance of athletes may increase when they are part of a team. The opposite of social facilitation is *social inhibition*, sometimes called social impairment. This phenomenon is experienced when an individual's performance of a difficult task is worse when performed in the presence of others. When people give speeches, they may experience social impairment.

Have you ever been in a group where it seemed that you were doing more than your fair share of the work? If so, you have experienced the group dynamic of *social loafing*. Social loafing is when individuals in a group do not expend as much effort in the group as they would when working alone. Many people in groups think that others in the group will make up for their reduced effort by doing more work, so they lack motivation to contribute much effort.

When individuals in a group act in a more extreme manner than they would on their own, this is the dynamic of *group polarization*. Think of group polarization as being an exaggeration of the attitudes of the members. For example, if people who engage in antisocial behaviors are placed in the same group, the antisocial behaviors of the members may be even more extreme as a result of group interaction.

Similar to this idea is the concept of *deindividuation*. When people are parts of groups and they get carried away by the group's activities, they often lose self-restraint and engage in activities or behaviors that they would never do on their own. This type of behavior is more likely to occur when members of a group feel aroused by the group's activities and when group members feel anonymous. Examples of deindividuation are when group members loot stores but they would not otherwise engage in this activity individually.

Muzafer Sherif conducted an experiment, known as the *Robbers Cave study*, in order to understand how conflicts in a group can be resolved. Sherif's study was based on the *contact theory*. Although the contact theory was proposed as a way to reduce prejudice, it is beneficial in understanding how working toward a common, mutually beneficial goal can reduce tension and animosity between groups. In this study, groups of campers who were hostile to each other were able to find a solution to staged camp emergencies by working toward a *superordinate goal*. A superordinate goal is one that will benefit all members of the group and requires the participation of all members. *Graduated and Reciprocated Initiatives in Tension-Reduction (GRIT)* is another way conflicts can be resolved. With GRIT, different groups will demonstrate their intention to reduce conflict, and each group will take steps to accomplish the stated goal, so long as the actions are reciprocated by the other groups.

Groupthink is a term created by **Irving Janis** to describe the actions of groups who make bad decisions because members do not consider the implications of the group's choices. Groups are more prone to exhibiting this type of thinking when leaders are biased, when the group is isolated from others, when members of the group are similar, and when the group is under a great deal of pressure to make a decision. Members of a group lose objectivity and cannot recognize fallacies in the group's decisions. In instances of groupthink, group members may not share their concerns about ideas supported by the group. When members who express disagreement share their reservations, a member of the group may criticize them. This member is called a *mindguard*.

Attribution Theory and Motives

Attribution refers to how we ascribe motives behind behavior. *Attribution theory* attempts to explain the processes individuals use to determine the causes of behavior. Attributions fall into two categories: dispositional or situational attribution. When the cause of a behavior is assumed to be internal, the attribution is *dispositional* or person. *Situational attribution* assumes that the behavior is a result of external factors.

Harold Kelley's co-variation model proposes that there are three kinds of information people use in order to form attributions: consistency, distinctiveness, and consensus.

Consensus Information:	Consistency Information:	Distinctiveness Information:
asks how others in the same situation would have responded	refers to how a person behaves under the same circumstances over time	refers to how similar the situation is to other situations
Do other people behave this way in this situation?	Is the person's behavior consistent across time in this situation?	Is the person's behavior unique to this situation?

By doing a kind of mental math people take into account these 3 factors that lead to an internal or situational attribution. For example, suppose you observe a stranger heaping great praise on a film, the chart below explains how the factors lead to different attributions.

	Consensus	Distinctiveness	Consistency	Attribution
The stranger raves about the film.	Low	Low	High	Personal/Internal
	Other people do not rave about the film.	The stranger raves about many other films	The stranger always raves about this film.	Something about the stranger caused the behavior.
	High	High	High	Situational/External
	Other people rave about the film.	The stranger does not rave about many other films.	The stranger always raves about this film.	Something about the film caused the behavior.

What people think about others can have great impact on a person's behavior. This concept is referred to as *self-fulfilling prophecy*. If a person expects another person to behave in a certain manner, the other person will most likely behave in the manner anticipated. An area where this concept is very evident is education. Students will often perform in a manner consistent with the teacher's expectations. This phenomenon in education is called the Rosenthal effect.

In the *"Pygmalion in the Classroom"* experiment, **Robert Rosenthal** and **Lenore Jacobson** investigated the impact of others expectations on student performance. Rosenthal and Jacobson gave students an IQ test and told the students that the test would demonstrate which students were on the verge of academic growth. Then, the researchers chose a random sample from among these students and told their teachers that the students were ripe for intellectual growth. The students chosen for the random sample were not any different than the students in the original sample. When the researchers administered the IQ test at the end of the year, the students from the random sample had a greater increase in their test scores than the other students. The teachers' expectations of these students affected the students' performance.

Four typical attributional biases are self-serving bias, fundamental attribution error, false consensus effect, and just-world bias. A *self-serving bias* occurs when a person takes more credit for good outcomes than bad. When a positive outcome is the result, the person attributes the good outcome to his innate qualities, but when the outcome is bad, the same person blames the outcome on situational factors. A concept closely related to self-serving bias is *fundamental attribution error,* which is demonstrated when a person overestimates dispositional factors and underestimates situational factors. Fundamental attribution errors are not as common as once believed. In fact, in cultures that are *collectivist*, this bias is less common than in *individualistic* cultures. When a person overestimates the number of people who will agree with them, that person is demonstrating *false-consensus effect.* The *just-world bias* is evidenced when people believe that bad things only happen to bad people. If something bad happens to a person, the person deserved what happened. This bias often results in people assigning blame to victims.

Attitude Formation and Change

An *attitude* is an organized set of cognitions, emotions, and behaviors towards people, places, things or beliefs. Attitudes can be changed and influenced by others through persuasion or persuasive messages. The marketing and advertising industry are relevant examples for the power of persuasive messages. One central idea of advertising is that the more someone is exposed to something, the more they will like it. This is called the *mere exposure effect* and has been consistently demonstrated in research.

The ELM model stands for *Elaboration Likelihood Model* and it states that persuasive messages can be cognitively processed by one of two routes: in the *central route*, people think deeply about the content of the message before making a decision, in the *peripheral route*, people are persuaded by superficial factors, such as the appeal of the messenger. The ELM model identifies when each route will be taken and the resulting change in attitudes and behavior.

Persuasive Message	*Audience Factors*	*Processing Approach*	*Persuasion Outcome*
Central Route Processing	High motivation or cognitive ability to think about message	Deep processing Focused on strength and quality of arguments in message	Lasting attitude change Resists fading and counterarguments
Peripheral Route Processing	Low motivation or ability to think about the message	Shallow processing Focused on superficial elements of message such as speaker's attractiveness or number of arguments	Temporary attitude change Susceptible to fading and counterarguments

Although attitudes can affect behavior, the interaction between attitudes and behavior cannot perfectly predict behavior. **Richard LaPiere** conducted a study in which he examined how people's attitudes about Asians would affect their treatment of Asian people. LaPiere visited hotels and restaurants with an Asian couple. He observed how the couple was treated. The couple was treated poorly only one time. LaPiere later contacted all the hotels and restaurants that had been visited and asked about their attitude toward Asians. Over 90 percent of the establishments indicated that they would not serve Asian people, although these establishments had served Asian people. In this case, attitudes did not predict behavior.

Attitudes can also be changed by *cognitive dissonance,* which is a term created by Leon Festinger. Cognitive dissonance occurs when people experience uncomfortable mental tension because their attitudes conflict with their behaviors. **Festinger** and **James Carlsmith** conducted an experiment in which participants were told to perform a boring task. After each participant performed the task, the participant was instructed to tell the next subject that the task was enjoyable. The participants that were paid only $1 to lie had a more favorable opinion about the experiment than did participants who were paid $20. The participants who were paid less money had less external motivation to lie, so lying created cognitive dissonance, which resulted in those participants changing their attitude in order to relieve their cognitive dissonance.

Conformity, Compliance and Obedience

Conformity occurs when individuals go along with the attitudes and actions of others. One of the most interesting conformity experiments was conducted by **Solomon Asch**. Participants were placed in a room with confederates and were asked to make simple perceptual judgments. They were shown 3 vertical lines and asked which line matched the target line. Each participant was required to answer out loud. The confederates unanimously responded with obviously incorrect answers. Even though the participants knew the answers being given were incorrect, they gave the same incorrect answers. Approximately 70 percent of the of the participants conformed to the wrong answer on at least one trial. In one third of the cases, the participants conformed to the wrong answer given by the confederates. Research studies indicate that conformity is most likely to occur when the opinion is unanimous, but in groups which have more than three participants, conformity is not significantly affected. The higher the amount of group cohesion, the greater the conformity.

Conformity is influenced by cultural factors. People who live in individualistic cultures tend to conform less than those living in collectivist cultures. People who are more educated and view themselves as being of higher status are less likely to conform than are people who have a lower status, and men are less likely to conform than women. Lastly, if one group member refuses to conform, other members may be less likely to conform.

Compliance is giving in to the requests of others, often times at your own expense. Strategies that people use to get others to comply with their requests are called *compliance strategies.* One such strategy uses the *foot-in-the-door approach.* This strategy implies that if people will agree to a small request, they will have a greater likelihood of agreeing to a larger task. The opposite is also true. If someone refuses a large task, there exists a greater likelihood that they will agree to a small request that seems more reasonable. This concept is known as the *door-in-the-face approach*. Both of these strategies give the appearance that the one making the request is giving something to encourage the other person to comply.

Another compliance strategy relies on using what is referred to as *norms of reciprocity*. The premise of this strategy is that when people think someone has done something nice for them, they need to do something nice in return.

Stanley Milgram conducted *obedience studies*. In these studies, participants were told it was their job to administer electric shocks of increasing intensity to other participants if they performed poorly on a task. The other participant was a confederate and was deliberately performing poorly so that the other participant would have to administer a shock. The confederates acted like the shocks were painful and begged for them to stop. Despite the pain of the confederate, the other participant was told to continue to give the shocks. The study measured how willing participants were to continue to obey. Over 60 percent of the participants continued to administer the maximum number of shocks. Based on the results of this study, Milgram conducted additional studies to try to explain why a person might or might not continue to comply. Compliance decreased when participants had to sit in the room with the confederate while the shocks were being administered. If participants could see the confederate, willingness to comply decreased. If the participant had to force the learner's hand to administer the shock, compliance decreased, but 30 percent of the participants still continued to deliver shocks. Obedience also decreased if the participants perceived the authority of the test administrator as being less than another administrator. If other confederates in the room with the confederate who was being shocked objected to the shocks, a significant number of participants quit in the middle of the experiment.

Attraction

Social psychology also focuses on why people are attracted to others. When someone evaluates someone in a positive way, they will be drawn to that person, a tendency referred to as *interpersonal attraction*. There are three fundamental principles of attraction. The first principle is *similarity*. People like other people to whom they are similar. The second principle is *proximity*. People like others with whom they have frequent contact. The third principle is *reciprocal liking*, which means people like others who like them.

In addition, positive evaluation leads to attraction. *Positive evaluation* means that we like to be thought of positively, and, therefore, we like to be around those who have a good opinion of us. *Shared opinions* means we like to be around people who hold ideas, values, attitudes, and opinions similar to ours. Of course, physical attractiveness is important, too.

Altruism and Pro-social Behavior

Altruism is defined as selfless sacrifice. It is closely linked to *prosocial (helping) behavior*. One event that triggered research about what factors influence people to help others was the murder of **Kitty Genovese**. While Kitty Genovese was being murdered in her apartment complex, 38 neighbors saw or heard what was occurring but did not intervene. This type of indifference is called the *bystander effect*. The larger the group of people who witness a person in distress, the less likely anyone will help. The indifference of the bystanders led **John Darley** and **Bibb Latane** to study the factors that influenced the decision to help someone. The concept known as *diffusion of responsibility* partly explains bystander effect. The larger the number of people who witness a problem, there exists less likelihood that anyone will take responsibility for solving the problem. Pluralistic ignorance also helps explain the bystander effect. *Pluralistic ignorance* occurs when people look to others to determine what is appropriate behavior for the situation.

Aggression and Antisocial Behavior

Antisocial behavior is behavior that is harmful to others. Antisocial behavior can be divided into two categories: prejudice and aggression. Prejudice is often the result of stereotypes about groups of people. *Stereotypes* are ideas and attitudes about what other groups are like, and they influence how someone interacts with members of other groups. Stereotypes can be negative or positive. *Prejudice* is an undeserved and negative attitude towards members of certain groups. Prejudices are the result of stereotypes that are applied broadly to all members of a group. For example, if someone thinks that Sally, who is from the south, is ignorant, then all people from the south must be ignorant. When people believe their culture is superior to other cultures, they are displaying an attitude of *ethnocentrism*. While prejudice is an attitude, *discrimination* is an action taken against members from different groups.

Individuals prefer to be around other members of their group. This is known as *in-group bias*. An in-group is simply the group to which one belongs, and the *out-group* is every other group. *Outgroup homogeneity* is the assumption that every member of an outside group is similar.

Aggression is actions directed at another person with the intent of harming the other person. There are two types of aggression. *Hostile aggression* has no clear purpose and is driven by emotions. *Instrumental aggression*, on the other hand, is aggression that has the purpose of securing a certain outcome. Biological and hormonal factors can cause aggression, and aggression can be learned through modeling. **Albert Bandura** conducted the *Bobo Doll experiment* to demonstrate that the more someone is exposed to aggression, the more aggressive they will become. Another theory about what causes aggression is the *frustration-aggression hypothesis*, which postulates that feelings of frustration increase the likelihood of aggressive actions.

Numerous research studies have documented how humans have the ability to view victims of violence as less than human, which is called *dehumanization*. One study that investigated this concept is was conducted by **Phil Zimbardo**. In Zimbardo's *Stanford Prison experiment*, randomly selected participants were jailed in a simulated jail and other participants were randomly selected to be guards. All participants who were guards wore uniforms and the prisoners were assigned numbers, not names. Prisoners were locked up and the guards were put in charge. Within a short time, members of each group became so engrossed in their roles that they began to hate members of the other group. The members of each group experienced *deindividuation*, which means they lost their personal identities

and identified with their group's identity. Before long, participants in the guard group began to act violently towards the prisoner group members. To protect the well-being of the participants, Zimbardo ended the experiment prematurely.
Practice Questions

1. **When subjects in Milgram's obedience experiments received their orders from a research assistant, they**
   (Lower order)

   (A) conformed more easily
   (B) refused to participate
   (C) dropped out of the study
   (D) were less likely to obey
   (E) were slightly more obedient

The correct answer is D. were less likely to obey.
Participants were less likely to obey a person whom they perceived as having less authority. They conformed more easily when the person had more authority. Many participants dropped out of the study when other confederates in the room objected to the other confederate being shocked.

2. **Which of the following examples is an example of situational attribution?**
   (Higher order)

   (A) Mary takes a French exam and passes it and attributes her passing grade to her good study habits.
   (B) Jake gets ripped off by a rich man. He then assumes that every rich man is greedy.
   (C) Marlo is more aggressive when she is around other aggressive children.
   (D) Stanley likes Mr. Caruso because Mr. Caruso likes him.
   (E) Henry takes a Zoology test and fails it. He blames his poor score on disruptions by his classmates.

The correct answer is E. Henry takes a Zoology test and fails it. He blames his poor score on disruptions by his classmates.
When a person attributes success or failure to situations or external events, they are assigning situational attribution to the outcome. If someone attributes a positive outcome to personal characteristics, they are assigning dispositional attribution. Answer B describes a stereotype. Answer C is referring to the results of a study conducted by Albert Bandura. Answer D refers to the principle of reciprocal liking.

Challenge Question:

3. A group of teenagers is attending summer camp. During the camp, one of the adults deliberately manipulates situations to make the campers mistrust one another. Before long, the campers are being mean to each other and the environment is becoming hostile. Which of the following statements best describes how the groups can work out their differences?

    (A) The groups can play games that cause them to compete against each other for prizes.
    (B) There is nothing that can be done to help the groups work out their differences.
    (C) The leaders need to sit the groups down and have a discussion with them about how to resolve conflict.
    (D) The groups should work together to solve a problem that is affecting all of them.
    (E) The groups need to take some time away from each other to allow things to settle down.

The correct answer is D. The groups should work together to solve a problem that is affecting all of them.

Working together to solve a problem that is affecting all of them is working towards a superordinate goal. A superordinate goal is a goal that will benefit all members and will require the participation of all members. Competing against each other for prizes can create a hostile environment. While there is nothing wrong with leaders talking to the groups about how to resolve conflict, this type of strategy may do nothing to resolve the hostility and solve the problem. Taking some time away from each other may be helpful, but it does not require group members to work together to find a mutually beneficial resolution.

SECTION III:
Sample Tests

SUGGESTIONS FOR THE FREE-RESPONSE SECTION_____

ORGANIZING YOUR RESPONSE

1. Before you begin formulating your response, stop and think about what the question is asking you. On the question sheet, write down some notes or make an outline. Take a few minutes to think about your answer and organize your thoughts. Begin creating a mental image of what you need to cover. If your notes are organized and well thought out, writing your response should be relatively easy.

2. You should NOT use your outline as your response. This is prohibited in the free response instructions given by the College Board. You will not be awarded any points for answers written in outline form.

3. Write your response using complete sentences in paragraph form. Indent each paragraph. Organizing your paragraphs in the order implied in the question will help the AP scorers grade your response. Do not label the sections of your response with letters. Each paragraph of your response should clearly indicate which part of the question you are answering.

4. Make sure you cover every part of the question, even if you have to guess. If your response is an incorrect guess, it will not count against you. If it is correct, though, you will be awarded a point. Do not spend too much time, however, trying to think of something to write for a section. If you do not know the information, move to the next part of the question. Do not worry if you miss one part of the question. Your overall score for that question will not be greatly affected.

5. Do not worry about writing an introduction and conclusion. The first sentence in each paragraph should indicate which section of the question you are answering. Do NOT restate or reword the question in your answer.

6. Your answer will be scored based on accurate content knowledge and the ability to correctly apply that knowledge to various scenarios. You will not be penalized for your writing style, use of incorrect grammar or punctuation or your general writing ability. Of course, you should always do your best!

7. Write as legibly as possible. If your handwriting is too illegible, the reader will not know what you have written, and you will not be awarded any points you may have been awarded if you had written more neatly.

8. Make sure you cover every part of the question in an organized, cogent manner. Find a method for organizing your thoughts, whether by outline, checklist, or some other manner that works for you so that you will know you covered all elements of the question. Refer to your notes or outline or whatever method you choose frequently when answering the question. Doing this will help you organize your thoughts in your head and on paper, and it will serve as mental checklist. It may also help you identify parts of the question you did not answer or areas where you need to add information.

9. If you have time after you have answered BOTH free response questions, read through your answers to check for errors or omissions. If you forgot to cover something, neatly add it to your response in the appropriate place. If you need to delete something, make it clear that you are deleting that portion, but keep your writing as neat and legible as possible. Leaving a small space between the lines will give you room to add content and make corrections.

CONTENT SUGGESTIONS

1. Do only what is asked of you. If you are to discuss a concept and give an example, keep it simple. Elaborating too much will take up time that you may need to finish BOTH your responses.

2. Use psychological terms as much as possible. If you reference a theory or theorist, make sure you use the proper name.

3. Underline all important terms. This not only makes it easier for the reader to locate the information in your response, it also helps you know you covered that point.

4. Define all terms even though it may not be explicitly stated in the question. Make sure the definition is clear and to the point and within the proper context. Do not use the word you are defining in the definition. For example, when defining the word "conformity," do not use the word conform in your definition. The AP reader wants to know that you understand the meaning of the word you are defining. Using definitions shows the reader that you know the content.

5. Use examples or specific studies or cases to help support your arguments. The example must be used in the right context. Make sure examples demonstrate your understanding of the concept or term and are accurate. If you use an example incorrectly, it shows that you do not have a good grasp of that concept. Examples should not contradict definition of terms, concepts, or principles. Examples should come from content in your psychology courses or review books, not from your personal life. If the question asks you to give an example, make sure you give an example or you will not be awarded a point for that part of the question. Indicate that you are giving an example by using "for example" or "an example of.." This is especially important when giving an example is a required element of the question.

6. Keep the content relevant to the question. Decide the context of the question, and limit your response to the context. Adding unnecessary information will not help you score higher on a response. The readers are looking for specific information from a carefully designed rubric. You will not be awarded any additional points for providing information that was not required.

7. Make sure your writing is well-organized, clear, and to the point.

HOW YOUR ANSWER WILL BE GRADED

The AP readers use a rubric to score your answer. Most free response questions will be worth 6 to 10 points. As the scorers read your answer, they will award a point for every required element of the question that was covered accurately and thoroughly. After reading your answer, the reader will add up your points to arrive at your total score for that question. No points are deducted.

The rubric helps the readers score your work in an objective and fair way, but they do not determine exactly what content will earn you points or how many points each element of the question is worth. The rubric is their guide, and it will specify the information that should be included in the response. In most instances, you will earn a point for providing accurate and complete knowledge as required by the question unless you directly contradict yourself. Be consistent!

The free-response section of the AP exam will make up roughly 1/3 of your grade for the entire test. You must answer BOTH of the questions. You will be given 50 minutes to answer BOTH questions, so allow yourself enough time to answer each question adequately. Do not spend too much time on any one component of the question. Use all the time you are given, but if you do complete the free response answers before the 50 minutes is up, go back over your work and make any necessary changes.

AP Psychology Sample Test 1 _____

Sample Test Questions

Instructions: For each problem, select the choice that best answers the question

Section I: Multiple Choice

1. **A city council who deflects criticism for the way it handled an emergency situation in the city by responding, "It's just how things are done" describes which of the following terms?**
   (Higher order)

   [A] Mere exposure effect
   [B] Bystander effect
   [C] In-group bias
   [D] Diffusion of responsibility
   [E] Situational ignorance

2. **Which of the following statements about persuasive messages is NOT true?**
   (Higher order)

   [A] They can be processed one of two ways.
   [B] The persuasiveness of the messages is influenced by the likeability of the messenger.
   [C] Messages that play on people's emotions do not affect attitudes.
   [D] Repetitive messages are more likely to result in attitudinal change.
   [E] The length of the message is important.

3. **Experiments involving cognitive dissonance were conducted by which researcher(s)?**
   (Lower order)

   [A] Robert Rosenthal and Lenore Jacobson
   [B] Leon Festinger and James Carlsmith
   [C] Albert Bandura
   [D] Phil Zimbardo
   [E] Richard LaPiere

4. **A group of rioters begin looting neighborhood stores. The group members do not seem to realize that the stores' owners have nothing to do with the situation they are protesting, and they seem indifferent to any consequences of their actions. The leader of the group intimidates any member who expresses concerns about the group's actions. This scenario is an example of which phenomenon?**
   (Higher order)

   [A] Mindguard
   [B] Prejudice
   [C] Foot-in-the-door
   [D] Positive evaluation
   [E] Groupthink

5. **A dancer's performance improves when she is dancing as part of her ballet group. What is this an example of?**
   (Lower order)

   [A] Group polarization
   [B] Social inhibition
   [C] Social facilitation
   [D] Door-in-the-face
   [E] Deindividuation

6. **All of the following statements about conformity are true EXCEPT:**
(Higher order)

   [A] Groups with high levels of cohesion are more likely to have higher levels of conformity.

   [B] Women are more likely to conform than men.

   [C] People of high social status are less likely to conform than people of lower social status.

   [D] Conformity is the same thing as compliance.

   [E] If one group member refuses to conform, other members may be less likely to conform.

7. **Someone does something nice for you, and you feel that you need to do something nice for them in return. What is this called?**
(Lower order)

   [A] Norms of reciprocity

   [B] Shared opinions

   [C] In-group bias

   [D] Self-fulfilling prophecy

   [E] Altruism

8. **A fundamental attribution error is:**
(Lower order)

   [A] taking more credit for good outcomes than bad

   [B] overestimating dispositional factors and underestimating situational factors

   [C] overestimating the number of people who will agree with you

   [D] believing that bad things only happen to bad people

   [E] a set of feelings and beliefs

9. **Daniel is playing a game of marbles with his elementary school friends. He perceives the marbles on the playing surface as three main groups and a few individual scattered marbles. Daniel's perception is most likely:**
(Higher order)

   [A] an illusion related to distance consistency

   [B] based on monocular rather than binocular depth cues

   [C] an example of a gestalt principle

   [D] represented as a spatial map plotted in his parietal lobes

   [E] relying on visual input primarily from rod cells

10. **A sudden, unexpected and very loud sound can result in deafness that is limited to a narrow range of sound frequencies close to and including the frequency of the injury producing sound. Where is the most probable location of the injury that results in this type of deafness?**
(Higher order)

   [A] The tympanic membrane

   [B] The oval window

   [C] The basilar membrane

   [D] The spiral ganglia

   [E] The cochlear nerve

11. The Necker cube (shown below) is an optical illusion that top-down processing theorists claim cannot be explained by the principles of bottom-up processing. What type of perceptual concept is most likely NOT relevant to the perception of this specific optical illusion?

(Higher order)

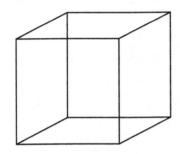

[A] Receptive fields
[B] Depth cues
[C] Figure-ground relationship
[D] Shape constancy
[E] The psi phenomena

12. Visual information from the retina does NOT travel directly to _____.

(Lower order)

[A] the lateral geniculate nucleus of the thalamus
[B] the superior colliculus of the midbrain
[C] the pretectum of the midbrain
[D] the suprachiasmatic nucleus of the hypothalamus
[E] the visual cortex of the occipital lobes

13. The moon appears larger when it is close to the horizon. This is an example of:

(Lower order)

[A] slow adaptation
[B] rapid adaptation
[C] transduction
[D] size constancy
[E] an illusion

14. Which sensory receptor cells are considered direct extensions of the brain?

(Lower order)

[A] Rod cells
[B] Cone cells
[C] Hair cells
[D] Olfactory receptor cells
[E] Pain receptor cells

15. Paul is at a football game. He receives a phone call from his wife asking him for the alarm code to their home. Paul would most likely:

(Higher order)

[A] access subconscious processes to retrieve the code
[B] access preconscious processes to retrieve the code
[C] provide the code based on his current conscious awareness
[D] experience interference in providing the code due to unconscious processes
[E] experience interference in providing the code due to a subconscious conflict.

16. **Which theorist is most closely associated with the concept of dissociation as a proposed mechanism to explain hypnotic states?**
    (Lower order)

    [A] William James
    [B] Sigmund Freud
    [C] J. Allan Hobson
    [D] Ernest Hilgard
    [E] Alexander Luria

17. **Claire is a 4-year-old girl who for several months has had episodes of sudden awakenings late at night where she is crying and seems terrified. In the morning she has no recollection of the awakening episodes. Claire's episodes are:**
    (Higher order)

    [A] probably related to airway obstruction
    [B] occurring during the REM stage of sleep
    [C] a form of reverse wish fulfillment
    [D] unlikely to be accompanied by heavy sweating
    [E] associated with stage 3 sleep

18. **Based only on the fact that a psychoactive drug is well-known to produce exceptionally severe withdrawal symptoms, the drug is:**
    (Higher order)

    [A] not a neurotransmitter agonist
    [B] exceptionally permeable to the blood-brain barrier
    [C] likely causing suppression of normal neurotransmitter activity
    [D] unlikely to be reversed by the administration of naloxone
    [E] one with an effective dose that is relatively close to its lethal dose.

19. **Which brain region plays an important role in generating and regulating circadian rhythms?**
    (Lower order)

    [A] Hypothalamus
    [B] Basal ganglia
    [C] Cerebellum
    [D] Amygdala
    [E] Pons

20. **Alpha waves are brainwave patterns that are:**
    (Lower order)

    [A] the highest frequency of the five major brainwave patterns
    [B] associated with states of relaxation and light sleep
    [C] required to generate sleep spindles
    [D] the dominant wave pattern during stage 2 sleep
    [E] the dominant wave pattern during REM stage sleep

21. Jason administers a questionnaire at the end of the school year, on the same day at the same time in the school auditorium, to all the students in his elementary school grades 2 through 6. One of the questions asks: "On average, how many days per week did you eat breakfast during the past school year?" He then plots the average number of days students ate breakfast, 0 through 7, against the average GPA of students for each day average. For instance, a 3.4 average GPA was found for all students who reported eating breakfast 5 times per week. All of the students responded to the survey. The total survey response number was 600. Ten students were absent on the day the questionnaire was administered. Among the choices below, what is the most likely source of error in Jason's study?

(Higher order)

[A] A sampling error
[B] An observational bias
[C] An experimenter bias
[D] A situation-relevant confounding variable
[E] A participant-relevant confounding variable

22. Which of the following is true regarding an independent variable?

(Lower Order)

[A] It cannot be controlled in an experiment
[B] It cannot be changed during an experiment
[C] It is the observer in a naturalistic study
[D] It does not correlate with a dependent variable
[E] It may cause a change in a dependent variable

23. Which choice below describes a means to control for the Hawthorne effect?

(Higher order)

[A] Providing a control group with sugar pills that have an identical appearance to the pills with an active ingredient that are provided to an experimental group.
[B] Designing a study so that the participants serve alternately as the experimental group and the control group.
[C] Ensuring that the participants of a study are randomly assigned to either the control or the experimental group.
[D] Choosing a dependent variable that can be observed in subjects while they are asleep.
[E] Stratifying the subject population according to age ranges, gender and ethnic background.

24. A set of experimental data has the following values: 2, 3, 4, 4, 5, 6, 6, 12. This set of data has a:

(Lower order)

[A] bimodal distribution
[B] negatively skewed distribution
[C] standard deviation of ten
[D] standard deviation of twelve
[E] median of five

25. Jack is a 35-year-old man who is offered opportunity to participate in a research study in which he will be interviewed by the researcher. According to APA ethical guidelines, Jack must NOT be:
(Higher order)

[A] misled about the purpose of the study

[B] provided with a means to contact the researcher after the conclusion of the study

[C] intentionally subjected to any painful stimuli during the study

[D] denied anonymity during and after the study.

[E] told the results of his specific participation the study

26. Which of the following is NOT an example of a naturalistic research methodology?
(Lower order)

[A] Using a video camera to record children's reactions to distant thunder while they are playing in a park

[B] Providing a food source for nocturnal animals only at night

[C] Constructing an artificial structure to hide an observer

[D] Recording only clearly abnormal behavior of persons at a rock concert

[E] Observing the behavior of animals following a natural disaster.

27. All of the following statements about psychoanalytic theory are true EXCEPT:
(Higher order)

[A] Psychoanalytic theory focuses on the unconscious.

[B] Psychoanalytic theory is not based on empirical research.

[C] Psychoanalytic theory emphasizes the importance of childhood.

[D] Psychoanalytic theory uses assessments that are objective and reliable.

[E] Psychoanalytic theory seems to be biased against women.

28. The model of triadic reciprocality focuses on the interaction between:
(Higher order)

[A] mind, body, and spirit.

[B] the therapist, the client, and the environment.

[C] the person, behavior, and the environment.

[D] the id, ego, and superego.

[E] biology, person, and situations.

29. Traits that are unique to each person are called:
(Lower order)

[A] nomothetic

[B] collective

[C] idiographic

[D] complexes

[E] personality

30. The following list of traits are not part of the Big Five EXCEPT:
    (Higher order)

    [A] Extraversion, openness, honesty, conscientiousness, and neuroticism
    [B] Conscientiousness, curiosity, extraversion, agreeableness, and psychoticism
    [C] Extraversion, neuroticism, openness, agreeableness, and conscientiousness
    [D] Extraversion, psychoticism, honesty, trustworthiness, and openness
    [E] Idiographic, nomothetic, extraversion, honesty, and openness

31. Albert Bandura's theory of personality falls into which category?
    (Lower order)

    [A] Cognitive
    [B] Humanistic
    [C] Psychoanalytic
    [D] Social-cognitive
    [E] Trait theory

32. A psychologist interested in measuring and describing personality traits would use which of the following assessment tools?
    (Lower order)

    [A] Stanford-Binet
    [B] DSM
    [C] Myers-Briggs
    [D] MMPI
    [E] Rorschach Inkblot

33. Which of the following statements best describes learning?
    (Higher order)

    [A] Learning occurs when two stimuli are repeatedly paired and an association is made between the two stimuli.
    [B] Learning is an entirely cognitive process.
    [C] Learning is based on the consequences resulting from one's actions.
    [D] Learning produces changes in behavior.
    [E] Learning is a result of biological processes.

34. Miguel hates going to physical education. On P.E. day, he acts sick, hoping his father will write a note asking for Miguel to be excused from P.E. class for that day. Which of the following terms describes Miguel's actions?
    (Higher order)

    [A] Garcia effect
    [B] Imitation
    [C] Escape learning
    [D] Classical conditioning
    [E] Avoidance learning

35. Which psychologist demonstrated that emotions can be learned?
    (Lower order)

    [A] B.F. Skinner
    [B] John B. Watson
    [C] John Garcia
    [D] Edward Thorndike
    [E] Edward Tolman

36. **Which reinforcement schedule is best to use if you want to teach your dog to rollover?**
    (Lower order)

    [A] Variable-ratio
    [B] Fixed-ratio
    [C] Continuous
    [D] Fixed-interval
    [E] Contingency

37. **According to classical conditioning, extinction has occurred when:**
    (Lower order)

    [A] similar stimuli elicit the same response as the initial stimuli
    [B] behavior suddenly reappears
    [C] the conditioned stimulus no longer elicits the conditioned response
    [D] the conditioned stimulus becomes aversive
    [E] distinctions between similar stimuli can be made

38. **Which of the following best states the difference between positive reinforcement and negative reinforcement?**
    (Higher order)

    [A] Positive reinforcement is likely to increase the behavior; negative reinforcement is likely to decrease the behavior.
    [B] Positive reinforcement means something rewarding is taken away, while negative reinforcement means something unpleasant is taken away.
    [C] Positive reinforcement involves adding something rewarding and negative reinforcement means taking away something unpleasant.
    [D] Positive reinforcement uses primary reinforcers and negative reinforcement uses secondary reinforcers.
    [E] Positive reinforcement involves rewarding positive behaviors, while negative reinforcement involves rewarding negative behaviors.

39. **A biological psychologist might be interested in which of the following?**
    (Higher order)

    [A] How unconditional positive regard affects self-concept
    [B] How dopamine affects thought processes
    [C] How a person's perception of events affects behavior
    [D] How social roles impact development
    [E] How to improve an employee's motivation

40. **In what way would a behaviorist disagree with an evolutionary psychologist about the cause of fearful behavior?**
    (Higher order)

    [A] A behaviorist would argue that fear is caused by repressed unconscious memories, while an evolutionary psychologist would say that fear is the result of how someone interprets experiences.
    [B] A behaviorist would attribute fear to biological processes, but an evolutionary psychologist would argue it is the result of receiving some type of positive reward for it in the past.
    [C] A behaviorist would argue that fear results from receiving a positive reward for fearful behavior in the past, while an evolutionary psychologist would say that fear is an adaptive response that promotes survival.
    [D] A behaviorist would say that fear is an adaptive response, but an evolutionary psychologist would argue that fear is caused by biological, social, and psychological factors.
    [E] A behavioral psychologist and an evolutionary psychologist would both agree that fear is a learned response that has been consistently reinforced.

41. **Which of the following two people are closely associated with humanistic psychology?**
(Lower order)

[A] John B. Watson and B.F. Skinner

[B] Sigmund Freud and Erik Erikson

[C] Max Wertheimer and Rene Descartes

[D] Carl Rogers and Abraham Maslow

[E] Charles Darwin and John Locke

42. **Who was the first woman to be awarded a Ph.D. in psychology?**
(Lower order)

[A] Dorothea Dix

[B] Margaret Floy Washburn

[C] Karen Horney

[D] Mary Whiton Calkins

[E] Mary Ainsworth

43. **In which way are structuralism and functionalism different?**
(Higher order)

[A] Structuralism recognizes a distinction between the mind and body and functionalism does not.

[B] Structuralism assumes that only matter and energy exist and functionalism assumes that observation and experiences are the only way to acquire knowledge.

[C] Structuralism breaks the mind down into its most basic components. Functionalism asserts that the uses of the mind are more important than the individual components of the mind.

[D] Structuralism focuses only on cognitive functions and functionalism is concerned with social structures and cognitive functions.

[E] There is no difference between the two.

44. **In what major way is behaviorism different from other theoretical perspectives?**
(Lower order)

[A] It is only concerned with observable behavior.

[B] Its concepts are based on empirical research.

[C] Its principles are of no use today.

[D] It is not considered scientific.

[E] There is no specific way behaviorism is different from other perspectives.

45. **A researcher wants to know how metacognition changes over time. He groups participants according to their ages. Based on your understanding of cross-sectional research, which of the following statements is true?**
(Higher order)

[A] The researcher will be able to measure individual differences.

[B] The researcher will be able to determine how participants change over time.

[C] The researcher will be able to determine what is normal for each group.

[D] The researcher does not have to consider how cultural differences effect the results.

[E] The researcher will have to assess the participants at set intervals of time to see what changes have occurred.

46. **All of the following statements about development are true EXCEPT:**
(Higher order)

[A] Development occurs in multiple contexts.

[B] Cognitive development does not affect social development.

[C] Cultural factors impact development.

[D] Development is affected by genetic and environmental factors.

[E] Each stage of development has a critical period.

47. **At birth, which sense is the least developed?**
    (Lower order)

    [A] Vision
    [B] Hearing
    [C] Smell
    [D] Taste
    [E] Touch

48. **Jane's family has a cat. Jane knows the cat is an animal and has four legs. When Jane's family visits a pond, Jane sees a duck waddling on the shoreline. Jane does not think the duck is an animal. Jane is confused when she is told the duck is an animal. Based on Piaget's cognitive learning theory, how can Jane achieve equilibration?**
    (Higher order)

    [A] Assimilation
    [B] Conservation
    [C] Theory of Mind
    [D] Static reasoning
    [E] Accommodation

49. **Zone of proximal development is a concept proposed by which cognitive learning theorist?**
    (Lower order)

    [A] Albert Bandura
    [B] Lev Vygotsky
    [C] Harry Harlow
    [D] Jean Piaget
    [E] Erik Erikson

50. **Andy is doing a lot of self-evaluation. He is questioning some of the values and beliefs of his parents and realizes there are some things his parents value that he does not value. He is trying to make a decision about how he wants to live his life. Which stage of Erikson's psychosocial theory describes Andy's crisis?**
    (Higher order)

    [A] Generativity versus Stagnation
    [B] Trust versus Mistrust
    [C] Independence versus Dependence
    [D] Identity versus Role Confusion
    [E] Industry versus Inferiority

51. **Which parenting style is the healthiest for children?**
    (Lower order)

    [A] Authoritative
    [B] Permissive
    [C] Neglectful
    [D] Authoritarian
    [E] Organized

52. **Which reflex is elicited when the bottom of baby's foot is stroked?**
    (Lower order)

    [A] Moro reflex
    [B] Babinski reflex
    [C] Rooting reflex
    [D] Orienting reflex
    [E] Palmar reflex

53. **Nativist theories of language acquisition prominently feature:**
    (Lower order)

    [A] principles of long-term potentiation
    [B] grammar acquisition devices
    [C] mnemonics
    [D] elaboration rehearsal
    [E] heuristic thinking

54. Quincy is preparing for a high school history examination. During his preparation, memorization of a list of dates will most likely:

(Higher order)

[A] require primarily automatic processing

[B] occur during a critical phase

[C] generate procedural memories

[D] require divided attention

[E] improve with chunking techniques

55. Following her recovery from meningitis, a serious infection of the membranes that surround the brain, a 25-year-old woman is no longer able to form new explicit memories. She is able to subsequently learn to needlepoint as a hobby. The woman will most likely:

(Higher order)

[A] have damage to her cerebellum

[B] not have permanent brain damage

[C] also have difficulty with speech fluency

[D] be able to describe in words how she needlepoints

[E] have damage to her hypothalamus

56. Brian is a 35-year-old father of three teenage daughters. What statement about teenage girls would represent a belief bias of Brian's?

(Higher order)

[A] "Since all of my daughters are irresponsible, any teenage girl is probably irresponsible."

[B] "My friends all say my daughters are very responsible. I can't prove it but I am sure my daughters are actually irresponsible at heart."

[C] "All teenage girls are irresponsible. My daughters are teenagers. Therefore my daughters are irresponsible."

[D] "Based on my observations, genetic factors are the cause of my daughter's irresponsibility."

[E] "For every example that indicates my daughters are responsible, which I don't even need to hear to know they are wrong, I can show twenty examples that prove my daughters are irresponsible."

57. Among the choices below, which is most precisely associated with the process of selective attention?

(Lower order)

[A] Sensory memory

[B] Phoneme enunciation

[C] The order effect

[D] Constructed memories

[E] Cued recall

58. Which researcher has made the most significant contributions to the understanding of nature of constructed memories?

(Lower order)

[A] George Sperling
[B] George Miller
[C] Alexander Luria
[D] Elizabeth Loftus
[E] Benjamin Whorf

59. Damage to Wernicke's area of the brain is most likely to cause which of the following?

(Lower order)

[A] Receptive aphasia
[B] Expressive aphasia
[C] Global aphasia
[D] Dysphagia
[E] Aphagia

60. What process explains how acetylcholine release at a localized region of the body can directly trigger a generalized sympathetic response throughout the body?

(Higher order)

[A] Acetylcholine release at cardiac neuromotor junctions can result in increased blood pressure and heart rate.
[B] Acetylcholine release in the pancreas causes release of insulin into the bloodstream.
[C] Acetylcholine release in the adrenal medulla causes epinephrine and norepinephrine release into the bloodstream.
[D] Acetylcholine release at synapses in ganglia in the brainstem can result in activation of all sympathetic ganglia neurons.
[E] Acetylcholine reuptake by sympathetic neurons results in the release of norepinephrine into the bloodstream.

61. Phineas Gage was a railroad worker who suffered a traumatic brain injury in the 1800s. This is a famous example of brain injury resulting in:

(Lower order)

[A] unilateral neglect
[B] word blindness
[C] personality changes
[D] inability to consolidate new memories
[E] enhanced mathematical performance

62. Jennifer is a 27-year-old woman with two children who is suffering from the recent onset of cold intolerance, weight gain, inability to conceive another child and blurred vision. Among the choices listed below, which would be the most likely cause of Jennifer's symptoms?

(Higher order)

[A] Exposure to pesticides
[B] A tumor in the hypothalamus
[C] Heavy, long-term alcohol consumption
[D] Lack of adequate blood flow to the amygdala
[E] Early onset of menopause

63. What diagnostic study is able to evaluate the rate of blood flow to a localized region of the brain?

(Lower order)

[A] Computerized tomography (CT) scan
[B] Pneumoencephalography
[C] Electroencephalography (EEG)
[D] Positron emission tomography (PET) scan
[E] Functional magnetic resonance imaging (fMRI)

64. An example of the gambler's fallacy is the common belief that if a coin that has come up heads on 9 consecutive coin tosses, it is more likely than a 50-50 chance that the coin will come up tails on the tenth toss. How would an evolutionary psychologist explain the persistence of this common misconception?
(Higher order)

[A] Gambling behavior is associated with high risk behavior.

[B] During human evolution, successful decision making rarely required identification of truly random events.

[C] Individuals who show persistence at a given task have a survival advantage over those who do not.

[D] There is likely to be less competition for rewards that are rarely available.

[E] Gambling behavior was a socially enjoyable activity that enhanced cooperativity among early human groups.

65. Karl Lashley's experiments with rhesus monkeys in 1923 demonstrated evidence for which of the following?
(Lower order)

[A] Lateralization of brain function

[B] Detrimental consequences of sensory deprivation

[C] Altruistic behavior in nonhuman primates

[D] Neuroplasticity

[E] Self-awareness in nonhuman primates

66. If all of the statements below were true, which one would represent the strongest argument that a hypothetical human behavior has no genetic component?
(Higher order)

[A] The behavior always instantly results in the death of the individual who engages in the behavior.

[B] The behavior only occurs in individuals who are under the influence a synthetic chemical compound that has never been known to exist in the natural environment.

[C] The behavior occurs only in individuals who have not had human contact.

[D] The behavior can only be elicited by physical torture.

[E] The behavior is completely random in individuals and occurs randomly in any experimental subject population.

67. According to the DSM-5, for a diagnosis of schizophrenia, there must be:
(Lower order)

[A] a response to medical treatment.

[B] symptoms of delusions, hallucinations, and disorganized speech for at least 1 month.

[C] continuous signs of the disturbance that persist for at least 6 months.

[D] no other comorbid conditions present.

[E] agreement by at least two independent licensed mental health practitioners' evaluations.

68. Among the conditions listed below, _____ is most likely to require hospitalization.
(Lower order)

[A] a manic episode

[B] a panic attack

[C] a derealization episode

[D] a purging episode

[E] a major depressive episode

69. The disorder that most closely resembles the popular term "split personality" is:
(Lower order)

[A] schizophrenia
[B] bipolar disorder
[C] borderline personality disorder
[D] dissociative identity disorder
[E] depersonalization/derealization disorder

70. Among the conditions listed below, which has the LEAST diagnostic similarity to the other four?
(Higher order)

[A] Participant-relevant confounding variable (pica)
[B] Binge eating disorder
[C] Bulimia nervosa
[D] Avoidant/restrictive food intake disorder
[E] Anorexia nervosa

71. Jeremy is a highly intelligent 17-years-old male. He has been expelled from school for a second episode of theft from other students' lockers in the past year. In the latest incident, he initially blamed another student for the theft but was then shown security camera footage that proved he was the culprit. Among the choices below, which is the most likely response from Jeremy when confronted with this evidence?
(Higher order)

[A] Puzzlement
[B] Pleading
[C] Suspicion
[D] Denial
[E] Laughter

72. _____ is NOT a typical characteristic of persons with obsessive-compulsive disorder.
(Higher order)

[A] distress
[B] lack of awareness
[C] concealment behavior
[D] efforts to restrain behavior
[E] empathy

73. To treat Madeline's schizophrenia, her doctors put her on an antipsychotic medication, conduct talk therapy in which they help Madeline and her family learn to deal with Madeline's illness, have her participate in social skills training, and send her to group therapy. Which of the following best describes this approach?
(Higher order)

[A] Psychoanalytic
[B] Cognitive-behavioral
[C] Humanistic
[D] Eclectic
[E] Biological

74. After seeing a therapist for a few months, Jake suddenly begins arriving late for sessions or misses his appointments. When asked why he is behaving this way, Jake tells his friends he disagrees with his therapist about the source of his problems. Jake's behavior is an example of _____.
(Higher order)

[A] transference
[B] distorted thinking
[C] resistance
[D] depression
[E] countertransference

75. **Cognitive triad is a concept developed by which psychologist?**
(Lower order)

[A] Sigmund Freud
[B] Abraham Maslow
[C] Aaron Beck
[D] Albert Ellis
[E] Fritz Perls

76. **Which of the following is an example of tertiary prevention?**
(Higher order)

[A] Providing job training for the unemployed
[B] Educating adolescents about the dangers of smoking
[C] Educating women about the dangers of consuming alcohol during pregnancy
[D] Removing a child from an abusive home
[E] Providing counseling to a woman who was sexually abused and has post-traumatic stress disorder

77. **Kathy has a bad habit of biting her fingernails. Her mother applies a bitter tasting polish to Kathy's nails to help Kathy break this habit. What therapeutic technique is Kathy's mother using?**
(Lower order)

[A] Flooding
[B] Aversion therapy
[C] Systematic desensitization
[D] Token economy
[E] Rational-emotive therapy

78. **All of the following are examples of biological therapies EXCEPT:**
(Lower order)

[A] Pre-frontal lobotomy
[B] Aversion therapy
[C] Electroconvulsive therapy
[D] Monoamine oxidase inhibitors
[E] Prozac

79. **According to Sternberg's Triarchic theory, an individual's intelligent behavior, in general is:**
(Higher order)

[A] generated by three independent socio-cultural matrices
[B] predetermined to eliminate the effects of novelty in social contexts
[C] comprised of metacognition, performance and knowledge acquisition thought processes.
[D] resolved into final actions that are primarily analytic, primarily componential or primarily componential/analytic.
[E] visual-spatial and/or logical-mathematical and/or Interpersonal-intrapersonal

80. **Among the descriptions below, which would be considered the most serious weakness in the construct validity of a standardized test?**
    (Higher order)

    [A] The consensus expert opinion is that the test's constructed content does not include questions sufficient to test for the full range of what is being tested for

    [B] The consensus expert opinion is that the test content as it is constructed includes a large percentage of questions that are irrelevant to what is being tested for

    [C] The test questions are constructed on the basis of a theory that has not yet been validated

    [D] The results of the test administration shows a strong negative correlation with predictions of the theory upon which the test was constructed

    [E] After the first administration of the test, there is a low calculated correlation coefficient with an older test's results, AND the older test measures for what the new test is intended to measure for AND expert consensus is that the older test is almost perfectly valid.

81. **Which statement below would be most consistent with a historically well-documented characterization of Alfred Binet's earliest concepts of human intelligence?**
    (Higher order)

    [A] "What we think, we must ultimately thing in words."

    [B] "There is a great diversity in individual intelligence, but there is a common element of practical judgement that influences the intellectual functions in all individuals."

    [C] "When we actually analyze the results of intelligence tests, the evidence indicates there are several independent types of intelligence."

    [D] "When we actually analyze the results of intelligence tests, the evidence indicates there is one fundamental intelligence that can operate in many specific modes."

    [E] "The intelligence measured in children is fundamentally different than the intelligence measured in adults"

82. **Charles Spearman is most directly associated with which of the following?**
    (Lower order)

    [A] Factor analysis of correlations related to intelligence

    [B] The concept of crystallized intelligence

    [C] The concept of fluid intelligence

    [D] Development of the Culture Fair Intelligence Test

    [E] Development of The Three Stratum Model of Intelligence

83. Zach is a 17-year-old high school student. He has recently been administered the latest age appropriate version of the Stanford-Binet Intelligence Test and his overall score is 95. Zach is therefore:

(Lower order)

[A] unqualified for enlistment in the regular U.S. armed forces

[B] within one standard deviation from the mean of the test population

[C] Less likely to have a coexisting diagnosis of antisocial personality disorder than a typical student who would have taken the Stanford-Binet exam during the same year that Zach took the exam.

[D] more likely to score higher on his SATs than a typical student who would have taken the Stanford-Binet exam during the same year that Zach took the exam

[E] more likely to be an only child than is a typical student who would have taken the Stanford-Binet exam during the same year that Zach took the exam

84. A test that features questions that are sequentially increasingly difficult to solve due to their complexity and not due to the total amount of time allotted to answer all of the questions is:

(Lower order)

[A] an achievement test

[B] an aptitude test

[C] a non-standardized test

[D] a reliability test

[E] a power test

85. According to the research of Masters and Johnson, among the statements below, the most accurate and direct evidence for a significant psychological effect on sexual function is:

(Higher order)

[A] demonstrated by a sexual repose to erotic materials in men with erectile dysfunction

[B] most apparent during the resolution phase of the sexual response cycle

[C] expressed as a secondary learned drive

[D] resistance to habituation effects during the plateau phase of the sexual response cycle

[E] most apparent in women with a history of sexual abuse

86. Imagine that research has strongly supported one of the following effects. Which of those in the choices below would be most similar to the proposed mechanism for the Garcia effect?

(Higher order)

[A] Persons with previous long term exposure to violent video games have decreased emotional response to violent images.

[B] The motivation to pursue self-actualization is less apparent in persons who have never experience a 1-month or longer period of homelessness compared to those that have.

[C] Persons who experience a traumatic event during a holiday experience extreme anxiety on subsequent occurrences of that particular holiday.

[D] The re-experiencing of a previously fearful event as an enjoyable but exhilarating event.

[E] Persons with a history of digestive disorders are less likely to engage in social activities related to states of high arousal.

87. **What is most clearly a criticism of opponent processes theory of motivation?**
    (Higher order)

    [A] The effects of opiate withdrawal can be almost instantly eliminated by the administration of the drug naloxone
    [B] Research indicates persons do not think of their needs in terms of a hierarchy
    [C] To attain a relatively preferred high baseline state of arousal requires that the novelty of arousing situation remains high
    [D] Depending on the overall context in which an event occurs the immediate removal of a highly joyful experience can result in multiple strongly experienced emotions including relief and not including sadness.
    [E] The exact same experience can produce exactly opposite emotional responses in different individuals

88. **Stanley Schachter is most directly associated with which of the following?**
    (Lower order)

    [A] The hierarchy model of motivation
    [B] The two-factor theory of emotion
    [C] The general adaptation syndrome
    [D] The principle of optimum arousal for peak performance
    [E] The Opponent-Process Theory

89. **The ventromedial hypothalamus is most closely identified with which physiological process?**
    (Lower order)

    [A] The generation of the sensation of satiety
    [B] The generation of the sensation of hunger
    [C] The establishment of a metabolic set point
    [D] The regulation of heart rate
    [E] The regulation of blood pressure

90. **The general adaptation syndrome is most closely associated with:**
    (Lower order)

    [A] Jerome Singer
    [B] Abraham Maslow
    [C] Richard Solomon
    [D] Hans Selye
    [E] William Masters and Virginia Johnson

91. **Which approach deals with issues of self-concept and free choice?**
    (Lower order)

    [A] Sociocultural approach
    [B] Biological approach
    [C] Humanistic approach
    [D] Functionalism
    [E] Gestalt psychology

92. **Which early theoretical perspective had the greatest influence on the field of behavioral psychology?**
    (Higher order)

    [A] Empiricism
    [B] Dualism
    [C] Natural selection
    [D] Materialism
    [E] Tabula rasa

93. Linda is seeing a therapist because she is having problems in her relationships. Linda reports being moody and grouchy due to a problem with her thyroid. Linda also states that she feels like she has no one to talk to because her family has never been one that talks about feelings. Linda expresses some negative and self-defeating thoughts. Which of the following statements best reflects the approach Linda's therapist should take?

[A] The therapist needs to treat Linda from a cognitive psychology approach because Linda's thoughts are what is causing her problems.

[B] The therapist should use a sociocultural approach to help Linda understand how her family's views have caused her interpersonal difficulties.

[C] The therapist should help Linda improve her self-concept and take responsibility for her choices.

[D] The therapist should focus more on making sure Linda is being treated for her thyroid problem since that problem is affecting her moods, which affect her relationships.

[E] The therapist should take an approach that addresses Linda's medical issues, familial influences, and thought processes because they are all contributing to Linda's problems.

94. Amelia is angry with her boss for adding a new project to her tasks. When Amelia arrives home, she argues with her children, gets mad at them, and sends them to bed early. Which defense mechanism is Amelia using?

(Lower order)

[A] Reaction formation
[B] Sublimation
[C] Rationalization
[D] Compensation
[E] Displacement

95. Which of the following statements best describes incongruence?

(Higher order)

[A] Ken's marriage is ending so he throws himself into his work.

[B] Marcy sees one group of her classmates as "cool" and the other group as "uncool."

[C] Henry believes in having a good work ethic but he steals from his boss.

[D] Candi makes a high score on her SAT and attributes her success to her intelligence.

[E] Adam distances himself from his son when his son fails to make the football team.

96. Max is known across many settings for being dishonest, grouchy, funny, intelligent, overly emotional, and ambitious. Which of the following statements is true?

[A] These characteristics indicate that Max needs to work on self-actualization.

[B] These characteristics probably show that Max has a mental disorder.

[C] These characteristics show that Max has a high level of self-esteem.

[D] These characteristics describe Max's central dispositions.

[E] These characteristics can change if Max explores his unconscious.

97. The idea that cognitive development is impacted by both biological and environmental factors best represents the theoretical perspective of which person?

(Lower order)

[A] Jean Piaget
[B] Sigmund Freud
[C] Lawrence Kohlberg
[D] Konrad Lorenz
[E] Lev Vygotsky

98. Alicia's curfew is 10:00. When she arrives home 30 minutes late, her parents express concern and frustration. They remind Alicia about the importance of rules and the reason for the rule. They let Alicia know that there will be consequences for her actions, but they first want to know why Alicia was out past her curfew. Which type of parenting style do Alicia's parents have?

    (Higher order)

    [A] Permissive
    [B] Insecure
    [C] Authoritative
    [D] Authoritarian
    [E] Indulgent

99. Amelia is angry with her boss for adding a new project to her tasks. When Amelia arrives home, she argues with her children, gets mad at them, and sends them to bed early. Which defense mechanism is Amelia using?

    (Lower order)

    [A] Reaction formation
    [B] Sublimation
    [C] Rationalization
    [D] Compensation
    [E] Displacement

100. Which of the following statements best describes incongruence?

     (Higher order)

     [A] Ken's marriage is ending so he throws himself into his work.
     [B] Marcy sees one group of her classmates as "cool" and the other group as "uncool."
     [C] Henry believes in having a good work ethic but he steals from his boss.
     [D] Candi makes a high score on her SAT and attributes her success to her intelligence.
     [E] Adam distances himself from his son when his son fails to make the football team.

Section II: Free Response Questions

SAMPLE QUESTION ONE

1. The Wilson's four-year old daughter, Missy, has begun throwing tantrums when she does not get her way. The tantrums are increasing in frequency and intensity; sometimes Missy gets aggressive during her tantrums. Missy's parents are frustrated and say they have tried everything they know to do to decrease or eliminate the tantrums, including arguing with Missy and bribing her with a fun activity. Sometimes, they give in to Missy just to get her to stop throwing a tantrum.

    A. **Summarize the main idea(s) of each of the following: (3 points)**
- Operant conditioning (1 points)
- Albert Bandura's Bobo Doll experiment (1 points)
- Piaget's cognitive theory— preoperational stage-egocentrism (1 point)

    B. **Discuss how the Wilson's could use their knowledge of the concepts to address their daughter's behavior. Provide examples for each one. (3 points)**
- Operant conditioning—Tantrums (1 point)
- Modeling—aggression (1 point)
- Egocentrism—arguing/reasoning (1 point)

    C. **Of the methods you provided, which method would you use and why? (1 point)**

2. In a classic psychological study, Loftus and Palmer (1974) conducted experiments to determine the reliability of eyewitness accounts of events. In the second experiment, 150 American students were shown a one-minute film in which a car was being driven through the countryside. That scene was followed by a four-second scene that showed a multiple car accident. After viewing the film, students were questioned about it. One group consisting of 50 students, was asked, "How fast were the cars going when they hit each other?" A second group of 50 students was asked, "How fast were the cars going when they smashed each other?" The remaining 50 students were not questioned about the film. The participants returned a week later, and without viewing the film again, were asked ten questions about the accident depicted on the film. The critical question, "Did you see any broken glass? Yes or no?" was randomly placed on each student's paper. There was no broken glass in the film. As was expected, the participants who were asked, "How fast were the cars going when they smashed each other?" were almost twice as likely to report seeing broken glass. Loftus and Palmer explained the results of this experiment by stating that there are two types of information that go into a person's memory after a complex occurrence. The first is information obtained during the perception of the event, and the second is external information supplied after the event. Over time, information from both sources becomes integrated in such a way that it becomes impossible to tell the original source of the information from which specific details are recalled. The information becomes one "memory."

(Reference: Loftus, E.F. & Palmer, J.C. (1974) Reconstruction of auto-mobile destruction: An example of the interaction between language and memory. Journal of Verbal Learning and Verbal Behaviour, 13, 585 -589)

   A. **Based on this information, identify the following elements of the study. (6 pts)**
   - Independent variable (1 point)
   - Dependent variable (1 point)
   - Experimental group(s) (1 point)
   - Control group(s) (1 point)
   - Hypothesis (1 point)
   - Confounding variables (1 point)

   B. **Discuss a limitation of the study. (1 point)**

   C. **Discuss a strength of the study. (1 point)**

SAMPLE TEST I
Answer Key

Question Number	Correct Answer	Your Answer	Question Number	Correct Answer	Your Answer	Question Number	Correct Answer	Your Answer
1	D		35	B		69	D	
2	C		36	C		70	A	
3	B		37	C		71	E	
4	E		38	C		72	B	
5	C		39	B		73	D	
6	D		40	C		74	C	
7	A		41	D		75	C	
8	B		42	B		76	E	
9	C		43	C		77	B	
10	C		44	A		78	B	
11	E		45	C		79	D	
12	E		46	B		80	D	
13	E		47	A		81	B	
14	D		48	E		82	C	
15	B		49	B		83	B	
16	D		50	D		84	E	
17	E		51	A		85	A	
18	C		52	B		86	C	
19	A		53	B		87	D	
20	B		54	E		88	B	
21	E		55	E		89	A	
22	E		56	C		90	D	
23	D		57	A		91	C	
24	A		58	D		92	D	
25	D		59	A		93	D	
26	B		60	C		94	E	
27	D		61	C		95	C	
28	C		62	B		96	D	
29	C		63	E		97	E	
30	C		64	A		98	C	
31	D		65	D		99	E	
32	D		66	E		100	C	
33	D		67	C				
34	E		68	A				

AP Psychology Sample Test 1

Answers and Explanations

Instructions: For each problem, select the choice that best answers the question.

1. **A city council who deflects criticism for the way it handled an emergency situation in the city by responding, "It's just how things are done" describes which of the following terms?**
   (Higher order)

   [A] Mere exposure effect
   [B] Bystander effect
   [C] In-group bias
   [D] Diffusion of responsibility
   [E] Situational ignorance

   The correct answer is D.
   When many people fail to properly handle a situation and no one takes responsibility for it, they are engaging in diffusion of responsibility. Mere exposure effect refers to the idea that the more someone is exposed to something, the more they will like it. Bystander intervention explains that the larger the group that observes an emergency situation, the greater likelihood that no one will help. In-group bias means individuals prefer to be around others in their same group. Situational ignorance is not a term related to social psychology.

2. **Which of the following statements about persuasive messages is NOT true?**
   (Higher order)

   [A] They can be processed one of two ways.
   [B] The persuasiveness of the messages is influenced by the likeability of the messenger.
   [C] Messages that play on people's emotions do not affect attitudes.
   [D] Repetitive messages are more likely to result in attitudinal change.
   [E] The length of the message is important.

   The correct answer is C.
   Messages that play on the emotions of others can result in attitudinal change, as can messages that are repetitive. Persuasive messages can be processed through the central route or peripheral route. The appeal and knowledge of the messenger is important, as is the length of the message.

3. **Experiments involving cognitive dissonance were conducted by which researcher(s)?**
   (Lower order)

   [A] Robert Rosenthal and Lenore Jacobson
   [B] Leon Festinger and James Carlsmith
   [C] Albert Bandura
   [D] Phil Zimbardo
   [E] Richard LaPiere

   The correct answer is B.
   Leon Festinger and James Carlsmith conducted studies to investigate cognitive dissonance. Rosenthal and Jacobson's studies investigated the impact of others' expectations on student performance. Albert Bandura studied aggression. Phil Zimbardo conducted the Stanford Prison experiment, and Richard LaPiere conducted studies to see how well attitudes predict behavior.

4. **A group of rioters begin looting neighborhood stores. The group members do not seem to realize that the stores' owners have nothing to do with the situation they are protesting, and they seem indifferent to any consequences of their actions. The leader of the group intimidates any member who expresses concerns about the group's actions. This scenario is an example of which phenomenon?**
(Higher order)

[A] Mindguard
[B] Prejudice
[C] Foot-in-the-door
[D] Positive evaluation
[E] Groupthink

The correct answer is E.
Groupthink is thinking evidenced by an entire group in which group members often make bad decisions and use poor judgment, failing to consider the implications of their actions. Members of the group are often reluctant to go against the group's decision because of the mindguard, or the member who may intimidate them or ostracize them for disagreeing. Prejudice refers to negative and undeserved attitudes towards a particular group. Positive evaluation refers to a principle of interpersonal attraction that states that we like to be thought of highly, so we like to be around those who have a high opinion of us.

5. **A dancer's performance improves when she is dancing as part of her ballet group. What is this an example of?**
(Lower order)

[A] Group polarization
[B] Social inhibition
[C] Social facilitation
[D] Door-in-the-face
[E] Deindividuation

The correct answer is C.
Social facilitation occurs when someone's performance increases or improves when in the presence of others. Group polarization refers to the tendency of group members to act more extreme than they would on their own. Social inhibition means that someone's performance decreases when in the presence of others. Door-in-the-face is a compliance strategy, and deindividuation refers to group members losing their identities and assuming the identity of the group.

6. **All of the following statements about conformity are true EXCEPT:**
(Higher order)

[A] Groups with high levels of cohesion are more likely to have higher levels of conformity.
[B] Women are more likely to conform than men.
[C] People of high social status are less likely to conform than people of lower social status.
[D] Conformity is the same thing as compliance.
[E] If one group member refuses to conform, other members may be less likely to conform.

The correct answer is D.
Conformity and compliance are not the same thing. Conformity occurs when people go along with the actions and attitudes of others; compliance means giving in to the requests of others, even at your own expense. Women and individuals of low to middle social status are more likely to conform. If even one group member refuses to conform, other group members may refuse to conform.

7. Someone does something nice for you, and you feel that you need to do something nice for them in return. What is this called?

(Lower order)

[A] Norms of reciprocity
[B] Shared opinions
[C] In-group bias
[D] Self-fulfilling prophecy
[E] Altruism

The correct answer is A.

Norms of reciprocity explain the behavior of someone who returns the kindness of someone else. Shared opinions is our tendency to want to be around others who value and like the same things as we do. In-group bias refers to our preference to be around people who are similar to us. Self-fulfilling prophecy is when the expectations of someone effects the behavior of someone else. Altruism is selfless sacrifice.

8. A fundamental attribution error is:

(Lower order)

[A] taking more credit for good outcomes than bad
[B] overestimating dispositional factors and underestimating situational factors
[C] overestimating the number of people who will agree with you
[D] believing that bad things only happen to bad people
[E] a set of feelings and beliefs

The correct answer is B.

When someone overestimates the influence of dispositional factors and underestimates the effect of situational factors, they are making a fundamental attribution error. Taking more credit for good outcomes than bad is called self-serving bias. When you overestimate the number of people who agree with you, you are demonstrating the false-consensus effect. A just-world bias assumes that bad things only happen to bad people. A set of feelings and beliefs defines attitude.

9. Daniel is playing a game of marbles with his elementary school friends. He perceives the marbles on the playing surface as three main groups and a few individual scattered marbles. Daniel's perception is most likely:

(Higher order)

[A] an illusion related to distance consistency
[B] based on monocular rather than binocular depth cues
[C] an example of a gestalt principle
[D] represented as a spatial map plotted in his parietal lobes
[E] relying on visual input primarily from rod cells

The correct answer is C.

The Gestalt Principles of visual perception are based on observations that there are general categories of fundamental visual phenomena. These include the principle of *proximity*, which describes the tendency to perceive objects as belonging to the same group based on their closer proximity to each other compared to other objects in the visual field. *Distance constancy* uses visual reference features to that include the relative sizes of apparently nearby objects. Although it can create optical illusions, Daniel's perception is not an illusion. He is probably relying more on binocular rather than monocular depth cues, but the playing surface is 2-dimensional so neither are likely to contribute to the grouping perception. Visual mapping occurs in the occipital rather than the parietal lobe. A tonotopic map of the sound environment does occur in the auditory cortex of the parietal lobes. Daniel is focusing on the marbles and observing high resolution features. This is more likely cone cell visual input from the fovea, which provides the highest acuity vision.

10. **A sudden, unexpected and very loud sound can result in deafness that is limited to a narrow range of sound frequencies close to and including the frequency of the injury producing sound. Where is the most probable location of the injury that results in this type of deafness?**

    (Higher order)

    [A] The tympanic membrane
    [B] The oval window
    [C] The basilar membrane
    [D] The spiral ganglia
    [E] The cochlear nerve

    The correct answer is C.

    Sound vibrations are indirectly transmitted to the basilar membrane of the cochlea. Specific frequencies cause vibrations of specific regions of the basilar membrane. This is called the *resonate frequency* of that membrane region. A very loud sound would most likely cause damage to hair cells at its resonant frequency site on the basilar membrane. This would explain the preservation of hearing at other sound frequencies. There is no frequency specific type of damage that the energy of a loud sound would be likely at the other anatomical sites. The tympanic membrane and oval window membrane may be ruptured by a very loud sound, but this would lead to impairment of hearing at all frequencies. The spiral ganglion and the cochlear nerve are anatomically separate from the pressure wave energy of sound and frequency specific deafness would unlikely be related to the injury producing sound frequency.

11. **The Necker cube (shown below) is an optical illusion that top-down processing theorists claim cannot be explained by the principles of bottom-up processing. What type of perceptual concept is most likely NOT relevant to the perception of this specific optical illusion?**

    (Higher order)

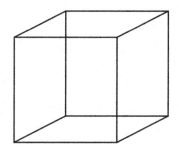

    [A] Receptive fields
    [B] Depth cues
    [C] Figure-ground relationship
    [D] Shape constancy
    [E] The psi phenomena

    The correct answer is E.

    This is a difficult basic knowledge question, but it can still be answered by a process of elimination even if you do not know what the psi phenomena is. The psi phenomena is a dynamic optical illusion of motion. A string of lights with a precisely timed sequential blinking pattern can produce the psi phenomenon. Receptive fields are required to see and more particularly are involved in the detection of object borders in processing systems in the retina. The illusion is a 3-dimensional effect, so depth cues are obviously important. The figure-ground relationship is less obviously true but the image flips between perceptions where inner surfaces of the cube become outer surfaces of the cube and inner vs. outer are related to what the figure is and what the background is. Shape constancy relates to the orientation of an object relative to the eyes it is involved or more likely involved in the illusion since the orientation of the object appears to change.

12. Visual information from the retina does NOT travel directly to _____.
(Lower order)

[A] the lateral geniculate nucleus of the thalamus

[B] the superior colliculus of the midbrain

[C] the pretectum of the midbrain

[D] the suprachiasmatic nucleus of the hypothalamus

[E] the visual cortex of the occipital lobes

The correct answer is E.

The fibers of the optic nerve do not travel directly to the visual cortex. Instead they synapse in one of four locations: the lateral geniculate nucleus of the thalamus where visual perception begins, the superior colliculus of the midbrain which is a center for complex automatic and voluntary control of eye movements, the pretectum of the midbrain for control of the pupillary light reflex and the suprachiasmatic nucleus of the hypothalamus for control of diurnal rhythms and hormonal changes.

13. The moon appears larger when it is close to the horizon. This is an example of:
(Lower order)

[A] slow adaptation

[B] rapid adaptation

[C] transduction

[D] size constancy

[E] an illusion

The correct answer is E.

Since the size of the moon does not change in terms of the size its image occupies on the retina, the perception of a size change is not real, so it is an illusion. Slow adaptation of visual receptor cells occurs during dark adaptation. Rapid adaptation of visual receptor cells occurs during light adaptation. However, neither explains the illusion of change in size of the moon. Transduction is a process of conversion of one type of information to another within the nervous system. Again, this does not explain the illusion of change in size of the moon. Size constancy is a feature of visual perception that an object's intrinsic size does not change, so this a violation of, not an example of the perception of a size change of the moon

14. Which sensory receptor cells are considered direct extensions of the brain?
(Lower order)

[A] Rod cells

[B] Cone cells

[C] Hair cells

[D] Olfactory receptor cells

[E] Pain receptor cells

The correct answer is D.

Olfactory receptor cells are considered to be central nervous system neurons are therefore a direct anatomical extension of the brain. Rod and cone cells synapse with bipolar cells in the retina. Hair cells synapse with ganglia cells of the acoustic and vestibular nerves. The neural pathways of pain receptor or (nociceptor) cells are generally routed through the spinothalamic tracts (three types of spinothalamic tracts, actually). Although this was not discussed, pain receptors are not considered direct extensions of the brain nor should any information you are responsible for suggest that this would be true.

15. **Paul is at a football game. He receives a phone call from his wife asking him for the alarm code to their home. Paul would most likely:**

    (Higher order)

    [A] access subconscious processes to retrieve the code

    [B] access preconscious processes to retrieve the code

    [C] provide the code based on his current conscious awareness

    [D] experience interference in providing the code due to unconscious processes

    [E] experience interference in providing the code due to a subconscious conflict.

    The correct answer is B.
    The preconscious level is a repository of readily accessible information or potential elements of our consciousness that we are not currently aware of but we are aware that they are available. Details such as names and dates are stored in memories that can be retrieved if you wish to do so. Subconscious processes may assist in retrieving information but are not recognized as a source of interference with conscious processes. It is unlikely Paul is actively thinking about his home's alarm code while watching a football game so this is not information his current conscious state is entertaining. Subconscious processes, if they exist, are unlikely to include a conflict in providing Paul's wife a code to enter their home but, if so, it is even less likely than answer B, which is a definitional characteristic of the preconscious level.

16. **Which theorist is most closely associated with the concept of dissociation as a proposed mechanism to explain hypnotic states?**

    (Lower order)

    [A] William James

    [B] Sigmund Freud

    [C] J. Allan Hobson

    [D] Ernest Hilgard

    [E] Alexander Luria

    The correct answer is D.
    Ernest Hilgard's Neodissociation Theory hypothesizes that the hypnotic state is not an alteration of a state of consciousness but occurs due a voluntary division of consciousness into 2 simultaneous streams: one which responds to the hypnotist and the other that retains an awareness of reality. Freud's explanation for hypnotic states were not discussed nor are they widely known. He did use hypnosis for a time in an attempt to elicit subconscious memories but abandoned the technique when it proved ineffective. William James was interested in hypnosis and wrote about the effect, but he is not recognized as closely as Higard with the Dissociation Principle, although he did agree it was a reasonable hypothesis. J. Allan Hobson and Robert McClarley developed the activation-synthesis model to explain dreams. They have no connection to theories regarding hypnotic phenomena. Alexander Luria is an important figure in memory research, but is not associated with theories of hypnosis.

17. **Claire is a 4-year-old girl who for several months has had episodes of sudden awakenings late at night where she is crying and seems terrified. In the morning she has no recollection of the awakening episodes. Claire's episodes are:**

    (Higher order)

    [A] probably related to airway obstruction
    [B] occurring during the REM stage of sleep
    [C] a form of reverse wish fulfillment
    [D] unlikely to be accompanied by heavy sweating
    [E] associated with stage 3 sleep

    ### The correct answer is E.

    Night terrors occur during deep sleep or stage 3 sleep. Night terrors occur mostly in children beginning at the age of three and cause the child to awaken abruptly in a confused, inconsolable state of panic. The child is often sweating profusely and has an elevated heart rate and blood pressure. The child is usually unable to recall any details of the night terror experience and generally does not recall that the episode happened upon awakening in the morning. Sleep apnea is related to airway obstruction. Most dreams occur during REM sleep, but night terrors do not and are not even verified to be dreams.

18. **Based only on the fact that a psychoactive drug is well-known to produce exceptionally severe withdrawal symptoms, the drug is:**

    (Higher order)

    [A] not a neurotransmitter agonist
    [B] exceptionally permeable to the blood-brain barrier
    [C] likely causing suppression of normal neurotransmitter activity
    [D] unlikely to be reversed by the administration of naloxone
    [E] one with an effective dose that is relatively close to its lethal dose.

The correct answer is C.

Drugs that mimic the effects of neurotransmitters often cause the neurons that normally release those neurotransmitters to decrease or even stop releasing the neurotransmitter entirely. If users attempt to stop using a drug there will be a lack of the normal levels of the neurotransmitter at the areas where the drug was acting as an agonist and this can cause various unpleasant and potentially dangerous psychological and physiological consequences. As a group these effects constitute the *withdrawal* symptoms for a given drug. All psychoactive drugs are permeable to the blood-brain barrier. The relative permeability of a drug is not related to the severity of withdrawal symptoms. Naloxone is a endorphin receptor blocker that reverses the effects of opioid drugs. There are many other drugs that are associated with severe withdrawal that are unaffected by naloxone administration. The efficacy or ED50 is the dose of the drug that will produce the desired effect 50% of the time it is administered. Lethality or the LD_{50} is the dose of a drug that will result in death 50% of the time. Lethality is not a measure of the effects that occur when a drug is withheld.

19. **Which brain region plays an important role in generating and regulating circadian rhythms?**

    (Lower order)

    [A] Hypothalamus
    [B] Basal ganglia
    [C] Cerebellum
    [D] Amygdala
    [E] Pons

The correct answer is A.

Circadian rhythms are 24-hour day-night light cycles that oscillate between neurological and other biological activities that correspond to wakeful and sleep associated schedules. In addition to sleep patterns, circadian rhythms regulate feeding patterns, core body temperature, cell regeneration and repair activity, hormone production and brain wave activity. The cycle is regulated by the hypothalamus through the secretion of the hormone melatonin. Increasing melatonin levels lead to greater activation of sleep processes and decreasing levels lead to greater activation of wakeful processes. The basal ganglia is associated with basic motor functions and the cerebellum with coordination of muscle activities. The amygdala is closely associated with memory processing that are functions that occur while asleep and the pons is a brainstem relay center. None of these are known to generate or regulate circadian rhythms.

20. **Alpha waves are brainwave patterns that are:**
    (Lower order)

    [A] the highest frequency of the five major brainwave patterns

    [B] associated with states of relaxation and light sleep

    [C] required to generate sleep spindles

    [D] the dominant wave pattern during stage 2 sleep

    [E] the dominant wave pattern during REM stage sleep

The correct answer is B.

Alpha waves correspond to relaxed wakeful states and are the waves that are most prominent just before the onset of sleep. They are also are present in stage 1 or light sleep. Alpha waves are slower frequency waves than gamma or beta waves. Sleep spindles occur most commonly in stage 2 sleep and

appear to be spontaneous, but definitely do not rely on alpha waves for any purpose. The dominant wave patterns during stage 2 sleep theta and delta waves. REM sleep is characterized by high frequency combination waves that produce a sawtooth pattern. They are not associated with alpha waves.

21. **Jason administers a questionnaire at the end of the school year, on the same day at the same time in the school auditorium, to all the students in his elementary school grades 2 through 6. One of the questions asks: "On average, how many days per week did you eat breakfast during the past school year?" He then plots the average number of days students ate breakfast, 0 through 7, against the average GPA of students for each day average. For instance, a 3.4 average GPA was found for all students who reported eating breakfast 5 times per week. All of the students responded to the survey. The total survey response number was 600. Ten students were absent on the day the questionnaire was administered. Among the choices below, what is the most likely source of error in Jason's study?**
    (Higher order)

    [A] A sampling error

    [B] An observational bias

    [C] An experimenter bias

    [D] A situation-relevant confounding variable

    [E] A participant-relevant confounding variable

The correct answer is E.

A sampling error is not defined for this question, since the researcher has not specified a population that the sample is drawn from. The population could be all students in the school grades 2 through 6 or it could be meant to represent a random sample of all grade school children in the United States. The only observation Jason makes is the observation of the question responses and the average GPAs. This is an unlikely source of error. The study is not an experimental study so there can be no experimenter error. The situation or environment of the study is well controlled. All of the participants were administered the questionnaire on the same day and at the same location. There are many types of participant-relevant confounding variables that questionnaire studies cannot control. For instance, the participants may have colluded to give inaccurate information or individually tended to give inaccurate information for various reasons.

22. **Which of the following is true regarding an independent variable?**
(Lower order)

[A] It cannot be controlled in an experiment
[B] It cannot be changed during an experiment
[C] It is the observer in a naturalistic study
[D] It does not correlate with a dependent variable
[E] It may cause a change in a dependent variable

The correct answer is E.

The main purpose of most research studies is to show that changes in an independent variable are most likely the cause of changes in a dependent variable. To say that an independent variable cannot be controlled in an experiment is an imprecise and ambiguous statement. Experiments strive to be well-controlled and the independent variable is under the control of the experimenter. In no sense is an independent variable something that cannot be "controlled." Variables in any study should not be observers. If they are, they are confounding variables and not independent variables. An independent variable MAY not correlate a dependent variable, i.e. there proves to be a correlation coefficient of zero between the dependent

and independent variable in a particular experiment, but often there is a strong correlation between independent and dependent variables.

23. **Which choice below describes a means to control for the Hawthorne effect?**
(Higher order)

[A] Providing a control group with sugar pills that have an identical appearance to the pills with an active ingredient that are provided to an experimental group.
[B] Designing a study so that the participants serve alternately as the experimental group and the control group.
[C] Ensuring that the participants of a study are randomly assigned to either the control or the experimental group.
[D] Choosing a dependent variable that can be observed in subjects while they are asleep.
[E] Stratifying the subject population according to age ranges, gender and ethnic background.

The correct answer is D.

The Hawthorne effect is the tendency of study participants to alter their normal behavior specifically because they know that they are being observed. By definition, subjects who are asleep cannot know (or are surely less likely to know) that they are being observed. In all other choice options, you should be able to recognize that the measures described would not decrease the likelihood that the subjects are aware that they are being observed.

24. **A set of experimental data has the following values: 2, 3, 4, 4, 5, 6, 6, 12. This set of data has a:**
    (Lower order)

    [A] bimodal distribution
    [B] negatively skewed distribution
    [C] standard deviation of ten
    [D] standard deviation of twelve
    [E] median of five

    The correct answer is A.
    The mode of a sequence of values is the value that occurs with the highest frequency, in the data set the values 4 and 6 occur with the greatest but equal frequency (twice for each value). The sequence has two modes, 4 and 6. This corresponds to a bimodal distribution. If you are able to calculate the sample standard deviation for the data set you would see that it is rounds to 3.05. The median value for a set of values is the value where half of the other values are less than the median value and half of the other values are greater than the median value. If there are an even number of values as is the case here (8 values) the median is the average of the highest lowest value and the lowest highest value, in this case 5 and 6. The average of 5 and 6 is 5.5. The set of values has an extreme greatest value outlier, 12, that is much further from the mean, 5.5, than the lowest value, 2 this is defined in a distribution graph as a positively, not negatively, skewed distribution.

25. **Jack is a 35-year-old man who is offered opportunity to participate in a research study in which he will be interviewed by the researcher. According to APA ethical guidelines, Jack must NOT be:**
    (Higher order)

    [A] misled about the purpose of the study
    [B] provided with a means to contact the researcher after the conclusion of the study
    [C] intentionally subjected to any painful stimuli during the study
    [D] denied anonymity during and after the study.
    [E] told the results of his specific participation the study

    The correct answer is D.
    APA guidelines require that participants in an interview study be guaranteed confidentiality, not anonymity. In interview studies, it is impossible to guarantee anonymity because there is no means to ensure that it would be impossible to for an interviewer of Jack to identify that Jack was a participant in the study. The interviewer must guarantee that he will not disclose Jack's participation in the trial. This is a guarantee of confidentiality. Within very narrowly defined limits, participants may be misled about the purpose of a study before and during the study, (but not after the study) and may be subjected to temporary physical discomfort including mildly painful forms of discomfort. APA guidelines state the participants should be told the personal results of their study and should be provided with a means to contact the researcher after the conclusion of the study.

26. Which of the following is NOT an example of a naturalistic research methodology?
(Lower order)

[A] Using a video camera to record children's reactions to distant thunder while they are playing in a park

[B] Providing a food source for nocturnal animals only at night

[C] Constructing an artificial structure to hide an observer

[D] Recording only clearly abnormal behavior of persons at a rock concert

[E] Observing the behavior of animals following a natural disaster.

The correct answer is B.

In naturalistic research, the researcher should observe subjects in their natural environment with as little interference as possible with the subjects. Introducing a food source is interfering in the natural environment. The other choices describe subjects in their natural environment, including following a natural disaster which is a natural occurrence within a natural environment. The construction of an artificial concealment is intended to reduce the likelihood that subjects will notice things that are not part of their natural environment.

27. All of the following statements about psychoanalytic theory are true EXCEPT:
(Higher order)

[A] Psychoanalytic theory focuses on the unconscious.

[B] Psychoanalytic theory is not based on empirical research.

[C] Psychoanalytic theory emphasizes the importance of childhood.

[D] Psychoanalytic theory uses assessments that are objective and reliable.

[E] Psychoanalytic theory seems to be biased against women.

The correct answer is D.

The assessments used by psychoanalytic therapists are subjective and are not reliable. All the other statements are true. This approach does focus on the unconscious, emphasizes the importance of childhood in shaping personality, and does seem to be biased against women. Some research supports certain aspects of psychoanalytic theory. However, some research does not support other aspects of this approach.

28. The model of triadic reciprocality focuses on the interaction between:
(Higher order)

[A] mind, body, and spirit.

[B] the therapist, the client, and the environment.

[C] the person, behavior, and the environment.

[D] the id, ego, and superego.

[E] biology, person, and situations.

The correct answer is C.

At any given point, there is a reciprocating, ongoing relationship between the environment, the person, and the person's behavior, with each one affecting the others. The id, ego, and superego are terms used by Freud to describe the three parts of the mind. Although there is an interaction between biological factors/heredity, the person and situations, this is not part of triadic reciprocality.

29. Traits that are unique to each person are called:
(Lower order)

[A] nomothetic

[B] collective

[C] idiographic

[D] complexes

[E] personality

The correct answer is C.

Idiographic traits are not universal but are unique to the individual. Nomothetic traits are common to all people. Collective traits is not a term used to describe personality traits. Complexes is a term related to Jung's psychodynamic theory. Personality is made up of traits, both nomothetic and idiographic; while personality is unique for each individual, some traits are not unique.

30. **The following list of traits are not part of the Big Five EXCEPT:**
    (Higher order)

    [A] Extraversion, openness, honesty, conscientiousness, and neuroticism

    [B] Conscientiousness, curiosity, extraversion, agreeableness, and psychoticism

    [C] Extraversion, neuroticism, openness, agreeableness, and conscientiousness

    [D] Extraversion, psychoticism, honesty, trustworthiness, and openness

    [E] Idiographic, nomothetic, extraversion, honesty, and openness

    The correct answer is C.

    These traits are considered nomothetic because all people have each trait to some degree. Honesty, curiosity, and trustworthiness are not common to all people. Extraversion, neuroticism, and psychoticism were the three traits proposed by Hans Eysenck.

31. **Albert Bandura's theory of personality falls into which category?**
    (Lower order)

    [A] Cognitive
    [B] Humanistic
    [C] Psychoanalytic
    [D] Social-cognitive
    [E] Trait theory

The correct answer is D.

Albert Bandura saw personality as being formed and shaped by social and cognitive factors. Cognitive theories explain cognitive processes. Maslow and Rogers were humanistic theorists. Psychoanalytic theories were proposed be Freud, Jung, Adler, and Horney. Trait theories were proposed by Eysenck, Cattell, Allport, Costa and McCrae, and Mischel.

32. **A psychologist interested in measuring and describing personality traits would use which of the following assessment tools?**
    (Lower order)

    [A] Stanford-Binet
    [B] DSM
    [C] Myers-Briggs
    [D] MMPI
    [E] Rorschach Inkblot

The correct answer is D.

The MMPI stands for the Minnesota Multiphasic Personality Inventory. This self-report questionnaire is used to measure personality traits. The Stanford-Binet is an IQ test. The DSM-6 is the Diagnostic and Statistical Manual of Mental Disorders that is published by the American Psychological Association. The Myers-Briggs is a personality inventory but it is not one studied in this manual. The Rorschach Inkblot test is a projective test used mostly in psychoanalysis.

33. **Which of the following statements best describes learning?**
(Higher order)

[A] Learning occurs when two stimuli are repeatedly paired and an association is made between the two stimuli.

[B] Learning is an entirely cognitive process.

[C] Learning is based on the consequences resulting from one's actions.

[D] Learning produces changes in behavior.

[E] Learning is a result of biological processes.

The correct answer is D.
Learning is defined as long-lasting changes in behavior that occur as result of experience or study. Research has demonstrated that learning involves more than making an association between paired stimuli, and it is more complex than simply receiving consequences for one's actions. Learning involves cognitive and biological processes.

34. **Miguel hates going to physical education. On P.E. day, he acts sick, hoping his father will write a note asking for Miguel to be excused from P.E. class for that day. Which of the following terms describes Miguel's actions?**
(Higher order)

[A] Garcia effect

[B] Imitation

[C] Escape learning

[D] Classical conditioning

[E] Avoidance learning

The correct answer is E.
Miguel wants to avoid P.E. so he feigns illness. If Miguel were to go to P.E. and act up in hopes of being asked to leave class, he would be demonstrating escape learning. The Garcia effect is also known as conditioned taste aversion. Avoidance learning is associated with operant conditioning, not classical conditioning.

35. **Which psychologist demonstrated that emotions can be learned?**
(Lower order)

[A] B.F. Skinner

[B] John B. Watson

[C] John Garcia

[D] Edward Thorndike

[E] Edward Tolman

The correct answer is B.
John B. Watson's experiment with Little Albert demonstrated that a fearful response can be conditioned. Skinner is known for his theory of operant conditioning. Garcia conducted experiments on conditioned taste aversions. Thorndike's work laid the foundation for Skinner's work on operant conditioning. Edward Tolman is credited for his work on latent learning.

36. **Which reinforcement schedule is best to use if you want to teach your dog to rollover?**
(Lower order)

[A] Variable-ratio

[B] Fixed-ratio

[C] Continuous

[D] Fixed-interval

[E] Contingency

The correct answer is C.
Continuous reinforcement is best to use when teaching a new behavior. Continuous reinforcement involves rewarding the behavior every time it occurs until it is learned. Variable-ratio would administer a reward after a changing and unpredictable number of responses, whereas fixed-ratio would administer a reward after a set amount of responses has occurred. Fixed-interval would deliver reinforcement after a set amount of time had passed. The contingency approach is associated with classical conditioning and asserts that the presence of one stimulus predicts the presence of the other.

37. According to classical conditioning, extinction has occurred when:
(Lower order)

[A] similar stimuli elicit the same response as the initial stimuli

[B] behavior suddenly reappears

[C] the conditioned stimulus no longer elicits the conditioned response

[D] the conditioned stimulus becomes aversive

[E] distinctions between similar stimuli can be made

The correct answer is C.
Extinction is when a behavior is unlearned because the conditioned stimulus is repeatedly presented without the unconditioned stimulus until it no longer elicits the conditioned response. When similar stimuli elicit the same response as the initial stimuli, generalization has occurred. Behavior suddenly reappearing after it was extinguished is spontaneous recovery. A stimulus becoming aversive does not mean extinction has occurred. Discrimination involves being able to tell the difference between two very similar stimuli.

38. Which of the following best states the difference between positive reinforcement and negative reinforcement?
(Higher order)

[A] Positive reinforcement is likely to increase the behavior; negative reinforcement is likely to decrease the behavior.

[B] Positive reinforcement means something rewarding is taken away, while negative reinforcement means something unpleasant is taken away.

[C] Positive reinforcement involves adding something rewarding and negative reinforcement means taking away something unpleasant.

[D] Positive reinforcement uses primary reinforcers and negative reinforcement uses secondary reinforcers.

[E] Positive reinforcement involves rewarding positive behaviors, while negative reinforcement involves rewarding negative behaviors.

The correct answer is C.
Reinforcement is anything that increases the likelihood that a behavior will be repeated. Positive reinforcement adds something rewarding to strengthen the behavior, whereas negative reinforcement removes an aversive stimulus (which is rewarding). Both positive and negative reinforcement increase the likelihood of the behavior occurring again, but punishment decreases the likelihood of the behavior being repeated. The type of reinforcers used have nothing to do with whether the reinforcement is positive or negative. Positive reinforcement can be used to reward undesirable behaviors, not just desirable behaviors.

39. A biological psychologist might be interested in which of the following?
(Higher order)

[A] How unconditional positive regard affects self-concept

[B] How dopamine affects thought processes

[C] How a person's perception of events affects behavior

[D] How social roles impact development

[E] How to improve an employee's motivation

The correct answer is B.
Dopamine is a neurotransmitter in the brain that is linked to thoughts and emotions. Because neurotransmitters are controlled by physiological processes, studying how a neurotransmitter affects thought processes is within the scope of a biological psychologist. Unconditional positive regard is a concept proposed by Carl Rogers, a humanistic

psychologist. A cognitive psychologist would be interested in how a person's perceptions of events affect behavior. A sociocultural psychologist would be interested in how social roles impact development. An industrial-organizational psychologist would be interested in how to improve an employee's motivation.

40. **In what way would a behaviorist disagree with an evolutionary psychologist about the cause of fearful behavior?**
(Higher order)

[A] A behaviorist would argue that fear is caused by repressed unconscious memories, while an evolutionary psychologist would say that fear is the result of how someone interprets experiences.

[B] A behaviorist would attribute fear to biological processes, but an evolutionary psychologist would argue it is the result of receiving some type of positive reward for it in the past.

[C] A behaviorist would argue that fear results from receiving a positive reward for fearful behavior in the past, while an evolutionary psychologist would say that fear is an adaptive response that promotes survival.

[D] A behaviorist would say that fear is an adaptive response, but an evolutionary psychologist would argue that fear is caused by biological, social, and psychological factors.

[E] A behavioral psychologist and an evolutionary psychologist would both agree that fear is a learned response that has been consistently reinforced.

The correct answer is C.
A behavioral psychologist believes behavior is a learned response for which one has been rewarded in the past; evolutionary psychology is based on Darwinian Theory that behavior has an adaptive function which ensures survival of the species. The psychodynamic approach focuses on the unconscious; a cognitive psychologist is concerned with how someone thinks about, perceives, and interprets events and experiences. A biological psychologist attributes behaviors, emotions, and cognitive processes to biological processes. A biopsychosocial psychologist attributes behaviors, cognitive processes, and emotions to biological, psychological and social factors.

41. **Which of the following two people are closely associated with humanistic psychology?**
(Lower order)

[A] John B. Watson and B.F. Skinner
[B] Sigmund Freud and Erik Erikson
[C] Max Wertheimer and Rene Descartes
[D] Carl Rogers and Abraham Maslow
[E] Charles Darwin and John Locke

The correct answer is D.
Rogers and Maslow are known as humanistic psychologists. Watson and Skinner are associated with behavioral psychology. Sigmund Freud is the founder of psychodynamic theory, and Erik Erikson was a developmental psychologist. Max Wertheimer helped found Gestalt psychology; Rene Descartes was a philosopher who held the view that the mind and body interact, but the mind is not subject to natural laws. Charles Darwin's theory of natural selection is the basis of evolutionary psychology, and John Locke is known for the theory of empiricism, which asserts that truth and knowledge can be acquired through observations and experiences.

42. **Who was the first woman to be awarded a Ph.D. in psychology?**
    (Lower order)

    [A] Dorothea Dix
    [B] Margaret Floy Washburn
    [C] Karen Horney
    [D] Mary Whiton Calkins
    [E] Mary Ainsworth

    The correct answer is B.
    Washburn was the first female to receive a Ph.D. in psychology. Dorothea Dix advocated for the establishment of and expansion of hospitals for the mentally ill. Karen Horney was a critic of Freud's psychoanalytic theory and developed her own psychodynamic theory. Mary Whiton Calkins was the first woman to be president of the American Psychological Association. Mary Ainsworth was a social psychologist who studied infant attachment using the "strange situation."

43. **In which way are structuralism and functionalism different?**
    (Higher order)

    [A] Structuralism recognizes a distinction between the mind and body and functionalism does not.
    [B] Structuralism assumes that only matter and energy exist and functionalism assumes that observation and experiences are the only way to acquire knowledge.
    [C] Structuralism breaks the mind down into its most basic components. Functionalism asserts that the uses of the mind are more important than the individual components of the mind.
    [D] Structuralism focuses only on cognitive functions and functionalism is concerned with social structures and cognitive functions.
    [E] There is no difference between the two.

The correct answer is C.
Structuralism breaks the mind down into its most basic parts, or structures, then combines those structures in order to understand the sum total of mental processes. Functionalism argues that understanding the function of the parts of the mind is more important. The distinction between mind and body refers to the concept of dualism. Materialism is the theory that only matter and energy exist. The theory of empiricism states that the only way to acquire knowledge is through observations and experiences. Both structuralism and functionalism were theories that pertained to cognitive processes, or the mind, only.

44. **In what major way is behaviorism different from other theoretical perspectives?**
    (Lower order)

    [A] It is only concerned with observable behavior.
    [B] Its concepts are based on empirical research.
    [C] Its principles are of no use today.
    [D] It is not considered scientific.
    [E] There is no specific way behaviorism is different from other perspectives.

The correct answer is A.
Behaviorism defines psychology as the science of observable behavior. All the other theoretical approaches studied in this chapter recognize the importance of unobservable behavior and processes. Research supports many of the principles and concepts of behaviorism, and some principles are used today in behavior modification. Behavioral psychology is considered scientific.

45. A researcher wants to know how metacognition changes over time. He groups participants according to their ages. Based on your understanding of cross-sectional research, which of the following statements is true?

(Higher order)

[A] The researcher will be able to measure individual differences.

[B] The researcher will be able to determine how participants change over time.

[C] The researcher will be able to determine what is normal for each group.

[D] The researcher does not have to consider how cultural differences effect the results.

[E] The researcher will have to assess the participants at set intervals of time to see what changes have occurred.

The correct answer is C.

Cross-sectional research helps researcher recognize when certain skills, tasks, or cognitive processes occur. By studying different age groups, the researcher can determine what development is normal for certain groups. Cross-sectional research does not account for individual differences, but rather for differences among certain age groups. Longitudinal research, not cross-sectional research, helps researcher determine how participants change over time. A researcher who uses a cross-sectional method must consider historical trends and cultural differences because these factors can affect the validity of the results. Longitudinal research assesses participants at set intervals of time to see what changes have occurred.

46. All of the following statements about development are true EXCEPT:

(Higher order)

[A] Development occurs in multiple contexts.

[B] Cognitive development does not affect social development.

[C] Cultural factors impact development.

[D] Development is affected by genetic and environmental factors.

[E] Each stage of development has a critical period.

The correct answer is B.

Physical, social, and cognitive development interact, with each domain influencing and being influenced by the other domains. Development occurs in multiple contexts, and includes the home, schools, social constructs, gender, and culture. Genetic and environmental factors both affect development. Each stage of development has a critical period in which certain things must occur for an individual to develop normally.

47. **At birth, which sense is the least developed?**
(Lower order)

[A] Vision
[B] Hearing
[C] Smell
[D] Taste
[E] Touch

The correct answer is A.
Babies are born "legally blind." There is no need for babies to be able to see in the womb, which is why vision is not well developed when they are born. Unless there is a vision problem, infants have normal vision around the age of twelve months. Hearing is the most developed sense at birth because babies are able to hear while still in the womb. Babies are born with innate preferences for taste and smell. The sense of touch is not as developed as hearing, smell, and taste, but it quickly develops after birth. Babies learn how to distinguish their mother's touch from the touch of others.

48. **Jane's family has a cat. Jane knows the cat is an animal and has four legs. When Jane's family visits a pond, Jane sees a duck waddling on the shoreline. Jane does not think the duck is an animal. Jane is confused when she is told the duck is an animal. Based on Piaget's cognitive learning theory, how can Jane achieve equilibration?**
(Higher order)

[A] Assimilation
[B] Conservation
[C] Theory of Mind
[D] Static reasoning
[E] Accommodation

The correct answer is E.
Jane mentally represents animals as having four legs. When she is faced with new information, she must change her mental representation of animals through the process of accommodation. When Jane sees another animal with four legs, she categorizes it as an animal because it fits her existing schema. In this case, Jane is using assimilation. Conservation refers to understanding that something does not change in quantity even though its appearance changes. Theory of Mind is an individual's theory about what other people may be thinking. Static reasoning is when a young child thinks that nothing changes. It occurs in the pre-operational stage.

49. **Zone of proximal development is a concept proposed by which cognitive learning theorist?**
(Lower order)

[A] Albert Bandura
[B] Lev Vygotsky
[C] Harry Harlow
[D] Jean Piaget
[E] Erik Erikson

The correct answer is B.
Lev Vygotsky believed that cognitive development is impacted by social factors. Children are able to develop cognitively with help and guidance from others. The zone of proximal development refers to the range of skills and tasks a person is close to acquiring but cannot perform without some help from others. Albert Bandura was a social learning theorist. Harry Harlow conducted research on attachment. Jean Piaget's theory of cognitive development did not address social influences on learning. Erik Erikson focused on psychosocial development, not cognitive development.

50. **Andy is doing a lot of self-evaluation. He is questioning some of the values and beliefs of his parents and realizes there are some things his parents value that he does not value. He is trying to make a decision about how he wants to live his life. Which stage of Erikson's psychosocial theory describes Andy's crisis?**

    (Higher order)

    [A] Generativity versus Stagnation
    [B] Trust versus Mistrust
    [C] Independence versus Dependence
    [D] Identity versus Role Confusion
    [E] Industry versus Inferiority

    The correct answer is D.
    In this stage, the adolescent engages in self-evaluation and tries to forge an identity based on his own values and beliefs. Generativity and Stagnation is the stage in which individuals are attempting to find productive and meaningful ways to contribute to society and to the next generation. Trust versus mistrust is the first stage of psychosocial theory and deals with infants determining if they can trust adults to meet their needs. Independence versus Dependence is not a stage of Erikson's theory. Industry versus Inferiority is the stage in which children try to master new skills and abilities.

51. **Which parenting style is the healthiest for children?**

    (Lower order)

    [A] Authoritative
    [B] Permissive
    [C] Neglectful
    [D] Authoritarian
    [E] Organized

    The correct answer is A.
    Authoritative parenting is the only parenting style that balances setting limits and enforcing rules with responsive listening

and flexibility. Permissive parents give their children a lot of nurture but little guidance or discipline. Neglectful parents seem to not care about their children and often are unaware of what their children are doing. Authoritarian parenting is characterized by excessive control and high behavioral standards with little to no affection. Organized parenting is not a parenting style.

52. **Which reflex is elicited when the bottom of baby's foot is stroked?**

    (Lower order)

    [A] Moro reflex
    [B] Babinski reflex
    [C] Rooting reflex
    [D] Orienting reflex
    [E] Palmar reflex

    The correct answer is B.
    When the bottom of a baby's foot is stroked, his toes will bend and splay upward. The Moro reflex occurs when an infant flails his legs and arms outward as if to hold on to something as a response to being startled. The rooting reflex causes the baby to turn his mouth to anything that touches his cheek. The orienting reflex occurs when a baby turns his head toward a loud noise. The palmar reflex is when a baby tightly grips objects that are placed in his hand.

53. **Nativist theories of language acquisition prominently feature:**

    (Lower order)

    [A] principles of long-term potentiation
    [B] grammar acquisition devices
    [C] mnemonics
    [D] elaboration rehearsal
    [E] heuristic thinking

The correct answer is B.

If you are considering two or more answer choices for a given question it is often because you believe a case could be made for each as being potentially correct. One way to make a decision between these alternatives is to imagine that you are explaining to someone else why a choice is the correct choice. The more complex your explanation for an answer option, the less likely it is to be the correct answer choice. Probably none of the choices are completely irrelevant to language acquisition but it would require a lot of explanation to describe precisely how they are relevant. Grammar acquisition devices are relevant to nativist language acquisition theories because they are the basis of the theory. That is all the explaining required to demonstrate that the choice is relevant.

54. **Quincy is preparing for a high school history examination. During his preparation, memorization of a list of dates will most likely:**

(Higher order)

[A] require primarily automatic processing

[B] occur during a critical phase

[C] generate procedural memories

[D] require divided attention

[E] improve with chunking techniques

The correct answer is E.

You usually must to pay attention to the information you intend to memorize then actively try to memorize it by rehearsing it either through rote memorization or by using other a mnemonic or chunking or association memory techniques. George Miller showed that the capacity of short term memory is limited to on average 5 to 7 specific new or random items such as individual digits of a phone number. Much larger amounts of memory can be held in short term memory by various memory enhancement techniques. Chunking is a technique where specific units

of information including dates are grouped into larger conceptual units. Automatic processing does not require conscious effort. Quincy may have some eidetic memory ability and this could allow an automatic visual memorization of a list of dates, but less than 10% of children have this ability and it tends to disappear as they grow older. Critical phases are often a feature of cognitive development but are not directly relevant to the question of memorizing a list in the context that it is presented in the question. Procedural memories are usually a type of implicit memory. They are memories of how to perform a task such as the sequences of movements required to tie a shoelace. Cognitive processes that require conscious effort typically require focused attention. Attention that alternates or switches between two or more task is divided attention. Information processing tasks that require focused attention are disrupted or terminated by divided attention. Divided attention is not required for any memory functions.

55. **Following her recovery from meningitis, a serious infection of the membranes that surround the brain, a 25-year-old woman is no longer able to form new explicit memories. She is able to subsequently learn to needlepoint as a hobby. The woman will most likely:**

(Higher order)

[A] have damage to her cerebellum

[B] not have permanent brain damage

[C] also have difficulty with speech fluency

[D] be able to describe in words how she needlepoints

[E] have damage to her hypothalamus

The correct answer is E.

Damage to the hypothalamus can cause anterograde amnesia where explicit new memories cannot be formed but implicit procedural memories such as new skill can be. Implicit procedural memories are shown in animal models to be closely associated with processing that occurs in the cerebellum, so not likely the woman has damage to the cerebellum. Difficulty with speech fluency would not be surprising following a serious brain infection, but the woman definitely has retrograde amnesia, so an injury to the hypothalamus is more likely -- within the context of the question. Whether brain damage in retrograde amnesia is permanent is less relevant since it is not emphasized as a central feature of retrograde amnesia within the scope of the AP Psychology exam. In fact, it is almost certainly permanent. If the choice was phrased as *likely permanent* it would be a valid correct answer. In general, statements that are true but outside the scope of knowledge expected of the AP Psychology examination will not conflict with a correct answer choice that is within the scope of knowledge expected for the AP exam. As the answer choice is stated, it is a fair question because it is not true. Similarly, if speech fluency was more likely it would either be covered in your coursework or is specific information that is outside the scope of a freshman psychology course, but is nevertheless true and a reasonable answer choices compared to others. To be unable to describe in words how a new skill is accomplished is a typical impairment of retrograde amnesia.

56. Brian is a 35-year-old father of three teenage daughters. What statement about teenage girls would represent a belief bias of Brian's? *(Higher order)*

[A] "Since all of my daughters are irresponsible, any teenage girl is probably irresponsible."

[B] "My friends all say my daughters are very responsible. I can't prove it but I am sure my daughters are actually irresponsible at heart."

[C] "All teenage girls are irresponsible. My daughters are teenagers. Therefore my daughters are irresponsible."

[D] "Based on my observations, genetic factors are the cause of my daughter's irresponsibility."

[E] "For every example that indicates my daughters are responsible, which I don't even need to hear to know they are wrong, I can show twenty examples that prove my daughters are irresponsible."

The correct answer is C.
The belief bias is the bias to make illogical judgments because of your belief system. The bias is most precisely an illogical judgment in choice C, which is the only statement that is phrased as a formal logical argument. There are two premises, 1) All teenage girls are irresponsible and 2) my daughters are teenagers. The conclusion of the argument is "therefore my daughters are irresponsible". Belief bias can result in an incorrect evaluation of any logical statement. Brian's belief system causes him to consider the statement "all teenage girls are irresponsible" to be so likely to be true that he actually believes it is true. The conclusion that his daughters are therefore irresponsible is based on this belief. He may have other reasons for believing his daughters are irresponsible, but the belief bias is the reason for his conclusion in choice C. The other choices are more or

less obviously other types of biases. Choice A is an estimation of probability and probably results from an error of representative or availability heuristic thinking. Choice B is most consistent with the definition of belief perseveration. His belief is contradicted by the consensus of others and persists despite the lack of any evidence Brian has to support his belief. Choice D is the illusion of correlation bias and is well described in the methods chapter. Choice E is a clear example of confirmation bias where one tends to ignore or undervalue the significance of evidence that contradicts what one already believes to be so and to actively search for evidence to support that belief.

57. **Among the choices below, which is most precisely associated with the process of selective attention?**
(Lower order)

[A] Sensory memory
[B] Phoneme enunciation
[C] The order effect
[D] Constructed memories
[E] Cued recall

The correct answer is A.
There is an immense amount of raw information detected by sensory systems at a given point in time. The three box model proposes that there is a *filtering* or buffering mechanism that selects a small amount of this information for packaging and transfer to short term memory. This selection process requires the active attention of the perceiver. In other words, you remember the information that attracts your attention or that for which you are searching. This is known as *selective attention*. The definitions of choices C, D and E are found in the chapter. Choice B, phoneme enunciation, is a topic that is not necessarily related to selective attention. It can be argued that it does or does not involve selective attention, but it is

not an explicitly fundamental process as it is for sensory memory.

58. **Which researcher has made the most significant contributions to the understanding of nature of constructed memories?**
(Lower order)

[A] George Sperling
[B] George Miller
[C] Alexander Luria
[D] Elizabeth Loftus
[E] Benjamin Whorf

The correct answer is D.
Elizabeth Loftus' research has shown that memories are highly malleable and vulnerable to suggestion. This has provided powerful evidence that any recovered memories are likely to be false or constructed memories. George Sperling's iconic memory tests supported for his hypothesis that human beings store a perfect image of the visual world for a brief moment, before it is discarded from memory. The research of George Miller showed that the capacity of short term memory is limited to on average 5 to 7 specific new or random items such as individual digits of a phone number. Alexander Luria's case study of an individual with an exceptional ability to almost instantly memorize lists of random letters or digits up to 70 items long and to perfectly recall these as long as 15 years later. Edward Sapir and Benjamin Whorf's linguistic relativity hypothesis (the Sapir-Whorf Hypothesis) proposes that the unique patterns of one's native language result in thought patterns that are unique to native speakers of a particular language.

59. **Damage to Wernicke's area of the brain is most likely to cause which of the following?**

   (Lower order)

   [A] Receptive aphasia
   [B] Expressive aphasia
   [C] Global aphasia
   [D] Dysphagia
   [E] Aphagia

   The correct answer is A.

   Damage to Wernicke's area is associated with receptive aphasia. Sufferers of receptive aphasia have no difficulty enunciating words or forming fluent sequences of words, but the sequences are often a string of meaningless words that sound like a sentence but don't make sense. Expressive aphasia is typically seen in patients with damage to Broca's area of the brain. These persons can verbally convey sensible statements but have great difficulty forming complete sentences. Global aphasia is usually the result of a stroke that affects an extensive portion of the frontal and occipital regions of the left hemisphere. It is the most severe form of aphasia. Victims are often incapable of any type of coherent speech. Dysphagia and aphagia refer to impairment of the ability to swallow. Damage localized to Wernicke's area is not reported to cause dysphagia or aphagia.

60. **What process explains how acetylcholine release at a localized region of the body can directly trigger a generalized sympathetic response throughout the body?**

   (Higher order)

   [A] Acetylcholine release at cardiac neuromotor junctions can result in increased blood   pressure and heart rate.
   [B] Acetylcholine release in the pancreas causes release of insulin into the bloodstream.
   [C] Acetylcholine release in the adrenal medulla causes epinephrine and norepinephrine release into the bloodstream.
   [D] Acetylcholine release at synapses in ganglia in the brainstem can result in activation of all sympathetic ganglia neurons.
   [E] Acetylcholine reuptake by sympathetic neurons results in the release of norepinephrine into the bloodstream.

   The correct answer is C.

   Epinephrine and norepinephrine secreting endocrine cells in the adrenal medulla are considered to be specialized postsynaptic sympathetic neurons. They release epinephrine and norepinephrine into the bloodstream in response to acetylcholine release from presynaptic sympathetic neurons. Norepinephrine can reach and activate other sympathetic target cells through the bloodstream. This can cause a generalized activation of the sympathetic nervous system. Acetylcholine receptors in cardiac tissue cells are generally part of the parasympathetic nervous system. Acetylcholine release in the heart would antagonize the effects of sympathetic stimulation. Autonomic innervation of the pancreas is complex, but there is no well-defined mechanism whereby acetylcholine can directly stimulate secretion of insulin. The mechanisms described in choices D and E do not exist.

61. **Phineas Gage was a railroad worker who suffered a traumatic brain injury in the 1800s. This is a famous example of brain injury resulting in:**
    (Lower order)

    [A] unilateral neglect

    [B] word blindness

    [C] personality changes

    [D] inability to consolidate new memories

    [E] enhanced mathematical performance

    The correct answer is C.

    Phineas Gage was injured by a railroad spike that penetrated his brain and destroyed most of his left frontal lobe. For many years afterward he seemed a "different person" to those who had known him prior to his injury. Specifically, he underwent a radical change in fundamental individualistic features of his personality. Unilateral neglect is a phenomenon that is common in patients following large strokes of the left or right hemisphere. Word blindness is a complex phenomenon associated with dysfunction or injury to the occipital lobes. Inability to consolidate new memories is well described in persons with abnormalities of the hippocampus. Enhanced mathematical performance after brain injuries is sporadically reported, but no specific mechanism other than extreme neuroplasticity or loss of inhibition from competing mental process seems to explain how this can occur.

62. **Jennifer is a 27-year-old woman with two children who is suffering from the recent onset of cold intolerance, weight gain, inability to conceive another child and blurred vision. Among the choices listed below, which would be the most likely cause of Jennifer's symptoms?**
    (Higher order)

    [A] Exposure to pesticides

    [B] A tumor in the hypothalamus

    [C] Heavy, long-term alcohol consumption

    [D] Lack of adequate blood flow to the amygdala

    [E] Early onset of menopause

    The correct answer is B.

    Jennifer's symptoms indicate dysfunction of two or more endocrine glands. Cold intolerance and weight gain are common symptoms of low levels of thyroid hormone. Inability to conceive suggests an abnormality of the ovaries or the adrenal gland. Weight gain can also be due to low levels of steroid hormones -- an additional indication of adrenal gland dysfunction. The regulation of all of these endocrine glands is under the influence of hormones synthesized in the hypothalamus. Blurred vision is a frequent symptom of a brain tumor. All of the evidence taken together makes a tumor of the hypothalamus the most likely cause of Jennifer's symptoms.

63. **What diagnostic study is able to evaluate the rate of blood flow to a localized region of the brain?**
    (Lower order)

    [A] Computerized tomography (CT) scan

    [B] Pneumoencephalography

    [C] Electroencephalography (EEG)

    [D] Positron emission tomography (PET) scan

    [E] Functional magnetic resonance imaging (fMRI)

The correct answer is E.

Among the choices above, only fMRI is capable of evaluating the rate of blood flow to localized areas of the brain. The technical distinctions between an fMRI and a conventional MRI are beyond the scope of the AP Psychology exam, but you are expected to know the differences in their capabilities.

64. **An example of the gambler's fallacy is the common belief that if a coin that has come up heads on 9 consecutive coin tosses, it is more likely than a 50-50 chance that the coin will come up tails on the tenth toss. How would an evolutionary psychologist explain the persistence of this common misconception?**

(Higher order)

[A] Gambling behavior is associated with high risk behavior.

[B] During human evolution, successful decision making rarely required identification of truly random events.

[C] Individuals who show persistence at a given task have a survival advantage over those who do not.

[D] There is likely to be less competition for rewards that are rarely available.

[E] Gambling behavior was a socially enjoyable activity that enhanced cooperativity among early human groups.

The correct answer is A.

In psychology, gambling is considered to be an undesirable activity that is generally harmful to individuals and societies. This is an example of a mismatch, where there is an apparently disadvantageous trait or cognitive misperception that persists among individuals and groups despite the obvious negative consequences. All of the choices provided are arguably plausible evolutionary explanations for gambling behavior, but only choice B would explain why persons actually

believes the fallacy. Presumably it is an advantage to recognize that certain events are truly random, but during human evolution that may not have been true. In other words there was no selective advantage to evolving this cognitive ability. After all, if an event is truly random, what is one to do about it? It is only in recent times that humans are paying the price for a cognitive ability they never previously needed in order to survive. Unfortunately the advanced cognitive abilities we have evolved are sufficient to conceive of and participate in gambling activities.

65. **Karl Lashley's experiments with rhesus monkeys in 1923 demonstrated evidence for which of the following?**

(Lower order)

[A] Lateralization of brain function

[B] Detrimental consequences of sensory deprivation

[C] Altruistic behavior in nonhuman primates

[D] Neuroplasticity

[E] Self-awareness in nonhuman primates

The correct answer is D.

Lashley's experiments showed that changes occurred in the structure of neurons in rhesus monkeys after they learned a new task. This was one of the earliest studies to provide evidence that the neural structure of the brain can change during the process of learning a new task. Recent studies suggest lateralization of visuospatial and vocal processing occurs in some species of monkeys. Harry Harlow's experiments with maternal deprivation in infant rhesus monkeys resulted in grossly abnormal adult behavior of the subjects of the study. Several researchers have published studies that suggest rhesus monkeys engage in altruistic behavior. Evidence for self-awareness in nonhuman species is a controversial subject, but several species have passed the *mirror test*, where they appear to be aware that their mirror shows images of themselves and no other members of their species.

66. If all of the statements below were true, which one would represent the strongest argument that a hypothetical human behavior has no genetic component?
(Higher order)

[A] The behavior always instantly results in the death of the individual who engages in the behavior.

[B] The behavior only occurs in individuals who are under the influence a synthetic chemical compound that has never been known to exist in the natural environment.

[C] The behavior occurs only in individuals who have not had human contact.

[D] The behavior can only be elicited by physical torture.

[E] The behavior is completely random in individuals and occurs randomly in any experimental subject population.

The correct answer is E.
Perhaps the only argument that proves a behavior has no genetic component is that the behavior would always instantly result in the extinction of all life on earth forever. Even then one could argue the behavior resulted from a spontaneous mutation in the individual's DNA. Ultimately it is a question of whether or not humans possess free will. Truly random behavior can have only one genetic argument in its favor: that somehow random behavior can be genetically encoded. There is, unfortunately, some evidence that it can be. Some species of bacteria can be randomized in their motion by changing the direction that their flagella rotate. This is possible due to the spatial arrangement of structural subunits of the flagella. There is an argument that purely random behavior

can be encoded in DNA. One strong argument is that the behavior occurs with the same frequency in identical twins as it does in a random population sample. The counterargument is that the behavior is encoded in every human's DNA.

67. According to the DSM-5, for a diagnosis of schizophrenia, there must be:
(Lower order)

[A] a response to medical treatment.

[B] symptoms of delusions, hallucinations, and disorganized speech for at least 1 month.

[C] continuous signs of the disturbance that persist for at least 6 months.

[D] no other comorbid conditions present.

[E] agreement by at least two independent licensed mental health practitioners' evaluations.

The correct answer is C.
According to the DSM-5, a diagnosis of schizophrenia requires at least 2 of the following symptoms: delusions, hallucinations, disorganized speech, disorganized or catatonic behavior, negative symptoms. At least 1 of the symptoms must be the presence of delusions, hallucinations, or disorganized speech. Continuous signs of the disturbance must persist for at least 6 months, during which at least 1 month of active symptoms (or less if successfully treated) must be present. One are not expected to memorize every DSM-5 set of diagnostic criteria for every condition. For major disorders, including schizophrenia, one should be aware or strongly suspect that signs of the condition have been present for a reasonable period of time before making such a critical diagnosis.

68. Among the conditions listed below, _____ is most likely to require hospitalization.

(Lower order)

[A] a manic episode

[B] a panic attack

[C] a derealization episode

[D] a purging episode

[E] a major depressive episode

The correct answer is A.

Manic episodes, particularly those that occur in bipolar type-I disorder, can be dangerous to the sufferers and to those around them. Such episodes almost always require hospitalization. Panic attacks may result in hospitalization, particularly if the sufferer feels that a heart attack is occurring, but usually not. Derealization episodes occur most often in persons with depersonalization/derealization disorder. The sufferers are usually accustomed to the eerie quality of the episode and it is not otherwise dangerous. Purging episodes are almost always covert. Over time, chronic purging behavior will likely cause conditions that require hospitalization. Sometimes a single episode can cause an esophageal tear or rupture of an esophageal blood vessel and can be fatal, but this occurs infrequently for a given episode. A major depressive episode can often be a reason for hospitalization, particularly if it is the first such episode in a patient, but most episodes do not require hospitalization.

69. The disorder that most closely resembles the popular term "split personality" is:

(Lower order)

[A] schizophrenia

[B] bipolar disorder

[C] borderline personality disorder

[D] dissociative identity disorder

[E] depersonalization/derealization disorder

The correct answer is D.

In dissociative identity disorder there is a feeling of possession by another identity or that there are two or more identities or personality traits within a single person. Often there is an apparent transfer of behavioral control to the particular personality that seems to have the best capacity to function in specific social situations or other sets of circumstances.

70. Among the conditions listed below, which has the LEAST diagnostic similarity to the other four?

(Higher order)

[A] Participant-relevant confounding variable (pica)

[B] Binge eating disorder

[C] Bulimia nervosa

[D] Avoidant/restrictive food intake disorder

[E] Anorexia nervosa

The correct answer is A.

Feeding and eating disorders feature persistent abnormalities of perception and behavior related to the normal physiological and psychological functionality of eating. These include eating non-food items such as clay, paint, etc., as occurs in pica. The other conditions involve consumption of actual food.

71. **Jeremy is a highly intelligent 17-years-old male. He has been expelled from school for a second episode of theft from other students' lockers in the past year. In the latest incident, he initially blamed another student for the theft but was then shown security camera footage that proved he was the culprit. Among the choices below, which is the most likely response from Jeremy when confronted with this evidence?**
(Higher order)

[A] Puzzlement
[B] Pleading
[C] Suspicion
[D] Denial
[E] Laughter

The correct answer is E.

In order to answer this question, one needs to make a likely diagnosis. Persons with antisocial personality disorder by definition have a pervasive pattern of disregard for and violation of the rights of others. This often begins by age 15, as indicated by 3 or more of the following characteristics: failure to conform to social norms with respect to lawful behaviors, irritability and aggressiveness, reckless disregard for safety of self or others, consistent irresponsibility and a lack of remorse. The next step in answering the question requires some consideration of how an intelligent antisocial person would likely react to irrefutable evidence of a crime he had committed. There is no point in reactions such as puzzlement or denial, they could be mock reactions or tactics to appear innocent if there was doubt about his guilt, but in this case they would just make him seem stupid to the authorities. Pleading would probably be a distasteful reaction for Jeremy, as it would be degrading and likely make him look weak and an object of scorn by the authorities. Reacting with suspicion may be plausible, perhaps to give the appearance he has a different mental disorder,

like paranoia, but it's not a scheme he should have any reason to believe would result in a better outcome for himself. Laughter seems a likely response among the other choices. Presumably, antisocial personalities enjoy who they are and what they do and they don't appear to be concerned about what others think about them. Since he has no way out of the situation, he would likely reveal his true nature through laughter, showing that that he just doesn't care.

72. **_____ is NOT a typical characteristic of persons with obsessive-compulsive disorder.**
(Higher order)

[A] distress
[B] lack of awareness
[C] concealment behavior
[D] efforts to restrain behavior
[E] empathy

The correct answer is B.

Persons with obsessive-compulsive disorder are remarkable for how acutely aware that their intrusive thoughts and repetitive rituals are abnormal. This is often not the case in other mental disorders. OCD sufferers find their condition extremely distressful and this often results in depression. They go to great efforts to conceal their rituals, which may take hours to complete. They will cooperate with therapists and make lifelong commitments to use self-restraint to limit their abnormal, compulsive activities and they are often successful in doing so. Lack of empathy is not a diagnostic criterion for OCD nor is it even mentioned as a feature of OCD. It is NOT true that empathy is NOT a typical characteristic of persons with OCD because it is a typical characteristic of normal people and there is no evidence that OCD would make an otherwise normal person less empathetic.

73. To treat Madeline's schizophrenia, her doctors put her on an antipsychotic medication, conduct talk therapy in which they help Madeline and her family learn to deal with Madeline's illness, have her participate in social skills training, and send her to group therapy. Which of the following best describes this approach?

(Higher order)

[A] Psychoanalytic
[B] Cognitive-behavioral
[C] Humanistic
[D] Eclectic
[E] Biological

The correct answer is D.
Madeline's doctors are using techniques from different types of therapy and choosing which methods that will work best for Madeline. A psychoanalytic approach would focus on Madeline's childhood experiences and her unconscious conflicts. A cognitive-behavioral approach would focus solely on Madeline's cognitions and behaviors. A humanistic approach would center on issues of self-fulfillment, personal choice and personal responsibility, and a biological approach would focus on using medical methods and drugs that affect mental states.

74. After seeing a therapist for a few months, Jake suddenly begins arriving late for sessions or misses his appointments. When asked why he is behaving this way, Jake tells his friends he disagrees with his therapist about the source of his problems. Jake's behavior is an example of _____.

(Higher order)

[A] transference
[B] distorted thinking
[C] resistance
[D] depression
[E] countertransference

The correct answer is C.
A psychoanalytic therapist would argue that since Jake's tardiness and truancy began after the therapist shared her interpretations about the cause of Jake's problems, he is demonstrating resistance. Transference would involve Jake redirecting strong emotions from conflictual relationships onto his therapist, and countertransference involves the therapist redirecting her feelings onto Jake. Jake's thinking may be distorted, and he may be suffering from depression, although those things could only be assumed since they are not clearly stated, but those factors do not explain his behavior.

75. Cognitive triad is a concept developed by which psychologist?

(Lower order)

[A] Sigmund Freud
[B] Abraham Maslow
[C] Aaron Beck
[D] Albert Ellis
[E] Fritz Perls

The correct answer is C.
Aaron Beck developed cognitive therapy, which is based on the idea that depressed people form a negative cognitive triad about themselves, the world and the future. Sigmund Freud is associated with psychoanalysis. Abraham Maslow developed the hierarchy of needs. Albert Ellis developed rational-emotive behavior therapy, and Fritz Perls developed Gestalt therapy.

76. **Which of the following is an example of tertiary prevention?**
    (Higher order)

    [A] Providing job training for the unemployed
    [B] Educating adolescents about the dangers of smoking
    [C] Educating women about the dangers of consuming alcohol during pregnancy
    [D] Removing a child from an abusive home
    [E] Providing counseling to a woman who was sexually abused and has post-traumatic stress disorder

The correct answer is E.
The goal of tertiary prevention is to keep existing mental illnesses from becoming more severe, so counseling someone who already has a mental illness would fit this category. Job training for the unemployed and removing a child from an abusive home are examples of secondary prevention, which focuses on people who are at risk for developing a mental illness. Educating adolescents about the dangers of smoking and women about the dangers of drinking during pregnancy are primary preventions because both are ways to proactively work to decrease the incidence of mental illness.

77. **Kathy has a bad habit of biting her fingernails. Her mother applies a bitter tasting polish to Kathy's nails to help Kathy break this habit. What therapeutic technique is Kathy's mother using?**
    (Lower order)

    [A] Flooding
    [B] Aversion therapy
    [C] Systematic desensitization
    [D] Token economy
    [E] Rational-emotive therapy

The correct answer is B.
Kathy's mother is applying a bitter polish to Kathy's nails in the hopes that the aversive taste of the polish will stop Kathy from biting her nails. Every time Kathy bites her nails, she will experience a bitter taste and will associate this taste with nail-biting, which should extinguish this behavior. Flooding is an extinction procedure that applies to phobias and anxiety. Systematic desensitization is used to treat phobias and anxiety. A token economy is a behavioral therapy approach. Rational-emotive therapy is a cognitive-behavioral technique that is used to help people change irrational thinking.

78. **All of the following are examples of biological therapies EXCEPT:**
    (Lower order)

    [A] Pre-frontal lobotomy
    [B] Aversion therapy
    [C] Electroconvulsive therapy
    [D] Monoamine oxidase inhibitors
    [E] Prozac

The correct answer is B.
Aversion therapy is a type of classical conditioning in which an aversive stimulus is repeatedly paired with a behavior the person wants to stop. A pre-frontal lobotomy is a type of psychosurgery. Electroconvulsive therapy involves passing brief electrical currents through the brain. Monoamine oxidase inhibitors are a class of antidepressant drugs, and Prozac belongs to the class of antidepressants known as serotonin-reuptake inhibitors.

79. According to Sternberg's Triarchic theory, an individual's intelligent behavior, in general is:
(Higher order)

[A] generated by three independent socio-cultural matrices

[B] predetermined to eliminate the effects of novelty in social contexts

[C] comprised of metacognition, performance and knowledge acquisition thought processes.

[D] resolved into final actions that are primarily analytic, primarily componential or primarily componential/analytic.

[E] visual-spatial and/or logical-mathematical and/or Interpersonal-intrapersonal

The correct answer is D.
Sternberg's theory describes intelligent behavior as behavior that requires fundamental thought processes that can be categorized as metacognition, performance and knowledge acquisition processes. This is the primary level of understanding of Sternberg's Theory that is expected for the AP examination. The remaining answer choices are to varying degrees misstatements of principles of the theory or other theories of intelligence or just frankly nonsense statements. You could be seduced into considering these other statements as somehow even more correct than choice C, but you should be adequately prepared to recognize that C is correct. If you choose another option you have made at least two major mistakes. The first is to decide that you are wrong about you basic understanding of the theory and concluded that C is not true. The choice cannot be used in this question if there is another correct answer. If you trust your own knowledge that C is correct, the other choices cannot be otherwise it is a invalid question. There is never more

than one correct answer choice. So if you trust your own basic understanding of the theory you are done with this question. After this first mistake the second is to convince yourself that one of the other choices is true. At some point you fail to recognize you are expending a ridiculous amount of effort in explaining to yourself why any one of these other choices actually are more true than choice C. If you are just guessing then just guess. Any guessing strategies you attempt to employ will just chew up valuable time and undermine your overall test performance.

80. Among the descriptions below, which would be considered the most serious weakness in the construct validity of a standardized test?
(Higher order)

[A] The consensus expert opinion is that the test's constructed content does not include questions sufficient to test for the full range of what is being tested for

[B] The consensus expert opinion is that the test content as it is constructed includes a large percentage of questions that are irrelevant to what is being tested for

[C] The test questions are constructed on the basis of a theory that has not yet been validated

[D] The results of the test administration shows a strong negative correlation with predictions of the theory upon which the test was constructed

[E] After the first administration of the test, there is a low calculated correlation coefficient with an older test's results, AND the older test measures for what the new test is intended to measure for AND expert consensus is that the older test is almost perfectly valid.

The correct answer is D.
Construct validity can show a clear

connection to a theory about what the test is intended to measure and the content of the test. Based on the theory, the expert can make a rational argument to explain why the content of an exam will likely measure what the test is intended to measure. After trial runs or actual administration of the new test, the construct validity of the test can be assessed retroactively. For instance the theory may predict that an overall test score should increase as the age of the test taker increases or that one type of subscore in the test should decrease as the birth order of test takers increase. If the results of the test administration shows a strong negative correlation ("negative" in this case meaning "does not agree") with predictions of the theory upon which the test was constructed this would by definition be a specific and severe weakness in the construct validity of a standardized test. For choices A and B, content validity is based on expert opinion of completeness - that the content fairly and proportionately tests for the full range of the thing that is being tested for and appropriateness (choice A) - that the content is focused on the this thing and does not include content that is extraneous or unrelated to what is being tested for (choice B).For choice E, concurrent validity is often the degree to which a new test correlates with older tests that are agreed to be valid for measuring what the new test is intended to measure. Choice C is remarkable in that construct validity may be poor if it is based on a bad theory, but if it is based a new theory that has not been well-validated scientifically, it may or may not be a construct weakness. In fact the new test may provide a positive correlation between the theories predictions and the results of the test and thereby improve the validity of the theory itself. This is essentially a central element of the scientific method - to evaluate the validity of a hypothesis through experimentation.

81. **Which statement below would be most consistent with a historically well-documented characterization of Alfred Binet's earliest concepts of human intelligence?**
(Higher order)

[A] "What we think, we must ultimately thing in words."

[B] "There is a great diversity in individual intelligence, but there is a common element of practical judgement that influences the intellectual functions in all individuals."

[C] "When we actually analyze the results of intelligence tests, the evidence indicates there are several independent types of intelligence."

[D] "When we actually analyze the results of intelligence tests, the evidence indicates there is one fundamental intelligence that can operate in many specific modes."

[E] "The intelligence measured in children is fundamentally different than the intelligence measured in adults"

The correct answer is B.

The question can be most easily answered based on basic knowledge that is expected by the AP psychology exam. You are expected to have a historical awareness of the major figures in IQ testing and intelligence theory. Binet was the first to develop a standardized IQ test. For choices B, C and D, his contributions precede the historical stage of factor analysis of IQ tests and Binet is not identified as a strong advocate of either the single intelligence or multiple intelligence theories of intelligence. One of his most well-documented and relevant positions on the matter of intelligence is paraphrased, namely that he felt either view "a great diversity in individual intelligence" and "a common element of practical judgement" was worth serious consideration. Perhaps he eventually became to be a supporter of one view over the other, but the question asks for his earliest views. Choice A distracts because it is true that Binet's test measured primarily verbal abilities, but that does not directly indicate he believed a more specific verbal mechanism existed for intelligence at a fundamental level and there is no record he actually did believe this. For choice E, Binet's test was intended to test school children but that does not indicate Binet thought children's intelligence was fundamentally different than adult intelligence, and again there is no well documented record that he held this view.

82. Charles Spearman is most directly associated with which of the following?

(Lower order)

[A] Factor analysis of correlations related to intelligence

[B] The concept of crystallized intelligence

[C] The concept of fluid intelligence

[D] Development of the Culture Fair Intelligence Test

[E] Development of The Three Stratum Model of Intelligence

The correct answer is C.

Charles Spearman published the first factor analysis of the correlation of grades for individuals among specific school subjects and proposed that although there were specific types of intelligence or mental abilities, called s intelligence there appeared to by an underlying general or g intelligence. For choices B, C and D, Raymond Cattell proposed that Spearman's general intelligence was composed of two fundamental types of intelligence; 1) fluid intelligence that utilized a reasoning capacity to solve novel problems or to otherwise function well in a changing external environment, and 2) crystallized

intelligence that was adapted to utilize an individual's general fund of knowledge acquired through study and through life experience. He also developed the Culture Fair Intelligence Test (CFIT) in an effort measure of cognitive abilities in a manner that was independent of sociocultural and environmental influences. For choice E, John Carroll developed The Three Stratum Model of Intelligence.

83. Zach is a 17-year-old high school student. He has recently been administered the latest age appropriate version of the Stanford-Binet Intelligence Test and his overall score is 95. Zach is therefore:

(Lower order)

[A] unqualified for enlistment in the regular U.S. armed forces

[B] within one standard deviation from the mean of the test population

[C] Less likely to have a coexisting diagnosis of antisocial personality disorder than a typical student who would have taken the Stanford-Binet exam during the same year that Zach took the exam.

[D] more likely to score higher on his SATs than a typical student who would have taken the Stanford-Binet exam during the same year that Zach took the exam

[E] more likely to be an only child than is a typical student who would have taken the Stanford-Binet exam during the same year that Zach took the exam

The correct answer is B.

The exact correlations for IQ scores are not specified by the AP Examination authorities but in general you should either know or strongly suspects that some or all of the other answer choices are perhaps false. Regardless, you have a extremely basic expectation to know that the single score IQ number of 100 is the mean score of the examination and that the standard deviation from the mean is 15, therefore Zack's deviation from the mean (100-95 = 5) is within one standard deviation from the mean.

84. **A test that features questions that are sequentially increasingly difficult to solve due to their complexity and not due to the total amount of time allotted to answer all of the questions is:**

    (Lower order)

    [A] an achievement test
    [B] an aptitude test
    [C] a non-standardized test
    [D] a reliability test
    [E] a power test

    The correct answer is E.

    This is an explicit description of what a power test and how it differs from a speed test. We will not repeat the very basic definitions of terms that make the wrong answer choices wrong. If you are having trouble with this question you require extensive review of the material presented in this chapter. If so, do not panic, perhaps you have taken this practice exam to diagnose your weakness. Otherwise you now realize you have a long way to go in terms of preparation for the AP exam. One way we feel you may do this is to read this book and do the all problems in it, then read the explanations; not only to see why you may have answered a problem incorrectly, but also to be sure that you got a question right for the right reasons. In any case, this question is at the very lowest level of difficulty that you can expect for the AP Psychology Examination.

85. **According to the research of Masters and Johnson, among the statements below, the most accurate and direct evidence for a significant psychological effect on sexual function is:**

    (Higher order)

    [A] demonstrated by a sexual repose to erotic materials in men with erectile dysfunction
    [B] most apparent during the resolution phase of the sexual response cycle
    [C] expressed as a secondary learned drive
    [D] resistance to habituation effects during the plateau phase of the sexual response cycle
    [E] most apparent in women with a history of sexual abuse

    The correct answer is A.

    The Masters and Johnson Study was notable for this avenue of investigation and it remains as a very reliable clinical indicator that a physiological response is not due to a direct physical impairment. If a man has the response in certain circumstances - namely when viewing erotic material he clearly has the physical capability to do so - he just proved he can. So, if this is not the case in other circumstances, it is a logical conclusion that the problem is not physiological, but most likely psychological. Choices B and D are constructed to appear reasonable and related to the question but at a fundamental level are nonsense. Choice C is clearly wrong in the context of the question - the response is, if anything, an almost instinctive behavior or automatic physiological response. That is not to say that all sorts of factors may influence the behavior but the analytical processes to conclude this is the correct answer are too esoteric for the level of the AP Psychology exam and there is already a perfectly obviously correct answer if you are familiar with the Masters and Johnson research. Choice E is fair choice in this question only because it is not addressed in the Masters and Johnson research and for that reason alone it must be wrong.

86. **Imagine that research has strongly supported one of the following effects. Which of those in the choices below would be most similar to the proposed mechanism for the Garcia effect?**
(Higher order)

[A] Persons with previous long term exposure to violent video games have decreased emotional response to violent images.

[B] The motivation to pursue self-actualization is less apparent in persons who have never experience a 1-month or longer period of homelessness compared to those that have.

[C] Persons who experience a traumatic event during a holiday experience extreme anxiety on subsequent occurrences of that particular holiday.

[D] The re-experiencing of a previously fearful event as an enjoyable but exhilarating event.

[E] Persons with a history of digestive disorders are less likely to engage in social activities related to states of high arousal.

The correct answer is C.
The Garcia effect is considered to be a physiologic classical conditioning repose of nausea or vomiting associated with a particular food that was associated with a single exposure to a stimulus of an illness that resulted in nausea and vomiting. Choice C describes an emotional state, anxiety, which has a primarily physiological character, increased heart rate nervousness and possibly sweating. The response was conditioned by a traumatic single event that occurred on a particular holiday. The food item in the Garcia effect and the holiday in the question did not cause nausea or anxiety but were associated with a nausea inducing event -illness and an anxiety inducing event that is a traumatic event by definition. Subsequently, exposure to these conditioned stimuli, the food item and the specific holiday, generate the conditioned responses, nausea and anxiety respectively. Choice A is better interpreted as an example of habituation or desensitization. Choice B is a scenario which would tend to refute one of the tenets of Maslow's theory of motivation based on hierarchical needs. Rather than fulfilling a lower need for security that allows for progression to attain higher level needs of self-actualization, there is an actual deficiency of a lower need that seems to correlate with an increased desire to fulfill a higher level need. Choice D describes a phenomena that is proposed to be accounted for by the opponent processes theory of motivation, it is not clearly a conditioned response and even less clearly classical conditioning. Choice E is a hypothetical correlation that is designed to introduce unpleasant experiences that may be eating related with a response that is very general. It could be somewhat analogous to the Garcia effect, but not nearly as specific as choice C.

87. **What is most clearly a criticism of opponent processes theory of motivation?**
    (Higher order)

    [A] The effects of opiate withdrawal can be almost instantly eliminated by the administration of the drug naloxone

    [B] Research indicates persons do not think of their needs in terms of a hierarchy

    [C] To attain a relatively preferred high baseline state of arousal requires that the novelty of arousing situation remains high

    [D] Depending on the overall context in which an event occurs the immediate removal of a highly joyful experience can result in multiple strongly experienced emotions including relief and not including sadness.

    [E] The exact same experience can produce exactly opposite emotional responses in different individuals

The correct answer is D.
All of the answer choices are strongly defensible criticisms of various motivation theories. Choice D directly attacks the central premise of the opponent processes theory. The theory states there are pairs of opposite emotions and that when one is strongly felt and suddenly removed the opposite emotion is strongly experienced in response to this sudden absence of the original emotion. Presumably the opposite emotion of joy is sadness and if persons often do not have this as an immediate emotion upon the withdrawal of the joy emotion that strongly undermines the mechanism proposed by the theory. Furthermore there is more than one type of emotional responses that can replace the joy emotion so this contradict a precise opposing pair theory of emotion. The fact that there can be a mix of emotions that replace the joy emotion also contradicts the opposite emotion pair concept of the theory.

88. **Stanley Schachter is most directly associated with which of the following?**
    (Lower order)

    [A] The hierarchy model of motivation
    [B] The two-factor theory of emotion
    [C] The general adaptation syndrome
    [D] The principle of optimum arousal for peak performance
    [E] The Opponent-Process Theory

The correct answer is B.
Stanley Schachter and Jerome E. Singer proposed The Schachter–Singer theory, or two-factor theory of emotion. For choice A, there is no one hierarchical theory of motivation but a prominent theory of this types is Abraham Maslow's hierarchy of needs model of motivation. For choice C, Hans Selye was the first to characterize the general adaptation syndrome. For choice D, the Yerkes-Dodson Law states that one's performance will increase as one's level of arousal increases, but only to a certain point. After that point, increasing levels of arousal will progressively impair performance. For choice E, Richard Solomon's opponent-process theory is based on his premise that that emotions exist as opposing pairs.

89. **The ventromedial hypothalamus is most closely identified with which physiological process?**
    (Lower order)

    [A] The generation of the sensation of satiety
    [B] The generation of the sensation of hunger
    [C] The establishment of a metabolic set point
    [D] The regulation of heart rate
    [E] The regulation of blood pressure

The correct answer is A.
The ventromedial hypothalamus generates the signal to stop eating. This is perceived as satiety -the sense of fullness. The lateral

hypothalamus generates of the sensation of hunger. The establishment of a metabolic set point is believed to be a hypothalamic function but has not been clearly localized to the ventromedial hypothalamus. The regulation of heart rate and blood pressure occurs in the medulla oblongata

90. **The general adaptation syndrome is most closely associated with:**
(Lower order)

[A] Jerome Singer
[B] Abraham Maslow
[C] Richard Solomon
[D] Hans Selye
[E] William Masters and Virginia Johnson

The correct answer is D.
Hans Selye was the first to characterize the general adaptation syndrome. Stanley Schachter and Jerome E. Singer proposed The Schachter–Singer theory, or two-factor theory of emotion. Abraham Maslow proposed the hierarchy of needs model of motivation. Richard Solomon's opponent-process theory is based on his premise that that emotions exist as opposing pairs. William Masters and Virginia Johnson research characterized the human sexual response cycle.

91. **Which approach deals with issues of self-concept and free choice?**
(Lower order)

[A] Sociocultural approach
[B] Biological approach
[C] Humanistic approach
[D] Functionalism
[E] Gestalt psychology

The correct answer is C.
Humanistic psychology focuses on studying free will, self-concept, awareness of the human condition, and aspects of consciousness. The sociocultural approach studies how social and cultural factors influence thoughts and behavior. The biological approach views behavior as being caused by biological and genetic factors. Functionalism is a theory that states that the functions of the mind are more important than the actual components of the mind. Gestalt psychology seeks to understand the individual in view of the person's total experiences. Although very similar to humanistic psychology, gestalt psychology does not focus on self-concept.

92. **Which early theoretical perspective had the greatest influence on the field of behavioral psychology?**
(Higher order)

[A] Empiricism
[B] Dualism
[C] Natural selection
[D] Materialism
[E] Tabula rasa

The correct answer is D.
Materialism is the belief that matter and energy are the only things that exist. It rejects the idea of a soul and spirit and proposes that all things in a person's conscious awareness are results of processes of the brain. Since behavioral psychology focuses only on what can be observed, no attention is given to cognitive processes, emotions, or any other part of the human experience, such as the soul and spirit. Empiricism refers to the belief that truth and knowledge can be acquired through experiences and observations. Dualism refers to the idea that the world and human nature can be divided into two parts, the body and the spirit. Natural selection is a theory proposed by Charles Darwin that states that only behaviors and thoughts that promote survival and adaptation are selected and passed down to other generations. Tabula rasa is the theory that all humans are born knowing nothing; they are essentially

blank states. Knowledge is gained through experiences.

93. **Linda is seeing a therapist because she is having problems in her relationships. Linda reports being moody and grouchy due to a problem with her thyroid. Linda also states that she feels like she has no one to talk to because her family has never been one that talks about feelings. Linda expresses some negative and self-defeating thoughts. Which of the following statements best reflects the approach Linda's therapist should take?**

[A] The therapist needs to treat Linda from a cognitive psychology approach because Linda's thoughts are what is causing her problems.

[B] The therapist should use a sociocultural approach to help Linda understand how her family's views have caused her interpersonal difficulties.

[C] The therapist should help Linda improve her self-concept and take responsibility for her choices.

[D] The therapist should focus more on making sure Linda is being treated for her thyroid problem since that problem is affecting her moods, which affect her relationships.

[E] The therapist should take an approach that addresses Linda's medical issues, familial influences, and thought processes because they are all contributing to Linda's problems.

The correct answer is D.
The problem with Linda's thyroid affects her moods, which has a negative impact on her relationships. However, Linda's culture does not seem to value discussing feelings, but Linda needs to be able to talk about her feelings and how things are affecting her. Linda's thoughts are also negatively affecting her feelings and her relationships. Therefore, the therapist should not ignore any one of these areas because all of these areas are contributing to Linda's difficulties. Linda's thoughts are not the only factor contributing to her interpersonal problems, nor is her family environment the only contributing factor. While there is nothing wrong with addressing self-concept issues with a client or working with a client to help the client accept responsibility for her problems, there is no indication that either of these scenarios is what is causing Linda's problems. Linda does need to be receiving treatment for her thyroid problem because it is affecting her moods, but focusing more on that issue will not address the cognitive or sociocultural factors that are also contributing to Linda's difficulties.

94. **Amelia is angry with her boss for adding a new project to her tasks. When Amelia arrives home, she argues with her children, gets mad at them, and sends them to bed early. Which defense mechanism is Amelia using?**
(Lower order)

[A] Reaction formation
[B] Sublimation
[C] Rationalization
[D] Compensation
[E] Displacement

The correct answer is E.
Amelia is taking her unwanted feelings towards her boss out on people who are less threatening, her children. In reaction formation, the person acts the opposite of how she feels. Sublimation is redirecting one's sexual and aggressive drives to more socially acceptable goals. Rationalization involves creating excuses in order to justify one's actions or feelings.

Compensation is used when a person who fails in one area directs energy to succeeding in another area.

95. **Which of the following statements best describes incongruence?**
(Higher order)

[A] Ken's marriage is ending so he throws himself into his work.

[B] Marcy sees one group of her classmates as "cool" and the other group as "uncool."

[C] Henry believes in having a good work ethic but he steals from his boss.

[D] Candi makes a high score on her SAT and attributes her success to her intelligence.

[E] Adam distances himself from his son when his son fails to make the football team.

The correct answer is C.
Incongruence refers to the gap that exists between who one wishes to be and who one actually is. Henry may wish to have a good work ethic, but he actually does not have a good work ethic, as evidenced by stealing from his boss. Choice A is an example of the defense mechanism of compensation. Choice B describes a personal construct. Choice D is an example of an internal locus-of-control, and Choice E illustrates the concept of conditions of worth.

96. **Max is known across many settings for being dishonest, grouchy, funny, intelligent, overly emotional, and ambitious. Which of the following statements is true?**

[A] These characteristics indicate that Max needs to work on self-actualization.

[B] These characteristics probably show that Max has a mental disorder.

[C] These characteristics show that Max has a high level of self-esteem.

[D] These characteristics describe Max's central dispositions.

[E] These characteristics can change if Max explores his unconscious.

The correct answer is D.
Central dispositions are those that stand out the most in an individual. Since Max demonstrates these traits across different settings and is known for these traits, these are the traits that people associate with Max. It will not hurt Max to work on self-actualization, but the type of traits someone has does not make achieving self-actualization any more or less important for them. There is no evidence that Max has a mental disorder. Some of his central dispositions are good and some are bad, but that does not indicate a mental disorder since all humans have good and bad personality traits. These traits also do not support the idea that Max has high self-esteem, and there is not enough information to make that assumption. Most likely, these characteristics will not change significantly, regardless of what type of therapy Max receives, especially that of exploring his unconscious mind.

97. **The idea that cognitive development is impacted by both biological and environmental factors best represents the theoretical perspective of which person?**
    (Lower order)

    [A] Jean Piaget
    [B] Sigmund Freud
    [C] Lawrence Kohlberg
    [D] Konrad Lorenz
    [E] Lev Vygotsky

    The correct answer is E.
    Vygotsky believed that social factors greatly affect a child's cognitive development. He was critical of Piaget's cognitive development theory because it did not consider social factors. Sigmund Freud's theory focused on psychosexual development, and Kohlberg's theory centered on moral development. Konrad Lorenz contributed to attachment theory with his concept of imprinting.

98. **Alicia's curfew is 10:00. When she arrives home 30 minutes late, her parents express concern and frustration. They remind Alicia about the importance of rules and the reason for the rule. They let Alicia know that there will be consequences for her actions, but they first want to know why Alicia was out past her curfew. Which type of parenting style do Alicia's parents have?**
    (Higher order)

    [A] Permissive
    [B] Insecure
    [C] Authoritative
    [D] Authoritarian
    [E] Indulgent

The correct answer is C.
Authoritative parents set clear and reasonable behavioral standards, and they consistently enforce the rules. However, they also care about the thoughts of their children and allow their children to have some role in setting the rules. They discuss the rationale for the rules. These parents are warm and nurturing and communicate with their children. Permissive parents are warm and nurturing but they have few, if any rules. Insecure refers to an attachment pattern, not a parenting style. Authoritarian parents have strict rules and high behavioral expectations. They do not discuss the reason for the rules, and they are rigid and inflexible. They are not very nurturing or supportive. The term indulgent is often used to describe permissive parents.

99. Amelia is angry with her boss for adding a new project to her tasks. When Amelia arrives home, she argues with her children, gets mad at them, and sends them to bed early. Which defense mechanism is Amelia using?

(Lower order)

[A] Reaction formation
[B] Sublimation
[C] Rationalization
[D] Compensation
[E] Displacement

The correct answer is E.
Amelia is taking her unwanted feelings towards her boss out on people who are less threatening, her children. In reaction formation, the person acts the opposite of how she feels. Sublimation is redirecting one's sexual and aggressive drives to more socially acceptable goals. Rationalization involves creating excuses in order to justify one's actions or feelings. Compensation is used when a person who fails in one area directs energy to succeeding in another area.

100. Which of the following statements best describes incongruence?

(Higher order)

[A] Ken's marriage is ending so he throws himself into his work.
[B] Marcy sees one group of her classmates as "cool" and the other group as "uncool."
[C] Henry believes in having a good work ethic but he steals from his boss.
[D] Candi makes a high score on her SAT and attributes her success to her intelligence.
[E] Adam distances himself from his son when his son fails to make the football team.

The correct answer is C.
Incongruence refers to the gap that exists between who one wishes to be and who one actually is. Henry may wish to have a good work ethic, but he actually does not have a good work ethic, as evidenced by stealing from his boss. Choice A is an example of the defense mechanism of compensation. Choice B describes a personal construct. Choice D is an example of an internal locus-of-control, and Choice E illustrates the concept of conditions of worth.

Sample Test 1

SAMPLE QUESTION ONE

1. The Wilson's four-year old daughter, Missy, has begun throwing tantrums when she does not get her way. The tantrums are increasing in frequency and intensity; sometimes Missy gets aggressive during her tantrums. Missy's parents are frustrated and say they have tried everything they know to do to decrease or eliminate the tantrums, including arguing with Missy and bribing her with a fun activity. Sometimes, they give in to Missy just to get her to stop throwing a tantrum.

    A. **Summarize the main idea(s) of each of the following: (3 points)**

    *   Operant conditioning (1 points)
    *   Albert Bandura's Bobo Doll experiment (1 points)
    *   Piaget's cognitive theory—preoperational stage-egocentrism (1 point)

    B. **Discuss how the Wilson's could use their knowledge of the concepts to address their daughter's behavior. Provide examples for each one. (3 points)**

    *   Operant conditioning—Tantrums (1 point)
    *   Modeling—aggression (1 point)
    *   Egocentrism—arguing/reasoning (1 point)

    C. **Of the methods you provided, which method would you use and why? (1 point)**

BEFORE WRITING YOUR RESPONSE

Before you begin formulating your response, stop and think about what the question is asking you. On the question sheet, write down some notes or make an outline. Following these suggestions will help you organize your thoughts. Let the implied organization of the question guide the organization of your response.

There are 3 bulleted points to be addressed in Part A, and three bulleted elements to be addressed in Part B. There is one point to cover in Part C. Those bulleted points should serve as the organization for your response. You should NOT use your outline as your response. This is prohibited in the free response instructions given by the College Board. Write your response using complete sentences in paragraph form. Organizing your paragraphs in the order implied in the question will help the AP scorers grade your response.

In Part A of this question, there are 3 points you need to cover: operant conditioning, Bobo Doll experiment, and preoperational stage-egocentrism. You are to summarize each of these concepts. In Part B, there are 3 concepts you need to cover: operant conditioning, modeling, and egocentrism. You are to describe how each of those concepts can be used to address the corresponding behavior, and you are to give an example for each one. In some cases, a good example can serve as the description. Your answers must reflect the context of the question.

You may find it helpful to underline each bulleted element when you write your response. While this is not required, underlining these words will not only help you organize your response, it will also help the AP readers be able to score your response more easily and quickly. You can apply these suggestions to both the response questions you will answer.

The important thing is to make sure you address every part of the question in an organized, cogent manner. If you prefer not to underline the terms, find a method that works for you so that you will know you covered all elements of the question.

Refer to your notes or outline or whatever method you choose frequently when answering the question. Doing this will help you organize your thoughts in your head and on paper, and it will serve as mental checklist. It may also help you identify parts of the question you did not answer or areas where you need to add information. If you have time after you have answered BOTH free response questions, read through your answers to check for errors or omissions. If you forgot to cover something, neatly add it to your response in the appropriate place. If you need to delete something, make it clear that you are deleting that portion, but keep your writing as neat and legible as possible. Leaving a small space between the lines will give you room to add content and make corrections.

Before you read the sample response to this question, you may find it beneficial to write your response. After you have written your response, read over your answer. Use the following rubric to make sure you covered the information given to you in the question. If you realize there is something in the question that you did not cover in your response, go back and add the missing information to your response. Once you have read through your response and are certain you adequately covered all the points of the question, use the following rubric to score your response.

RUBRIC FOR SAMPLE QUESTION ONE

This question is worth 7 points. Part A is worth 3 points. Part B is worth 3 points, and Part C is worth 1 point.

Point 1: *Operant conditioning.* The response can include any principle of operant conditioning (reinforcement, shaping, punishment, consequences, contingencies, schedules of reinforcement). Reinforcement must be described as increasing behavior, and punishment must be described as decreasing behavior.

Point 2: *Bobo Doll experiment.* The response should mention observational learning (vicarious learning, social learning), modeling, and violent or aggressive behavior. The response should demonstrate that the student understands that children learn behaviors from watching others.

Point 3: *Preoperational stage-egocentrism.* The response should indicate that children Missy's age (age 4) cannot understand or share the point of view (perspective) of others and they are not able to understand how their actions affect others. The response should indicate that they are not capable of logic and reasoning.

Point 4: *Operant conditioning.* The response should establish that the student understands how to apply principles of operant conditioning to modify behavior. The student can discuss positive and negative reinforcement, punishment, shaping, schedules of reinforcement, consequences, contingencies. The student must demonstrate knowledge that reinforcement strengthens/increases behavior and punishment weakens/decreases behavior. Examples must correctly describe these concepts.

Point 5: *Modeling-Aggression.* The response should mention observational/social learning of behavior by watching/seeing it. Examples should provide practical suggestions for avoiding/eliminating modeling of aggressive behavior.

Point 6: *Egocentrism-Arguing/Reasoning.* The response should establish that the child cannot take the point of view of others or use logic or reason to solve problems. Examples should present a practical and reasonable alternative to arguing or reasoning with the child.

Point 7: *Student opinion and reason.* The response should clearly present the student's opinion and argument for the opinion. Any reasonable argument and explanation is acceptable so long as it does not contradict something the student stated earlier and as long as it demonstrates accurate understanding and application of the concepts.

SAMPLE RESPONSE ONE

Operant conditioning is learning that occurs because a behavior has been reinforced or strengthened. According to Skinner, behavior is a function of its consequences. If a behavior is rewarded, it is more likely to occur again, but if it is punished, it is likely to weaken and be eliminated. Reinforcement is a major principle of operant conditioning. Behavior can be changed by administering the right kind of reinforcement. Positive reinforcement increases the likelihood a behavior will be repeated by presenting a desirable reinforcer after the behavior. Negative reinforcement occurs when the removal of something unpleasant increases the chance the behavior will be repeated. With both types of reinforcement, the behavior is strengthened. A behavior can be weakened through punishment. Positive punishment involves presenting an unpleasant consequence after an undesirable behavior occurs, and negative punishment means a pleasant stimulus is removed after an undesirable behavior is exhibited. Both types of punishment decrease the likelihood the behavior will be repeated.

Albert Bandura was a social learning theorist who conducted an experiment involving Bobo Dolls. In this experiment, one group of children watched a male or female model acting violently or aggressively toward a Bobo doll. Children in another room watched a non-aggressive adult male or female playing quietly with toys and ignoring the Bobo doll. The children that watched the aggressive models were far more likely to act aggressively toward the Bobo doll, even when the adults who modeled the behavior were absent. The children who witnessed the violent behavior imitated it hours after they it. The presence or absence of reinforcement that were given to the models made no difference. This experiment demonstrated that children learn behavior, even violent behavior, from watching others.

Egocentrism is a concept proposed by Piaget. Children develop egocentrism in what Piaget called the preoperational stage. Children enter this stage around the age of two and leave this stage around age seven. During the preoperational stage, children do not have the ability to reason or use logic. Egocentrism means that a child does not have the ability to think of others or understand perspectives that are different than theirs.

The Wilsons can use positive punishment to decrease the frequency of Missy's tantrums. By giving in to Missy and bribing her, the Wilson's are actually strengthening her tantrum behavior. What they should do is take away something Missy finds fun or pleasant after she has a tantrum. For example, if Missy enjoys watching a certain television show, the Wilson's can take away the chance of watching that television show from Missy. If Missy throws a tantrum, she does not get to watch the show. Before long, Missy's tantrums will disappear, or at least occur much less frequently. The Wilson's could also use positive reinforcement with Missy. If Missy does not throw a tantrum for not getting her way, the Wilson's can let Missy do something she enjoys or reward her in some way. For example, the Wilson's may let Missy draw or color every time she cooperates instead of throwing a tantrum.

One possible reason for Missy's aggressive behavior is that she is seeing that kind of behavior, whether it is from watching television or from seeing her parents get frustrated and angry with her. Her parents may be arguing or exhibiting other signs of aggression in front of Missy, and Missy is learning that aggression is a way to act when she does not get what she wants. Missy's parents should be careful what they watch on television when Missy is in the room, and they should learn to respond to Missy in a calm way. If Missy's parents are acting verbally or physically aggressive in front of her, they need to stop it. They need to make an extra effort to learn to handle conflict in a positive way. For example, if the Wilson's are watching a show with a lot of bad language and physical aggression and Missy walks in

the room, the Wilson's need to turn off the television and watch the show later.

Missy's parents need to stop arguing with her and trying to reason with her. Missy does not yet have the ability to reason. She will not understand an adult's reasons. She is incapable at her age of seeing things from any point of view other than her own. She does not understand how her behavior is affecting others. The Wilson's should avoid arguing with Missy for any reason. An example is if Missy begins to throw a tantrum, the Wilson's should find another way to deal with Missy instead of arguing with her.

If I were the Wilson's I would use punishment to try to change Missy's behavior. Punishment should decrease the frequency of Missy's tantrums. If Missy loses something she enjoys every time she has a tantrum, she will quickly learn that her tantrums are not going to help her get her way. I think that punishment would be more effective, though, if the Wilson's use it with positive reinforcement. But, the quickest way to extinguish the tantrums is punishment. After that the change can be maintained by the Wilson's also using positive reinforcement. If Missy throws a tantrum, something she enjoys should be taken away every time at first until the change is significant, and the Wilson's can reward Missy for not throwing a tantrum by allowing her to do something she enjoys. In combination, these methods should be very effective in changing Missy's behavior.

END OF RESPONSE

GRADING THE SAMPLE RESPONSE

The AP readers will use the rubric to score your response. The readers will look at the rubric as they read your answer. As the readers go over your response, they will award a point for each correct answer. The readers will not penalize you for inaccurate information unless you directly contradict something you wrote earlier in your response.

The scorers will use a "grid" to indicate how many points a response has been awarded. The grid is organized just as the question is and will reflect what is on the rubric. It may help you to think of the grid as a sort of checklist. Every time the reader sees a correct answer in your response, they will give you a checkmark. At the end of reading your response, the scorer will count the checkmarks to arrive at your total grade for that question.

How well do you think the fictitious student did? Let's examine this response based on the rubric.

Point 1: Awarded—The student discussed operant conditioning, positive and negative reinforcement and punishment. The student demonstrated understanding that reinforcement increases the likelihood of a behavior being repeated or strengthened, and punishment weakens the behavior and makes it less likely to be repeated.

"Positive reinforcement increases the likelihood a behavior will be repeated by presenting a desirable reinforcer after the behavior. Negative reinforcement occurs when the removal of something unpleasant increases the chance the behavior will be repeated. With both types of reinforcement, the behavior is strengthened. A behavior can be weakened through punishment. Positive punishment involves presenting an unpleasant consequence after an undesirable behavior occurs, and negative punishment means a pleasant stimulus is removed after an undesirable behavior is exhibited. Both types of punishment decrease the likelihood the behavior will be repeated."

Point 2: Awarded—The student covered all the important aspects of the Bobo doll experiment.

"In this experiment, one group of children watched a male or female model acting violently or aggressively toward a Bobo doll. Children in another room watched a non-aggressive adult male or female playing quietly with toys and ignoring the Bobo doll. The children that watched the aggressive models were far more likely to act aggressively toward the Bobo doll, even when the adults who modeled the behavior were absent. The children who witnessed the violent behavior imitated it hours after they it. The presence or absence of reinforcement that were given to the models made no difference. This experiment demonstrated that children learn behavior, even violent behavior, from watching others."

Point 3: Awarded—The student summarized the preoperational stage and the concept of egocentrism.

"During the preoperational stage, children do not have the ability to reason or use logic. Egocentrism means that a child does not have the ability to think of others or understand perspectives that are different than theirs."

Point 4: Awarded—The student applied the concepts of positive punishment as a way of modifying Missy's behavior and gave an accurate example.

"The Wilsons can use positive punishment to decrease the frequency of Missy's tantrums. By giving in to Missy and bribing her, the Wilson's are actually strengthening her tantrum behavior. What they should do is take away something Missy finds fun or pleasant after she has a tantrum. For example, if Missy enjoys watching a certain television show, the Wilson's can take away the chance of watching that television show from Missy."

Point 5: Awarded—The student correctly applied the results of the Bobo doll experiment and modeling to Missy's behavior and gave an accurate example.

"One possible reason for Missy's aggressive behavior is that she is seeing that kind of behavior, whether it is from watching television or from seeing her parents get frustrated and angry with her. Her parents may be arguing or exhibiting other signs of aggression in front of Missy, and Missy is learning that aggression is a way to act when she does not get what she wants."

Point 6: Awarded—The student adequately discussed the concept of egocentrism and applied it to Missy's situation and gave an accurate example.

"Missy's parents need to stop arguing with her and trying to reason with her. Missy does not yet have the ability to reason. She will not understand an adult's reasons. She is incapable at her age of seeing things from any point of view other than her own."

Point 7: Awarded—The student stated his position and presented a strong argument explaining his choice. His response reflected the context of the situation and demonstrated that he understood the principles of positive reinforcement and punishment.

"Punishment should decrease the frequency of Missy's tantrums. If Missy loses something she enjoys every time she has a tantrum, she will quickly learn that her tantrums are not going to help her get her way. I think that punishment would be more effective, though, if the Wilson's use it with positive reinforcement. But, the quickest way to extinguish the tantrums is punishment. After that the change can be maintained by the Wilson's also using positive reinforcement."

For this answer, the student would have earned all possible points.

SAMPLE QUESTION TWO

2. In a classic psychological study, Loftus and Palmer (1974) conducted experiments to determine the reliability of eyewitness accounts of events. In the second experiment, 150 American students were shown a one-minute film in which a car was being driven through the countryside. That scene was followed by a four-second scene that showed a multiple car accident. After viewing the film, students were questioned about it. One group consisting of 50 students, was asked, "How fast were the cars going when they hit each other?" A second group of 50 students was asked, "How fast were the cars going when they smashed each other?" The remaining 50 students were not questioned about the film. The participants returned a week later, and without viewing the film again, were asked ten questions about the accident depicted on the film. The critical question, "Did you see any broken glass? Yes or no?" was randomly placed on each student's paper. There was no broken glass in the film. As was expected, the participants who were asked, "How fast were the cars going when they smashed each other?" were almost twice as likely to report seeing broken glass. Loftus and Palmer explained the results of this experiment by stating that there are two types of information that go into a person's memory after a complex occurrence. The first is information obtained during the perception of the event, and the second is external information supplied after the event. Over time, information from both sources becomes integrated in such a way that it becomes impossible to tell the original source of the information from which specific details are recalled. The information becomes one "memory."

(Reference: Loftus, E.F. & Palmer, J.C. (1974) Reconstruction of auto-mobile destruction: An example of the interaction between language and memory. Journal of Verbal Learning and Verbal Behaviour, 13, 585 -589)

A. Based on this information, identify the following elements of the study. (6 pts)
- Independent variable (1 point)
- Dependent variable (1 point)
- Experimental group(s) (1 point)
- Control group(s) (1 point)
- Hypothesis (1 point)
- Confounding variables (1 point)

B. Discuss a limitation of the study. (1 point)

C. Discuss a strength of the study. (1 point)

BEFORE YOU WRITE YOUR RESPONSE

Before you begin formulating your response, stop and think about what the question is asking you. On the question sheet, write down some notes or make an outline. Following these suggestions will help you organize your thoughts. Let the implied organization of the question guide the organization of your response.

There are 6 bulleted points to be addressed in Part A, and 1 bulleted point to be addressed in Part B. There is one point to cover in Part C. Those bulleted points should serve as the organization for your response. You should NOT use your outline as your response. This is prohibited in the free response instructions given by the College Board. Write your response using complete sentences in paragraph form. Organizing your paragraphs in the order implied in the question will help the AP scorers grade your response.

In Part A of this question, you are asked to identify the following elements of the experiment: independent variable, dependent variable, experimental group(s), control group(s), hypothesis, and confounding variables. In Part B, you are to discuss a limitation of the study, and in Part C, you are to discuss a strength of the study.

RUBRIC FOR SAMPLE QUESTION TWO

Point 1: *Independent variable.* Student must correctly identify the independent variable(s) (IV). For this study the independent variable is the how the questions are worded. One question uses the word "hit" and the other uses the word "smashed."

Point 2: *Dependent variable.* Student must correctly identify the dependent variable(s). In this study, the DV is whether the student thought they saw glass.

Point 3: *Experimental group.* Student must correctly identify two experimental groups: one in which the word "hit" was used and one in which the word "smashed" was used in the question.

Point 4: *Control group.* Student must correctly identify the control group as the one that was not asked any questions.

Point 5: *Hypothesis.* Student must correctly state a hypothesis similar to "The way questions are worded can distort memory of the event."

Point 6: *Confounding variables.* The student should list any of the following as a confounding variable: drugs/alcohol, hunger, lack of sleep, environment, emotional or mental state, meaning of the event, the presence of others, and similar things as long as they could reasonably affect memory.

Point 7: *Limitations.* Student should establish either of the following: student participants (not representative sample), results not generalizable (either because of sample or because of unnatural environment), or low ecological validity (not true to real life).

Point 8: *Strengths.* Student should establish that any of the following are strengths: precise control of variables, operationally defined variables, use of standardized procedures, and can be replicated.

SAMPLE RESPONSE

In the Loftus and Palmer experiment, the <u>independent variable</u> was how the question was asked. One question used the word hit and the other used the word smashed. The <u>dependent variable</u> was how fast the students thought the cars were going. There are two <u>experimental groups</u>: one group that was asked a question using the word hit and one that was asked a question using the word smashed. The <u>control group</u> was the group that was not asked any questions. The <u>hypothesis</u> was that how the questions are worded can distort someone's memory. Using stronger verbs, like smashed, might make a person think the wreck was worse than it was, which might make the person think the drivers were going faster than they actually were. There are no <u>confounding variables</u>. The experimenters just showed the participants a film and asked them questions about it. The types of questions and the wording were controlled by the experimenters and they randomly placed questions on the page. The results of this study cannot be applied to the larger population because the participants were all students. If the researchers had used people of different ages, in different stages of life, and with a broader spectrum of backgrounds, the results might be more applicable to others. The amount of control the researcher's maintained over the variables makes it easier for the study to be replicated.

END OF RESPONSE

GRADING THE SAMPLE RESPONSE

Point 1: Awarded—The student cor-rectly iden-tified the independent variable as being how the questions were worded.

"In the Loftus and Palmer experiment, the in-dependent variable was how the question was asked. One question used the word "hit" and the other used the word "smashed.""

Point 2: Not awarded—The student did not correctly identify the dependent variable as being whether the students remembered seeing glass.

"The dependent variable was how fast the stu-dents thought the cars were going."

Point 3: Awarded—The student correctly identi-fied the two experimental groups.

"There are two experimental groups: one group that was asked a question using the word hit and one that was asked a question using the word smashed."

Point 4: Awarded—The student correctly identi-fied the control group.

"The control group was the group that was not asked any questions."

Point 5: Awarded—The student correctly stated the hypothesis.

"The hypothesis was that how the questions are worded can distort someone's memory."

Point 6: Not Awarded—The student did not identify any confounding variables.

"There are no confounding variables."

Point 7: Awarded—The student correctly identi-fied one limitation of the study.

"The results of this study cannot be applied to the larger population because the participants were all students."

Point 8: Awarded—The study correctly identi-fied a strength of the study.

"The amount of control the researcher's main-tained over the variables makes it easier for the study to be replicated."

Out of a possible 8 points, this student earned 6 points. Overall, this student's answer was not strong. The student seemed confused at times, and not all of his explanations were solid. The student should have taken more time to critically evaluate the sum-mary of the research and consider if there were any other possible ways the results of the study could be explained. **When determining how to respond to the free response questions, remember that most of the questions cover content from at least two chapters of the book.** Therefore, if the student had considered the information presented in the chap-ters about Motivation & Emotion, Biological Bases of Behavior, Cognition, and Sensation and Percep-tion, the student may have realized that physiological states and emotional and mental states, for example, affect memory and perception, and could have used that information to determine possible confounding variables.

For more practice writing free response answers, visit the College Board's AP central website: http://apcentral.collegeboard.com/apc/public/exam/exam_information/2088.html

AP Psychology Sample Test 2

Sample Questions

Instructions: For each problem, select the choice that best answers the question.

Section 1: Multiple Choice

1. Shelley is opening an ice cream shop. She states in her advertisements that she will rent out her shop for birthday parties to anyone. She also says that anyone is welcome in her ice cream shop so long as they are fully dressed and have on shoes. She claims she values diversity and appreciates the individuals who have supported her business. After a little league soccer game, a Filipino family comes to Shelley's shop. Shelley nods at the family when they come in but she feels uncomfortable. She serves the family because she does not want to create a negative image for her business, but a week later, she changes her policy regarding diversity. Shelley's actions best illustrate which statement?
    (Higher order)

    [A] Shelley believes her group is superior to others.
    [B] Shelley is experiencing self-serving bias.
    [C] Shelley's attitudes did not predict her behavior.
    [D] Shelley's behavior has been influenced by the expectations of others.
    [E] Shelley is exhibiting the just-world bias.

2. What did the Bobo Doll experiment demonstrate?
    (Lower order)

    [A] The more someone is exposed to aggression, the more aggressive they can become.
    [B] The persuasiveness of the messages is influenced by the expertise of the messenger.
    [C] People will obey orders only if others are not being hurt.
    [D] Giving people a common goal to work toward helps with conflict resolution.
    [E] People like to be around those with whom they are similar.

3. An unpleasant mental state that is the results when attitudes and behavior are not consistent is known as:
    (Lower order)

    [A] cognitive dissociation
    [B] self-fulfilling prophecy
    [C] cognitive dissonance
    [D] prejudice
    [E] central tension

4. A student asked her teacher to allow her to take a test five days after it was due. The teacher denied the student's request. The next day, the student asked the teacher to allow her to take the test the following day. The teacher agreed to the request. The student is using which compliance strategy?
(Higher order)

   [A] Groupthink
   [B] Door-in-the-face
   [C] Foot-in-the-door
   [D] Graduated and reciprocated initiatives
   [E] Mere exposure effect

5. Two categories of antisocial behavior are:
(Lower order)

   [A] prejudice and discrimination
   [B] prejudice and racism
   [C] stereotypes and aggression
   [D] aggression and prejudice
   [E] social inhibition and sexism

6. Phil Zimbardo's Stanford Prison Experiment suggested which of the following:
(Higher order)

   [A] People in authority abuse their power.
   [B] If one member of a group refuses to conform, other members may be less likely to conform.
   [C] Prison guards are prejudiced against inmates.
   [D] People can justify violence against others by dehumanizing them.
   [E] Carrying out an assigned role has no impact on attitude.

7. The "Pygmalion in the Classroom" experiment which investigated how expectations influence behavior was conducted by whom?
(Lower order)

   [A] Leon Festinger and James Carlsmith
   [B] Bibb Latane and John Darley
   [C] Stanley Milgram
   [D] Janis Irving
   [E] Robert Rosenthal and Lenore Jacobson

8. Consistency, distinctiveness, and consensus are three factors that relate to which area of social psychology?
(Higher order)

   [A] Conformity
   [B] Aggression
   [C] Group dynamics
   [D] Attribution theory
   [E] Attraction

9. What would be the most specific role theorists' criticism of the dissociation theory interpretation of ice-bath immersion experiments?
(Higher order)

   [A] When subjects raise their finger they are demonstrating an observer role
   [B] The subjects are in a single altered state but responding to two separate roles
   [C] The subjects do perceive pain and wish to follow the directions to raise a finger
   [D] There is a subconscious post-hypnotic cue for the raising of the finger
   [E] The subjects do not remember the first response due to post hypnotic amnesia

10. During REM sleep the voluntary muscles are essentially paralyzed. What is the most probable explanation for this phenomena among those provided in the answer choices below?

(Higher order)

[A] Dreams often feature a sense of paralysis or inability to physically escape from physical danger in dream scenarios.

[B] Experiments with cats with specific neurosurgical procedures result in. reproduction of physical prey stalking behavior during REM sleep.

[C] REM sleep states have high beta and gamma wave activity.

[D] There is a lack of spindle in brainwave activity during REM sleep.

[E] Infants spend up to 18 hours in REM sleep per day.

11. What is a difference between priming effects and mere-exposure effects?

(Higher order)

[A] Priming effects can occur without the conscious perception of the subject.

[B] Mere-exposure effects are related to the same stimulus as the initial stimulus.

[C] A mere-exposure effect requires more than one pre-effect exposure.

[D] Mere-exposure effects do not indicate that the effects are unconscious.

[E] Priming effects require a longer initial stimulus exposure duration.

12. In Freud's wish fulfillment explanation of the nature of dreams, latent content is:

(Lower order)

[A] the literal storyline of dreams

[B] the unconscious meaning of meaning of dreams

[C] the conflict between the preconscious and the unconscious

[D] the conflict between the preconscious and the conscious

[E] the unchanging theme of a dream

13. Which statement is NOT true concerning the sleep cycle?

(Lower order)

[A] There are 4 types of sleep cycles

[B] Delta waves occur during the deepest stages of the sleep cycle

[C] A progressively larger percentage of time is spent in REM sleep as the cycle progresses toward wakefulness.

[D] The final sleep cycle before awakening may not include stage 3 sleep

[E] Theta waves are the first sleep stage brainwaves to occur after onset of sleep

14. What is a common feature of psychedelic drugs?

(Lower order)

[A] They are primarily depressants

[B] They are primarily stimulants

[C] They are endorphin receptor agonists

[D] Their effects may increase with continued use

[E] They are water soluble compounds

15. **Which of the following is NOT a characteristic of a p value?**
    (Higher order)

    [A] it is a descriptive statistic
    [B] it may be used to determine the statistical significance of a result
    [C] it can not be calculated for a correlation coefficient
    [D] it can not be calculated for a Z score
    [E] it is a measure of variance

16. **What element of an experimental design will most likely control for the order effect?**
    (Higher order)

    [A] Debriefing
    [B] Counterbalancing
    [C] Single blinding
    [D] Double blinding
    [E] Blindfolding

17. **What correlation coefficient in the following answer choices shows the least correlation of data to a regression line calculated for that data?**
    (Lower order)

    [A] 0.5
    [B] 0.01
    [C] 10
    [D] -0.001
    [E] -100

18. **Choose they answer that identifies likely the LEAST well-controlled study among the choices below.**
    (Higher order)

    [A] A standardized test study
    [B] A questionnaire study
    [C] A non-blind study (not single blinded or double blinded)
    [D] An observational study
    [E] A case study

19. **What is a true statement regarding anecdotal evidence?**
    (Lower order)

    [A] It cannot be used as a basis for forming a hypothesis
    [B] It is considered, by definition, to be a type of archival evidence
    [C] It can disprove a null hypothesis
    [D] It can correlate with an independent variable
    [E] It is considered to be hypothetically provable

20. **What type of statistic can be directly compared between distribution curves from two or more separate research studies?**
    (Lower order)

    [A] Standard deviation
    [B] Mean
    [C] Median
    [D] Mode
    [E] Z score

21. **Linda is a 16-year-old who has developed a complete loss of vision in her left visual field but still has normal vision in her right visual field. Her doctors have identified a tumor in her pituitary gland. What visual sensory information is not being perceived by Linda?**
    (Higher order)

    [A] Signals from the left side of the right retina and the right side of the left retina
    [B] Signals from the right side of the right retina and the left side of the left retina
    [C] Signals from the right retina only
    [D] Signals from the right side of the right retina and the right side of the left retina.
    [E] Signals from the left side of the right retina and the left side of the left retina

22. **Which researcher is most closely associated with the visual cliff studies?**

    (Lower order)

    [A] Linda Buck
    [B] Gustav Fechner
    [C] Eleanor Gibson
    [D] Richard Gregory
    [E] Richard Nisbett

23. **Videos of experiments in microgravity aboard the international space station show close-up, real-time sequences of fist-sized globules of water with an undulating surface. The globules as a cohesive unit are also rotating and moving in a linear direction within the space station environment. What principle among those listed below is most specifically relevant to an accurate perception of this phenomena?**

    (Higher order)

    [A] The figure-ground relationship
    [B] Absolute thresholds
    [C] Signal transduction in the vestibular sensory system
    [D] Size constancy
    [E] Rapid adaptation

24. **The degree of stretch of extraocular muscles during perception of depth is a feature of:**

    (Lower order)

    [A] stereopsis
    [B] convergence
    [C] the pupillary light reflex
    [D] bottom-up processing
    [E] receptive fields

25. **According to Fechner's law, the minimum change in intensity required to be perceived as a change is:**

    (Lower order)

    [A] a constant absolute quantity
    [B] lower for higher intensity levels
    [C] applicable only to frequency dependent stimuli
    [D] proportional to the logarithm of the stimulus intensity
    [E] a function of the attention level of the perceiver

26. **One means of evaluating the functional status of the cochlea is to determine whether sound can be produced by the cochlea. What mechanism of those stated below is most likely to explain the production of sounds by the cochlea?**

    (Higher order)

    [A] Motor signals to muscles of the ossicles from the central nervous system
    [B] Motor signals to the muscles of Reissner's membrane from the central nervous system
    [C] Direct efferent triggering of outer hair cell contraction by the central nervous system
    [D] A reflex feedback mechanism between muscles of the ossicles and neurons in the spiral ganglia
    [E] An increase in the potassium concentration in endolymph is the cochlear duct.

27. According to the multi-store (3-box) theory of memory, the transfer of sensory information to the short-term store (short term memory) does NOT require:
(Higher order)

[A] selective attention

[B] filtering

[C] specific sensory registries

[D] rehearsal

[E] sensory receptor cells

28. A nativist language acquisition theory criticism of behaviorism language acquisition theories is:
(Higher order)

[A] Studies have shown there is no absolute critical period for language acquisition.

[B] There are language specific concepts that are not present in other languages.

[C] There are potentially millions of specific ways to misuse grammar when constructing a specific statement.

[D] Speakers of different languages actually do not perceive that phonemes not included in their native language sound differently than any and all of the native language phonemes.

[E] Broca's aphasia can be localized damage in the frontal lobe and it causes impairment of speech fluency but comprehension of language is retained.

29. Whitney is a 22-year-old woman who works for a new technology firm. During a meeting she offers a statement that illustrates her pattern of thinking includes an understanding of the concept of framing. Among the choices below, Whitney's statement was most likely:
(Higher order)

[A] "We can use this process for a different application"

[B] "The question is not is this something that people currently know that they WANT to buy, but rather is this something that people WILL buy once the see it?"

[C] "If we just take a day or so and simply think about this problem in the broadest general way, the solution may just pop into one of our heads."

[D] "This is not something that can be physically measured."

[E] "The fact that this approach has worked in the past does not mean that it will work in the future."

30. What is a valid reason for someone to choose to use an algorithm to solve a problem?
(Higher order)

[A] An algorithm can be easily adapted under rapidly changing circumstances.

[B] The consequences of a wrong solution to the problem are of little concern to the problem solver.

[C] There is an algorithm to solve the problem and the solution to the problem requires expertise that the problem solver does not possess.

[D] Using a rule of thumb, the problem can be solved 99% of the time.

[E] The problem does not require a moral judgment.

31. What specific type of heuristic relies on solutions that are based on how easily things are brought to mind?

(Lower order)

[A] The availability heuristic

[B] The representativeness heuristic

[C] The anchoring and adjustment heuristic

[D] The affect heuristic

[E] The contagion heuristic

32. In language theories, the most fundamental unit of meaning is the _____.

(Lower order)

[A] idea

[B] syllable

[C] phoneme

[D] icon

[E] morpheme

33. Patricia is a 22-year-old woman who is about to undergo an electroencephalogram (EEG) study. Among the choices below, what disorder would this study best be able to diagnose?

(Higher order)

[A] REM sleep disorder

[B] An injury to a peripheral motor nerve

[C] A narrowing of a cerebral artery

[D] A region of the brain with abnormal glucose uptake

[E] Increased intracranial pressure

34. Thomas is a 15-year-old boy who, at the age of 3 years, underwent a radical type of brain surgery as a last resort to control an extreme and dangerous form of epilepsy. Since his surgery, he has been unable to follow verbal commands to perform specific tasks involving only his non-dominant hand. He is otherwise normal. What surgical procedure could account for this long-term impairment?

(Higher order)

[A] A left frontal lobotomy

[B] A severing of the corpus callosum

[C] A right frontal lobectomy

[D] A lumbar laminectomy

[E] A bilateral occipital lobectomy

35. What are the two major neurotransmitters of the peripheral motor nervous systems?

(Lower order)

[A] Norepinephrine and epinephrine

[B] Serotonin and dopamine

[C] Acetylcholine and serotonin

[D] Acetylcholine and dopamine

[E] Norepinephrine and acetylcholine

36. All of the following statements are true for endocrine glands EXCEPT:

(Lower order)

[A] They all release hormones into the bloodstream.

[B] At least one gland is also an exocrine gland.

[C] At least one gland releases epinephrine.

[D] They are all independent of the peripheral nervous system.

[E] At least one gland synthesizes more than one type of hormone.

37. Clinical observations suggest that some blind persons may be able to perceive their surroundings through echolocation. What experimental findings in these blind persons would most strongly support the claim that their echolocation ability is an example of neuroplasticity?

(Higher order)

[A] Auditory stimuli causes increased activity in the occipital cortex

[B] Auditory stimuli causes dilation of the iris

[C] Flashes of light are perceived as snapping or popping sounds

[D] The auditory cortices of blind echolocators are larger than the auditory cortices of blind persons who cannot echolocate

[E] The visual cortices of blind echolocators are larger than the visual cortices of blind persons who cannot echolocate

38. What experimental evidence described below best demonstrates the functional organization of the autonomic nervous system?

(Higher order)

[A] The same stimulus causes both increased heart rate and blood pressure in many test subjects

[B] The same stimulus always causes the same response in all randomly chosen test subjects

[C] Microscopic examination shows two synapses with a smooth muscle cell

[D] Fear inducing stimuli causes pupil dilation and pleasant stimuli causes pupil constriction

[E] A rapid application of force to a flexed tendon causes involuntary extension of the associated appendage

39. Identical vs. fraternal twin studies have shown:

(Lower order)

[A] no evidence that schizophrenia is a biologically influenced trait

[B] no evidence that IQ is an environmentally influenced trait

[C] evidence for a genetic basis for some types of psychological behavior

[D] evidence that nutritional deficiencies are more common in fraternal twins

[E] evidence that there are structural differences in the chromosomes of identical twins

40. Among the choices below, what type of psychological theory is best supported by evidence that shows there are lower levels of warfare between hunter-gatherer societies compared to agrarian societies?

(Lower order)

[A] Classical conditioning theories

[B] Stage theories

[C] Evolutionary theories

[D] Psychoanalytic theories

[E] Emergent theories

41. What is NOT true with regard to a cataleptic state?

(Higher order)

[A] It may appear to be a trance-like state.

[B] Purposeless agitation may be present.

[C] It may constitute the primary character of a catatonic state.

[D] Waxy flexibility may be present.

[E] Persons in a cataleptic state are often unresponsive to stimuli.

42. **A person with a diagnosis of borderline personality disorder most likely has:**
    (Higher order)

    [A] delusions of grandeur

    [B] perseveration

    [C] a very mild form of schizophrenia-like symptoms

    [D] episodes of disoriented and aimless wandering

    [E] difficult interactions with others

43. **Which statement is a direct sociocultural based criticism of a behaviorist based theory?**
    (Higher order)

    [A] Differences in one's household ethnicity correlate more strongly with depression than does one's birth order.

    [B] Antisocial behavior is higher in males who have lower than average IQ levels than in females who have lower than average IQ levels.

    [C] Women who were raised in a matriarchal society are more likely to be rewarded for having spiritual visions than those in patriarchal societies.

    [D] Pica behavior is never rewarded but it does correlate with increased incidence rates in women who were raised in male dominated cultures.

    [E] Compulsive rituals are rewarded when they are more acceptable in a given culture.

44. **What neurotransmitter has been most strongly identified to be likely playing an important role in schizophrenia?**
    (Lower order)

    [A] Serotonin

    [B] Acetylcholine

    [C] GABA

    [D] Beta-endorphins

    [E] Dopamine

45. **Which term is most specifically associated with the expression of inappropriate types of emotional responses?**
    (Lower order)

    [A] A blunted affect

    [B] A delusional episode

    [C] A labile affect

    [D] A disordered thinking process

    [E] A disorganized thinking process

46. **Choose the answer that represents a correct sequence of increasing abnormality or severity beginning with the least abnormal or least severe form and progressing to the most abnormal or most severe form.**
    (Lower order)

    [A] A flat affect, then a blunted affect and then a restricted affect

    [B] A restricted affect, then a labile affect, and then a broad affect

    [C] An illusion, then a delusion and then a hallucination

    [D] Cyclothymic disorder, then bipolar 2 disorder, and then bipolar 1 disorder

    [E] A dissociative disorder, a phobia and then a panic attack

47. **Which concept of Jung's can explain some of the similarities seen among all people?**

(Higher order)

[A] Complexes

[B] Striving for success

[C] Basic anxiety

[D] Temperament

[E] Collective unconscious

48. **Which of the following statements is true based on Alfred Adler's theory?**

(Higher order)

[A] Individuals with an inferiority complex have a high level of social interest.

[B] Individuals with an inferiority complex strive for success.

[C] Individuals with a superiority complex are concerned about the welfare of others.

[D] Individuals with a superiority complex think they are better than others.

[E] All individuals are born with a superiority complex.

49. **Two main concerns of humanistic theories are:**

(Lower order)

[A] self-efficacy and self-actualization

[B] inferiority and self-understanding

[C] self-understanding and unconditional positive regard

[D] objective experiences and self-esteem

[E] self-esteem and self-concept

50. **A woman takes a personality assessment three separate times over the course of six months. Each time she takes the test, the results are different. What statement best explains the problem?**

(Higher order)

[A] The test does not measure what it is supposed to measure.

[B] The test is valid but not reliable.

[C] Mary is lying on the test.

[D] The test is not reliable.

[E] Mary's locus-of-control is external.

51. **Which trait theorist believed that not all personality traits are consistent in all situations?**

(Lower order)

[A] Karen Horney

[B] Walter Mischel

[C] Carl Rogers

[D] Gordon Allport

[E] B.F. Skinner

52. **Ways of relating to others and the environment that are present at birth are called?**

(Lower order)

[A] Idiographic traits

[B] Personality traits

[C] Temperament

[D] Central dispositions

[E] Archetypes

53. **A mother who is potty training her child initially rewards her child for going near the bathroom, then she rewards the child for touching the bathroom door, then she rewards the child for walking into the bathroom. She continues to reward the child until the child engages in the desired behavior. Which principle of conditioning is the mother using?**

(Lower order)

[A] Generalization

[B] Shaping

[C] Modeling

[D] Cognitive mapping

[E] Aversion

54. **Albert Bandura asserted that four conditions must be met in order for observational learning to be effective. All of the following statements describe the four conditions EXCEPT:**

(Higher order)

[A] Jimmy was fascinated at how his brother dribbled the basketball so he paid close attention.

[B] Valerie wants to learn the dance steps she saw her sister doing because she wants to impress her boyfriend at the prom.

[C] After Jody watched the video tape his guitar instructor gave him, he knew where to place his fingers and was able to play the chords.

[D] Abby hit her sister because her best friend hit her brother without getting into any trouble with her parents.

[E] Timmy remembered how his mother showed him to fold the towels two weeks ago.

55. **Which of the following statements would most closely match Donald Hebb's theory about learning?**

(Higher order)

[A] Learning occurs as a result of behaviors being reinforced.

[B] Learning occurs when a person connects two events that have been paired repeatedly.

[C] Learning occurs as a result of neural activity in the brain.

[D] Learning requires cognitive insight.

[E] Learning occurs by watching others.

56. **Why are variable schedules of reinforcement more resistant to extinction?**

(Higher order)

[A] A fixed amount of time must pass before a response is rewarded.

[B] Responses are not immediately reinforced.

[C] Responses are continuous.

[D] A reward is administered after a set number of responses.

[E] A response can be rewarded at any time.

57. **Mental institutions, schools, and prisons often use which of the following as a way to modify behavior?**

(Lower order)

[A] Token economy

[B] Variable schedules of reinforcement

[C] Punishment

[D] Aversion therapy

[E] Biofeedback

58. The Garcia effect refers to which of the following:

    (Lower order)

    [A] stimulus discrimination
    [B] Premack principle
    [C] Conditioned taste aversion
    [D] Latent learning
    [E] successive approximations

59. Which theory offers a way to explain differences between species?

    (Lower order)

    [A] Cognitive
    [B] Evolutionary
    [C] Biological
    [D] Psychoanalytic
    [E] Dualism

60. Which of the following statements about cognitive psychology is NOT true?

    (Higher order)

    [A] It is interested in how people perceive and interpret events and experiences.
    [B] It is interested in the smaller components of mental processes.
    [C] It often combines principles from this approach with other approaches.
    [D] It developed as a reaction against behaviorism's focus on only what is observable.
    [E] It is interested in the function of mental processes.

61. Which subfield of psychology deals with diagnosing, assessing, and evaluating emotional, behavioral, and psychological disorders?

    (Lower order)

    [A] Industrial-organizational psychology
    [B] Counseling psychology
    [C] Human factors psychology
    [D] Clinical psychology
    [E] Educational psychology

62. A sociocultural psychologist might be interested in which of the following?

    (Higher order)

    [A] How hormones contribute to aggression levels
    [B] How sleep deprivation affects memory
    [C] How different ethnic groups respond to violence
    [D] How painful memories are repressed
    [E] How personal needs direct behavior

63. Which early psychologist is the founder of child psychology and educational psychology?

    (Lower order)

    [A] William James
    [B] Edward Titchener
    [C] Wilhelm Wundt
    [D] G. Stanley Hall
    [E] Margaret Floy Washburn

64. **Wilhelm Wundt is the founder of the science of psychology. Which of the following statements best describes why psychology was first considered a science under Wundt?**
(*Higher order*)

   [A] Wundt developed a theory based on general laws.
   [B] Wundt's work influenced other psychologists.
   [C] Wundt based his theory on his own experiences.
   [D] Wundt developed his theory by using experimental methods.
   [E] Wundt acquired knowledge about the mind.

65. **The two broad categories that developmental theories can be divided into are:**
(*Lower order*)

   [A] nature and nurture
   [B] continuous and discontinuous
   [C] social and physical
   [D] maturation and environmentalism
   [E] psychosocial and psychodynamic

66. **Johnny, an infant, does not cry or fuss when his mother leaves. When a person he is not familiar with enters the room, Johnny allows the stranger to hold him and play with him. When Johnny's mother returns, he avoids her and does not want her to hold him. Which of the following statements best explains Johnny's behavior?**
(*Higher order*)

   [A] Johnny is begin abused.
   [B] Johnny knows his mother will be responsive to his needs.
   [C] Johnny does not think his mother will be responsive to his needs.
   [D] Johnny is not sure if his mother will be responsive to his needs.
   [E] Johnny feels secure with his mother.

67. **Which of following did Carol Gilligan believe was crucial to moral progress?**
(*Lower order*)

   [A] Caring relationships
   [B] Environmental stability
   [C] Concept of justice
   [D] Bargaining
   [E] Reasoning

68. **According to Freud's psychosexual theory, a person who is too dependent on others might be preoccupied by behaviors that occur in which stage?**
(*Lower order*)

   [A] Phallic stage
   [B] Genital stage
   [C] Anal stage
   [D] Oral stage
   [E] Oedipal stage

69. **David's mother pours cream into a tall pitcher. She then pours the cream into a bowl. When she asks David if the amount of cream in the bowl is the same amount of cream that was in the pitcher. David seems confused at first, but he thinks about the situation. He then walks over to the bowl and pours the cream back into the pitcher before responding that the amount of cream is the same. David is in what stage of cognitive development according to Piaget?**
(*Higher order*)

   [A] Formal operational stage
   [B] Sensorimotor stage
   [C] Concrete operational stage
   [D] Preoperational stage
   [E] Preconventional stage

70. A researcher wants to conduct research using the longitudinal method. All of the following statements are true things EXCEPT:

(Higher order)

[A] He will have to assess changes at set intervals of time.

[B] He can assume that any changes are the result of cultural differences.

[C] He can measure specific aspects of development.

[D] He can assume any changes are the result of aging.

[E] He should use participants who are close in age.

71. Harmful substances that can have serious effects on a developing fetus are called:

(Lower order)

[A] carcinogens

[B] schemas

[C] zygotes

[D] stereotyped ingestive responses

[E] teratogens

72. Abigail and her mother, Amy, are great friends. Amy devotes much of her time to promoting Abigail's career and buying luxurious items for Abigail. Amy is very warm and affectionate toward Abigail, and they talk every day. Abigail stays out late and hangs out with peers who use drugs and alcohol. Amy only has a few rules for Abigail to follow, but she does not enforce the rules. Amy frequently subjects Abigail to potentially dangerous situations and then leaves the room. What characteristics might Abigail demonstrate as a result of Amy's permissive parenting?

(Higher order)

[A] Abigail will be organized, able to regulate her emotions and will have a good work ethic.

[B] Abigail will exhibit a great deal of self-control, will take responsibility for her choices and will appreciate the things she has.

[C] Abigail will have difficulty taking responsibility for her choices, will lack self-control, and may feel as if she is entitled to things.

[D] Abigail will be withdrawn, have difficulty making friends, and will have problems making decisions.

[E] Abigail will be confident, have good communication skills, and will be able to make her own choices.

73. **Holly is a 29-year-old woman who demonstrates defining features of interpersonal intelligence described in Howard Gardner's theory of multiple intelligences. Which summary of her behavior most closely matches Holly's utilization of her interpersonal intelligence?**

(Higher order)

[A] Holly finds ways to persuade homeless persons to seek assistance that is available to them but requires the homeless to cooperate with the assistance agencies.

[B] Holly learns to function in unfamiliar situations by generalizing from the experience of others.

[C] Holly relies on an acute emotional understanding of others to persuade her boss to give her a raise in salary.

[D] Holly integrates her exceptional fund of knowledge to identify a subtle behavior in her daughter as a potential sign of severe mental illness.

[E] Holly is able to use highly analytical thought processes to discourage an attack on her by an enraged coworker.

74. **The Flynn effect is a verified phenomena that has been observed for the past seven decades. It shows an increase in the average IQ scores of the human population that is approximately 3 points per decade. This effect is seen to be particularly evident in the increase in IQ scores among relatively less well-developed industrial societies. What statement below is the most reasonable conclusion that may be draw based on the information provided in this passage?**

(Higher order)

[A] The effect provides more support for a general intelligence than for multiple intelligences.

[B] The effect provides support for a primarily environmental component to intelligence rather than a primarily genetic component to intelligence

[C] The effect demonstrates that environmental conditions can result in increased intelligence

[D] The effect demonstrates that nutritional factors are not involved in relative levels of intelligence among individuals.

[E] The effect demonstrates that IQ testing is not culturally biased.

75. From the choices below, select the most significant theoretical distinction between the original Stanford Binet and Wechsler intelligence tests.
(Higher order)

[A] The statistical normalization of the score distributions curve of the Wechsler test

[B] The inclusion of non-intellectual factors in the structural design of the Wechsler test

[C] The factor analysis based questions to detect differences between fluid intelligence and crystallized intelligence of the Stanford-Binet test

[D] The non-verbal intelligence measurement of the Stanford-Binet test

[E] The hierarchical intelligence theory based construction of the Wechsler test

76. The contrasting category of test in comparison to an achievement test is a(n) _____.
(Lower order)

[A] psychometric test
[B] pilot test
[C] IQ test
[D] standardized test
[E] aptitude test

77. According to Raymond Cattell's definition, what is true regarding crystallized intelligence?
(Lower order)

[A] It may continue to increase over the entire normal adult lifespan.

[B] It is equivalent to the concept of a single intelligence or "g" intelligence.

[C] It is equivalent to verbal intelligence.

[D] It is best assessed with questions intended to measure the upper limit of complexity that an individual is capable of solving within a reasonable time limit.

[E] It is thinking that features intuition, wisdom, and motivation. It also involves thinking with a strong will, strong opinions and confidence.

78. Regarding the reliability and validity of a test, which of the following is NOT true?
(Lower order)

[A] Correlation coefficients can be calculated for the reliability of tests

[B] Reliability requires that a test be valid

[C] Construct validity may be based on a interpretation of a theory

[D] Predictive validity may not be present on the first administration of a test

[E] Validity of psychometric tests are never perfect

79. Max is known across many settings for being dishonest, grouchy, funny, intelligent, overly emotional, and ambitious. Which of the following statements is true?

[A] These characteristics indicate that Max needs to work on self-actualization.
[B] These characteristics probably show that Max has a mental disorder.
[C] These characteristics show that Max has a high level of self-esteem.
[D] These characteristics describe Max's central dispositions.
[E] These characteristics can change if Max explores his unconscious.

80. Which type of psychotropic drug depresses the central nervous system?
(Lower order)

[A] Antipsychotic
[B] Anxiolytic
[C] Antidepressant
[D] Monoamine oxidase inhibitor
[E] Neurotransmitters

81. Which of the following statements would a humanistic therapist be most likely to make?
(Higher order)

[A] "Tell me about your childhood."
[B] "I want you to imagine your worst fear."
[C] "What I hear you saying is that you feel worthless."
[D] "What proof do you have that everyone hates you?"
[E] "I want you to observe someone being kind and then practice being kind."

82. A behavioral therapist would be most likely to agree with which of the following criticisms of psychoanalytic therapy?

[A] Psychoanalytic therapy wastes too much time on exploring present experiences.
[B] Psychoanalytic therapy does not address thought patterns.
[C] Psychoanalytic therapy is not based on observable, objective data.
[D] Psychoanalytic therapy does not address issues of self-fulfillment.
[E] Psychoanalytic therapy relies too heavily on drug therapy.

83. When subjects in Milgram's obedience experiments received their orders from a research assistant, they:
(Lower order)

[A] conformed more easily
[B] refused to participate
[C] dropped out of the study
[D] were less likely to obey
[E] were slightly more obedient

84. Which of the following examples is an example of situational attribution?
(Higher order)

[A] Mary takes a French exam and passes it and attributes her passing grade to her good study habits.
[B] Jake gets ripped off by a rich man. He then assumes that every rich man is greedy.
[C] Marlo is more aggressive when she is around other aggressive children.
[D] Stanley likes Mr. Caruso because Mr. Caruso likes him.
[E] Henry takes a Zoology test and fails it. He blames his poor score on disruptions by his classmates.

85. A group of teenagers is attending summer camp. During the camp, one of the adults deliberately manipulates situations to make the campers mistrust one another. Before long, the campers are being mean to each other and the environment is becoming hostile. Which of the following statements best describes how the groups can work out their differences?

[A] The groups can play games that cause them to compete against each other for prizes.

[B] There is nothing that can be done to help the groups work out their differences.

[C] The leaders need to sit the groups down and have a discussion with them about how to resolve conflict.

[D] The groups should work together to solve a problem that is affecting all of them.

[E] The groups need to take some time away from each other to allow things to settle down.

86. The following list of traits are not part of the Big Five EXCEPT:
   (Higher order)

[A] Extraversion, openness, honesty, conscientiousness, and neuroticism

[B] Conscientiousness, curiosity, extraversion, agreeableness, and psychoticism

[C] Extraversion, neuroticism, openness, agreeableness, and conscientiousness

[D] Extraversion, psychoticism, honesty, trustworthiness, and openness

[E] Idiographic, nomothetic, extraversion, honesty, and openness

87. A biological psychologist might be interested in which of the following?
   (Higher order)

[A] How unconditional positive regard affects self-concept

[B] How dopamine affects thought processes

[C] How a person's perception of events affects behavior

[D] How social roles impact development

[E] How to improve an employee's motivation

88. In what major way is behaviorism different from other theoretical perspectives?
   (Lower order)

[A] It is only concerned with observable behavior.

[B] Its concepts are based on empirical research.

[C] Its principles are of no use today.

[D] It is not considered scientific.

[E] There is no specific way behaviorism is different from other perspectives.

89. Which theorist proposed the concept of zone of proximal development?
   (Lower order)

[A] Albert Bandura

[B] Lev Vygotsky

[C] Harry Harlow

[D] Jean Piaget

[E] Erik Erikson

90. **For a diagnosis of schizophrenia (according to the DSM-5), there MUST be:**
(Lower order)

[A] a response to medical treatment.

[B] symptoms of delusions, hallucinations, and disorganized speech for at least 1 month.

[C] continuous signs of the disturbance that persist for at least 6 months.

[D] no other comorbid conditions present.

[E] agreement by at least two independent licensed mental health practitioners' evaluations.

91. **_____ resembles the popular term "split personality" is:**
(Lower order)

[A] Schizophrenia

[B] Bipolar disorder

[C] Borderline personality disorder

[D] Dissociative identity disorder

[E] Depersonalization/derealization disorder

92. **_____ best describes incongruence?**
(Higher order)

[A] Ken's marriage is ending so he throws himself into his work.

[B] Marcy sees one group of her classmates as "cool" and the other group as "uncool."

[C] Henry believes in having a good work ethic but he steals from his boss.

[D] Candi makes a high score on her SAT and attributes her success to her intelligence.

[E] Adam distances himself from his son when his son fails to make the football team.

93. **Cognitive triad is a concept developed by _____.**
(Lower order)

[A] Sigmund Freud

[B] Abraham Maslow

[C] Aaron Beck

[D] Albert Ellis

[E] Fritz Perls

94. **Charles Spearman is most directly associated with _____.**
(Lower order)

[A] factor analysis of correlations related to intelligence

[B] the concept of crystallized intelligence

[C] the concept of fluid intelligence

[D] development of the Culture Fair Intelligence Test

[E] development of The Three Stratum Model of Intelligence

95. Debra is a consultant who is evaluating the performance of employees for her client company. She recommends a change in policy that substitutes a theory X management principle for a theory Y management principle. Choose the policy change that would correspond to Debra's recommendation.

(Higher order)

[A] Substitute a percentage commission for hourly wage on new client sales.

[B] Institute careful documentation policy to identify specific individuals associated with poor implementation of a business model in place of a nonexistent documentation policy.

[C] Assess career advancement potential based on past work history that shows individual initiative and problem solving rather than current emphasis on detail oriented and focused commitment to carry out specific tasks.

[D] Provide a rolling point system that tracks late arrival and absent work AND has an absolute employment termination point limit BUT subtracts points for voluntary overtime in place of an absolute policy that does not allow employees to improve job security by future behavior.

[E] Set high achievement goals that earn high value socially based rewards such as vacation packages that can not be redeemed for cash, traded or used by others in place of a vacation or cash equivalent choice option reward.

96. Amber, an intelligent, success-oriented, 24-year-old woman who has just resigned from her highly paid position as a junior partner in a hedge fund investment firm. She has lost interest in daily activities and is unconcerned for her future despite serious consequences to her financial and personal life that are likely to result from her seemingly foolish choice to leave her high-paced, high-risk but very successful career. Based on this information, Amber most likely has:

(Higher order)

[A] abnormally high baseline levels of epinephrine and/or norepinephrine

[B] a serious undiagnosed-stress related physical illness

[C] a preceding prolonged period of abnormally high cortisol levels

[D] an unresolveable multiple approach-avoidance conflict

[E] failed to fulfill basic security needs that are unique to a young adult compared to those of a teenager who is younger than the age of eighteen.

97. **Which statement below provides a rebuttal to a Cannon-Bard advocates criticism of the James-Lange theory of emotion?**
   (Higher order)

   [A] If the definition of a physiological state is broadened, this can account for correspondingly wider range and more complex character of emotional experiences.

   [B] There is not enough time for physiological changes to occur and then be detected to allow them to generate a corresponding emotional experience based on how quickly the those emotions are experienced.

   [C] In experiments, subjects have received injections of epinephrine in neutral controlled environments. The subjects report that they sense the increased arousal that the epinephrine produces but they do not have any particular emotional experience that occurs with this sensation.

   [D] In experiments with epinephrine injections in subjects, in one environment subjects found the experience to be funny as in amusing. In the other environment subjects found that the experience made them angry.

   [E] Although an individual's performance will initially increase as his or her level of arousal increases, after a certain point. Increasing levels of arousal will progressively impair performance.

98. **A behavior that is instinctive is most specifically a behavior that:**
   (Lower order)

   [A] is driven by an internal or intrinsic motivation

   [B] directly satisfies a drive state urge such as hunger or thirst

   [C] is genetically determined, precise and predictable

   [D] results from neurological processes that do not require the participation of the cerebral cortex

   [E] always overrides behaviors that are not directly required for immediate self-preservation

99. **The hypothalamus, amygdala and cingulate cortex are included in a higher level organization of neurological structures known as:**
   (Lower order)

   [A] the limbic system
   [B] the striate cortex
   [C] Broca's area
   [D] the corpus callosum
   [E] the cerebellum

100.Which theorist categorizes needs as deficiency or "d" needs and being or "b" needs?

(Lower order)

[A] William James

[B] Jerome Singer

[C] Richard Solomon

[D] Abraham Maslow

[E] Hans Selye

SAMPLE QUESTION ONE

1. Psychology is a field that relies heavily on research. As such, it is important to know the different methods of research used by psychologists, including the strengths and weaknesses of each method. All of the following are different methods of research used by psychologists:

    - Case study
    - Correlational study
    - Experiment
    - Longitudinal study
    - Cross-sectional study

    A. Discuss one advantage of each of the above kinds methods of research. (5 points)

    B. Discuss one limitation of each of the above kinds methods of research. (5 points)

SAMPLE QUESTION TWO

2. A. Define each of the following concepts and discuss how each one contributes to the phenomenon of prejudice. Be sure to define prejudice in your response. (4 points)

    - Conformity
    - Stereotypes
    - Ethnocentrism

    B. Define each of the following concepts and explain how each one relates to changing the attitude of prejudice. Be sure to define attitude in your response. (4 points)

    - Mere exposure effect
    - Superordinate goal
    - Cognitive dissonance

SAMPLE TEST 2
Answer Key

Question Number	Correct Answer	Your Answer	Question Number	Correct Answer	Your Answer	Question Number	Correct Answer	Your Answer
1	C		35	E		69	C	
2	A		36	D		70	B	
3	C		37	A		71	E	
4	B		38	D		72	C	
5	D		39	C		73	A	
6	D		40	A		74	C	
7	E		41	B		75	B	
8	D		42	E		76	E	
9	C		43	C		77	B	
10	B		44	E		78	B	
11	B		45	C		79	D	
12	B		46	D		80	B	
13	A		47	E		81	C	
14	D		48	C		82	C	
15	A		49	E		83	D	
16	B		50	D		84	E	
17	A		51	B		85	D	
18	E		52	C		86	C	
19	D		53	B		87	B	
20	E		54	D		88	A	
21	D		55	C		89	B	
22	C		56	E		90	C	
23	A		57	A		91	D	
24	B		58	C		92	C	
25	D		59	B		93	C	
26	C		60	D		94	C	
27	D		61	D		95	D	
28	C		62	C		96	C	
29	B		63	D		97	B	
30	C		64	D		98	B	
31	A		65	B		99	A	
32	E		66	C		100	D	
33	A		67	A				
34	B		68	D				

Sample Test 2

AP Psychology Sample Test 2
Answers and Explanations

Instructions: For each problem, select the choice that best answers the question.

1. **Shelley is opening an ice cream shop. She states in her advertisements that she will rent out her shop for birthday parties to anyone. She also says that anyone is welcome in her ice cream shop so long as they are fully dressed and have on shoes. She claims she values diversity and appreciates the individuals who have supported her business. After a little league soccer game, a Filipino family comes to Shelley's shop. Shelley nods at the family when they come in but she feels uncomfortable. She serves the family because she does not want to create a negative image for her business, but a week later, she changes her policy regarding diversity. Shelley's actions best illustrate which statement?**

   (Higher order)

   [A] Shelley believes her group is superior to others.

   [B] Shelley is experiencing self-serving bias.

   [C] Shelley's attitudes did not predict her behavior.

   [D] Shelley's behavior has been influenced by the expectations of others.

   [E] Shelley is exhibiting the just-world bias.

   The correct answer is C.
   Shelley claims to have a positive attitude about diversity and people of all ethnic and racial backgrounds. However, this attitude is not consistent with Shelley's actions; therefore, her attitude could not have predicted her behavior. There is no evidence that Shelley thinks her group is superior to others. There is no indication that she is taking credit for more good outcomes than bad, nor does she think that good things can only happen to good people, or vice versa, which is the just-world bias. Her behavior has not necessarily been influenced by the expectations of others, although she is concerned with how people will view her.

2. **What did the Bobo Doll experiment demonstrate?**
   (Lower order)

   [A] The more someone is exposed to aggression, the more aggressive they can become.

   [B] The persuasiveness of the messages is influenced by the expertise of the messenger.

   [C] People will obey orders only if others are not being hurt.

   [D] Giving people a common goal to work toward helps with conflict resolution.

   [E] People like to be around those with whom they are similar.

   The correct answer is A.
   Bandura's Bobo Doll experiment helped people understand the impact of seeing violence and aggression. The more violence and aggression a person sees, the greater the chance they will become violent and aggressive. The Bobo Doll experiment shed some light on the importance of modeling in teaching and reinforcing both social and antisocial behavior. Persuasiveness of messages deals with attitudinal change. Obedience was studied by Stanley Milgram. The importance of working toward a superordinate goal was the focus of studies

Sample Test 2

by Muzafer Sherif. That people like to be around those with whom they are similar is a principle of interpersonal attraction.

3. **An unpleasant mental state that is the results when attitudes and behavior are not consistent is known as:**
   (Lower order)

   [A] cognitive dissociation
   [B] self-fulfilling prophecy
   [C] cognitive dissonance
   [D] prejudice
   [E] central tension

   The correct answer is C.
   Cognitive dissonance is an unpleasant state of mental tension created when attitudes are not consistent with behaviors. Cognitive dissonance is one way that attitudinal change occurs. Cognitive dissociation is not a term related to social psychology. Self-fulfilling prophecy occurs when the expectations of others affect someone's behavior. Prejudice is undeserved and negative attitudes towards a group of people. Central tension is not a term related to social psychology.

4. **A student asked her teacher to allow her to take a test five days after it was due. The teacher denied the student's request. The next day, the student asked the teacher to allow her to take the test the following day. The teacher agreed to the request. The student is using which compliance strategy?**
   (Higher order)

   [A] Groupthink
   [B] Door-in-the-face
   [C] Foot-in-the-door
   [D] Graduated and reciprocated initiatives
   [E] Mere exposure effect

The correct answer is B.
The idea behind door-in-the-face strategy is that if someone is asked to agree to a large request and refuses, when asked to accommodate a smaller request that is more reasonable, the person will likely agree. Groupthink is thinking by an entire group in which group members often make bad decisions and use poor judgment, failing to consider the implications of their actions. Foot-in-the-door strategy states that when someone agrees to a smaller request, the likelihood is greater that the person will agree to a larger request. Graduate and reciprocated initiatives is part of the GRIT acronym. Graduated and reciprocated Initiatives in Tension-Reduction is a conflict resolution strategy. Mere exposure effect states that the more someone is exposed to something, the more the person will come to like it.

5. **Two categories of antisocial behavior are:**
   (Lower order)

   [A] prejudice and discrimination
   [B] prejudice and racism
   [C] stereotypes and aggression
   [D] aggression and prejudice
   [E] social inhibition and sexism

The correct answer is D.
Aggression and prejudice are two categories of antisocial behavior. Prejudice is an undeserved and negative attitude towards members of a certain group; aggression is actions directed at another person with the intent of harming the other person. Prejudice and racism are similar, but one can be prejudiced and not racist, as racism is prejudice based on someone's race or ethnic group, but not based on other characteristics of a group. Stereotypes are ideas about members of other groups and often leads to prejudice. Social inhibition is when someone's performance decreases in the presence of others and sexism is prejudice against females or males.

6. **Phil Zimbardo's Stanford Prison Experiment suggested which of the following:(**
   Higher order)

   [A] People in authority abuse their power.
   [B] If one member of a group refuses to conform, other members may be less likely to conform.
   [C] Prison guards are prejudiced against inmates.
   [D] People can justify violence against others by dehumanizing them.
   [E] Carrying out an assigned role has no impact on attitude.

   The correct answer is D.
   Zimbardo began his study in order to help understand the effects of dehumanization. While some people in authority abuse their power, not all do. Even though one member of a group refusing to conform may make other members less likely to conform, Zimbardo's study did not investigate this aspect of conformity. Some prison guards are prejudiced against inmates, but not all are. Carrying out an assigned role can impact someone's attitudes and behavior, as was the case with the "guards" in Zimbardo's experiment.

7. **The "Pygmalion in the Classroom" experiment which investigated how expectations influence behavior was conducted by whom?**
   (Lower order)

   [A] Leon Festinger and James Carlsmith
   [B] Bibb Latane and John Darley
   [C] Stanley Milgram
   [D] Janis Irving
   [E] Robert Rosenthal and Lenore Jacobson

The correct answer is E.
Rosenthal and Jacobson conducted an experiment to see how student performance would be affected by teacher expectations. Festinger and Carlsmith studied cognitive dissonance. Stanley Milgram conducted obedience studies. Janis Irving coined the word "groupthink." Darley and Latane studied possible causes of the bystander effect.

8. **Consistency, distinctiveness, and consensus are three factors that relate to which area of social psychology?**
   (Higher order)

   [A] Conformity
   [B] Aggression
   [C] Group dynamics
   [D] Attribution theory
   [E] Attraction

   The correct answer is D.
   Harold Kelley used these three words to describe the types of information people use to form attributions. Conformity refers to people going along with the actions and attitudes of others. Aggression is one category of antisocial behavior. Group dynamics examine how people are affected by the presence and absence of others, and attraction investigates the factors that attract people to other people.

9. **What would be the most specific role theorists' criticism of the dissociation theory interpretation of ice-bath immersion experiments?**
   (Higher order)

[A] When subjects raise their finger they are demonstrating an observer role

[B] The subjects are in a single altered state but responding to two separate roles

[C] The subjects do perceive pain and wish to follow the directions to raise a finger

[D] There is a subconscious post-hypnotic cue for the raising of the finger

[E] The subjects do not remember the first response due to post hypnotic amnesia

The correct answer is C.

The relevant position of role theorist regarding this question is that the subjects are not in an altered state of consciousness but are acting out a role within a social context. In choice C the role is complex, first denting they feel pain but act as if they do not then following directions to raise a finger. Essentially, they are playing a role that is intended to please the researchers assuming the researcher wants them to say they do not perceive pain and that they want them to indicate that some part of them (the subjects) does feel pain. It provides a role theory explanation as an alternative to the dissociation theory that a splitting of consciousness explains the subject's behavior. Choice A indicates an observer role for raising a finger but the term role is not an act in this context and dissociation theorists also refer to this as an outside observer or an observer role. For choice B, role theorists reject the notion that the subjects are in an altered state of consciousness, which is the premise of state theorists. For choice D, all theorists agree that post-hypnotic cues are a feature of the hypnotic phenomenon. It is not specifically a role theorist criticism as compared to choice C. Choice E is also a general criticism, if it even is a criticism since it is difficult to determine how post hypnotic amnesia would affect a hypnotic state.

10. **During REM sleep the voluntary muscles are essentially paralyzed. What is the most probable explanation for this phenomena among those provided in the answer choices below?**

(Higher order)

[A] Dreams often feature a sense of paralysis or inability to physically escape from physical danger in dream scenarios.

[B] Experiments with cats with specific neurosurgical procedures result in. reproduction of physical prey stalking behavior during REM sleep.

[C] REM sleep states have high beta and gamma wave activity.

[D] There is a lack of spindle in brainwave activity during REM sleep.

[E] Infants spend up to 18 hours in REM sleep per day.

The correct answer is B.

This experiment shows that REM activity will result in physical activities that could be dangerous during the REM state if they are not suppressed by paralysis. Although we are not cats, it is reasonable to assume that if we were not paralyzed we would probably thrash about, try to run or otherwise do thing that would injure us. Choice A may explain why we have dreams about paralysis, but it does not explain why we would actually be paralyzed during REM sleep. Choice C is partially true. Gamma wave activity is not well documented during REM sleep, but even if true the question indicates that REM is a high arousal state and it is another step in logic to arrive at an explanation for the REM paralytic state compared to answer B. Spindle activity is thought to play a role in preserving the sleep state but they (spindles) are not present in REM sleep. Infants do spend up to 18 hours in REM sleep but again it is one or two steps to connect this with an explanation for paralysis.

11. What is a difference between priming effects and mere-exposure effects?
(Higher order)

[A] Priming effects can occur without the conscious perception of the subject.

[B] Mere-exposure effects are related to the same stimulus as the initial stimulus.

[C] A mere-exposure effect requires more than one pre-effect exposure.

[D] Mere-exposure effects do not indicate that the effects are unconscious.

[E] Priming effects require a longer initial stimulus exposure duration.

The correct answer is B.

Mere-exposure effects are related to the same stimulus as the initial stimulus while priming effects are related to different types of stimuli that are affected by the initial type of stimuli. Both effects can occur with a single exposure to the initial stimulus. Both effects can occur without the conscious perception of the subject therefore unconscious processes are occurring during both effects. Priming effects have been shown to occur at the minimum exposure duration that can be perceived by visual receptors.

12. In Freud's wish fulfillment explanation of the nature of dreams, latent content is:
(Lower order)

[A] the literal storyline of dreams

[B] the unconscious meaning of meaning of dreams

[C] the conflict between the preconscious and the unconscious

[D] the conflict between the preconscious and the conscious

[E] the unchanging theme of a dream

The correct answer is B.

Freud's wish fulfillment interpretation of dreams describes latent content as the **latent content** or true meaning of the dream that is transposed by the ego into a **manifest content** or the literal storyline of the dream. This occurs to protect us from the secret knowledge of the subconscious.

13. Which statement is NOT true concerning the sleep cycle?
(Lower order)

[A] There are 4 types of sleep cycles

[B] Delta waves occur during the deepest stages of the sleep cycle

[C] A progressively larger percentage of time is spent in REM sleep as the cycle progresses toward wakefulness.

[D] The final sleep cycle before awakening may not include stage 3 sleep

[E] Theta waves are the first sleep stage brainwaves to occur after onset of sleep

The correct answer is A.

There are not 4 types of sleep cycles, rather there are 4 stages of a complete sleep cycle, the REM stage and three stages of non-REM stages. Each cycle typically lasts about 90 minutes and repeats four to six times over the course of a night. A progressively larger percentage of time is spent in REM sleep as the cycle progresses toward wakefulness. It is common for the last cycle before awakening to lack the stage 3 sleep level. Delta waves occur during the deepest stages of the sleep cycle. Theta waves are the first sleep stage brainwaves to occur after onset of sleep.

14. **What is a common feature of psychedelic drugs?**
   (Lower order)

   [A] They are primarily depressants
   [B] They are primarily stimulants
   [C] They are endorphin receptor agonists
   [D] Their effects may increase with continued use
   [E] They are water soluble compounds

   The correct answer is D.
   Many Psychedelics remain in the body for long periods of time repeated doses can build up to produce larger effects than would be anticipated from a single dose. Psychedelics have very unpredictable effects and are considered neither primarily stimulants nor depressants. Opiate drugs are endorphin receptor agonists, but psychedelic drugs are not. Psychoactive drugs such as psychedelics must cross the blood-brain barrier and are therefore not soluble in water as these type of molecules are generally unable to cross the blood-brain barrier.

15. **Which of the following is NOT a characteristic of a p value?**
   (Higher order)

   [A] it is a descriptive statistic
   [B] it may be used to determine the statistical significance of a result
   [C] it can not be calculated for a correlation coefficient
   [D] it can not be calculated for a Z score
   [E] it is a measure of variance

   The correct answer is A.
   A p value is an inferential, not a descriptive statistic. The p value is a measure of the probability of the null hypothesis i.e. that the results of a study are due to random chance. This allows one to make inferences about whether research results can generalized to a larger population. Measures of variance describe attributes of a distribution curve, usually related to the mean of the distribution. P values can be calculated for many types of measures of variance, including Z scores and standard deviations, and other descriptive statistics, such as correlation coefficients. P values of .05 or lower are often the definition of statistical significance for research results.

16. **What element of an experimental design will most likely control for the order effect?**
   (Higher order)

   [A] Debriefing
   [B] Counterbalancing
   [C] Single blinding
   [D] Double blinding
   [E] Blindfolding

   The correct answer is B.
   The order effect occurs when subjects are required to perform two separate tasks in sequential order, i.e., first this and next that.

Subjects may behave differently depending on what order they perform the tasks. Counterbalancing controls for the order effect by dividing the subjects into two groups and assigning one task to one group as the first task and the same task to the second group as the second task. Single and double blinding conceal the group assignment (ex control group or experimental group) from subjects in single blinding and from subjects and researchers in double blinding. In each case, subjects would still be aware of the order in which they perform tasks. Blindfolding may conceal visual information about tasks, but again, subjects would be aware of in what order their tasks are performed. Debriefing is an APA guideline for conduct of researchers after the conclusion of a study.

17. **What correlation coefficient in the following answer choices shows the least correlation of data to a regression line calculated for that data?**

    (Lower order)

    [A] 0.5
    [B] 0.01
    [C] 10
    [D] -0.001
    [E] -100

    The correct answer is A.
    The range of correlation coefficient scores is from -1 to +1. Perfect correlations are -1 and +1. Scores show less correlation to a regression line as they approach a 0.0 (zero) value. A zero value shows no correlation at all. Scores of greater than +1 or less than -1 are not possible for correlation coefficients. Among all answer choices, 0.5 is the nearest value to either +1 or -1.

18. **Choose they answer that identifies likely the LEAST well-controlled study among the choices below.**

    (Higher order)

    [A] A standardized test study
    [B] A questionnaire study
    [C] A non-blind study (not single blinded or double blinded)
    [D] An observational study
    [E] A case study

    The correct answer is E.
    Case studies are studies where very detailed information about a single individual is collected, often completely without controls. There are no controls required for case studies and any possible controls are less than those for the other answer choices Standardized testing should be conducted in a very well controlled environment i.e. same time, same place. Questionnaire studies are the least well controlled of the choices except for case studies. There are usually attempts to increase the likelihood that the pool of respondents are a random sample of a larger population. A non-blind study as defined in the answer choice lacks the controls provided by single and double blinding, but all other possible control method can and should be used, and there are likely many such possible controls. A case study may be considered a special type of observational study but in general, observational studies often can be very well controlled and are certainly more likely to be better controlled than case studies.

19. What is a true statement regarding anecdotal evidence?

(Lower order)

[A] It cannot be used as a basis for forming a hypothesis

[B] It is considered, by definition, to be a type of archival evidence

[C] It can disprove a null hypothesis

[D] It can correlate with an independent variable

[E] It is considered to be hypothetically provable

The correct answer is D.

Anecdotal evidence can correlate with an independent variable. You should know that eyewitness reports can be considered anecdotal evidence and often could correlate with an independent variable. For instance, eyewitness UFO reports can correlate with missile launchings. You should be able to infer other scenarios where this would be true. Eye witness reports are frequently the basis upon which a hypothesis is formed. There is no definition of anecdotal evidence that includes that it is archival evidence, it may be or it may not be. For instance, a direct verbal report of an eyewitness to a researcher is not archival evidence. The null hypothesis can never be disproven. It is always theoretically possible that any set of data could have occurred by random chance. It is also considered theoretically impossible to ever prove any conclusion including the truth of anecdotal statements because there is always the possibility of the null hypothesis.

20. What type of statistic can be directly compared between distribution curves from two or more separate research studies?

(Lower order)

[A] Standard deviation

[B] Mean

[C] Median

[D] Mode

[E] Z score

The correct answer is E.

Z scores were designed to be comparable among different research studies, standard deviations are part of a Z score but they cannot be directly compared between two different research studies, the same is true for the mean, median and mode of a distribution curve. This is basic knowledge and the mathematics that explain why this is so is beyond the scope of the AP Psychology Exam.

21. Linda is a 16-year-old who has developed a complete loss of vision in her left visual field but still has normal vision in her right visual field. Her doctors have identified a tumor in her pituitary gland. What visual sensory information is not being perceived by Linda?

(Higher order)

[A] Signals from the left side of the right retina and the right side of the left retina

[B] Signals from the right side of the right retina and the left side of the left retina

[C] Signals from the right retina only

[D] Signals from the right side of the right retina and the right side of the left retina.

[E] Signals from the left side of the right retina and the left side of the left retina

The correct answer is D.

The left visual field corresponds to the right side of the right retina and the right side of the left retina. The left visual field information is most likely blocked at or behind the optic chiasm after the the left visual field information has crossed over from the left eye and is en route along with the left visual field information from the right eye to the right visual cortex.

22. **Which researcher is most closely associated with the visual cliff studies?**

(Lower order)

[A] Linda Buck
[B] Gustav Fechner
[C] Eleanor Gibson
[D] Richard Gregory
[E] Richard Nisbett

The correct answer is C.

Psychologist Eleanor Gibson was the most notable early contributor to the bottom-up theory of visual perception. This was based in large part on the results of her research studies with infants and a "visual cliff." Linda Buck and Richard Axel won the Nobel Prize in Physiology In 2004 for their work on olfactory receptors. Gustav Fechner developed Fechner's law, or Fechner's scale, which states that a subjective change in sensation is proportional to the logarithm of the stimulus intensity. Richard Gregory, in his "Perception as Hypothesis" theory, argued that top down visual processing is required due to the heavy filtering of visual information. Gregory criticized Gibson's and other's bottom up theory, arguing that it could not account for many features the perception of certain optical illusions. Richard Nisbett's theory of culture and perception cites psychological experiments that compared perceptual and attentional differences between Westerners and Asians. These studies showed large differences in change blindness between Westerners and Asians.

23. **Videos of experiments in microgravity aboard the international space station show close-up, real-time sequences of fist-sized globules of water with an undulating surface. The globules as a cohesive unit are also rotating and moving in a linear direction within the space station environment. What principle among those listed below is most specifically relevant to an accurate perception of this phenomena?**

(Higher order)

[A] The figure-ground relationship
[B] Absolute thresholds
[C] Signal transduction in the vestibular sensory system
[D] Size constancy
[E] Rapid adaptation

The correct answer is A.

An ability to clearly perceive what is the object - the water globule, and what is the background - the space station environment is essential for an accurate perception of the phenomena. An absolute threshold is the minimum stimulus intensity required to detect or perceive any sensory information but that is the most generally, not specifically relevant principle. Signal transduction in the vestibular sensory system is involved in sensing one's own motion in space, not in observing the motion of objects. Size constancy is not likely relevant because the absolute size of the globules image on the retinae should remain relatively constant in the video recording, the question stated "close-up" so one needn't quibble that the globules may become larger or smaller as they move nearer or further away from the recording device. Shape constancy would be a difficult topic for this question. Fortunately, it is not a choice. Rapid adaptation is a phenomena relating to how quickly thresholds can change, it is not clear that any adaptation is required for an accurate perception of this phenomena.

24. **The degree of stretch of extraocular muscles during perception of depth is a feature of:**
(Lower order)

[A] stereopsis
[B] convergence
[C] the pupillary light reflex
[D] bottom-up processing
[E] receptive fields

The correct answer is B.
The overall perception of depth involves the principle of size constancy and binocular and monocular cues to estimate the absolute and relative size and distances of objects from the eyes. When you focus directly on an object, the spatial separation between the pupils of your eye requires each eye to move inward by a precise angle to converge on an object. The kinesthetic sense of the amount of stretching of extraocular muscles that occurs when the eyes turn inward. The greater the stretch the closer the object. This cue is called convergence. The comparative disparity between the left and right images is a binocular depth cue called stereopsis. The closer the object, the greater the difference in the image relative to the visual background. The pupillary light reflex is a visual adaptive reflex that is not related to depth perception. Bottom-up processing may require depth perception, but it is not directly related to convergence. Receptive fields is a general term for regions of sensory input.

25. **According to Fechner's law, the minimum change in intensity required to be perceived as a change is:**
(Lower order)

[A] a constant absolute quantity
[B] lower for higher intensity levels
[C] applicable only to frequency dependent stimuli
[D] proportional to the logarithm of the stimulus intensity
[E] a function of the attention level of the perceiver

The correct answer is D.
Fechner's law, or Fechner's scale, states that a subjective change in sensation is proportional to the logarithm of the stimulus intensity. In absolute terms it would be higher for higher intensity levels and it would by definition not be an unchanging amount. It does not apply to some types of stimuli such as light frequency and is independent of the attention level of the perceiver, although this may change the precise amount of change required to be perceived

26. One means of evaluating the functional status of the cochlea is to determine whether sound can be produced by the cochlea. What mechanism of those stated below is most likely to explain the production of sounds by the cochlea?
    (Higher order)

    [A] Motor signals to muscles of the ossicles from the central nervous system
    [B] Motor signals to the muscles of Reissner's membrane from the central nervous system
    [C] Direct efferent triggering of outer hair cell contraction by the central nervous system
    [D] A reflex feedback mechanism between muscles of the ossicles and neurons in the spiral ganglia
    [E] An increase in the potassium concentration in endolymph is the cochlear duct.

The correct answer is C.
Direct efferent triggering of outer hair cell contraction by the central nervous system would cause mechanical movement of the tectorial membrane resulting in production of pressure waves in the cochlea, which could be transmitter in the reverse of the process of sound wave reception. This actually is the mechanism for the phenomena described in the question and the absence of this phenomena shows there is a serious dysfunction of central or cochlear hearing processes. Choices A and D might cause sound production but it would be produced by the ossicles which are middle ear structures. The cochlea is an inner ear structure. Reissner's membrane has no muscles. An increase in potassium in endolymph is a concept beyond the scope of the AP examination, but answer C is sufficiently likely to explain the phenomena based on knowledge that is within the scope of the AP Exam.

27. According to the multi-store (3-box) theory of memory, the transfer of sensory information to the short-term store (short term memory) does NOT require:
    (Higher order)

    [A] selective attention
    [B] filtering
    [C] specific sensory registries
    [D] rehearsal
    [E] sensory receptor cells

The correct answer is D.
The sensory memory or sensory register is the entryway for sensory information into the memory processing system. There are actually separate sensory memories or specific sensory registries for each type of sensory stimuli. Therefore, choice D is true. Obviously to collect this sensory information, sensory receptor cells are required, so choice E is true. The three box model proposes that there is a filtering or buffering mechanism that selects a small amount of this information for packaging and transfer to short term memory, so choice B is true. This selection process requires the active attention of the perceiver. In other words, you remember the information that attracts your attention or that you are actively searching for. This is known as selective attention, so choice A is true. Short term memories are encoded for long term memory with increasing strength by the process of rehearsal or actively repeating them over and over. The longer that items are stored in short term memory the more strongly they are encoded for long term memory. The hypothesis is that rehearsal throws short term information back into sensory memory where it is again immediately retrieved into short term memory. This resets the clock for the information in short term memory. This is not however, a process that is required to transfer sensory information to short term memory, so choice C is false. The question

was asking for the answer choice that was false, so this is the correct answer.

28. A nativist language acquisition theory criticism of behaviorism language acquisition theories is:
(Higher order)

[A] Studies have shown there is no absolute critical period for language acquisition.

[B] There are language specific concepts that are not present in other languages.

[C] There are potentially millions of specific ways to misuse grammar when constructing a specific statement.

[D] Speakers of different languages actually do not perceive that phonemes not included in their native language sound differently than any and all of the native language phonemes.

[E] Broca's aphasia can be localized damage in the frontal lobe and it causes impairment of speech fluency but comprehension of language is retained.

The correct answer is C.
Depending on the authority that establishes guidelines for distractors (incorrect answer choices) for a particular standardized examination, distractors must be more or less true and more or less relevant. This is usually of no help to the test taker because these standards are a matter of judgment and sometimes there are no standards. In other words, a distractor can be anything, completely untrue or incorrect for any reason within the context of the question. Also the test developers may or may not wish to divulge aspects of how they construct tests, including standards they use to screen distractor choices. For this question you may conclude choice A is wrong because you know (or you think you know) it is actually not true that studies have shown there is no..., but this is a common pitfall

for very well informed test takers. Often, it does not matter whether the statement is actually true or untrue in the context of the question. Always begin with the "there is one best answer" approach. You should have a sense of what the level of difficulty is for the AP Psychology exam. This is an extremely difficult question if you overlook that choice C is just a specific way of stating the nativist's fundamental criticism of behaviorist theories. If a question seems extremely difficult it is usually constructed to only appear difficult. This is the "illusion of difficulty" principle that may be used when constructing distractors. The intent is to distract you from recognizing that there is actually a rather obvious correct choice.

29. Whitney is a 22-year-old woman who works for a new technology firm. During a meeting she offers a statement that illustrates her pattern of thinking includes an understanding of the concept of framing. Among the choices below, Whitney's statement was most likely:
(Higher order)

[A] "We can use this process for a different application"

[B] "The question is not is this something that people currently know that they WANT to buy, but rather is this something that people WILL buy once the see it?"

[C] "If we just take a day or so and simply think about this problem in the broadest general way, the solution may just pop into one of our heads."

[D] "This is not something that can be physically measured."

[E] "The fact that this approach has worked in the past does not mean that it will work in the future."

The correct answer is B.

How we precisely state a problem in words is how we frame the problem. If we restate the problem or state the problem using different word or in a different way, we are reframing the problem. By reframing a problem, we may be able to arrive at a solution more easily or in completely different and unexpected way. Whitney changes a few words and completely changes the basis for deciding whether or not to proceed with a product's development. The other statements are for your consideration, most involve concepts of the thinking process including rigidity, insight and functional fixedness. It could take a fair amount of time to think about the other answer choices but it would be a good way to semantically process the concepts and make them easier to remember and understand during the AP Psychology exam. None of them provided a precise example of reframing as is the case for choice B, so there is one clearly best answer that should jump out at you as is often the case during the exam.

30. **What is a valid reason for someone to choose to use an algorithm to solve a problem?** *(Higher order)*

[A] An algorithm can be easily adapted under rapidly changing circumstances.

[B] The consequences of a wrong solution to the problem are of little concern to the problem solver.

[C] There is an algorithm to solve the problem and the solution to the problem requires expertise that the problem solver does not possess.

[D] Using a rule of thumb, the problem can be solved 99% of the time.

[E] The problem does not require a moral judgment.

The correct answer is C.

An algorithm is a method to solve problems or arrive at answers that begins with an initial query:" is this problem either one thing or one of these other things?" The either or process continues as the initial problem is narrowed down to one of all of the possible answers or solutions to the initial problem. They are basically automatic problem solving methods that do not require much in terms of higher cognitive thinking but they do require continuous focused attention and are therefore effortful problem solving methods. They are designed to be a fool-proof problem solving method that guarantees a correct solution. One advantage to an algorithm is that it does not require specific expert knowledge to use them. In other words, you can make an expert decision even though you are not an expert. For choice A, they are carefully and laboriously constructed for specific problems so are not easily adapted to rapidly changing circumstances. For choice B, since they are slow and require continuous attention they would not be an obvious choice for problems that can be solved with easier and quicker methods that have a higher error rate when the consequences of those errors are not significant. For choice D, they are anything but rules of thumb. If anything they are the opposite of rules of thumb. For choice E, moral judgments may seem irrelevant to the topic of algorithms but some of the most famous philosophical methods of arriving at moral judgments use algorithms. That is outside the range of your expected knowledge for the AP Psychology exam, but it is true, so you have no useful basis for concluding that choice E is correct. It is therefore a fair answer option.

31. **What specific type of heuristic relies on solutions that are based on how easily things are brought to mind?**
(Lower order)

[A] The availability heuristic
[B] The representativeness heuristic
[C] The anchoring and adjustment heuristic
[D] The affect heuristic
[E] The contagion heuristic

The correct answer is A.
The availability heuristics allow us to make quick decisions based on how easy it is to bring something to mind. Typically things are easier to bring to mind if you were exposed to accounts of these things how frequent, how recent and if they were highly unusual or had a powerful emotional effect upon you. The representativeness or representative heuristic use your personal past experiences or the model or prototypes of things that are the consensus of other people's past experiences. You make generalizations about things because they share similarities with other things you have experienced in the past or because they have similarities to models or prototypes of things that you assume are true. You are expected to know what these two heuristics types are for the AP Psychology exam. There are many other well described types of heuristics; choices C, D, and E are examples of these. There are probably as many actual heuristics as the human imagination allows.

32. **In language theories, the most fundamental unit of meaning is the _____.**
(Lower order)

[A] idea
[B] syllable
[C] phoneme
[D] icon
[E] morpheme

The correct answer is E.
In terms of the level of difficulty of the AP Psychology exam, this question is as easy as things get. Either you know it or you do not. You might confuse this with a phoneme, which is the most fundamental unique type of sound that is used to form words, but phonemes have no intrinsic meaning outside of the words that they form. The other choices are in some sense fundamental but not in the context of language theory as the question is phrased.

33. **Patricia is a 22-year-old woman who is about to undergo an electroencephalogram (EEG) study. Among the choices below, what disorder would this study best be able to diagnose?**
(Higher order)

[A] REM sleep disorder
[B] An injury to a peripheral motor nerve
[C] A narrowing of a cerebral artery
[D] A region of the brain with abnormal glucose uptake
[E] Increased intracranial pressure

The correct answer is A.
Electroencephalograms (EEGs) record the electrical activity of the brain over a span of time. EEG recordings can show abnormalities in REM sleep because REM sleep has a characteristically rapid, low-voltage desynchronized wave pattern that will be recorded by an EEG. Injuries to peripheral nerves can be diagnosed with an electromyograph (EMG). Imaging studies such as angiography are required to diagnose narrowing of cerebral arteries. Glucose uptake in regional areas of the brain are demonstrated with positron emission tomography. Increased intracranial pressure can be detected by computerized tomography (CT) scans or magnetic resonance imaging (MRI) scans.

34. Thomas is a 15-year-old boy who, at the age of 3 years, underwent a radical type of brain surgery as a last resort to control an extreme and dangerous form of epilepsy. Since his surgery, he has been unable to follow verbal commands to perform specific tasks involving only his non-dominant hand. He is otherwise normal. What surgical procedure could account for this long-term impairment?

(Higher order)

[A] A left frontal lobotomy
[B] A severing of the corpus callosum
[C] A right frontal lobectomy
[D] A lumbar laminectomy
[E] A bilateral occipital lobectomy

The correct answer is B.

An inability to convert auditory information into voluntary movement that is restricted to one side of the body strongly suggests there is major disruption of the neural connections between the two cerebral hemispheres. In a corpus callosotomy, the fibers of the corpus callosum are severed, which effectively eliminates the majority of the functional connections between the right and left hemispheres of the cerebral cortex. This is why the procedure is sometimes referred to as "split-brain" surgery. Such general categories of deficits are well-documented in historic and current research and accounts of persons with a naturally occurring absence of the corpus callosum or whose corpus callosum was accidentally or surgically severed. Choices A and C would not affect the corpus callosum. Choice E would result in total blindness, so the boy would not be described as "otherwise normal." The term "lumbar" which is used in choice D is not used in the terminology of the brain, so it is not a brain surgery.

35. What are the two major neurotransmitters of the peripheral motor nervous systems?

(Lower order)

[A] Norepinephrine and epinephrine
[B] Serotonin and dopamine
[C] Acetylcholine and serotonin
[D] Acetylcholine and dopamine
[E] Norepinephrine and acetylcholine

The correct answer is E.

In the two major divisions of the peripheral nervous system, acetylcholine is the only major neurotransmitter except at most sympathetic motor neuron target cell junctions, where the postganglionic sympathetic motor neurons release norepinephrine. Dopamine and serotonin are major neurotransmitters of the central nervous system, but have almost no role in the peripheral nervous system.

36. All of the following statements are true for endocrine glands EXCEPT:

(Lower order)

[A] They all release hormones into the bloodstream.
[B] At least one gland is also an exocrine gland.
[C] At least one gland releases epinephrine.
[D] They are all independent of the peripheral nervous system.
[E] At least one gland synthesizes more than one type of hormone.

The correct answer is D.

Most of the endocrine glands of the body are influenced, if not directly innervated by, the sympathetic and/or parasympathetic nervous system. In fact, the epinephrine and norepinephrine secreting cells of the adrenal medulla are considered to be postganglionic neurons of the sympathetic nervous system. The definition of an endocrine gland is a gland that secretes hormones into the bloodstream. The pancreas is an endocrine gland because it secretes insulin, glucagon and other hormones into the bloodstream. It is also an exocrine gland because it secretes substances through a duct or canal to the surface of an organ - namely digestive enzymes to the lumen of the small intestine. Many endocrine glands, such as the adrenal gland and the pituitary gland, synthesize two or more types of hormones.

37. **Clinical observations suggest that some blind persons may be able to perceive their surroundings through echolocation. What experimental findings in these blind persons would most strongly support the claim that their echolocation ability is an example of neuroplasticity?**

    (Higher order)

    [A] Auditory stimuli causes increased activity in the occipital cortex
    [B] Auditory stimuli causes dilation of the iris
    [C] Flashes of light are perceived as snapping or popping sounds
    [D] The auditory cortices of blind echolocators are larger than the auditory cortices of blind persons who cannot echolocate
    [E] The visual cortices of blind echolocators are larger than the visual cortices of blind persons who cannot echolocate

    The correct answer is A.
    Neuroplasticity is the ability of the nervous system to form new neural connections and alter the functions of the nervous system in response to new situations, changes in environment and to compensate for injuries or disease that impair normal neurological activity. Choice A shows a direct response to auditory input in an area of the brain previously dedicated to processing visual input. Choice B describes an autonomic response that could occur in persons

with normal vision. Choice C describes a synesthesia like phenomena that could be evidence of neuroplasticity, but also implies that there remains some direct visual input capability and is difficult to explain as a mechanism for echolocation. Choices D and E could be interpreted as innate differences between echolocators and non-echolocators and not alterations of the nervous system over time.

38. **What experimental evidence described below best demonstrates the functional organization of the autonomic nervous system?**

    (Higher order)

    [A] The same stimulus causes both increased heart rate and blood pressure in many test subjects
    [B] The same stimulus always causes the same response in all randomly chosen test subjects
    [C] Microscopic examination shows two synapses with a smooth muscle cell
    [D] Fear inducing stimuli causes pupil dilation and pleasant stimuli causes pupil constriction
    [E] A rapid application of force to a flexed tendon causes involuntary extension of the associated appendage

    The correct answer is D.
    The demonstration of two different autonomic responses at the same organ to two different classes of stimuli indicates there are two separate functional motor pathways in the autonomic nervous system, one that responds to fearful stimuli and one that responds to pleasant stimuli. Choice A could represent a single functional pathway operating by two different physiological mechanisms. Choice B describes a single type of response to a stimulus. Choice C provides no evidence that the two synapses are capable of inducing different functional effects.

Choice E also shows only a single functional response to a single type of stimuli.

39. **Identical vs. fraternal twin studies have shown:**

    (Lower order)

    [A] no evidence that schizophrenia is a biologically influenced trait
    [B] no evidence that IQ is an environmentally influenced trait
    [C] evidence for a genetic basis for some types of psychological behavior
    [D] evidence that nutritional deficiencies are more common in fraternal twins
    [E] evidence that there are structural differences in the chromosomes of identical twins

    The correct answer is C.
    Twin studies show more similarity in many types of psychological behaviors in identical twins raised apart than in fraternal twins raised together. This is strong evidence for a biological rather than environmental influence on some psychological traits. there are greater differences in IQs between identical twins raised apart than in identical twins raised together This is evidence for an environmental influence on a trait. There are no well reported studies that show the results described for choices D and E.

40. **Among the choices below, what type of psychological theory is best supported by evidence that shows there are lower levels of warfare between hunter-gatherer societies compared to agrarian societies?**

    (Lower order)

    [A] Classical conditioning theories
    [B] Stage theories
    [C] Evolutionary theories
    [D] Psychoanalytic theories
    [E] Emergent theories

    The correct answer is A.
    Evolutionary theories postulate that human social behavior is the result of evolutionary adaptation to the historical human environment, which has strongly favored behaviors appropriate for hunter-gatherer societies. This suggests there must be significant genetically programed predispositions to behaviors that enhance the survival of these types of societies. In comparatively modern societies, these predispositions can be maladaptive, leading to dysfunctional and harmful social behavior. Classical conditioning theories, stage theories and psychoanalytic theories have difficulty accounting for the abundant examples of lower civil and cultural strife in longstanding ancient societies compared to modern societies. Emergent theories focus on the appearance of new complex phenomena in a system that could not be predicted to occur based on the individual properties of elements of the system. In other words, they explain situations where the sum is greater than the parts.

41. What is NOT true with regard to a cataleptic state?
(Higher order)

[A] It may appear to be a trance-like state.

[B] Purposeless agitation may be present.

[C] It may constitute the primary character of a catatonic state.

[D] Waxy flexibility may be present.

[E] Persons in a cataleptic state are often unresponsive to stimuli.

The correct answer is B.

Catalepsy is often characterized by lack of response to stimuli. Persons in a cataleptic state may have a fixed body posture that can be rearrange by others. This phenomenon is called waxy flexibility. Those in a cataleptic state are also generally unresponsive to stimuli. A cataleptic state is the more common primary character of a catatonic state, but not always. Alternatively, a constant movement pattern called *purposeless agitation*, in combination with extreme negativism, may replace a cataleptic state as the primary character of catatonic state.

42. A person with a diagnosis of borderline personality disorder most likely has:
(Higher order)

[A] delusions of grandeur

[B] perseveration

[C] a very mild form of schizophrenia-like symptoms

[D] episodes of disoriented and aimless wandering

[E] difficult interactions with others

The correct answer is E.

We did not discuss the details of borderline personality disorder. It's possible a person with borderline personality disorder could have any of these other features. There is no reason to conclude they are more likely to occur in persons with a specific diagnosis of borderline personality unless the DSM-5 states that this is so, or you could draw a conclusion that it is likely to be true based on the DSM-5 description of the disorder. In fact, DSM-5 does not so state for borderline personality disorder but does so state for schizotypal personality disorder and choice C "a very mild form of schizophrenia-like symptom". For choice D, a state of disoriented and aimless wandering is a defining element of dissociative fugue, which is one type of dissociative disorder. For choice B We mentioned perseveration is as a type of speech pattern abnormality that may represent disorganized thinking as occurs in a psychosis. Choice A is by definition a delusion which is also more closely associated with psychotic states. Choice E is true for all specific personality disorders by definition and for many other disorders as well.

43. **Which statement is a direct sociocultural based criticism of a behaviorist based theory?**
   (Higher order)

   [A] Differences in one's household ethnicity correlate more strongly with depression than does one's birth order.

   [B] Antisocial behavior is higher in males who have lower than average IQ levels than in females who have lower than average IQ levels.

   [C] Women who were raised in a matriarchal society are more likely to be rewarded for having spiritual visions than those in patriarchal societies.

   [D] Pica behavior is never rewarded but it does correlate with increased incidence rates in women who were raised in male dominated cultures.

   [E] Compulsive rituals are rewarded when they are more acceptable in a given culture.

   The correct answer is C.
   Behaviorist theories most likely involve aspects of conditioned learning such as reward and punishment concepts in operant conditioning. Choices A and B could be sociocultural based criticism of a behaviorist based theory, but it is not directly stated what principles of conditioned learning were proposed for depression or antisocial behavior. Choices C and E explain a conditioned learning mechanism that results from a sociocultural context, so these are not really criticisms. Choice D directly refutes a behavioral mechanism, reward, as being not possible and provides evidence for a sociocultural mechanism i.e. abnormal behavior due to gender based factors instead.

44. **What neurotransmitter has been most strongly identified to be likely playing an important role in schizophrenia?**
   (Lower order)

   [A] Serotonin
   [B] Acetylcholine
   [C] GABA
   [D] Beta-endorphins
   [E] Dopamine

   The correct answer is E.
   The dopamine hypothesis proposes that psychotic symptoms of schizophrenia are due in part to abnormal dopamine receptor activity in certain brain regions. This is based on observations that a large number of antipsychotics have dopamine-receptor blocking. High acetylcholine levels are associated with depression, and low levels in the hippocampus have been associated with dementia. Low serotonin levels are associated with depression and some anxiety disorders and obsessive-compulsive disorder. Low GABA levels are is associated with anxiety disorders. Endorphin levels are not well established as relevant in any mental disorder.

45. **Which term is most specifically associated with the expression of inappropriate types of emotional responses?**
   (Lower order)

   [A] A blunted affect
   [B] A delusional episode
   [C] A labile affect
   [D] A disordered thinking process
   [E] A disorganized thinking process

   The correct answer is C.
   A labile affect describes emotional instability with sudden mood swings and inappropriate or paradoxical emotional responses such a laughing aloud in public upon hearing of a tragic occurrence. A blunted affect is the term for a very limited intensity and range of

emotional displays. A delusion is a strongly held belief that is obviously almost certainly untrue. A disordered or disorganized thinking process is a feature of psychosis, usually displayed by strange repetitive speech patterns.

46. **Choose the answer that represents a correct sequence of increasing abnormality or severity beginning with the least abnormal or least severe form and progressing to the most abnormal or most severe form.**

    (Lower order)

    [A] A flat affect, then a blunted affect and then a restricted affect
    [B] A restricted affect, then a labile affect, and then a broad affect
    [C] An illusion, then a delusion and then a hallucination
    [D] Cyclothymic disorder, then bipolar 2 disorder, and then bipolar 1 disorder
    [E] A dissociative disorder, a phobia and then a panic attack

    The correct answer is D.
    Bipolar 1 disorder is the most severe of bipolar and related disorders. The primary symptoms are those of extreme mania or rapid mood swings between mania and depression. The less severe bipolar 2 disorder, features recurrent depression alternating with hypomanic episodes, a milder state of mania in which the symptoms are not severe enough to cause marked impairment or need for hospitalization. Cyclothymic disorder is a chronic state of cycling between hypomanic and depressive episodes that are less severe than those of bipolar disorders.

47. **Which concept of Jung's can explain some of the similarities seen among all people?**

    (Higher order)

    [A] Complexes
    [B] Striving for success
    [C] Basic anxiety
    [D] Temperament
    [E] Collective unconscious

    The correct answer is E.
    The collective unconscious contains ancestral knowledge and experiences that have been passed down from generation to generation. As such, the content of the collective unconscious is common to all people. Complexes are part of the personal unconscious. Basic anxiety is not a Jungian concept, nor is temperament.

48. **Which of the following statements is true based on Alfred Adler's theory?**

    (Higher order)

    [A] Individuals with an inferiority complex have a high level of social interest.
    [B] Individuals with an inferiority complex strive for success.
    [C] Individuals with a superiority complex are concerned about the welfare of others.
    [D] Individuals with a superiority complex think they are better than others.
    [E] All individuals are born with a superiority complex.

    The correct answer is C.
    Individuals with a superiority complex care about others and have levels of social interest. Individuals with an inferiority complex have low levels of social interest and strive for superiority, not success. Superiority complex does not mean that one thinks he is better than others. All individuals, according to Adler, are born with physical deficiencies that create inferiority complexes.

49. Two main concerns of humanistic theories are:

(Lower order)

[A] self-efficacy and self-actualization
[B] inferiority and self-understanding
[C] self-understanding and unconditional positive regard
[D] objective experiences and self-esteem
[E] self-esteem and self-concept

The correct answer is E.

The main purpose of life, according to humanistic theory, is to achieve self-actualization. In order to accomplish this task, individuals must have positive self-concepts and high levels of self-esteem. Self-efficacy is a term used by Albert Bandura, a social-cognitive theorist. Inferiority was the focus of Alfred Adler's work. Self-understanding is linked to self-esteem and self-concept, but humanistic theory does not focus on self-understanding. Unconditional positive regard, which means to love and accept others with no conditions, was a term used by Carl Rogers. Although it affects self-concept and self-esteem, it is not a concern of both the humanistic theorists studied in this review. Humanistic theories are interested in subjective, not objective, experiences.

50. A woman takes a personality assessment three separate times over the course of six months. Each time she takes the test, the results are different. What statement best explains the problem?

(Higher order)

[A] The test does not measure what it is supposed to measure.
[B] The test is valid but not reliable.
[C] Mary is lying on the test.
[D] The test is not reliable.
[E] Mary's locus-of-control is external.

The correct answer is D.

A reliable test yields consistent and stable results across different settings and administrations. The test may be valid, which means it measures what it is supposed to measure. A test cannot be valid without also being reliable. Mary may be lying on some of responses, but that does not account for such different results. Mary may have an external locus-of-control, but that does not explain the inconsistent results.

51. Which trait theorist believed that not all personality traits are consistent in all situations?

(Lower order)

[A] Karen Horney
[B] Walter Mischel
[C] Carl Rogers
[D] Gordon Allport
[E] B.F. Skinner

The correct answer is B.

Mischel believed that situations and the person interact, with each affecting the other. Because of differences in situations, the person may not exhibit the same personality traits in different situations. Karen Horney was a psychoanalytic theorist who criticized Freud's theory and proposed her own theory based on security needs. Carl Rogers had a humanistic approach to personality. Gordon Allport was a trait theorist who proposed three levels of dispositions (cardinal, central, and secondary). B.F. Skinner espoused a behaviorist theory.

52. **Ways of relating to others and the environment that are present at birth are called?**

(Lower order)

[A] Idiographic traits
[B] Personality traits
[C] Temperament
[D] Central dispositions
[E] Archetypes

The correct answer is C.

Temperament is present a birth and has much influence over how one will interact with others and their environment. Temperament is one aspect of personality and can affect personality development, but not all personality traits are necessarily a result of one's temperament. Idiographic traits are those traits that are unique to each individual, and that may or may not be present at birth. Central dispositions are those traits that stand out the most in an individual. Archetypes are a concept proposed by Jung.

53. **A mother who is potty training her child initially rewards her child for going near the bathroom, then she rewards the child for touching the bathroom door, then she rewards the child for walking into the bathroom. She continues to reward the child until the child engages in the desired behavior. Which principle of conditioning is the mother using?**

(Lower order)

[A] Generalization
[B] Shaping
[C] Modeling
[D] Cognitive mapping
[E] Aversion

The correct answer is B.

In shaping, small, successive steps toward the behavior are rewarded until the

person engages in the desired behavior. Generalization refers to responding to similar stimuli in the same way. Modeling is a principle of social learning. Cognitive mapping is a term used to describe how people create mental representations that aid them in recalling information and forming associations between concepts. Aversion refers to something unpleasant.

54. **Albert Bandura asserted that four conditions must be met in order for observational learning to be effective. All of the following statements describe the four conditions EXCEPT:**

(Higher order)

[A] Jimmy was fascinated at how his brother dribbled the basketball so he paid close attention.
[B] Valerie wants to learn the dance steps she saw her sister doing because she wants to impress her boyfriend at the prom.
[C] After Jody watched the video tape his guitar instructor gave him, he knew where to place his fingers and was able to play the chords.
[D] Abby hit her sister because her best friend hit her brother without getting into any trouble with her parents.
[E] Timmy remembered how his mother showed him to fold the towels two weeks ago.

The correct answer is D.

The four conditions are attention, retention, reciprocation (reproduction), and motivation. In example A, Jimmy paid attention to his brother's actions. In Example B, Valerie was motivated by the desire to impress her boyfriend. Jody, in example C, was reproduced his instructor's actions and was able to play the chords. Example E stresses that Timmy remembered what he saw his mother doing. Observing the consequences of the behavior are not necessary for observational learning to occur.

55. **Which of the following statements would most closely match Donald Hebb's theory about learning?**
(Higher order)

[A] Learning occurs as a result of behaviors being reinforced.

[B] Learning occurs when a person connects two events that have been paired repeatedly.

[C] Learning occurs as a result of neural activity in the brain.

[D] Learning requires cognitive insight.

[E] Learning occurs by watching others.

The correct answer is C.
Hebb believed that all behavior can be explained in terms of how the brain functions. Hebb's research demonstrated that learning impacts and is impacted by neural networks in the brain. Skinner, a behaviorist, would assert that learning occurs through associating behaviors with consequences. Watson and Pavlov would argue that learning results from associations made by repeatedly pairing two stimuli. Wolfgang Kohler, who conducted experiments related to insight learning, would propose that in order for a problem to be solved, the individual must develop cognitive insight. Albert Bandura proposed social learning theory, which suggests that people can learn by observing others and their actions.

56. **Why are variable schedules of reinforcement more resistant to extinction?**
(Higher order)

[A] A fixed amount of time must pass before a response is rewarded.

[B] Responses are not immediately reinforced.

[C] Responses are continuous.

[D] A reward is administered after a set number of responses.

[E] A response can be rewarded at any time.

The correct answer is E.
With variable schedules of reinforcement, the individual never knows which response will lead to a reward. Because of the unpredictable nature of the reward, the behavior is harder to extinguish. Fixed schedules of reinforcement do not vary; rewards are administered after a certain number of responses or after a set number of times. Responses not being immediately reinforced does not necessarily make extinction more difficult. Only a continuous schedule of reinforcement provides reinforcement for every response. Continuous responses can be present, at least initially, with all these schedules. It is the unpredictable nature of variable schedules that makes extinction more difficult.

57. **Mental institutions, schools, and prisons often use which of the following as a way to modify behavior?**
(Lower order)

[A] Token economy

[B] Variable schedules of reinforcement

[C] Punishment

[D] Aversion therapy

[E] Biofeedback

The correct answer is A.

With a token economy every time the individual engages in a desired behavior, the person receives a token. Tokens serve as secondary reinforcers that can be exchanged for a reward. Token economies have proven to be effective in increasing positive behaviors. Variable schedules of reinforcement would make extinction of negative behaviors very difficult. Punishment is generally not as effective as reinforcement. Aversion therapy has not been mentioned in this chapter, but it should be used with caution. Because of the nature of biofeedback, it cannot be easily used in prisons, schools, and mental institutions.

58. **The Garcia effect refers to which of the following:**

    (Lower order)

    [A] stimulus discrimination
    [B] Premack principle
    [C] Conditioned taste aversion
    [D] Latent learning
    [E] successive approximations

    The correct answer is C.

    The Garcia Effect is also known as conditioned taste aversion. Stimulus discrimination is the ability to tell the difference between very similar stimuli. The Premack Principle states that the opportunity to engage in a more rewarding and pleasant activity or behavior can be used to reinforce less rewarding activities or behavior. Latent learning is learning that is not immediately outwardly obvious. Successive approximations are small, successive steps toward a desired behavior. Successive approximations are used in the process of shaping behavior.

59. **Which theory offers a way to explain differences between species?**

    (Lower order)

    [A] Cognitive
    [B] Evolutionary
    [C] Biological
    [D] Psychoanalytic
    [E] Dualism

    The correct answer is B.

    Evolutionary theory is based on the premise of natural selection, which basically states that the behaviors and characteristics of a species that help that species adapt and survive are the ones that are passed down. As characteristics are passed down, there exists some variations from previous generations. These variations explain differences between species. No other theory discussed in this study guide can provide an explanation for differences between species. Dualism refers to the idea that everything in the world can be divided into two parts—a body and a spirit.

60. **Which of the following statements about cognitive psychology is NOT true?**
    (Higher order)

    [A] It is interested in how people perceive and interpret events and experiences.
    [B] It is interested in the smaller components of mental processes.
    [C] It often combines principles from this approach with other approaches.
    [D] It developed as a reaction against behaviorism's focus on only what is observable.
    [E] It is interested in the function of mental processes.

    The correct answer is D.

    Humanistic psychology developed in response to behaviorism's view that thoughts and cognitive processes are not important and were ignored. Cognitive psychology deals with the mind, cognitive processes, perceptions, interpretations, and thoughts. Cognitive psychology is very popular, and it often blends its principles with principles from other approaches.

61. **Which subfield of psychology deals with diagnosing, assessing, and evaluating emotional, behavioral, and psychological disorders?**
(Lower order)

[A] Industrial-organizational psychology
[B] Counseling psychology
[C] Human factors psychology
[D] Clinical psychology
[E] Educational psychology

The correct answer is D.
Clinical psychologists diagnose, assess, evaluate, treat and try to prevent psychological disorders. Industrial-organizational psychology deals with human behavior in the workplace. Counseling psychology has a broad scope that focuses on helping people achieve and maintain healthy lifelong functioning, including educational, vocational, emotional, social and relational health. Human factors psychology uses scientific study to examine human behavior and capabilities to determine the best ways to design products, equipment and technology for maximum levels of safe, effective and satisfying use by humans. Educational psychology studies development, learning, motivation, instruction, assessment and evaluation that impact the interaction between teaching and learning. Educational psychology also includes dealing with psychological problems that influence a child's ability to learn and normally develop in an academic environment.

62. **A sociocultural psychologist might be interested in which of the following?**
(Higher order)

[A] How hormones contribute to aggression levels
[B] How sleep deprivation affects memory
[C] How different ethnic groups respond to violence
[D] How painful memories are repressed
[E] How personal needs direct behavior

The correct answer is C.
Sociocultural psychology studies how one's culture influences behavior. This branch of psychology also examines the differences between cultures and how those differences are expressed. The effects of hormones would be an interest of a biological psychologist. A cognitive psychologist might be interested in how memory is affected by sleep deprivation. Psychoanalytic theory focuses on the unconscious and defense mechanisms. Repression is a defense mechanism. Humanistic theory is interested in how personal needs, goals, and values motivate and direct behavior.

63. **Which early psychologist is the founder of child psychology and educational psychology?**
(Lower order)

[A] William James
[B] Edward Titchener
[C] Wilhelm Wundt
[D] G. Stanley Hall
[E] Margaret Floy Washburn

The correct answer is D.
Hall laid the foundation for child psychology and educational psychology. He was also interested in evolutionary psychology. William James developed the theory of functionalism. Edward Titchener expanded Wilhelm Wundt's study of the structures

of the mind and brought the science of psychology to the United States. Wilhelm Wundt founded the science of psychology in 1879 and conducted experiments that led to the development of his theory of structuralism. Margaret Floy Washburn was the first woman to receive a Ph.D. in psychology.

64. **Wilhelm Wundt is the founder of the science of psychology. Which of the following statements best describes why psychology was first considered a science under Wundt?**
    (Higher order)

    [A] Wundt developed a theory based on general laws.
    [B] Wundt's work influenced other psychologists.
    [C] Wundt based his theory on his own experiences.
    [D] Wundt developed his theory by using experimental methods.
    [E] Wundt acquired knowledge about the mind.

    The correct answer is D.
    In order for a field of study to be considered a science, knowledge must be acquired through systematic observation and experimentation. Wundt used an experimental method (introspection) to acquire knowledge about the mind. Developing a theory does not make one a scientist, even if the theory is based on general laws. General laws may be observed apart from experimentation. The influence of Wundt's work did not classify what he was doing as science. Basing a theory on personal experiences does not classify the theory as science. Wundt did acquire knowledge about the mind, but that fact alone does not classify his practice as science. What made Wundt's work "science" was that he acquired knowledge based on experimentation.

65. **The two broad categories that developmental theories can be divided into are:**
    (Lower order)

    [A] nature and nurture
    [B] continuous and discontinuous
    [C] social and physical
    [D] maturation and environmentalism
    [E] psychosocial and psychodynamic

    The correct answer is B.
    Developmental psychologists approach development from two different theoretical perspectives. Some psychologists see development as being a continuous and stable process, whereas others view it as being discontinuous or occurring in stages. Nature and nurture refers to how much a person's development is related to nurture and how much is a result of nature. Social and physical are two domains of development. Maturation and environmentalism refer to nature versus nurture. Psychosocial and psychoanalytic theory are two different types of theories that can help explain development.

66. **Johnny, an infant, does not cry or fuss when his mother leaves. When a person he is not familiar with enters the room, Johnny allows the stranger to hold him and play with him. When Johnny's mother returns, he avoids her and does not want her to hold him. Which of the following statements best explains Johnny's behavior?**
    (Higher order)

    [A] Johnny is begin abused.
    [B] Johnny knows his mother will be responsive to his needs.
    [C] Johnny does not think his mother will be responsive to his needs.
    [D] Johnny is not sure if his mother will be responsive to his needs.
    [E] Johnny feels secure with his mother.

The correct answer is C.

Johnny has an anxious-avoidant attachment to his mother and does not feel secure that she will meet his needs. If Johnny had a secure attachment to his mother, he would know she would be responsive to his needs. If the attachment was insecure, Johnny would not be sure that his mother would meet his needs. If Johnny was being abused, his behavior would be erratic, which indicates a disorganized attachment.

67. **Which of following did Carol Gilligan believe was crucial to moral progress?**
    (Lower order)

    [A] Caring relationships
    [B] Environmental stability
    [C] Concept of justice
    [D] Bargaining
    [E] Reasoning

The correct answer is A.

Gilligan criticized Kohlberg's theory of moral development, which was based on the concept of justice, because it did not address how gender differences could affect moral development. She thought that girls might consider the relationships of those involved in their moral reasoning. Environmental stability is not associated with a theory of moral development, nor is bargaining. Reasoning is not critical for moral development.

68. **According to Freud's psychosexual theory, a person who is too dependent on others might be preoccupied by behaviors that occur in which stage?**
    (Lower order)

    [A] Phallic stage
    [B] Genital stage
    [C] Anal stage
    [D] Oral stage
    [E] Oedipal stage

The correct answer is D.

The oral stage is the first stage in Freud's theory. In this stage, infants derive pleasure through their mouths. Because infants are helpless and depend on others for their care, someone who is too dependent on others would be fixated on this stage. In the phallic stage, boys experience the Oedipal complex and girls experience the Electra complex. In the genital stage, individuals obtain sexual pleasure through the genitals. Individuals in the anal stage seek pleasure from the process of elimination. There is no Oedipal stage in Freud's theory, but there is an Oedipal complex that occurs during the phallic stage.

69. **David's mother pours cream into a tall pitcher. She then pours the cream into a bowl. When she asks David if the amount of cream in the bowl is the same amount of cream that was in the pitcher. David seems confused at first, but he thinks about the situation. He then walks over to the bowl and pours the cream back into the pitcher before responding that the amount of cream is the same. David is in what stage of cognitive development according to Piaget?**
    (Higher order)

    [A] Formal operational stage
    [B] Sensorimotor stage
    [C] Concrete operational stage
    [D] Preoperational stage
    [E] Preconventional stage

The correct answer is C.

David demonstrated that the amount of liquid in both containers was the same by pouring the cream from the bowl back into the pitcher, or, in other words, he reversed the operation. Children who understand the concepts of conservation and reversibility are in the concrete operational stage. However, David does not yet have the ability to engage in abstract thinking, so he is not in the formal operational stage. The sensorimotor stage is from birth to about the age of two. In this stage, children learn through their senses and motor skills. If David was the in the preoperational stage, he would not have understood the concepts of reversibility or conservation. Preconventional stage is a stage of Kohlberg's moral development theory.

70. **A researcher wants to conduct research using the longitudinal method. All of the following statements are true things EXCEPT:**
    (Higher order)

    [A] He will have to assess changes at set intervals of time.
    [B] He can assume that any changes are the result of cultural differences.
    [C] He can measure specific aspects of development.
    [D] He can assume any changes are the result of aging.
    [E] He should use participants who are close in age.

The correct answer is B.

Longitudinal research studies participants who are of the same group and are close in age over the course of their lifetimes. Longitudinal research offers the advantage of being able to eliminate cultural differences.

This type of research requires the researcher to evaluate participants at set intervals of time to see if any changes have occurred. If any changes have occurred, the researcher can assume that changes are the result of aging. This type of research is advantageous because it can measure specific aspects of development.

71. **Harmful substances that can have serious effects on a developing fetus are called:**
    (Lower order)

    [A] carcinogens
    [B] schemas
    [C] zygotes
    [D] stereotyped ingestive responses
    [E] teratogens

The correct answer is E.

Teratogens are any harmful chemical or other types of substances that can negatively affect fetal development. Certain diseases and conditions of the mother can be considered teratogens. Carcinogens are harmful substances, but they are only one type of harmful substances. A schema is a mental representation of an object. A zygote is a fertilized egg. Stereotyped ingestive responses describe the sucking and smacking that are elicited when a sugary substance is placed in the mouth of infants.

72. Abigail and her mother, Amy, are great friends. Amy devotes much of her time to promoting Abigail's career and buying luxurious items for Abigail. Amy is very warm and affectionate toward Abigail, and they talk every day. Abigail stays out late and hangs out with peers who use drugs and alcohol. Amy only has a few rules for Abigail to follow, but she does not enforce the rules. Amy frequently subjects Abigail to potentially dangerous situations and then leaves the room. What characteristics might Abigail demonstrate as a result of Amy's permissive parenting?

(Higher order)

[A] Abigail will be organized, able to regulate her emotions and will have a good work ethic.

[B] Abigail will exhibit a great deal of self-control, will take responsibility for her choices and will appreciate the things she has.

[C] Abigail will have difficulty taking responsibility for her choices, will lack self-control, and may feel as if she is entitled to things.

[D] Abigail will be withdrawn, have difficulty making friends, and will have problems making decisions.

[E] Abigail will be confident, have good communication skills, and will be able to make her own choices.

The correct answer is C.
Children whose parents are permissive often have a good relationship with their parents, but their parents have few rules and do not hold their children to high behavior standards. These children often get their way. As a result, they have little to no self-control, think that they are entitled to things, and do not the blame for the consequences of their choices. Children from homes with authoritarian parents will be withdrawn, have

few friends and will lack the ability to make decisions. Authoritative parenting creates the best environment for children. These parents are nurturing and supportive but they have rules and hold their children accountable for the choices they make. As a result, children from homes with authoritative parents have self-control, take responsibility for their choices, are confident, have good communication skills and are able to make decisions.

73. Holly is a 29-year-old woman who demonstrates defining features of interpersonal intelligence described in Howard Gardner's theory of multiple intelligences. Which summary of her behavior most closely matches Holly's utilization of her interpersonal intelligence?
(Higher order)

[A] Holly finds ways to persuade homeless persons to seek assistance that is available to them but requires the homeless to cooperate with the assistance agencies.

[B] Holly learns to function in unfamiliar situations by generalizing from the experience of others.

[C] Holly relies on an acute emotional understanding of others to persuade her boss to give her a raise in salary.

[D] Holly integrates her exceptional fund of knowledge to identify a subtle behavior in her daughter as a potential sign of severe mental illness.

[E] Holly is able to use highly analytical thought processes to discourage an attack on her by an enraged coworker.

The correct answer is A.
In Howard Gardner's theory of multiple intelligences, the Interpersonal intelligence involves thinking that features street smarts, understanding and empathy for others,

interaction with others and learning through interaction. Choice A is hopefully a well-worded specific illustration of the use of street smarts - she is literally functioning on the street and interacting with others to achieve a practical goal; one that requires empathy for the homeless and learning how to accomplish a goal by interactions with them. This is at the highest levels of AP difficulty in terms of mastery of knowledge. You would require a very solid and clear understanding of Gardner's intrapersonal intelligence to discriminate among the other answer choices.

74. **The Flynn effect is a verified phenomena that has been observed for the past seven decades. It shows an increase in the average IQ scores of the human population that is approximately 3 points per decade. This effect is seen to be particularly evident in the increase in IQ scores among relatively less well-developed industrial societies. What statement below is the most reasonable conclusion that may be draw based on the information provided in this passage?**
    (Higher order)

    [A] The effect provides more support for a general intelligence than for multiple intelligences.

    [B] The effect provides support for a primarily environmental component to intelligence rather than a primarily genetic component to intelligence

    [C] The effect demonstrates that environmental conditions can result in increased intelligence

    [D] The effect demonstrates that nutritional factors are not involved in relative levels of intelligence among individuals.

    [E] The effect demonstrates that IQ testing is not culturally biased.

The correct answer is C.
When new information is provided by a question, it is often necessary to evaluate each answer choice. In a sense, these types of questions are designed to require this comparative process. Among the choices provided, choice D is the worst. It is the opposite of what may account for the Flynn effect. The Flynn effect is strong in underdeveloped societies. A rational explanation is that these societies are benefiting from improved diets as the decades have passed. Choice A is marginally better but it hardly seem relevant whether the effect is due to a general intelligence or multiple intelligences and it is difficult to understand how the effect could support one view over the other. The remaining choices are focused on the central issue of environmental and genetic factors in intelligence. at this comparative level choice E is arguable from either side. If the effect is universal, then how is it culturally biased? But perhaps this indicates all cultures are becoming more westernized. That seems to be at least as likely. Choice B is the most difficult to separate from the best answer. How is one to explain the Flynn effect except that it is the result of environmental effects? Consider that it could be possible that humans maximum IQs and everything about IQs is 100% determined by genetics. The environment however could have a profound effect on how this IQ is expressed. As societies become more socially complex there is a greater opportunity for intelligence to reach a higher level of its genetically evolved potential. This creates a mutually reinforced feedback cycle of more dynamically interactive sociocultural environments that increase the opportunities for intelligence to function at higher levels, resulting in an even more complex and interactive socio cultural environment. Choice C provides an easier way to choose - it

Sample Test 2

basically makes a logical conclusion. If the IQ of the human population is increasing over the decades, what other than environmental effects could account for this change? Natural selection requires millennia to evolve superior cognitive function.

75. **From the choices below, select the most significant theoretical distinction between the original Stanford Binet and Wechsler intelligence tests.**
(Higher order)

[A] The statistical normalization of the score distributions curve of the Wechsler test

[B] The inclusion of non-intellectual factors in the structural design of the Wechsler test

[C] The factor analysis based questions to detect differences between fluid intelligence and crystallized intelligence of the Stanford-Binet test

[D] The non-verbal intelligence measurement of the Stanford-Binet test

[E] The hierarchical intelligence theory based construction of the Wechsler test

The correct answer is B.
David Wechsler incorporated his theory of nonintellectual factors into the test's structural design and construction. This was present in the original version of his test and was not in the original Stanford-Binet test. For choice A, the Wechsler exam was calibrated so that the mean of the scoring distribution curve is always equal to score of 100 and 15 points was always equal to the standard deviation. This is not a theoretical distinction but rather a methodological distinction between the Wechsler and Stanford-Binet exams. For choice C, Wechsler was not necessarily in agreement with the concepts of fluid intelligence and crystallized intelligence and he did not include these concepts as a theoretical basis

for the construction of his exam. Both exams measured non-verbal cognitive functions. For choice E, the Hierarchical models of intelligence were many years in the future when the first versions of the two exams were created.

76. **The contrasting category of test in comparison to an achievement test is a(n) _____.**
(Lower order)

[A] psychometric test
[B] pilot test
[C] IQ test
[D] standardized test
[E] aptitude test

The correct answer is E.
One broad categorical distinction between tests is the achievement test vs aptitude test distinction. We refer you to the chapter if you are unsure of the definitions of terms in this lower level question.

77. **According to Raymond Cattell's definition, what is true regarding crystallized intelligence?**
(Lower order)

[A] It may continue to increase over the entire normal adult lifespan.

[B] It is equivalent to the concept of a single intelligence or "g" intelligence.

[C] It is equivalent to verbal intelligence.

[D] It is best assessed with questions intended to measure the upper limit of complexity that an individual is capable of solving within a reasonable time limit.

[E] It is thinking that features intuition, wisdom, and motivation. It also involves thinking with a strong will, strong opinions and confidence.

The correct answer is B.
This question probably represents about

the average level of difficulty on the AP Psychology exam. It does not ask for a straightforward definition of crystallized intelligence but a more specific distinctive element of the concept. The question choices are variable in their difficulty but usually relevant to the subject. Cattell proposed that general intelligence was composed of two fundamental types of intelligence; 1) fluid intelligence that utilized a reasoning capacity to solve novel problems or to otherwise function well in a changing external environment, and 2) crystallized intelligence that was adapted to utilize an individual's general fund of knowledge acquired through study and through life experience. Therefore, crystallized intelligence is one of two primary modes of general intelligence, but not synonymous with general intelligence. Verbal intelligence is not discussed as an explicit feature of crystallized intelligence and is not generally precisely defined as a specific type of intelligence by any of the major intelligence theorists. Choice D describes questions used in a power test and this may be used to assess crystallized intelligence, but it is several steps removed. To say this is a logically true feature of Cattell's definition and it is not definitely true as is choice A. Choice E is a description of Howard Gardner's theory of multiple intelligences, namely the Intrapersonal intelligence.

The correct answer is B.

It is possible for a test to be invalid, meaning that that the test does not measure what it is intended to measure. Nevertheless, the test may result in scores for individuals that are equivalent regardless of when, where how many times or which versions of the test the individuals take. Choice A is a statement of fact that is addressed in the chapter. Choice C is the definition of one type of construct validity. It is virtually impossible to prove that a psychometric standardized test is valid. Theoretically, it is impossible to prove anything but if you want to split hairs, we cannot ever have anywhere near the confidence that we are accurately testing for a psychological thing compared to the confidence that we are accurately testing for a physical quantity like temperature or mass. For choice D, The degree to which a test predicts future outcomes is called predictive validity. Depending on how far down the line a prediction of a test takes to be measured, the first assessment of predictive validity may not occur for many years after the first administration of the test. For choice E, there always must be an assumption that correct answers to questions are an indication of the amount of a psychological thing that a person possesses. We can never directly observe these internal qualities of the human mind. That is a built in fundamental uncertainty in the validity of any psychometric testing.

78. **Regarding the reliability and validity of a test, which of the following is NOT true?**
   (Lower order)

   [A] Correlation coefficients can be calculated for the reliability of tests
   [B] Reliability requires that a test be valid
   [C] Construct validity may be based on a interpretation of a theory
   [D] Predictive validity may not be present on the first administration of a test
   [E] Validity of psychometric tests are never perfect

79. Max is known across many settings for being dishonest, grouchy, funny, intelligent, overly emotional, and ambitious. Which of the following statements is true?

[A] These characteristics indicate that Max needs to work on self-actualization.

[B] These characteristics probably show that Max has a mental disorder.

[C] These characteristics show that Max has a high level of self-esteem.

[D] These characteristics describe Max's central dispositions.

[E] These characteristics can change if Max explores his unconscious.

The correct answer is D.
Central dispositions are those that stand out the most in an individual. Since Max demonstrates these traits across different settings and is known for these traits, these are the traits that people associate with Max. It will not hurt Max to work on self-actualization, but the type of traits someone has does not make achieving self-actualization any more or less important for them. There is no evidence that Max has a mental disorder. Some of his central dispositions are good and some are bad, but that does not indicate a mental disorder since all humans have good and bad personality traits. These traits also do not support the idea that Max has high self-esteem, and there is not enough information to make that assumption. Most likely, these characteristics will not change significantly, regardless of what type of therapy Max receives, especially that of exploring his unconscious mind.

80. Which type of psychotropic drug depresses the central nervous system?
(Lower order)

[A] Antipsychotic

[B] Anxiolytic

[C] Antidepressant

[D] Monoamine oxidase inhibitor

[E] Neurotransmitters

The correct answer is B.
Anxiolytic drugs reduce anxiety by depressing the central nervous system. Antipsychotic drugs block dopamine neural receptor sites; these drugs are used to treat schizophrenia. Antidepressants are used to treat mood disorders and work by altering the activity level of certain neurotransmitters in the brain. Monoamine oxidase inhibitors are a class of antidepressants. Neurotransmitters are chemicals in the brain that affect mental states.

81. Which of the following statements would a humanistic therapist be most likely to make?
(Higher order)

[A] "Tell me about your childhood."

[B] "I want you to imagine your worst fear."

[C] "What I hear you saying is that you feel worthless."

[D] "What proof do you have that everyone hates you?"

[E] "I want you to observe someone being kind and then practice being kind."

The correct answer is C.
A humanistic therapist using client-centered therapy is an active-listener. One aspect of active-listening is reflecting the client's feelings and helping the client clarify what she feels. Asking this type of question is seeking clarification and is letting the client know the therapist understands her feelings. A psychoanalytic or psychodynamic therapist would ask about childhood experiences. A

behavioral therapist who is using systematic desensitization to treat a phobia or anxiety would ask a client to imagine his worst fear. A cognitive therapist would challenge a client's thinking about how others feel about him by asking for evidence. A behavioral therapist would use modeling as a therapy technique.

82. **A behavioral therapist would be most likely to agree with which of the following criticisms of psychoanalytic therapy?**

[A] Psychoanalytic therapy wastes too much time on exploring present experiences.

[B] Psychoanalytic therapy does not address thought patterns.

[C] Psychoanalytic therapy is not based on observable, objective data.

[D] Psychoanalytic therapy does not address issues of self-fulfillment.

[E] Psychoanalytic therapy relies too heavily on drug therapy.

The correct answer is C.
A behavioral therapist focuses on what is observable and objective. Psychoanalytic therapy relies on the subjective interpretation of the therapist, so a behaviorist would make this criticism. Psychoanalytic theory focuses on past experiences, not the present. A behavioral therapist does not address thought patterns because thoughts are not observable, so they would not criticize psychoanalytic therapy for this issue. Humanistic therapy, not psychoanalytic therapy, addresses issues of self-fulfillment, so this would not be a criticism made by a behavioral therapist. Psychoanalytic therapy does not rely on drug therapy, so behaviorists would not make this criticism.

83. **When subjects in Milgram's obedience experiments received their orders from a research assistant, they:**
(Lower order)

[A] conformed more easily

[B] refused to participate

[C] dropped out of the study

[D] were less likely to obey

[E] were slightly more obedient

The correct answer is D.
Participants were less likely to obey a person whom they perceived as having less authority. They conformed more easily when the person had more authority. Many participants dropped out of the study when other confederates in the room objected to the other confederate being shocked.

84. **Which of the following examples is an example of situational attribution?**
(Higher order)

[A] Mary takes a French exam and passes it and attributes her passing grade to her good study habits.

[B] Jake gets ripped off by a rich man. He then assumes that every rich man is greedy.

[C] Marlo is more aggressive when she is around other aggressive children.

[D] Stanley likes Mr. Caruso because Mr. Caruso likes him.

[E] Henry takes a Zoology test and fails it. He blames his poor score on disruptions by his classmates.

The correct answer is E.
When a person attributes success or failure to situations or external events, they are assigning situational attribution to the outcome. If someone attributes a positive outcome to personal characteristics, they are assigning dispositional attribution. Answer B describes a stereotype. Answer C is referring

to the results of a study conducted by Albert Bandura. Answer D refers to the principle of reciprocal liking.

85. **A group of teenagers is attending summer camp. During the camp, one of the adults deliberately manipulates situations to make the campers mistrust one another. Before long, the campers are being mean to each other and the environment is becoming hostile. Which of the following statements best describes how the groups can work out their differences?**

[A] The groups can play games that cause them to compete against each other for prizes.

[B] There is nothing that can be done to help the groups work out their differences.

[C] The leaders need to sit the groups down and have a discussion with them about how to resolve conflict.

[D] The groups should work together to solve a problem that is affecting all of them.

[E] The groups need to take some time away from each other to allow things to settle down.

The correct answer is D.
Working together to solve a problem that is affecting all of them is working towards a superordinate goal. A superordinate goal is a goal that will benefit all members and will require the participation of all members. Competing against each other for prizes can create a hostile environment. While there is nothing wrong with leaders talking to the groups about how to resolve conflict, this type of strategy may do nothing to resolve the hostility and solve the problem. Taking some time away from each other may be helpful, but it does not require group members to work together to find a mutually beneficial resolution.

86. **The following list of traits are not part of the Big Five EXCEPT:**
(Higher order)

[A] Extraversion, openness, honesty, conscientiousness, and neuroticism

[B] Conscientiousness, curiosity, extraversion, agreeableness, and psychoticism

[C] Extraversion, neuroticism, openness, agreeableness, and conscientiousness

[D] Extraversion, psychoticism, honesty, trustworthiness, and openness

[E] Idiographic, nomothetic, extraversion, honesty, and openness

The correct answer is C.
These traits are considered nomothetic because all people have each trait to some degree. Honesty, curiosity, and trustworthiness are not common to all people. Extraversion, neuroticism, and psychoticism were the three traits proposed by Hans Eysenck.

87. **A biological psychologist might be interested in which of the following?**
(Higher order)

[A] How unconditional positive regard affects self-concept

[B] How dopamine affects thought processes

[C] How a person's perception of events affects behavior

[D] How social roles impact development

[E] How to improve an employee's motivation

The correct answer is B.
Dopamine is a neurotransmitter in the brain that is linked to thoughts and emotions. Because neurotransmitters are controlled by physiological processes, studying how a neurotransmitter affects thought processes is within the scope of a biological psychologist. Unconditional positive regard is a concept proposed by Carl Rogers, a humanistic

psychologist. A cognitive psychologist would be interested in how a person's perceptions of events affect behavior. A sociocultural psychologist would be interested in how social roles impact development. An industrial-organizational psychologist would be interested in how to improve an employee's motivation.

88. **In what major way is behaviorism different from other theoretical perspectives?**
    (Lower order)

    [A] It is only concerned with observable behavior.
    [B] Its concepts are based on empirical research.
    [C] Its principles are of no use today.
    [D] It is not considered scientific.
    [E] There is no specific way behaviorism is different from other perspectives.

    The correct answer is A.
    Behaviorism defines psychology as the science of observable behavior. All the other theoretical approaches studied in this chapter recognize the importance of unobservable behavior and processes. Research supports many of the principles and concepts of behaviorism, and some principles are used today in behavior modification. Behavioral psychology is considered scientific.

89. **Which theorist proposed the concept of zone of proximal development?**
    (Lower order)

    [A] Albert Bandura
    [B] Lev Vygotsky
    [C] Harry Harlow
    [D] Jean Piaget
    [E] Erik Erikson

    The correct answer is B.
    Lev Vygotsky believed that cognitive development is impacted by social factors.

Children are able to develop cognitively with help and guidance from others. The zone of proximal development refers to the range of skills and tasks a person is close to acquiring but cannot perform without some help from others. Albert Bandura was a social learning theorist. Harry Harlow conducted research on attachment. Jean Piaget's theory of cognitive development did not address social influences on learning. Erik Erikson focused on psychosocial development, not cognitive development.

90. **For a diagnosis of schizophrenia (according to the DSM-5), there MUST be:**
    (Lower order)

    [A] a response to medical treatment.
    [B] symptoms of delusions, hallucinations, and disorganized speech for at least 1 month.
    [C] continuous signs of the disturbance that persist for at least 6 months.
    [D] no other comorbid conditions present.
    [E] agreement by at least two independent licensed mental health practitioners' evaluations.

    The correct answer is C.
    According to the DSM-5, a diagnosis of schizophrenia requires at least 2 of the following symptoms: delusions, hallucinations, disorganized speech, disorganized or catatonic behavior, negative symptoms. At least 1 of the symptoms must be the presence of delusions, hallucinations, or disorganized speech. Continuous signs of the disturbance must persist for at least 6 months, during which at least 1 month of active symptoms (or less if successfully treated) must be present. One are not expected to memorize every DSM-5 set of diagnostic criteria for every condition. For major disorders, including schizophrenia, one should be aware or strongly suspect that

signs of the condition have been present for a reasonable period of time before making such a critical diagnosis.

91. _____ resembles the popular term "split personality" is:
(Lower order)

[A] Schizophrenia
[B] Bipolar disorder
[C] Borderline personality disorder
[D] Dissociative identity disorder
[E] Depersonalization/derealization disorder

The correct answer is D.
In dissociative identity disorder there is a feeling of possession by another identity or that there are two or more identities or personality traits within a single person. Often there is an apparent transfer of behavioral control to the particular personality that seems to have the best capacity to function in specific social situations or other sets of circumstances.

92. _____ best describes incongruence?
(Higher order)

[A] Ken's marriage is ending so he throws himself into his work.
[B] Marcy sees one group of her classmates as "cool" and the other group as "uncool."
[C] Henry believes in having a good work ethic but he steals from his boss.
[D] Candi makes a high score on her SAT and attributes her success to her intelligence.
[E] Adam distances himself from his son when his son fails to make the football team.

The correct answer is C.
Incongruence refers to the gap that exists between who one wishes to be and who one actually is. Henry may wish to have a good work ethic, but he actually does not have a good work ethic, as evidenced by stealing

from his boss. Choice A is an example of the defense mechanism of compensation. Choice B describes a personal construct. Choice D is an example of an internal locus-of-control, and Choice E illustrates the concept of conditions of worth.

93. Cognitive triad is a concept developed by _____.
(Lower order)

[A] Sigmund Freud
[B] Abraham Maslow
[C] Aaron Beck
[D] Albert Ellis
[E] Fritz Perls

The correct answer is C.
Aaron Beck developed cognitive therapy, which is based on the idea that depressed people form a negative cognitive triad about themselves, the world and the future. Sigmund Freud is associated with psychoanalysis. Abraham Maslow developed the hierarchy of needs. Albert Ellis developed rational-emotive behavior therapy, and Fritz Perls developed Gestalt therapy.

94. Charles Spearman is most directly associated with _____.
(Lower order)

[A] factor analysis of correlations related to intelligence
[B] the concept of crystallized intelligence
[C] the concept of fluid intelligence
[D] development of the Culture Fair Intelligence Test
[E] development of The Three Stratum Model of Intelligence

The correct answer is C.
Charles Spearman published the first factor analysis of the correlation of grades for individuals among specific school subjects and proposed that although there were

specific types of intelligence or mental abilities, called s intelligence there appeared to by an underlying general or g intelligence. For choices B, C and D, Raymond Cattell proposed that Spearman's general intelligence was composed of two fundamental types of intelligence; 1) fluid intelligence that utilized a reasoning capacity to solve novel problems or to otherwise function well in a changing external environment, and 2) crystallized intelligence that was adapted to utilize an individual's general fund of knowledge acquired through study and through life experience. He also developed the Culture Fair Intelligence Test (CFIT) in an effort measure of cognitive abilities in a manner that was independent of sociocultural and environmental influences. For choice E, John Carroll developed The Three Stratum Model of Intelligence.

95. **Debra is a consultant who is evaluating the performance of employees for her client company. She recommends a change in policy that substitutes a theory X management principle for a theory Y management principle. Choose the policy change that would correspond to Debra's recommendation.**

(Higher order)

[A] Substitute a percentage commission for hourly wage on new client sales.

[B] Institute careful documentation policy to identify specific individuals associated with poor implementation of a business model in place of a nonexistent documentation policy.

[C] Assess career advancement potential based on past work history that shows individual initiative and problem solving rather than current emphasis on detail oriented and focused commitment to carry out specific tasks.

[D] Provide a rolling point system that tracks late arrival and absent work AND has an absolute employment termination point limit BUT subtracts points for voluntary overtime in place of an absolute policy that does not allow employees to improve job security by future behavior.

[E] Set high achievement goals that earn high value socially based rewards such as vacation packages that can not be redeemed for cash, traded or used by others in place of a vacation or cash equivalent choice option reward.

The correct answer is D.
Distinguishing features of the X management style vs the Y management style includes that theory X management believe employees are high value as focused workers who follow directions to accomplish a task - in

other words they do what they are told to do and do it well. Theory Y management values employees for their ability to provide creative solutions to problems and an ability to work without close supervision. Choice A substitutes one monetary award for a more performance-based award. This is more of a theory X based principle that is being fine-tuned rather than a theory Y substitution. For the remaining choices there are similar rationales based on distinguishing features of Theory X and Theory Y management. You should be able to generate your own explanations for the remainder of the choices if you have a general understanding of the two management styles.

96. **Amber, an intelligent, success-oriented, 24-year-old woman who has just resigned from her highly paid position as a junior partner in a hedge fund investment firm. She has lost interest in daily activities and is unconcerned for her future despite serious consequences to her financial and personal life that are likely to result from her seemingly foolish choice to leave her high-paced, high-risk but very successful career. Based on this information, Amber most likely has:**

    (Higher order)

    [A] abnormally high baseline levels of epinephrine and/or norepinephrine
    [B] a serious undiagnosed-stress related physical illness
    [C] a preceding prolonged period of abnormally high cortisol levels
    [D] an unresolveable multiple approach-avoidance conflict
    [E] failed to fulfill basic security needs that are unique to a young adult compared to those of a teenager who is younger than the age of eighteen.

The correct answer is C.
The question describes all the elements that define the burnout phenomenon that results from persistent status in the stage 3 stress response exhaustion phase of the general adaptation syndrome (GAS). In a burnout episode, individuals typically become ineffective in their normal daily functions and perhaps incapable of continuing to function in their jobs and in their relationships with others. The stage 3 stress response is generally preceded by excessive exposure to the phase 2 resistance stage of the GAS during this stage the hypothalamus is stimulating the pituitary to release steroid releasing hormones that in turn stimulate the adrenal gland to produce increased amounts of the steroid hormone cortisol. For choice A, abnormally high baseline levels of epinephrine and/or norepinephrine are associated with the stage 1 alarm phase of the GAS. For choice B, Amber's high stress exposure makes her more prone to stress-related illnesses, but at her age these disease are less likely. That is somewhat beyond the scope of the AP Psychology exam but it is not beyond the level of analysis expected by higher-level questions. She may, in fact, have an undiagnosed stress related illness but it is almost certain she has recently experienced abnormally high cortisol levels. For choice D, She almost certainly faces multiple approach-avoidance conflicts, as do we all, but there is no reason to conclude she faces an unresolvable one. Choice E describes perhaps an issue related to hierarchy of needs models of motivation but it hardly seems likely to be relevant to a highly successful professional woman who was clearly fulfilling higher-level needs before her burnout experience.

97. **Which statement below provides a rebuttal to a Cannon-Bard advocates criticism of the James-Lange theory of emotion?**
    (Higher order)

    [A] If the definition of a physiological state is broadened, this can account for correspondingly wider range and more complex character of emotional experiences.
    [B] There is not enough time for physiological changes to occur and then be detected to allow them to generate a corresponding emotional experience based on how quickly the those emotions are experienced.
    [C] In experiments, subjects have received injections of epinephrine in neutral controlled environments. The subjects report that they sense the increased arousal that the epinephrine produces but they do not have any particular emotional experience that occurs with this sensation.
    [D] In experiments with epinephrine injections in subjects, in one environment subjects found the experience to be funny as in amusing. In the other environment subjects found that the experience made them angry.
    [E] Although an individual's performance will initially increase as his or her level of arousal increases, after a certain point. Increasing levels of arousal will progressively impair performance.

    The correct answer is B.
    Cannon of the Cannon-Bard theory criticized the James-Lange theory in part by stating that there are a very limited number of different physiological states that can correspond to different emotions. If there is a broader definition of physical states, that implies there are more physiological states that can be detected. That also implies there

may be sufficient number of detectably different physiological states to account for the total number of different emotions. Choice B is a Cannon-Bard criticism of the James-Lange Theory, not a rebuttal of a criticism of the theory. Choice C is evidence of support for the 2-factor theory of emotion. Choice D is also evidence of support for the 2-factor theory of emotion. Choice E describes the Yerkes-Dodson Law. This law states that one's performance will increase as one's level of arousal increases, but only to a certain point. After that point, increasing levels of arousal will progressively impair performance

98. **A behavior that is instinctive is most specifically a behavior that:**
    (Lower order)

    [A] is driven by an internal or intrinsic motivation
    [B] directly satisfies a drive state urge such as hunger or thirst
    [C] is genetically determined, precise and predictable
    [D] results from neurological processes that do not require the participation of the cerebral cortex
    [E] always overrides behaviors that are not directly required for immediate self-preservation

    The correct answer is B.
    The definition of an instinct includes the properties of genetic determination, specific or precise behavior and behavior that is highly predictable. For the other answer choices there may be instinctive behaviors that are included that match the defining characteristics, but there are many other non-instinctive behaviors that do so as well. None of the incorrect choices are specific types of instinctive behavior

99. The hypothalamus, amygdala and cingulate cortex are included in a higher level organization of neurological structures known as:

(Lower order)

[A] the limbic system
[B] the striate cortex
[C] Broca's area
[D] the corpus callosum
[E] the cerebellum

The correct answer is A.

At the lowest level of difficulty, the AP Psychology exam expects you to know these neurological regions or systems. The limbic system has a few other sub regions that constitute the system and you are not expected to know them all, you may not even need to know any of them. This is because you must know a lot about the hypothalamus and enough about the wrong answer choices to recognize they unquestionable do not include the hypothalamus. You are given the information in this chapter that specifically states these three structures are part of the limbic system. We can not confirm you are responsible for this specific knowledge, but it would be very surprising if you were not. Nevertheless, an elementary process of elimination would lead to the correct answer in this question, therefore it is a fair AP Psychology question.

100. **Which theorist categorizes needs as deficiency or "d" needs and being or "b" needs?**

(Lower order)

[A] William James
[B] Jerome Singer
[C] Richard Solomon
[D] Abraham Maslow
[E] Hans Selye

The correct answer is D.

Abraham Maslow's Hierarchy of Needs theory indicates that as needs become more complex they are increasingly psychological and social needs. At the lowest level are the purely biological need followed by the need for personal safety and security. After these needs are met there is the levels where are needs are of an interpersonal nature, needs for friendship, love and intimacy, at the highest levels are purely personal needs - a need for esteem and personal accomplishment. This processes of growth and personal development is termed self-actualization. Needs are also categorized as deficiency needs or "d" needs and the lack of these needs causes discomfort and other negative consequences. At the highest level, there are being or "B" needs. These type of needs are not perceived as a deficiency or lack of something, but as a desire to achieve a higher level of personal development. William James among other notable achievements is the James in the James-Lange theory of emotion. Stanley Schachter and Jerome Singer proposed in their two-factor theory that emotion is based on two factors: physiological arousal and cognitive assessment of the external context or environment of the arousal. Richard Solomon's opponent-process theory states that that emotions exist as opposing pairs. Hans Selye developed the general adaptation syndrome stress model that describes physiological process that occur in persons subjected to stress.

FREE RESPONSE ANSWER AND RUBRIC

SAMPLE QUESTION ONE

3. Psychology is a field that relies heavily on research. As such, it is important to know the different methods of research used by psychologists, including the strengths and weaknesses of each method. All of the following are different methods of research used by psychologists:

   - Case study
   - Correlational study
   - Experiment
   - Longitudinal study
   - Cross-sectional study

   C. Discuss one advantage of each of the above kinds methods of research. (5 points)

   D. Discuss one limitation of each of the above kinds methods of research. (5 points)

BEFORE YOU WRITE YOUR RESPONSE

Before you begin formulating your response, stop and think about what the question is asking you. On the question sheet, write down some notes or make an outline. Following these suggestions will help you organize your thoughts. Let the implied organization of the question guide the organization of your response.

There are five bulleted points to be addressed in this question. Those five bulleted points should serve as the organization for your response. You should NOT use your outline as your response. This is prohibited in the free response instructions given by the College Board. Write your response using complete sentences in paragraph form. For this question, you should have five paragraphs in this order: case-study, correlational study, experiment, longitudinal study, and cross-sectional study. Organizing your paragraphs in the order implied in the question will help the AP scorers grade your response.

When you begin crafting your response, you may find it helpful to underline the words, phrases, or concepts specifically mentioned in the question. In this question, there are five methods of research mentioned, so underline each of those terms: case-study(studies), correlational study(studies), experiment(s), longitudinal study(studies), and cross-sectional study (studies). For each of these methods, you are required to discuss one advantage and one limitation of that method. Underline the word advantage and the word limitation in your paragraphs. While this is not required, underlining these words will not only help you organize your response, it will also help the AP readers be able to score your response more easily and quickly. You can apply these suggestions to both the response questions you will answer.

The important thing is to make sure you address every part of the question in an organized, cogent manner. If you prefer not to underline the terms, find a method that works for you so that you will know you covered all elements of the question. Refer to your notes or outline or whatever method you choose frequently when answering the question. Doing this will help you organize your thoughts in your head and on paper, and it will serve as a checklist. It may also help you identify parts of the question you did not answer or areas where you need to add information. If you have time after you have answered BOTH free response questions, read through your answers to check for errors or omissions. If you forgot to cover something, neatly add it to your response in the appropriate place. If you need to delete something, make it clear that you are deleting that portion, but keep your writing as neat and legible as possible. Leaving a small space between the lines will give you room to add content and make corrections.

Before you read the sample response to this question, you may find it beneficial to write your response. After you have written your response, read over your answer. Use the following rubric to make sure you covered the information given to you in the question. If you realize there is something in the question that you did not cover in your response, go back and add the missing information to your response. Once you have read through your response and are certain you adequately covered all the points of the question, use the following rubric to score your response.

RUBRIC FOR SAMPLE QUESTION ONE

This is a 10-point question.

Point 1: *Case study advantage.* The response should clearly state one advantage to a case study method.

- Provide detailed and in-depth information about a single person, group or event
- Provide chance to study unique or unusual case
- Helps generate ideas for future research

- May help avoid ethical issues
- High ecological validity (real world validity)
- Changes can be seen as they happen

Point 2: Case study limitation. The response should clearly state one limitation of a case study.
- Results cannot be generalized
- Information may be reported inaccurately
- Cannot establish cause-effect relationships
- Researcher bias
- Difficult to replicate
- Time consuming

Point 3: Correlational study advantage. The response should clearly state one advantage of a correlational study.
- Examine the relationship between two or more naturally occurring variables
- Allow for collection of lots of data
- Inexpensive
- Saves time
- Predictions about variables can be made
- Pre-existing information can be used
- Require no participants
- Ethical considerations

Point 4: Correlational study limitation. The response should clearly state one limitation of correlational studies.
- Cannot establish a causal relationship or the direction of such a relationship
- Information may be reported inaccurately
- Difficult to determine the effects of extraneous variables
- No way to actively manipulate variables
- Subject to biasing factors

Point 5: Experiment advantages. The response should clearly state one advantage of an experiment.
- Possible to demonstrate cause-effect relationship
- Provide for operational definition of variables
- Allow for manipulation of variables
- Focus on the utilization of groups for purpose of comparison
- Allows variables to be precisely controlled
- Allows for participants to be randomly assigned to groups
- Can use double-blind or single-blind procedures
- Internal validity is high
- Provides for accurate and objective measurement of variables
- Placebo effects can be distinguished from effects of treatment
- Ability to be replicated
- Can control for biasing factors
- Ethical issues
- Use of standardized procedures

Point 6: Experiment limitations. Response should clearly state one limitation of an experiment.
- Lower ecological validity
- Hard to maintain control conditions
- Difficult to eliminate confounding variables
- Possibility of bias
- Can be expensive, time consuming
- Ethical issues

Point 7: Longitudinal study advantages. Response should clearly state one advantage of a longitudinal study.
- Allows for changes over time to be seen

- Allows for specific variables of development to be measured
- Eliminates cultural and historical differences among participants

Point 8: Longitudinal study limitations. Response should clearly state one limitation of a longitudinal study.

- Expensive
- Require lots of time
- Participants may drop out of the study (selective attrition)
- May not be able to generalize results
- Lower validity
- Data collected over long period of time
- Amount of data collected may be small

Point 9: Cross-sectional study advantages. Response should clearly state one advantage of cross-sectional research.

- Large amounts of data can be collected
- Data collected all at once
- Produces quick results
- Inexpensive
- Numerous variables can be studied at same time
- Can establish correlation among variables
- Can establish normative patterns

Point 10: Cross-sectional study limitations. Response should clearly state one limitation of cross-sectional studies.

- Requires large amount of participants
- Does not control for cultural or historical differences (cohort differences)
- Reveals little about the development of a single individual

SAMPLE RESPONSE

Case studies are detailed research of a person or event that occurs over a long period of time. Since the study lasts for years, any changes in the person or variables being investigated can be seen as they occur. Case studies are descriptive in nature and are based on observation or interviews. One advantage of a case study is that it helps researchers generate ideas that act as a basis for a hypothesis. From this hypothesis, the researcher can develop a more objective and controlled experiment. Case studies allow for the collection of a lot of information, but that information may not be helpful in other situations. One main limitation of a case study is that the results cannot be generalized to a larger group since the case study only investigates one person.

Correlational studies investigate the relationship between two or more variables. An advantage of this method is that it allows researchers to study variables that cannot be studied using a controlled experiment because it may be impractical or unethical to do so. For example, it would be unethical for a researcher to conduct an experiment to see if watching violence towards women on television causes domestic violence. Correlational studies may help the researcher determine patterns in a person's behavior or between the variables. One limitation of this method is that although it can show a relationship between variables, it does not demonstrate a cause-effect relationship between the variables. To use the example of domestic violence, there may be a relationship between seeing violence against women on television and domestic violence, but there is no way to determine if there is a direct cause-effect relationship. There may be other variables that need to be considered.

Experiments allow the researcher to establish a cause-effect relationship between variables by manipulating variables, which is one of the greatest advantages of this method. Experiments provide a high level of control for the variables. With experiments, variables are operationally defined, which helps future researchers replicate the study. Some limitations of experiments are the potential for subject and experimenter bias and the possibility for other confounding variables. For example, participants who know they are part of an experiment may respond in certain ways (response bias), or a researcher may treat participants differently based on which group the participants are in (experimenter bias).

A longitudinal study follows the same group of people over a long period of time. Participants are assessed at set intervals of time, like every five years, to see which changes have taken place over time. One advantage of this kind of research is that specific aspects of development can be measured, such as how children with a language impairment progress in building language skills over several years. Also, since this type of research takes place over years, the researcher can assume that any changes are a result of time. Because longitudinal research requires data to be acquired over the course of decades, a distinct limitation of this method is that it is expensive and requires more resources.

Cross-sectional research involves looking at groups of individuals of different ages at the same time to see which variables change over time. One advantage of this type of study is that it is objective and guards against bias. A limitation of this type of research is that it may not take into account the difference in experiences of individuals of different backgrounds. For example, a researcher may not consider how technological advances, such as the internet, have affected academic performance among people of the same age but with different socioeconomic status.

END OF RESPONSE

GRADING THE SAMPLE RESPONSE

The AP readers will use the rubric to score your response. The readers will look at the rubric as they read your answer. As the readers go over your response, they will award a point for each correct answer. The readers will not penalize you for inaccurate information unless you directly contradict something you wrote earlier in your response.

The scorers will use a "grid" to indicate how many points a response has been awarded. The grid is organized just as the question is and will reflect what is on the rubric. It may help you to think of the grid as a sort of checklist. Every time the reader sees a correct answer in your response, they will give you a checkmark. At the end of reading your response, the scorer will count the checkmarks to arrive at your total grade for that question.

How well do you think the fictitious student did? Let's examine this response based on the rubric.

Point 1: Awarded—The student correctly stated one advantage of a case study.

"One advantage of a case study is that it helps researchers generate ideas that act as a basis for a hypothesis."

Point 2: Awarded—The student correctly stated one limitation of a case study.

"One main limitation of a case study is that the results cannot be generalized to a larger group since the case study only investigates one person."

Point 3: Awarded—The student correctly identified an advantage of a correlational study.

"An advantage of this method is that it allows researchers to study variables that cannot be studied using a controlled experiment because it may be impractical or unethical to do so." The student's reference to research ethics, as well as her example, adequately covered this point.

Point 4: Awarded—The student correctly provided one limitation of a correlational study.

"A limitation of this method is that although it can show a relationship between variables, it does not demonstrate a cause-effect relationship between the variables."

Point 5: Awarded—The student correctly stated one advantage of an experiment.

"Experiments allow the researcher to establish a cause-effect relationship between variables by manipulating variables, which is one of the greatest advantages of this method."

Point 6: Awarded—The student correctly stated one limitation of an experiment.

"Some limitations of experiments are the potential for subject and experimenter bias and the possibility for other confounding variables."

Point 7: Awarded—The student correctly stated one advantage of a longitudinal study.

"One advantage of this kind of research is that specific aspects of development can be measured, such as how children with a language impairment progress in building language skills over several years." The student's example demonstrated that she understood the advantages of longitudinal research, so even if her answer did not specifically use the word "variable," her example earned her this point because language impairment is a variable that affects how language skills progress.

Point 8: Awarded—The study correctly stated one limitation of longitudinal research.

"Because longitudinal research requires data to be acquired over the course of decades, a distinct limitation of this method is that it is expensive and requires more resources."

Point 9: Not Awarded—The student did not correctly answer this part of the question.

"One advantage of this type of study is that it is objective and guards against bias."

Point 10: Awarded—The student answered the question about one limitation of cross-sectional research correctly.

"A limitation of this type of research is that it may not take into account the difference in experiences of individuals of the same age but with different socioeconomic status."

Out of a possible 10 points, the student earned 9. Overall, her response was strong, well-organized, and demonstrated that she has a good grasp of this material.

The student did not organize her answer in the same way the question was organized, but, for this question, her organization was logical and easy to follow. Discussing the advantages and limitations of a method in the same paragraph makes sense.

SAMPLE QUESTION TWO

4. **A. Define each of the following concepts and discuss how each one contributes to the phenomenon of prejudice. Be sure to define prejudice in your response. (4 points)**
    - **Conformity**
    - **Stereotypes**
    - **Ethnocentrism**
    C. Define each of the following concepts and explain how each one relates to changing the attitude of prejudice. Be sure to define attitude in your response. (4 points)
    - **Mere exposure effect**
    - **Superordinate goal**
    - **Cognitive dissonance**

SAMPLE QUESTION TWO RUBRIC

This is an 8-point question.

For Part A, 4 possible points can be awarded.

You are asked to define each of the concepts. For Points 2, 3, & 4, you must also discuss how those concepts contribute to prejudice.

Your response would be scored based on a similar rubric.

Point 1: *Define prejudice.* The response should establish that prejudice is an attitude and that is undeserved (or unjustified) and is negative AND should demonstrate that it is directed or applied toward all members of a certain group. Do not use the word prejudice to define the concept of prejudice.

Point 2: *Define conformity.* The response should establish that conformity means going along with attitudes or actions of others in a group AND that it is not a result of direct pressure (compliance or obedience) but is indirect; AND leads to changing or adjusting behavior to go along with the beliefs/attitudes/standards of the group. Do not use the word conform to define the concept of conformity. Discussion should indicate how conformity contributes to prejudice, either by using an example or by explanation.

Point 3: *Define stereotypes.* The response should establish that stereotypes are attitudes, beliefs, thoughts, or ideas about another group; AND establish impact on interactions/relationships with members of said group. Discussion must show relation to prejudice.

Point 4: *Define ethnocentrism.* The response should establish that this is a cultural or ethnic perspective (may include religion, nationality, or race) AND relates to ethnic judgment of being "better than" or "superior to" or "above" other ethnic groups. Must show relation to prejudice.

For Point B, 4 possible points can be awarded.

Point 5: *Define attitude.* The response should establish both cognitive and emotional component (ideas, beliefs, or thoughts, AND feelings) of attitudes.

Point 6: *Define mere exposure effect.* The response should establish exposure over time or with more frequency (not proximity) AND exposure leads to outcome of liking something more or becoming more comfortable with something. Must show relation to changing attitude.

Point 7: *Define superordinate goal.* The response should establish need to resolve conflict/tension among different groups AND common goals with mutual benefits. Must show relation to changing attitude.

Point 8: *Define cognitive dissonance.* The response should establish conflict/contradiction between thoughts/feelings AND actions/behaviors; AND establish result of tension, discomfort AND change/adjustment because of tension/discomfort. Must show relation to changing attitude.

SAMPLE RESPONSE TWO

Conformity, stereotypes and ethnocentrism all work together to contribute to prejudice. Prejudice is an undeserved attitude towards every member of another certain group. This attitude is usually negative. Conformity occurs when individuals conform with the attitudes and actions of others. Because people want to be liked by others, they will often conform even though they may not agree with others. If someone conforms to the attitudes of a group that are negative towards outsiders, they may adopt this attitude and become prejudiced even though the outsiders have not done anything to them to deserve the negative attitude. Prejudice is often the result of stereotypes about a group of people. Stereotypes are what someone thinks and feels about members of another group to the point that these things impact how the person responds to members of that group. Stereotypes are usually applied to all members of an outside group and may not have any factual basis. Many times people of one cultural group think their group is better than other cultural groups. This is called ethnocentrism. This attitude will make a person treat members of other ethnic groups in an unfair way. It may cause a group of people of one culture to try to keep themselves separate from other cultural groups.

Since prejudice is an attitude, it can be changed. An attitude is what someone feels and believes about something or someone. One way attitudes can be changed is by exposing someone to something or someone else more frequently. The mere exposure effect says that the more someone is exposed to something over time, the more they will like it. If this is true, then the more someone of one group is in contact with members of another group, the more that person should like the other group. Sometimes people of different groups do not like each other, and there is a lot of tension or conflict because of it. When this happens, it helps if members of those opposing groups work toward a common goal that will benefit all members of the groups. That goal is called a superordinate goal. Cognitive dissonance occurs when someone feels a lot of tension mentally because their attitudes do not line up with their actions. To relieve this tension, a person will change his attitude to match his actions.

 END OF RESPONSE

GRADING THE SAMPLE RESPONSE

Point 1: Awarded—"Prejudice is an undeserved attitude towards every member of a certain group. This attitude is usually negative."

Point 2: Not awarded—The student used the word conformity when defining the concept of conformity. The use of the word conformity does not indicate the student knows the definition of the word. If the student had used the words "goes along with" or something similar, the point would have been awarded.

"Conformity occurs when individuals conform with the attitudes and actions of others. Because people want to be liked by others, they will often conform even though they may not agree with others. If someone conforms to the attitudes of a group that are negative towards outsiders, they may adopt this attitude and become prejudiced even though the outsiders have not done anything to them to deserve the negative attitude."

Point 3: Awarded—" Prejudice is often the result of stereotypes about a group of people. Stereotypes are what someone thinks and feels about members of another group to the point that these things impact how the person responds to members of that group. Stereotypes are usually applied to all members of an outside group and may not have any factual basis."

Point 4: Awarded—" Many times people of one cultural group think their group is better than other cultural groups. This is called ethnocentrism. This attitude will make a person treat members of other ethnic groups in an unfair way. It may cause a group of people of one culture to try to keep themselves separate from other cultural groups."

Point 5: Awarded—" An attitude is what someone feels and believes about something or someone."

Point 6: Awarded—" One way attitudes can be changed is by exposing someone to something or someone else more frequently. The mere exposure effect says that the more someone is exposed to something over time, the more they will like it. If this is true, then the more someone of one group is in contact with members of another group, the more that person should like the other group."

Point 7: Awarded—"Sometimes people of different groups do not like each other, and there is a lot of tension or conflict because of it. When this happens, it helps if members of those opposing groups work toward a common goal that will benefit all members of the groups. That goal is called a superordinate goal."

Point 8: Awarded—"Cognitive dissonance occurs when someone feels a lot of tension mentally because their attitudes do not line up with their actions. To relieve this tension, a person will change his attitude to match his actions."

Out of 8 possible points, the student earned 7 points.

For more practice writing free response answers, visit the College Board's AP central website:

http://apcentral.collegeboard.com/apc/public/exam/exam_information/2088.html

CPSIA information can be obtained
at www.ICGtesting.com
Printed in the USA
BVOW04s0001140817
491837BV00049B/335/P